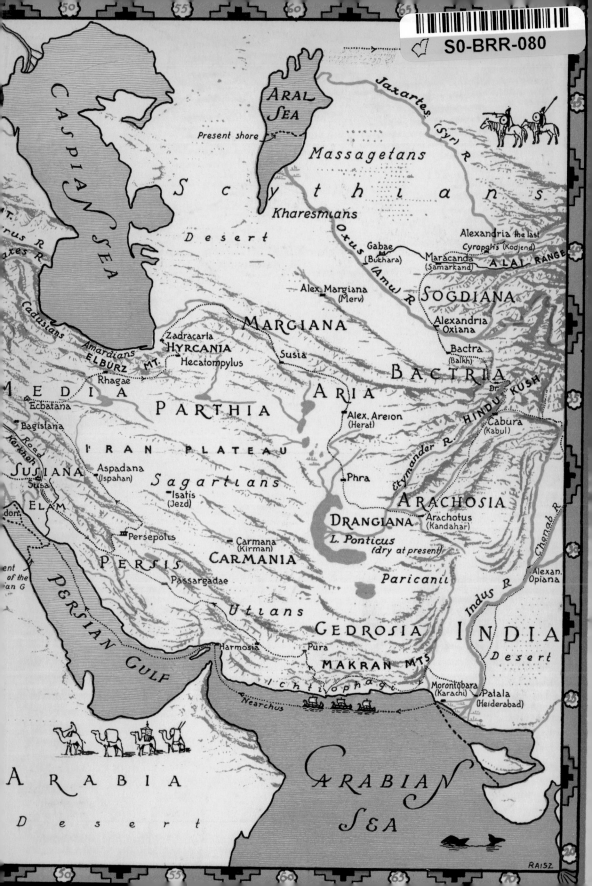

CASPIAN SEA

ARAL SEA

Present shore

Massagetans

Scythians

Kharesmians

Desert

Jaxartes (Syr) R.

Alexandria the last
Cyropghis (Kodjend)
ALAI RANGE

Gabae
(Bukhara)
Maracanda
(Samarkand)

SOGDIANA

Alex. Margiana
(Merv)

MARGIANA

Alexandria
Oxiana

Cadusians

Amardians
HYRCANIA
ELBURZ MT.
Zadracarla
Hecatompylus
Susia

Bactra
(Balkh)

BACTRIA

Rhagae

MEDIA

ARIA

HINDU KUSH

Dr.

Ecbatana

Bagistana

PARTHIA

Alex. Areion
(Herat)

Cabura
(Kabul)

Road
Kerkheh

IRAN PLATEAU

Etymander R.

SUSIANA

Aspadana
(Ispahan)

Sagartians

Phra

ARACHOSIA

Susa

ELAM

Isatis
(Jezd)

DRANGIANA

Arachotus
(Kandahar)

Chenab R.

don.

Persepolis

L. Ponticus
(dry at present)

Carmana
(Kirman)

CARMANA

Paricanii

Alexan.
Opiana

PERSIS

Passargadae

Indus R.

Utians

GEDROSIA

INDIA

PERSIAN GULF

Harmosia

Pura

Desert

MAKRAN MTS

Morontobara
(Karachi)

Patala
(Heiderabad)

Ichtiophagi

Nearchus

ARABIA

ARABIAN

SEA

Desert

RAISZ

A HISTORY
OF ANCIENT PERSIA

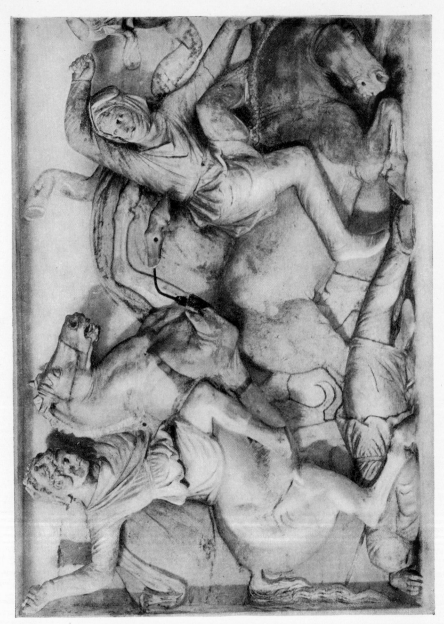

Alexander in Battle with the Persians.
From the Sarcophagus of Alexander.

A HISTORY
OF ANCIENT PERSIA

FROM ITS EARLIEST BEGINNINGS
TO THE DEATH OF ALEXANDER THE GREAT

BY

ROBERT WILLIAM ROGERS

PROFESSOR OF HEBREW AND OLD TESTAMENT EXEGESIS IN DREW UNIVERSITY
PROFESSOR OF ANCIENT ORIENTAL LITERATURE IN PRINCETON UNIVERSITY
PH.D., LEIPSIG ; HON. LITT.D., DUBLIN ; HON. D.LITT., OXFORD
HON. LITT.D., PENNSYLVANIA. MEMBER OF SAINT JOHN'S COLLEGE, OXFORD
AUTHOR OF "A HISTORY OF BABYLONIA AND ASSYRIA," 2 VOLS., SIXTH EDITION, 1915
"CUNEIFORM PARALLELS TO THE OLD TESTAMENT," SECOND EDITION, 1926

WITH ILLUSTRATIONS AND MAPS

CHARLES SCRIBNER'S SONS
NEW YORK · LONDON
1929

PREFACE

MOSTLY PERSONAL

In the sad years of 1913 and 1914 when war began to shatter the accumulations of civilization I rewrote for a sixth edition my History of Babylonia and Assyria whose friendly reception both by scholars and the public so greatly exceeded my hopes and dreams. As I came to the end of that task, and marked as its conclusion the taking of Babylon by Cyrus in the year 538 B. C., I felt my imagination stirred by the mighty figure of that great conqueror, and as I read the proofs my mind continually kept travelling backward to his origins in the little kingdom of Anshan, and forward to a far greater figure of Alexander the Great, and so there arose within me an appeal to write the story of the Persian Empire and its collapse under the genius of Alexander. I began slowly to collect material, and lay down the lines of such a survey.

But before I could begin to write weakness, weariness and pain took possession of me, and slowed my pace. Yet even with such a serious handicap the ambition to do this one final piece of serious work clung to me, and year after year my summers were spent in that most gentle, most kindly and most splendidly managed storehouse of learning the glorious Bodleian Library, while I found rest and refreshment in the hospitable High Table and the Common Room of St. John's College. These frequent journeys would not have been possible but for two subventions from the Carnegie Institution of Washington, and the repeated help of Mr. Arthur

vii

Curtiss James, and Mr. William W. Carman, to whom
I now express thus publicly my great and enduring
gratitude. It was they that kept me a-going at labors so
sorely handicapped by ill health. There were many dark
days when I was inclined to give over the effort, but
these dear and most kind friends kept me at it.

And now the work is done, after all the years of gathering and gleaning, and more than six years of writing.
Nobody will judge the result, however severe the stric-
tures may be, with such severity as I who now dedicate
it to friendly eyes and put it out into a world, that
yearly reads fewer histories and more novels. It is ill
done in many points and places, but it is all that I can
do, and I send it forth hoping that somewhere it may
find friends. The spirit with which I part with it finds
expression in the words of Herrick, which I here sub-
join:

> Go thou forth, my book, though late
> Yet be timely fortunate.
> It may chance good-luck may send
> Thee a kinsman or a friend,
> That may harbour thee, when I
> With my fates neglected lie.
> If thou know'st not where to dwell,
> See, the fire's by.—Farewell.

They who attempt to read it will, I fancy, not like the
foot-notes, but I plead their need and usefulness. By
them, and by them only, are scholars able at once to locate the source of some statement, and control it at its
origin, and from them must a new and better start be
commenced. If the beauty of the page seems marred by
them, let the reader who needs them not, nevertheless
suffer them gladly, and read on gaily, taking no heed
of their presence. To those who find some use for them,

there may occasionally arise a smile at the minute cita-
tion of the very page of a Teubner text. The excuse now
offered is that I have often found it difficult to locate a
reference, and was determined to give every possible
help, no matter how unnecessary it may in some instances appear.

Yet in spite of the paraphernalia of learning at the
bottom of the page the book was intended to be read,
not merely to be used for reference. These men of the
long ago have become very real to me, and I should
wish this book might help others to see them as they
were in life.

> "I have heard, but not believed, the spirits o' the dead
> May walk again." (*Winter's Tale*, iii, 3.)

The ghosts of Darius, Cyrus and Alexander are here
called to walk again, and the reader is besought to look
and see them.

To those who have helped in its making more thanks
is due in illustrations than in any other part. The Cura-
tors of the Bodleian Library, and the Trustees of the
British Museum have given permission to make pictures within their precincts, and several publishers have
authorized quotations from copyright material. To
them thanks are expressed at the proper places.

And so with such justification or defense as I can
offer I hand the book over to critics or friends. It is the
last big book that I shall ever attempt to write. Into
obscurity I slip away modestly and kindly.

ROBERT W. ROGERS.

THE BODLEIAN LIBRARY,
September 10, 1928.

CONTENTS

THE PERSIANS

THE PERSIAN KINGS

ALEXANDER THE GREAT

THE END

ILLUSTRATIONS

TEXT CUTS AND MAPS

THE PERSIANS

"In that admirable sytem of education which Xenophon ascribes to the Persians, we find that they taught virtue to their children as other nations teach them letters. Plato says that, in their royal family the eldest son was brought up thus: after his birth he was given into the hands, not of women, but of eunuchs of the highest reputation in the king's household because of their virtue. On these devolved the charge of making his body beautiful and sound, and after seven years they taught him to ride and to hunt. When he arrived at the age of fourteen, they entrusted him to the hands of four men: the wisest, the most upright, the most temperate, and the bravest of the nation. The first taught him religion; the second, to be always truthful; the third, to make himself master of his lusts; the fourth to fear nothing."

MONTAIGNE.

CHAPTER I

THE LAND AND PEOPLE

THE name Persia is applied in a broad sense in modern times among Western peoples to a vast territory from beyond the Caspian Sea in the west to the Hindu Kush in the east, and from the steppes of Turkestan, the Oxus, and the Jaxartes in the north to the Persian Gulf in the south. The name is preserved in modern Oriental usage in the form Fars, applied only to the southwestern portion of the larger territory, while the general name of Iran or Eran is given to the whole. For the purpose of this story the name Persia may, for convenience, be applied to the whole, for over it all, in greater or less degree for many centuries, Persian kings held sway, and from it came men of war and not insignificant contributions to the life of the world and the advance of civilization, or to its retardation. Of it as a unit Darius, one of its greatest kings, said it was "beautiful, possessing good horses, possessing good men," nor was this an idle boast, though it did not apply with anything like equal force to the land universally.

In the larger ancient sense Persia covers more than a million square miles, and provides almost every variety of land from the lowest coastal areas to mountain peaks nearly thirteen thousand feet in height, with long ranges nine thousand to ten thousand feet high and yet longer ones but fifteen to seventeen hundred feet above sea-level. Here and there these mountain ranges are broken by strips of desert, or, for the good of men

3

and cattle, by beautiful valleys. To these more especially do the proud words of Darius apply. They were
fitted to bear sturdy men and to produce noble horses,
both a contrast to those of the coastal strip by the Persian Gulf, which stretches for hundreds of miles seldom more than forty miles in width, and dominated by
abnormally high temperatures and sluggish winds.
Besides the lesser deserts of mountain valleys the land
has an immense stretch of desert "right across the high
plateau of Iran, going from northwest to southeast
and dividing the fertile provinces of the land into two
groups; for the desert is continuous from the southern
base of the Elburz Mountains, that to the north over-
look the Caspian, to the arid ranges of Makrân, which
border the Persian Gulf. Thus it measures nearly 800
m. in length, but the breadth varies considerably; for
in shape this immense area of drought is somewhat
that of an hour-glass with a narrow neck, measuring
only some 100 m. across, dividing Kermân from Seistân,
while both north and south of this the breadth expands
and in places reaches to over 200 m."[1]

The drainage of this vast region divides into five
principal distributions, of which by far the larger single part consists of rivers which do not reach the sea,
but are lost in central Persia in salt swamps now locally
known as *kavirs*. During the periods of snow melting
on the mountains or in torrential rains thousands of
such rivers flood violently and dash precipitately to
their ultimate destination in kavirs, and neither in ancient nor in modern times have they been successfully
used or controlled. In the summer they dwindle to rills
barely sufficient for irrigation, or disappear completely,
leaving no memorial but stony beds. Next in impor-

[1] Le Strange, *Lands of the Eastern Caliphate*, 1905.

FIG. 1.   The Zagros Gates.

FIG. 2.   Distant View of Behistun.

tance to these are the rivers of the southwestern region, which discharge their waters into the Persian Gulf or the Arabian Sea, the most important of them, the Diyala and the Kerkhek, both emptying into the Tigris. The remaining drainage areas are connected with the Caspian Sea, the Seistân, and Lake Urmia. The fluctuations in water volume between summer and winter, and the tortuous course of most of the rivers, have all conspired to render water-borne transport relatively small and always difficult. There was nowhere in the land any river to compare with the Nile or the Euphrates, and there is not one good natural harbor on the Persian Gulf or the Arabian Sea. For these reasons Persian history had a course widely different from those of Egypt and of Babylonia. During most of her history Persia was a land of men who kept ashore in the working out of their destiny, nor moved upon the great seas until her power had swept over Asia Minor to the Mediterranean or the Ægean. Then and there did her men of war learn from Greeks and Phœnicians the noble art of seafaring, and in it rose to no mean success. As they were unable to make an outlet for their energies over the sea on the southwest, so also on the north and east were they enclosed by the deserts and mountain ranges of Gedrosia, Carmania, and the Sagartii. Thus hemmed in they became a home-keeping folk and that too in small and scattered communities. Even their greatest kings built no great cities, and were content with massive buildings at Persepolis and Pasargadæ, which could in no sense vie either in size or magnificence with Babylon and Nineveh or with Memphis and Thebes.

The climate of Persia offers fewer variations of moment than might be expected from its great extent.

The prevailing winds are the northwest and southeast,
owing in considerable degree to the bearing of the great
mountain chains and to the position of the Black Sea,
the Mediterranean, and the Arabian Sea. As to temperature and living conditions there are three general
divisions. The first of these is a strip of country bordering upon the Caspian Sea and from twenty to sixty
miles wide. There the rainfall is heavy, the climate
damp and relaxing, but the temperature moderate.
There are numerous marshy or swampy parts, great
forests and heavy undergrowth. The second region,
with analogies to this, is in the lands about the Persian
Gulf and the Arabian Sea, in which the worst qualities
of the former are much exaggerated. Here from May
to October intense heat prevails, reaching its greatest
height during July and August. The temperature then
rises to 115° F. in the shade, trees are few, vegetation
scanty, the skies cloudless, the air humid. This district
has the reputation of being not only the most unfriendly, but almost the most unhealthful district of
anything like the same area in the world. Rainfall is
light, only six to nine inches per annum over most of
it, or in places even less. Considerable portions are un-
inhabitable even by natives of the same general region.
When these two areas are left out of the reckoning the
rest of Persia possesses a good climate. The great central plateau has a mild summer temperature, not far
above that of England, and the winters, though more
severe, do not have more than twenty degrees of frost
save in the mountain regions. Yet on the greater plains
there is considerable humidity which modern Euro-
peans often find very trying. When all deductions are
made Persia must still be allowed to possess a health-
ful and invigorating climate, in which was bred and

reared a race of might, of brawn, and vigorous also in mind. Herein lies the elemental secret of the vitality and initiative which they displayed when the Western world first came to know them. Unfortunately the natural advantages of wind and of water, of mountain and valley, have been lost in too large a measure in modern times by overcrowding of population and by fearfully insanitary conditions. The clear, cool waters of mountain streams are hopelessly defiled in transmission, and water-borne diseases, dysentery, enteric fever, and cholera, are common. Mosquitoes, including the Anopheles varieties, breed freely in marshy regions, and malaria, even of malignant type, is prevalent. Whether these and other conditions of similar import prevailed in the days of the great kings we know not and are left to conjecture. This only do we know—that great armies of virile men rose out of these valleys to follow kings in war hundreds of miles from home, rising superior to hardship, deprivations, and miseries innumerable. They would surely seem to have been better men than those who now inhabit their ancient homes.

The great extent of Persia and its wide diversities of terrain afford habitat to much diversity of fauna. Most of the animal life of southeastern Europe is represented, and to this many Asiatic and even African forms are added. Among the wild animals there are found the lion, tiger, leopard, brown bear, lynx, hyena, wild hog, porcupine, jackal, fox, hare, polecat, wild ass, wildcat, mountain-goat, gazelle, and deer. Among domesticated animals the horse ranks first in popular interest no less in ancient than in modern days. Though not bred into a perfection equal to the pure Arab, the native horse, more or less crossed with Arab, is a

strong, serviceable brute, and may well have been better during the great period, if we may venture a judgment based only upon the record of their service in
the western campaigns. Easily second in importance is
the camel, represented by the Bactrian two-humped,
the Arabian one-humped, and in modern times by the
Khorasan with long hair well fitted for cold mountain
journeys, and by various crosses, especially of the first
two. Sheep and goats come next in value and are now
generally good, while dogs are ill bred and the cat not
quite deserving of the rather fictitious repute obtained
as the result of good breeding in the west. In bird life
the country is rich, and though still imperfectly known
more than four hundred species have been noted. Fish
are scarce in the interior and none too plentiful, or
perhaps it were better to say none too well taken or
utilized elsewhere. In the Caspian Sea the sturgeon,
carp, trout, salmon, pike, perch, and even the herring
are taken along the southern shore.

In flora the land is rich. All the fruits of the temperate zone are or may be grown successfully. Some of
these, notably sugar melons and peaches, are famous
for their quality, while figs and pears are not far behind, and apples after them. Variety in vegetables is
far less and many are of comparatively recent introduction from Europe. The date-palm flourishes as far
north as Tabbas, and the olive is successfully cultivated
upon a small scale at Rudbar, and isolated specimens
are found even in central Persia. In the growth of the
great cereals Persia is but poor in comparison with
the Tigris-Euphrates Valley, whose amazing riches
startled Herodotus into praise.[1] How much of the modern riches in vegetation may have been available in an-

[1] Compare Rogers, *History of Babylonia and Assyria*, 6th ed., i, 418, 419.

cient times, or what proportion these had with flesh in the ancient dietary we cannot hope to know.

The people who made the greatest empire of the ancient world, until surpassed by Rome alone, are called Persians, but the origin of the word is not known. They and the Medes, once distinct, were blended into one people early in the career of empire-building, nor are afterward separated. Both belong to the same original stock, and so far as we know spoke the same language, with perhaps some minor dialectic variations. The two peoples belong to the Aryans, or, as they are sometimes called, Indo-Europeans or Indo-Iranians. They were proud to call themselves Aryans, and the name Indo-European is not happy. It is used only as a makeshift phrase to intimate that the modern representatives of this great and wide-spread stock are found in Europe in the west and in India in the southeast. But, as people of other stocks are to be found in Europe, the name Indo-Germanic was coined to restrict somewhat the application. This however restricts rather too much and is otherwise not quite descriptive. Indo-Iranian is better as covering the ancient representatives completely and as leaving out the more westerly and more modern spurs. But when all is said the old family name of Aryan meets all the conditions better than any other.

The original homeland of the Aryans still remains unknown, though debated with intensity and learning these many years. The indications are too few and much too uncertain to bear the weight of any sustained and sure conclusion. Anthropological material is exiguous, studies of crania are far too few, nor are any other general racial indications sufficiently clear. For all practical purposes we are restricted to words in the known

languages from which may be deduced what were the
animals, or vegetable growths, or early living conditions of these peoples. When these are all assembled
they prove to be few and applicable in greater or less
degree to several lands. The steppes of southern Russia meet fairly well some of the conditions so far as
they may be made out conjecturally, but objections are
easily found in their lack of some of the physical characteristics which unborrowed words seem to postulate.
No better does Europe serve, certainly not in its western portions, which seem in the early centuries to have
been covered with dense forests, unsuitable for the
horse and the cow, both animals of the plain and both
known to the early Aryans. The latest suggestion which
may be said to have some color of probability is the
"area which is bounded on its eastern side by the Carpathians, on the south by the Balkans, on its western
side by the Austrian Alps and the Böhmer Wald, and
on the north by the Erzgebirge and the mountains
which link them up with the Carpathians."[1] This land,
its fertility, its great steppe lands suitable for horses,
its highlands for the pasturing of sheep and its forests
affording sustenance for wild hogs and for domesticated swine, fills well a number of the conditions of
this vexatious problem.

Extended though this area is, and well adapted by
climatic and soil conditions for the sustenance of a
large population, it was nevertheless subject to the oft-
recurring problem of humanity in all lands and in all
ages. It was destined to be overpopulated from time to
time and men had to leave it and seek new homes. They
who move more readily are usually the young and the
strong, and in successive waves for many centuries they

[1]See Giles, *Cambridge History of India*, pp. 68 ff.

poured forth in the painful search for new homes. In
what directions the earliest waves moved we are little
likely ever to know. But analogies in later days, as for
example in the Arabian overflows after the life of Mo-
hammed, make it seem probable that those who went
first were pushed farther afield by later migrations; and
so it happened that far distant India on the one hand
and western Europe on the other each received its population.

From the ancient homeland there came the Medes
and the Persians, the former perhaps an earlier migra-
tion. If they came from the district already intimated
as possible if not probable, their line of march would
carry them southeastwardly toward the Bosphorus, and
over its narrow stream into Asia Minor. Before them,
as they moved with flocks and herds, with womenfolk
and children, they must have found the better and
more tempting areas of northern Asia Minor already
occupied. Pushing eastward, they would come to the
headwaters of the Euphrates and Tigris and, by that
strange and almost unearthly distribution of knowledge
among primitive, and especially among Eastern, peoples, would learn that these rivers flowed on into lands
of unparalleled fertility, and at the same time hear that
the whole land was already occupied. Their course then
would lie still a little further eastward and then beyond the Tigris toward the south. There, east of the
great river, the land was less fertile than in the valley
between the two rivers, and its population therefore
less dense, or less able to protect itself against invaders.
They who were dwelling in it may in part or wholly
have been pushed on toward India; and this new mi-
gration came to a halt, and prepared here to make a
new home. How early these movements, destined to

produce a new and great people, began we do not know,
but they may be recognized under the name of Manda
mentioned in the Hittite inscriptions as early or earlier
than 1300 B. C.[1] But the Babylonians knew them long
before this, even as early as the days of Naram-Sin
(2557–2520 B. C.). Their first emphatic appearance in
recorded history as a people in action is under the name
Amidai and Madai, and it was Shalmaneser III (859–
824 B. C.) who first gave them a taste of Assyrian warfare.[2] His successor, Shamshi-Adad V (824–811 B. C.),
marched through their land destroying twelve hundred
towns and receiving the submission of many of their
princes, otherwise unknown to us. Thenceforward they
were to know more of the depredations of the fierce
robber kings of the Tigris. Very fragmentary are the
allusions to them later, as we shall see, but their name
is found in the Cyprian Madoi, and in that form it
comes down among the Greeks. But how early they first
appeared in the lands afterward to be known under
their name we cannot learn, and how widely extended
were the territories which they occupied at first by

[1] For these Hittite texts found by Winckler at Boghaz Köi see his *Vorläufige
Nachrichten über die Ausgrabungen in Boghaz Köi im Sommer 1907*, in *Mitthei-
lungen der deutschen Orient Gesellschaft*, No. 35 (1908). Winckler died April 19,
1913, and the study of his important discovery has made rapid progress since
the end of the war. The most convenient display of the results may be found
in the work of D. G. Hogarth in the *Cambridge Ancient History*, vol. II, chap.
xi; vol. III, chaps. vi and vii. For individual texts see F. Hrozny, *Hethitische
Keilschrifttexte* (Boghazköi Studien 3); E. F. Weidner, *Politische Dokumente
aus Kleinasien* (Boghazköi Studien 8, 9), Leipzig, 1923; A. Götze, *Hattushilish*
(Mitt. d. Vorderasiat-Æg. Ges., 1924, 3), Leipzig, 1925; J. Friedrich, *Staatsverträge des Hatti-Reiches in hethitischer Sprache* (Mitt. d. Vorderas.-Æg. Ges.,
1926, 1), Leipzig, 1926; A. Götze, *Madduwattash* (Mitt. d. Vorderas.-Æg.
Ges., 1927, 1), Leipzig, 1928; while for more general discussions and results
these are especially useful: J. Friedrich, *Aus dem hethitischen Schrifttum*, I,
Historische Texte, Staatsverträge königl. Erlasse; Briefe, Gesetze, wirtschaft.
Texte; II, Religiose Texte (Der Alte Orient, 24.3 and 25.2); B. Landsberger,
Assyrische Handelskolonien in Kleinasien (ib., 24.2); H. Zimmern, *Hethitische
Gesetze aus dem Staatsarchiv von Boghazköi* (um 1300 v. Chr.), übersetzt unter
Mitwerkung von Johannes Friedrich, mit Nachträgen (ib., 23.2); and Al-
brecht Götze, *Das Hethiter-Reich, seine Stellung zwischen Ost und West* (ib.,
27.2), Leipzig, 1928.

[2] Rogers, *History of Babylonia and Assyria*, 6th ed., II, pp. 239 ff.

their scattered communities is also unknown. It must suffice for the present to say that they had gone as far eastward as to be in conflict with the people of Urartu, in the neighborhood of Lake Van, and in the south must early have occupied the area beyond the Tigris in which Susa was afterward to hold a prominent part. So soon as they had made a complete break with their kinsfolk in the original homeland they began to develop national identity and individuality, and in the notices of them left by their enemies we are able to discern a certain national unity.

If we know little of the early Medes, still less do we know of the early Persians. They were Aryans, close kinsfolk of the Medes, and they spoke the same language. But as to when they first appeared and settled on the eastern flank of the Medes it is hopeless to speculate. They burst suddenly upon us in the days of Cyrus. In the ninth century before Christ the Assyrians knew a district called Parshua, south of Lake Urmia, but there is no evidence sufficient to prove that its name is to be connected with that of the Persians, however similar its form. For hundreds of years they made no history, content to till their lands and tend their cattle, wringing a hard subsistence from unfriendly conditions. Like the Medes they suffered at the hands of the Assyrians and were silent. No leader arose among them to give unity in place of diversity, to imbue them with a sense of national life and pride in themselves. When he should come they could offer him sturdy men, toughened by daily toil, and armies of them would rise out of the soil and follow him willingly to the ends of the earth.

CHAPTER II

THE LANGUAGE OF THE PERSIANS

THE language spoken by the kings of the Achæmenian Dynasty belongs to the western division of the great Iranian family, which is in its turn a subdivision of the vast Aryan family. The Aryan family is represented by a congeries of tongues which may be set down in divisions as follows: (a) Indian, whereof Sanskrit is the best known and most important representative, (b) Iranian, of which Persian, old and new, has greatest significance. That we may see how wide are the ramifications and how interrelated are the forms of these different languages it may be useful to say that as sister or nearly related tongues of the great Aryan family there are to be enumerated (1) Armenian; (2) Greek; (3) Albanian; (4) Italic; (5) Celtic; (6) Germanic.

The kings whose history is now to be told have left us a very scant literature, far less in amount than did the Babylonians, Assyrians, and Chaldeans whom they displaced. These kings set down their story regularly in three languages, now all happily deciphered[1] and restored to modern study, viz., Persian, Elamite, and Babylonian. All three are written in cuneiform or wedge-shaped characters, whose relationship and order of development is still not quite clear. The most complicated script is the Babylonian, written in hundreds of characters, alphabetic, phonetic, and ideographic.[2] The Elamite is simpler and of it only one hundred and thirteen characters are identified in any of its texts.

[1]For the story of their decipherment see Rogers, *History of Babylonia and Assyria*, 6th ed., I, pp. 61–105, 216–245.
[2]For some description and examples see Rogers, *op. cit.*, I, pp. 354–376.

14

Yet much simpler is the Persian, which made use of only forty-one characters. It seems a probable hypothesis that this old Persian script was derived by a process of simplification from the other two, yet in no case is both sign and meaning identical with either. In old Persian there are thirty-six characters of syllabic value, each composed of from two to five elements. The elemental sign is always the cuneiform wedge. Besides these there are four ideograms of five or six elements each. There are two word dividers, and eighteen numerical signs. There are three vowel signs in the syllabary, while the remaining thirty-three signs represent a combination of a consonant with a vowel sound, twenty-two with "a," four with "i," and seven with "u." There are two signs which in form are identical with the Assyro-Babylonian, but have different meanings. One other closely resembles a Babylonian sign with a different meaning. Three of the old Persian signs are exactly the same as three Elamite signs, but with different meanings. The main and the significant point is that all these signs, whether Persian, Elamite, or Assyro-Babylonian, are composed of the same fundamental sign, in various combinations. It seems improbable that this sign was developed independently by three different peoples in three lands and at different times. The origin of it in Assyro-Babylonian is clear enough. The writing was originally picture writing, and had lines and curves. When it passed into use on soft clay by indentation the curved lines were found difficult and the wedge was developed. There is no reason for supposing any similar historic development in Elam or Persia, but it is probable that the Babylonian signs were simplified for Elamite and still further for Persian.

CHAPTER III

THE RELIGION

THE religion of the Iranians which the Medes and Persians brought with them from their ancestral home can be known to us only by more or less hazardous inferences from survivals in the later faith or practice. Fairly safe is the judgment that they were polytheists, for in the fourteenth century B. C. they were worshipping deities whose names Mitra, Varuna, Indra, and Nasatya are well known to us in the religious history of India.[1] Besides these there were probably many local deities, war gods, gods of agriculture, and of storms, with many more. Animistic ideas had also their place, for in the natural elements, and especially in fire, were their forces to be personified, adored, placated, or worshipped. These all, as in the case of other peoples, would tend to increase in number as time passed, until the common people would be entangled in a mass of superstition, and surrounded by clouds of divinities of good purport and hope and demons of evil. Nor were religious ecstasies and enthusiasms wanting, for on solemn occasions the drink soma (haoma) served to rouse passionate displays of emotion and intoxication.

In India the word for deity in the later Rig Veda period was *asura*, and to this among the Iranians corresponded the name *ahura*, with whom among these were evil spirits called *daēva*, though in the form *deva* it was the good spirits, the spirits of light, which were so

[1]Such were the deities worshipped by the Iranian kings of Mitani, kinsfolk of the Medes and Persians and in social contact with them. This is made known to us by the Boghaz Köi inscriptions, see p. 12, note, and add Eduard Meyer, *Sitzungsberichte der Preuss. Akademie*, 1908.

called. In India Asura-deva represented two distinct
ideas of deity combined in one term, the former ele-
ment expressing the sublime, the awful, the glorious
side, and the latter the more homely and anthropo-
morphic conceptions of the divine. Similar combinations found acceptance among the early Medes and
Persians, and the ideas which they represented needed
only to be purified by some master spirit, some great
religious leader, who could reanimate them with new
forces, drive down the lower conceptions, purify the
forms of worship, and so give his people a new religious
life and thought fitted to sustain them in dark days
and provide stimulus for great deeds. The man for this
great achievement comes suddenly upon a dark world
which had no reason to anticipate his appearance, and
little reason to profit by him save such a sense of need
as he himself might awaken by his own teaching. The
people must have a prophet, or there would be no
dawning of a better day.

The prophet appeared and his name was Zarathustra, which the Greeks finally wore down into Zoroaster.
The original meaning is unhappily not quite clear, but
the latter part is certainly *ushtra*, the camel, which ac-
cords well with the other names among family and
friends, such as his father *Pourushaspa* ("with gray
horses"), his mother *Dughdhova* ("who has milked
cows"), his patron *Vishta-aspa*, and his son-in-law
Jama-aspa from *aspa*, the horse, while his wife was
Hvovi ("having fine oxen"). The names suggest a simple pastoral and agricultural environment, and the
prophet appears dimly indeed, yet clear enough for a
general view, as a man born in humble surroundings
and living a simple life. The attempts to make him a
creation of myth, a shadow of unreality, have failed

completely and neither need nor deserve any discussion
or attempt at refutation.[1] The place of his birth is unknown, for the scanty allusions to it are conflicting.
The Avesta (Yasna, 9, 17) sets his home and the place
of his first appearance at Airyanem Vaējō on the river
Dāitya. There was his father's house on the bank of
the river Dareja. If this be correctly understood the
location would be the district Arrān on the river Araxes,
near the northwestern frontier of Media. There seems
however really solid historical basis for the tradition
that he preached in Bactria, whose king Vishtaspa was
his first important convert. This is not really inconsis-
tent with birth in the west, for the prophet may well
have been refused acceptance by his own people and
then wandered far away into the east, there to seek
followers whose minds were not held away from him
and his message by too great familiarity with his humble origin and simple life. There in far-distant Bactria
he found a woman ready to be devout who accepted
him and believed his mission, Hutaosa, queen of Vishtaspa. She became the intermediary and the king was
won. Here was the turning-point in the career of Zoroaster. The early poverty, the long and cruel struggle with men, the inward doubts of his own mission,
were crowned in a great victory. Yet was the victory
not without weakness and disadvantage. It made Zoroaster more or less dependent upon the king. In it lay
the germ of a state church. Zoroaster sought and received the great help and protection which the king
could give, but the conversion of the people was by so
much hindered rather than furthered. Could he first
have begun with them, first have won their hearts and
possessed their minds, the future would have been

[1]The most representative one of these is by Darmesteter in the *Sacred
Books of the East*, vol. iv, 1880, introduction 76.

Fig. 4. Manuscript of the Avesta.

Fig. 3. Supposed Figure of Zoroaster.

safer. The king would have then been a valuable and valued capstone on a structure already widely based on a great popular acceptance.

When did Zoroaster live and do his work? Few questions concerning the ancient world are more fiercely debated than this, and diverse are the answers. A date so early as 1000 B. C. has been proposed,[1] and perhaps largely on account of the authority of its sponsor found considerable acceptance. It is however supported by no clear evidence, and rests almost wholly upon inferences of doubtful weight or value. Tradition is reasonably clear in assigning his period of life at 660–583 B. C.[2] There are no relevant facts which may not reasonably be brought into agreement with this date for the prophet. It is not surprising that the religion preached by this extraordinary man moved swiftly; so have Oriental religions in other cases, and the seeds of life were in his doctrine. Unfortunately there remains one question to which only a conjectural answer may be given. Who was the so-called king Vishtaspa? The name is the same as Hystaspis, father of Darius, and it must be he, not any other.[3] No earlier Vishtaspa (Hystaspis) has perpetuated his memory in any historical or chronological document. It has been con-

[1]Eduard Meyer, *Encyclopædia Britannica*, xxi, 2053; accepted also by Clemen and Lehmann and by G. B. Gray, *Cambridge Ancient History*, iv, p. 207.

[2]The direct Persian tradition is found in the chronological chapter of the Bundahishn, 34, 1–9, and is supported by the Arta Viraf, 1, 2–5. This "places the opening of Zoroaster's ministry at 258 years before the era of Alexander, or 272 years before the close of the world-conqueror's dominion" (Jackson). This has been most learnedly and elaborately discussed by A. V. Williams Jackson (*Zoroaster, The Prophet of Ancient Iran*, New York, 1899, pp. 14–16, and especially in Appendix II, pp. 157–178). This seems to me conclusive.

[3]There can be no doubt of the historical existence of this Vishtaspa, known later as Gushtasp. He finds mention in Justin (Epistoma Pompei Trogi, I, 10, 6) as *Dareus, Hystaspi filius;* in Ammianus Marcellinus (xxiii, 6, 32) as *rex prudentissimus*, who had learned from the Brahmins in India the true manner of worshipping God, with which we may com-

jectured that he was a local king or prince in Bactria,
and that his name was given to or taken by the father
of Darius—a custom of adopting names for one reason
or another famous, which prevailed widely in the ancient orient. It was frequent enough among Babylonian and Assyrian kings, as Sargon I and Sargon II,
Tiglathpileser I, II, and III, and Shalmaneser I to V
show. But these are idle speculations. This is the king
whose distinguished son was Darius the Great, from
whom comes the first positive acknowledgment of the
acceptance of the new faith, the first determination to
propagate its message, and, it may well be inferred, to
live its precepts.

This new and glorious faith represents a complete
break with the earlier religion of the Iranians, with its
cult of demons, its pantheon of gods, and its sacrifices
of animals. No prophet until Jesus himself ever made
so complete a breach with the priestly side of religion
as did Zoroaster. It is not indeed so easily possible to
trace the strains of thought and of influence in his case
as in the dimly analogous case of Jesus, whose background of prophetic teaching is before us from Amos to
Jeremiah. We may indeed see how he who lived in the
simplicity of a pastoral and agricultural life, whose
family names enshrine the horse and cow, may well
have felt early a shiver of repulsion at the cultic
slaughter of beasts, but it is a perilous conjecture. The
operation of a mind, the well-springs of religious faith,
have not yet been solved by the psychologists. Failing
a knowledge of the prophet's early history we must be

pare Lactantius (div. inst., vii, 15, 19, 18, 2; epit. 68, 1), Ammian. Mar-
cell. (xxiii, 6, 32), and Agathias (II, 24). Ammianus quite clearly makes
him the father of Darius, but Agathias leaves it rather an open question.
There is no sufficient reason for considering him either as grandfather or
some other ancestor, or as some hypothetical early ruler of 1000 B. C., or
thereabout, and so to carry back the date of Zoroaster.

content to trace as well as we may the development
and deepening of his message.

From the early Iranian religion Zoroaster took over
the worship of one god, and found for him a name
among the materials used by his predecessors. It is
perhaps not an uncommon occurrence among founders
of religions. Moses found the name Yahweh, which existed long before his day as a name of a god, stripped
it of the rags and associations of polytheism, gave it
new life, and filled it with a new power whose influence
is not yet spent.[1] So also, though with a smaller but
still great success, did Zoroaster. From the ancient religion he took as the name of the god whom he would
preach *Mazda*, and to that name added the adjective
ahura, making the combined form, never again to be
separated, Ahura Mazda, the wise Lord. The important
question in Zoroaster's case is precisely the same as in
that of Moses. It matters little what name he adopted
for God, the greater question is what content did he
give it. In this he deserves a high place among the
prophets of God.

Ahura Mazda is the only God, here is monotheism
indeed and in truth. There is none other to worship and
none other than he presides over his kingdom, which
consists of the good among men, the clean among animals, and the plant or vegetable world. All these are his

---

[1] On the Divine name Yahweh it is very important to remember that
though the name, as I have said elsewhere, "covers a large extent of territory both geographically and ethnologically," the important point is not
as to the origin of the name, nor even as to its original meaning or con-
notation, but solely as to the content which a long line of priests and
prophets put into it. See on this point Rogers, *Religion of Babylonia and
Assyria*, 1908, pp. 92–97, noting especially the foot-notes, with quotations
from Marti and Driver. This use by Moses and his followers of an ancient
name for the God whom they revered is an interesting parallel to the use
of an older name for God by Zarathustra. The use he made of the name,
the religious content he put into it, the separation of the name from polytheism—these are the questions of moment.

works, he made them through the agency of Vohu
Mano, who fills a rôle somewhat vaguely similar to the
Logos of John's gospel. To increase this kingdom
(Khshathra), to call others into it, and have them acknowledge its laws, respect its demands, fulfil its order
of life, this is the chief business of those who believe
and come into the faith by their own choice. They are
to pursue Asha, 'the good,' righteousness. Whence the
name Ahura Mazda came originally we know not, it
may well have orginally been the name of some god or
goddess in the remote past among Iranians or Indians,
but for Zoroaster it is stripped of any personal or poly-
theistic encumbrance. It is not really a name, it is a
definition rather of the being of God, but would very
soon become a name of God and so it is in the Cuneiform texts, in the combined form Aurmazd, which
wears in use down into Ormuzd. In the earlier conception, in the purer use as Zoroaster himself may well
have used it, it is Wisdom, Divine Wisdom distinguishing between Good and Evil or between Truth and the
Lie. The old worship is a Lie. It belies the real Truth
of God, his real nature, it is satisfied with sacrifices and
offerings; but not so is Aurmazd pleased. He is moral,
and ethical are the demands which he makes upon men.
The principle of the divine life is purity and righteousness. These are the basis of his kingdom, and as
they are practised among men his kingdom advances,
and extends. He must teach men so to live that this end
of a world-wide kingdom may be builded, and so Aurmazda is conceived as the Teacher of men, who shows
them the difference between Truth and the Lie.

Aurmazda is also Creator, the world and man did he
make. But the good is especially to be ascribed to him,
and herein are the seeds of a difficulty from which a

rank growth was later to spring, for it was soon felt that it was difficult to make him the creator of the all, without the intellectual difficulty of making him also the creator of evil things. Here was the seed from which sprang the later Dualism. This came early and never again was laid low. It appears in one of the earliest religious hymns, the Gathas, and in this form.

"In the beginning there were two spirits, which were twins, and each existed for itself. These two spirits met and created as the first of all things, Life and Death, and at last Hell for the evil and Heaven for the just. These two spirits made choice, and the unbelieving chose evil doing, but the holy spirit chose justice, and for himself chose those who by their deeds should be grateful to Ahur-Mazda."[1] Here is a theological or philosophical position, destined to a long career, and likely to do much harm, and not good, to the simple doctrine of Zoroaster. The development of a dualistic conception readily supplied itself with a spirit of good, for that rôle could be given to Aurmazda, but name and personality were found for the evil spirit, and so by the side of the Spenta-mainyu or good spirit there was gleaned from the old demonology an evil spirit, Ako-mainyu, which was fully personified in the later Avesta under the Angro-mainyu, which then came to be Ahriman in a shortened form. So easy is it in religious thought to corrupt the simple by speculation until men's minds are again brought into a return to old superstitions which had been supposed to be outworn or destroyed.

In this characterization of the beginnings and the flowering of dualistic ideas we have wandered afield

[1] Yasna 30. Compare the translation by Lehmann in *Lehrbuch der Religionsgeschichte* of Chantepie de la Saussaye, 4th ed., by Alfred Bertholet and Eduard Lehmann. Tübingen, 1925, II, p. 230.

from the purer doctrine of the founder, and to it, in so far as it may be dissevered from later accretions or modification, we must return.

There remain only two observations more, the first practical, the second with a wider sweep. Zoroaster appears as a prophet, not as a lawgiver, or as a definer of cultus, or its observances. He is content to demand allegiance to the truth, to goodness, but he does not define them, limiting here, extending there. He may have been questioned, as was Jesus, concerning typical instances, or special matters of practice, but there is no record to substantiate the conjecture. If he had been thus plied with problems he might have defined more closely his attitude to sin. We may discern, however, some evidence that he laid emphasis on truth, in speech and in deed, for the Greek tradition is not likely to be wholly wrong.[1] Besides this he would seem to have laid stress upon the tilling of the land, and, wherever possible, the redemption of swamps or of desert or arid or waste spaces. He who redeems the land, and from it wins sustenance for man and beast, is pleasing to Mazda. Perhaps no great religion has ever more highly valued agriculture, and the need of this was great in such a land as Persia, whose waste lands filled areas so extensive.

Beyond and above these practical sides of the new religion and side by side with its Monotheism there ranges its Eschatology; and its beginning of rewards and punishment is in this life, but stretches thence onward into the next. Man who chooses the truth and

---

[1]"Die Ethik der Perser hat einen streng formalen Charakter; sie schätzt im Leben des Einzelnen Wahrheit, Sebstzucht und Tätigkeit, im gesellschaftlichen Leben Gerechtigkeit, Ordnung und Eintracht am höchsten." Bertholet und Lehmann, *Lehrbuch der Religionsgeschichte*, II, p. 246.

"They educate their boys from five to twenty years old, and teach them three things only, riding and archery and truth-telling." Herodotus, I, 136.

Fig. 5. Persian Fire Altars.

not the lie, is here rewarded by Ahura Mazda not merely with spiritual benefits but with temporal as well. The prophet who taught the good of agriculture has a thought of the kindly and useful beasts, and for himself even asks Ahura Mazda whether he may have the reward of his labors in "ten mares, a stallion, and a camel,"[1] while he is assured Salvation and Immortality in the life to come; and to a man who deserves the Future Life he promises here a pair of cows in calf.[2] This is all so simple, so reminiscent of the humble life from which the prophet came. Beyond this earthly life he was the first among the prophets of the great religions to preach a doctrine of a real life, immortal, beyond the grave. Thither by their own life determined do they who were mortal pass to the House of Praise, or to the House of a Lie. In a theology of later day there is provision for a judgment before Ahura Mazda in which Zoroaster is advocate and pleader, but it is only the simplest form of the future life that needs here concern us for the present purpose.

Beyond this hope or promise of future life for the individual there is the idea of a glorious consummation for the whole creation when Ahura Mazda shall triumph over all evil, and bring in his everlasting kingdom of Truth and Righteousness. It was Zoroaster's hope that this "Renovation of the World," toward which the whole creation moved, would come soon, even in the days of his mortal life. He can hear Ahura Mazda bidding him make speed with his work that the end may come. But he was not to see it, for the end was not to be in his day. He was to taste the same disappointment in the time allotted by God for the end, as

---

[1]Quoted by Moulton, *Early Zoroastrianism*, 1913, p. 155.
[2]Yasna, 46, 19. Also quoted by Moulton.

had all those who went before him or came after him.

There could be no better general statement of this faith which Zoroaster preached as its first and greatest prophet than is found in the noble and eloquent confession, whose warm and glowing words may thus be set down in English:[1]

I repudiate the Daevas. I confess myself a worshipper of Mazda, a Zoroastrian, as an enemy of the Daevas, a prophet of the Lord, praising and worshipping the Immortal Holy ones (Amesha Spentas). To the Wise Lord I promise all good; to him, the good, beneficent, righteous, glorious, venerable, I vow all the best; to him from whom is the cow, the law, the (celestial) luminaries, with whose luminaries (heavenly) blessedness is conjoined. I choose the holy, good Armaiti (Humble Devotion), she shall be mine. I abjure theft and cattle stealing, plundering and devastating the villages of Mazda-worshippers.

It is my duty to grant to the inmates of the house freedom of movement and residence, and to the cattle with which they live on earth. With due reverence I vow this to the Asha (Righteousness) by the consecrated water. I will henceforth not plunder nor lay waste the villages of Mazda worshippers, nor assail their persons and lives. I renounce fellowship with the wicked, lawless, evil-doing Daevas, the most deceitful, corrupt, and wicked of all, and with the adherents of the Daevas, with sorcerers and those who follow them, with every bad man, whoever he may be, in thoughts and words and deeds and deportment, as I hereby renounce fellowship with the mischievous heretic.

As the Wise Lord, in all his communings with Zoroaster instructed him, as he in all his communings with the Wise Lord renounced fellowship with the Daevas, so I also, as a worshipper of the Lord and follower of Zoroaster, renounce the fellowship of the Daevas, as Zoroaster, the representative of the true faith, renounced them.

Of the faith of the waters, the plants, the useful cow, the faith of the Wise Lord, who created the cow and the upright man, the faith of Zoroaster, of King Hyshtaspis, of Frashaostra[2] and Ja-

[1]Yasna, xii. Quoted by Moore, *History of Religions*, pp. 366, 367.
[2]Father-in-law of Zoroaster.

maspa,[1] the faith of all the messengers of salvation and their
helpers and of every right believer—in this faith and in this
promise I am a worshipper of Mazda. I confess myself a Mazda-
worshipper, a Zoroastrian, by vow and confession. I promise well-
thought thought, well-spoken word, well-done deed. I pledge myself to the religion of the Mazda worshippers, which makes an
end of strife and lays down weapons and promotes kindred marriage, which is the highest, best, and most beautiful of those that
are or shall be, the religion of faith in Ahura, the religion of Zoroaster. To the Wise Lord I promise all good. This is the profession of the Mazdæan religion.

Here then are the chief principles of the new faith.
Here are the fundamental theological presuppositions.
The break with ancient polytheism and its Daevas or
demons is complete, and that is glory enough on that
side. As to the rest there is emphasis on the ethical life,
with the brotherhood of man and kindness to animals
whose kinship with man is recognized. The cow comes
first and this is again the old touch with the early life
of Zoroaster himself. But the horse and even the unfriendly camel have their share in honor, and the dog
as man's nearest friend among so many peoples in all
ages has his good share in it all. If Zoroaster himself
has less to say the early Gathas make great play with
the goodness of the dog, and the later Vendidad is
crowded with him. Early Persian graves find dog and
man buried together. It is a good faith, and a good
practice in many ways resulted in the lives of those
who accepted and professed it.[2]

This great religion as we know it to-day is to be
sought in its Bible and prayer-book, mingled and commingled in a big composite work called the Avesta,

---

[1] The minister of the King.
[2] For a very able and lucid study of all these questions concerning Zoroaster,
see Jackson, *Zoroastrian Studies*, New York, 1928.

whose total literary content is more than twice as much
as the Iliad and Odyssey together. It is, however, only
a small portion of the original collection, made, so says
tradition, under the first Sassanian king (226–240
A. D.), one copy of which, so also says Parsi tradition,
was destroyed by Alexander the Great in the sack of
Persepolis. If he did destroy it the act was surely accidental, for he was not the man so to destroy ancient
documents of any kind. The surviving copy was subjected to some textual revision and was then canonized
in the fourth century of the Christian era. Then in the
seventh century Persia was invaded by the Mohammedans, and a fearful persecution began, in which the
Zoroastrians were compelled to choose between the
Quran with life and their own far greater religious
book with death. Many surrendered, while a few with
splendid valor gathered up whatever might be secured
of their sacred books and fled to India. It has been calculated[1] that two-thirds of their sacred literature had
already been destroyed, by their conquerors, and only
about one-third could be carried away into India by
the faithful. There in India quietness and peace were
found, but obscurity also, and the great outside world
neither knew nor cared about this people or about its
sacred book. So in darkness awaiting its re-creator lay
all that Zoroaster and his followers had taught.

The re-creation is one of the greatest romances of
literary rediscovery, and the world of learning owes
it all to the amazing patience and perseverance of a
son of the French people, the greatest culture folk of
Europe. He was Abraham Hyacinthe Anquetil Du Perron, born in Paris December 7, 1731, and was early destined for the priesthood, and for it began his prepara-

[1] By A. V. Williams Jackson.

tion. But he displayed keenest pleasure in the Hebrew of the Old Testament and from it crept out into Arabic and other languages of the Semitic family. As to many others of a later day the stories of travellers in the Orient were fascinating to him, and the early attempts to decipher copies of ancient inscriptions, and to penetrate beneath their solemn and mysterious externals into the faiths and emotions of the peoples who had written them roused his enquiring mind to a passion. Chiefest among all those who thus came to quicken and inspire and also to instruct was Thomas Hyde,[1] of the University of Oxford, more nearly related to the University of Paris in many respects than any other ancient foundation. An Avesta manuscript of the Yasna had been brought to Canterbury in 1633, and in 1723 George Boucher, an Englishman, had brought from the Parsis in Surat a copy of the Vendidad Sadah, which lay in the Bodleian Library at Oxford as a curiosity only, for Hyde could use only the later Parsi sources. But his book, great though it was, and as weak as it was great, sufficed to rouse Anquetil Du Perron to an unconquerable desire to visit India and seek original sources, and learn there the languages in which they might be written. Knowing no other way, he enlisted as a private November 2, 1754, in an expedition about to sail from L'Orient. Friends then arose to purchase his release, and he sailed a free man and seated at the captain's table. After six months' voyage he landed at Pondicherry August 10, 1755, and made his way to Surat. His sunny and eager spirit won the favor of the priests, who gave him facilities for learning to read their sacred books, and there for nearly seven years he remained, through a period of war and political dis-

[1]*Historia Religionis veterum Persarum*, 1700.

turbance, conquering obstacles, and surmounting every difficulty. He returned in an English vessel, spent a while in London and Oxford to see what they might possess, and on March 14, 1762, arrived in triumph at Paris, capital of the world of letters, carrying with him no less than one hundred and eighty Oriental manuscripts. With the same fortitude which he had displayed in India, he now set himself in loneliness and self-inflicted poverty to the task of collating, editing, and publishing his stores, and in 1771 there issued from the press in three volumes his Zend Avesta,[1] as he then called it, the first translation ever made. Its reception in France was splendid and with that he must perforce be content for the time. It is a sad reflection that the most distinguished among English Orientalists, Sir William Jones, published at once in French a letter assailing the work and declaring that the Parsis had palmed off on Anquetil worthless materials, void of any real scientific value. Jones it was who perpetrated the absurdity and it is not easy to find excuses for him. In his train there followed Sir John Chardin, who had done useful work as an explorer, but had no competence for a judicial decision on this problem. In Germany, though Meiners[2] was in agreement with the English, Kleuker[3] became a supporter and translated the work for the use of his countrymen. For fifty years the hopeless, helpless controversy dragged on, and on January 17, 1805, Anquetil laid down his weary body, still deprived of his just dues, and his fair meed of praise. But the reversal of unfavorable judgments must

[1]*Ouvrage de Zoroastre*, 3 vols., Paris, 1771.
[2]Christoph Meiners, Allgemeine Krische Geschichte der Religionen. 2 Bde., Hannover, 1806-7.
[3]Johann Friedrich Kleuker, Zend-Avesta, Zoroasters lebendiges Wort (Nach dem Französischen des Herrn Anquetil, von J. F. K.), 1776, 1777.

come, led on by Rask, a distinguished Danish philologist (1826) and carried to a triumphant conclusion by Eugène Burnouf, he of many and distinguished services to learning. His approach was by way of Sanskrit and an old translation of the Avesta in that venerable and related language. He demonstrated the soundness of Anquetil's general discussion and proved the immense importance of his primary contribution. He was, also, able to correct many mistakes, unavoidable indeed, which the pioneer had made, and when the Ancient Persian texts of the Achæmenian kings were successfully deciphered more confidence was gained and the public as well as scholars were satisfied. So came to the western world the rich and beautiful documents of one of the greatest and noblest faiths of mankind.

There remains only that we take a hasty glimpse at the religious literature of Zoroastrianism. This is as a whole called the Avesta, and its language Avestan, though much varying in age, dialectic variations, and character. It is usual to divide this combined Bible and Prayer Book into the following books:[1]

1. Yasna, including the Gathas.
2. Vispered.
3. Yashts.
4. Minor Texts (Nyaishes, Gahs, etc.).
5. Vendidad.
6. Fragments, from Hadhokt Nask, etc.

The Yasna, which means "sacrifice, worship," is the chief liturgical work of the sacred canon. In it are the prayers and hymns used by the priests in the sacred offices, and following upon them the Gathas, which is an Aryan word originally signifying poetical form,

[1] So A. V. Williams Jackson, An Avesta Grammar, 1892, p. xvi.

hymns, songs; but the word early lost this special meaning, for it appears also as covering seven short compositions in prose, which are far below the metrical portions in religious value. They came from a later date and in them the old deities reappear, and polytheism, and angelolatry are registered as a sad decadence from the pure faith of the great prophet.

The only portion of the Avesta which concerns our story is the little collection of Gathas now preserved in Yasna 28–34; 43–46; 47–50; 51, 53, omitting the prose forms in Yasna 35–42. Here in these little metrical compositions, preserved by faithful hands, are all that remain, or that tradition has secured, of the teaching of the prophet. They represent as nearly as may now be found the body of faith which possessed the earliest followers. These are they that preserve that life and truth which made Darius the Great the man of the new spirit. These show us what gave to the Persians of that age and for long after the spirit of ethical goodness which called forth the admiration of the cultivated and more highly civilized Greeks.

THE PERSIAN KINGS

CHAPTER IV

CYRUS THE GREAT

THE day of empire-building upon a scale undreamt before had come in the person of Cyrus, who well deserves the appellation Great. He was now about forty years of age, and he had thirty years of rule before his death at seventy. He had inherited from his father a kingdom small in extent and weak in power. Perhaps never before had any king destined to glory, honor, and majesty begun his career upon a promise so small.

The name which he made so great appears in the Persian inscriptions written *Kurush,* in Elamite *Kurash,* as also in Assyrian and Babylonian, in Hebrew *Koresh,* in Greek *Kuros,* and in Latin *Cyrus.* His is the only name ever borne by an Oriental king which passed into common use among Christians, probably because it was found in the Bible and has no unseemly sound in modern ears. The origin of the name is unknown, as is also its meaning. It has been supposed by some to be Elamite, and this may be the case, though there is no positive proof of it. It finds some support in that it does not seem to be Persian, and the Greeks preserved a tradition that his name was *Agradates,*[1] which is certainly Persian. If this really was the great king's name we are left to conjecture why he should have adopted an Elamite name in place of his own. Whatever the reason, it is as Cyrus and not as Agradates that he is known in ancient and in modern times.

[1] Strabo, *Geographica,* XV, III, 6, ed. Meineke, III, p. 1017 (Teubner).

It has served him well, for it rings melodiously down the corridors of time.

But whatever be the nationality of the name there is no doubt that Cyrus was a Persian, for on that point tradition never varies.[1] Cyrus was the son of Cambyses, and the stories[2] that make his mother Mandane, daughter of the Median king Astyages, may safely be dismissed as legends intended to comfort the Medes after their defeat. It will be safe to regard Cyrus as wholly Persian, able to say of himself, had he so chosen, what Darius was later to say of himself, "I am Darius, a Persian, son of a Persian, an Aryan, of Aryan race."

Of the childhood, youth, and education of Cyrus there is unhappily no knowledge for us. This is not strange, but it is surprising that we have no notice of his early manhood, of the years of preparation for a career so splendid. One may only wonder whether he had served as a soldier in the field under his father Cambyses, or had had some opportunity to observe or even participate in the government of the little country of his fathers. Whatever he did must have found expression in this tiny land of Anshan or Anzan, with its capital city of the same name and a rival in some measure of the city of Susa. What dreams he may have indulged of future greatness we may not divine, but it seems hardly probable that he should have come so suddenly without even the preparation of day-dreams, or the exercise in war or peace of talents so distinguished, into the beginnings of a power unparalleled.

The accession of Cyrus to his father's throne as King of Anshan was in 559 B. C., and the years immediately following were probably given, as in many

---

[1] Herodotus I, 107 ff.

[2] For the various legends concerning his origin and the dangers of his youth, see Appendix.

other cases in Oriental lands, to the consolidation of his rule, and in his case to preparations for the conquests which must long have been in his mind. Anshan was at this time only a small state, enjoying no untrammeled independence but living under the suzerainty of the Median king Astyages. To this situation a man such as Cyrus is later shown to be was not likely to submit tamely any longer than fate compelled. What gave the opportunity we do not know, but the Greeks, as Herodotus has held, had a tradition that Cyrus rebelled and was attacked by Astyages, with whom he had no less than three battles.

The sober narrative of the Babylonians gives no reason, stating simply the fact that Astyages attacked Cyrus, and that his own troops revolted and so gave the victory to Cyrus, and Astyages as his prisoner. The result was overwhelming and the whole kingdom lay helpless at the conqueror's feet. Cyrus entered Ecbatana, the capital city, and looted it, carrying off its silver and gold, its goods and possessions to Anshan. It was the year 550 B. C., a memorable year in the world's history, but they who stood nearest seem not to have been deeply moved, for the Babylonians contented themselves with the merest mention of the event, and without the slightest hint that it threatened any consequences of moment to themselves. The Ancient Orient was far less sensitive than the modern to a wave of fear or apprehension.

To the Medes and to the Persians the earliest results were not especially disturbing. The Medes had ruled over the Persians, the Persians were now to rule the Medes. The two peoples were of one blood and presumably of one speech, save for such dialectic variations as time or space had brought. The change would

not seem at first blush to be a great one. Time only
would show its momentous consequences. To Cyrus
personally it gave a mighty kingdom at one stroke.
He was indeed the chief ruler of western Asia, for he
had but two rivals. In Asia Minor west of the river
Halys was the kingdom of Lydia, whose ruler Crœsus
has bequeathed to posterity a fame founded chiefly on
riches, and his name as a proverb. From the Halys to
the Ægean Sea, a distance of about two hundred and
eighty miles, stretched his compact little kingdom. The
other rival was Nabonidus, a man of far less force or
capacity, ill fitted to rule any people in a world of disturbing or dangerous elements. His capital city was
Babylon and his kingdom touched the Persian Gulf in
the south and then following the Euphrates toward the
northwest embraced a portion only of the great Assyrian Empire, but not its capital, Nineveh. In Palestine and Syria he laid claim to rule as far as Gaza, "on
the border of Egypt," but it must have been a shadowy
power as he exercised it. His kingdom was at the best
both small and weak when compared with the vast territory which acknowledged the rule of such kings as
Sargon or Esarhaddon. In comparison with these two
rivals Cyrus ruled a dominion not merely greater than
either, but much greater than both combined. Beneath
his sway was his mother land of Anshan, as was also
the remainder of Elam; all of the Assyrian Empire was
his, including the ruined capital city of Nineveh, save
for the small portion to which Nabonidus might lay
some claim. From the mountains east of Elam to the
Halys on the west, and from Ararat on the north to
the Persian Gulf on the south stretched his territories
in great and almost unbroken sweeps. No king of any
Oriental people had ever before ruled a dominion so

vast or so rich. There were indeed stretches of desert within its wide extended boundaries, but they formed only a small, nay insignificant, portion of it. There were also portions wholly unsuited for agriculture, mountains, rough and stony hills, swamps, and woodlands or copses, the refuge of wild beasts. But these all taken together were but a small matter in comparison with the rich river bottoms, the ranging hillsides of fertile land, the forests of valuable timber, and the little cities of inhabitants who were laying the foundations of future riches and power. It is a pity that we do not know what steps Cyrus took to make the whole realm obedient to his will—what he did to organize its government and so to make it not a mere conglomeration of peoples, but an empire unified, controlled, pacified. There may be a useful hint as to the methods of Cyrus in the single phrase from Herodotus,[1] in the words, "As for Astyages, Cyrus did him no further harm, and kept him in his own house till Astyages died." If this be true, and we have no reason to doubt it, it shows a leniency and gentleness in dealing with the conquered which, applied to whole populations, would make them contented with changes in the central or dominating government and therefore less liable to incitement to rebellion. Failing all knowledge, and possessing only this small clue, we may only turn our eyes westward to see what was the scene of the next move on the part of Cyrus.

There were only two other kings on earth who might be considered rivals and therefore likely to provoke Cyrus to envy or to passion. Nabonidus was too weak to deserve any serious consideration unless some act of stupid folly might make him an object of concern. Sav-

[1] I, 130.

ing that, his kingdom might well be left to ripen and at
last, like fully matured fruit, fall into the mouth of
the eater. But in western Asia Minor there existed another kingdom which might well require of Cyrus and
his ambitions some serious reflection. We shall do well
to look at its position and significance.

About the year 660 B. C., the Assyrian king Ashurbanipal received tribute from Gyges, then king of a
territory in western Asia Minor. The people whom he
ruled were the Luddi, and their name was soon to be
given to a kingdom of no small moment for more than
a century later. The beginnings of new powers are ever
shadowy, and none more than this. The people were a
mixture of aborigines of unknown origin with whom
there had mingled a strong strain of Aryan immigrants, the result forming a virile people characterized
by a splendid bravery in war, an industrial capacity
scarcely to be paralleled at the period, and a commercial spirit which should soon give an excellent account
of itself. Concerning the processes of development of
these capacities we know nothing, and very little more
of their political growth. They had the great advantage of a land most of which was very fertile. The fir-
trees on the higher hilltops crowned slopes on which
the vine flourished, and in the broad plains grain grew
well, while in the soft and mild airs of the great river
bottoms of the Hermus cattle flourished on the lush
grass. Stranger than all this was another endowment
of nature destined to be of great importance in the development of the art of coinage, for the Pactolus, which
came from the Tmolus Mountains to discharge its
waters into the Hermus, bore washings of gold, and
was popularly believed to be full of golden sand. It

showed at least the way back into the mountains where gold mines were to be worked to yield their coveted treasure.

In this land of shifting and uncertain boundaries, but lying west of the Halys, tradition declared that three dynasties had ruled. The first, that of the Attiads, is clearly mythical, with a god at its head and as names of its kings words that are really place and not personal names, including among them such lengendary heroes as Cambletes, who devoured his own wife. The Second Dynasty was likewise of divine orgin, for they were descendants of the Heraclidæ, that is, of Heracles, which means that they came of the Asiatic sun-god with whom the Greeks had identified him. The Oriental origin of the dynasty is still further instanced by the reputed connections with the mythical Ninus, from whom comes Nineveh in the stories, and with Belus, the classical form of the god Bel Marduk. The last king of this Second Dynasty is called Candaules, which means "dog strangler," by the Greeks, but his name was really Sadyattes. He had a favorite named Gyges, so the stories go, who assassinated him, and founded the Third or Mermnad Dynasty. With Gyges history begins, and the long tale of divine interpositions closes. He made his people a military power and conquered the Troad, which gave the Lydians their first contact with the sea. This was followed by the siege of Smyrna, greatest of all prizes on that coast, and even to our own day desired by the peoples of Italy, Greece, and Turkey. The Lydians were not likely long to be content without it, nor satisfied with the alliances consummated by Gyges with Ephesus and Miletus. In these same days the power thus rapidly growing and strengthening was seriously threatened by an invasion

of the Cimmerians, who were ravaging great portions
of Asia Minor, but were successfully driven back by
Gyges. It was to oppose them that Gyges had appealed
for help from Ashurbanipal, but had not received it,
and was soon associated with the Egyptian king Psammeticus I in the effort to assist him in throwing off the
Assyrian yoke. The Cimmerians returned and Gyges
fell in battle (652 B. C.) against them.

These events had flung the Lydian kingdom into the
full stream of Oriental life and history, and his son
Ardys, and yet more his grandson Alyattes, sent it sailing grandly and powerfully. A reign of fifty-seven years
made Alyattes opportunities not easily matched, and
nobly did he seize them, and so became the real founder
of the Lydian Empire. He took Smyrna and in it gave
his people the advantage of the greatest port which
that whole coast-line of Asia Minor can show. One by
one the Greek towns on or near the same coast fell into
his hands, and very wisely as well as kindly were permitted to retain their own customs, institutions, and
local governments. They paid taxes and dues to the
Lydian monarch, and so not only Smyrna but every
other port was yielding a heavy toll to the Lydians.
It was not a cause for wonder that the Lydian king
became the richest monarch of his age.

A brief disturbance followed the successful reign of
Alyattes, in which a pretender disputed the succession
with the true son and heir, Crœsus, who defeated his
half-brother and ruled without dispute. The sceptre
had come into capable hands. He completed the capture of the Greek settlements on or near the Ægean Sea
by adding Ephesus and Miletus to his empire and
strengthened his eastern borders by settling them
finally at the Halys. His income from trade was so

great that his name has passed into a proverb; and this
rising increment of funds was used in part to secure
alliances with the Greek states. His fame spread over
Greece and legends clustered about his name, the best
of them being the story which ought to be true, but
alas is not, that he had a visit from Solon,[1] who left
with him a lesson concerning life by a series of illustrations usually summarized in the phrase, "Call no
man happy till he is dead." The prosperity of Crœsus
was not long-lived, for in the east there were portents
not lightly to be estimated. They summon us again to
look at Cyrus.

When Cyrus had conquered the Medes in 549 the
outer fringes of his empire touched the eastern bank
of the Halys. Crœsus recognized the danger with a
neighbor such as this, and took such steps as were possible to defend his kingdom. He made alliances with
Amasis, king of Egypt, and with Nabonidus, king of
Babylon, and from Sparta secured the promise of her
fleet. If Crœsus had now been dealing with a king of
ordinary force and character the precautions would
probably have been sufficient to deter the invader. To
Cyrus they were but an incitement to strike immediately and surely. The opportunity came through the
treachery of a much-trusted friend and emissary of
Crœsus, by name Eurybatos, of Ephesus, to whom had
been entrusted large sums of money to be used in the
raising of mercenaries in the Peloponnesus. He fled to
Persia with the gold, and betrayed the secret of the
confederacy.[2] Cyrus took immediate action before the
confederates could unite their forces. From Ecbatana
to the Halys was a march of appalling difficulties if he

[1]Herodotus, I, chaps 29–33.
[2]Diodorus Siculus, ix, 32 (ed. Vogel, II, p. 189. Teubner).

should attempt to move within the boundaries of his own empire, in order to avoid the danger of a flank attack on the part of Nabonidus. To cross the mountains of Armenia in the early spring when they were still covered deep with snow, perhaps just beginning to melt, seemed too great to be attempted; it was preferable to face the other possibility and boldly to march over the northern part of the great plain of Mesopotamia, with the left flank open to attack from the south from Babylonia. The issue showed the wisdom of the decision. Nisan, the first month of a new year, the month of early spring, found Cyrus on the march. His course was over the tangled highlands in a northwesterly direction past the slopes of Rowandiz to Arbela, and thence to the Tigris, which was crossed apparently without difficulty, and at Amidi, the modern Diarbekr. Thence the road lay open to Malatia on the upper waters of the Euphrates, here a small mountain stream, and so on to the sites where now stand Sivas and Tokat. The road he traversed has been known for centuries to moving bands of men bent on war or commerce from the days of the Romans to those of the Turks. When Cyrus swept over it the land was wild, and turbulent tribes must almost daily have been passed, but without any note or word of encounters. Cyrus was now in the great country which later history has made known under the name of Cappadocia. The next move was determined by the acts of Crœsus.

In the spring of 546 Crœsus left his capital city, Sardes, crossed the Halys to meet his enemy outside the limits of his empire. From a strategic point of view the move was wise, but the result disastrous. Crœsus had met with such brilliant successes that he might well have felt his veteran army invincible; but he took great pains to conciliate the gods, and to learn their will and secure their counsel by consulting the oracles. From two oracles he received the same reply that "if he should send an army against the Persians he would destroy a great empire."[1] He judged this to be a favorable response and did not pause to resolve its enigmatic meaning and to apply it to his own empire. With as great a force as he could muster among his own people he crossed the Halys and won an easy victory over the peoples of Cappadocia in the neighborhood of Pteria, and then took and destroyed the city. The place had in earlier centuries been the capital of one of the branches of the Hittite people, and the remains uncovered in our own time show that it had been a city of great importance in the time of the Hittites and was perhaps still in the days of Crœsus. The success would have turned the head of many another and Crœsus had already much to raise both pride and dignity. He was ill prepared for any concession to Cyrus, whose great march had brought him near. From him there came to Crœsus a conciliatory message,[2] which though humiliating would nevertheless have made him safe in any event. Cyrus offered him his life, his personal liberty, and appointment as satrap over the dominions he now held if he would accept the Persian king as his overlord, attaching Lydia to the Persian Empire. Crœsus indignantly refused, declaring that he had never obeyed any other, which was not the case with the Persians, who had been slaves of the Medes and would be the future slaves of the Lydians.[3] Such a taunt was ill suited to a man of the mettle of Cyrus, who brooked no insults and attacked at once. Crœsus was inferior in

[1] Herodotus, I, 53.
[2] Diodorus Siculus, IX, 31.3 (ed. Vogel, II, p. 188. Teubner).
[3] Ib., IX, 31.5.

the number of his forces and in their composition, for
they were mixed with foreign troops,[1] some of whom
must have come from the Greek cities on the Ægean
littoral, constrained to serve, and others of whom were
barbarians hired with gold. The fidelity of neither
might safely be trusted, and such a force could hardly
be fit to meet the Persians, hardy men of one race, who
served under the greatest captain of his age.

Cyrus gave battle and this issue, though indecisive,
was nevertheless rather on the side of Persia than of
Lydia;[2] and in a second battle Crœsus was driven from
the field in a hopeless rout, retreating under the cover
of the night and laying waste the country by fire. His
retirement carried him all the way to Sardes, to which
he supposed that Cyrus would not pursue, as the summer was now past and the cold and rains and snows of
the Anatolian highlands would compel him to take to
early winter quarters in Cappadocia. He therefore disbanded his army,[3] with orders not to reassemble until
the spring should make a new campaign against the
Persians both possible and successful. Surrounded only
by his personal bodyguard he awaited the snows with
composure.

Cyrus was not long in making decisions or in their
execution. He needed only to make sure that he should
not be attacked by one of the allies that Crœsus had
made, and of these only Nabonidus was likely by reason of location to be a menace, as his territories lay
upon the flank of the line between Persia and Lydia.
As we view Nabonidus in the light of his own inscrip-

---

[1]Herodotus, I, 77.
[2]Herodotus (I, 76) calls the battle indecisive, but Polyænus, *Stratagemata*,
VII, 8, 2 (ed. Woelfflin et Melber, p. 320. Teubner) mentions two battles, in
the first of which Crœsus was victorious, in the second was defeated.
[3]Herodotus, I, 77, 2.

tions he was not very likely to make any trouble, for his interests were rather in religion than in war. By some means, not known to us, Cyrus made sure of him,[1] and was ready at once for an invasion of Lydia, marching easily across Phrygia and entering Lydia unopposed. Crœsus was without means of adequate defense, and could only summon whatever men were hastily available to front Cyrus. The battle was joined in the valley of the Hermus, and probably where the Hyllus unites with it, with the city of Adala in the rear of the Persians, and Sardes behind the Lydians. Crœsus had great superiority in cavalry, world famous for horses and mounts, but was ill equipped in infantry because of the unfortunate decision to disband his forces at the beginning of the winter. He had the advantages of an intimate knowledge of the terrain, and of that subtle sense of defending one's own home which has often proved immensely important to kings on the defense. He had the prestige of success in former conflicts, but had never before met such an opponent. Cyrus, on the other hand, was even more sure of his own personal prowess, and of the men who fought beneath a banner never yet lowered before an enemy. The issue was perhaps never in doubt, but the immediate result was sudden and came out of a subterfuge, as the Greeks have described it,[2] nor is there any sound reason for doubting its truth.

The army of Cyrus had come over mountain and

---

[1] The only known allusion to this comes from Pompeius Trogus as reproduced by Justin (I, 7, 4, ed. Ruehl, p. 9. Teubner), who uses the sentence: "Cyrus quoque post victoriam, compositis in Babylonia rebus, bellum transfert in Lydiam."

[2] The story of the use of camels in the front line comes to us in its simplest form from Herodotus, I, 80 (ed. Dietsch et Kallenberg, I, p. 45. Teubner). It is confirmed, with certain variations, by Polyænus, *Strategemata*, VII, 6 (ed. Woelfflin et Melber, p. 317, Teubner); by Aelian, *De Natura Animal.*, III, 7 (ed. Hercher, p. 61. Teubner); and by Xenophon, *Cyropædia*, VII, 1, 48.

plain accompanied by a great train of camels to carry
the baggage. A suggestion of Harpagus, a Mede, was
adopted by Cyrus; the camels were unladen, and
mounted by men as a sort of camel corps, and these
were placed in the front line to face the far-famed
cavalry of Crœsus. The ill-smelling, ungainly big beasts
from the east, perhaps not seen before in this valley,
frightened the horses of Crœsus, threw them into hopeless disorder, and then into a flight. The stampede of
horses was sufficiently serious, but, as Herodotus says,
"The Lydians were no cowards," and the cavalrymen
leaped from their saddles to fight on foot. With too little infantry support, and in greater or less confusion,
the battle became a rout and the broken forces of
Crœsus took refuge in Sardes, their capital city.

Cyrus besieged, and Crœsus, who had lightheartedly
disbanded his own forces, and had given his allies in
Egypt, Greece, and Babylonia directions to unite in
five months, now found sore need for help, and sent off
messengers, with news of his plight, to seek immediate
succor. What were the answers, if any, from Egypt and
Babylonia we do not know, but the Lacedæmonians
made all haste to send a fleet. While it was still in
preparation the tragic news arrived that Sardes had
fallen and Crœsus was a prisoner in the Persian hands.
The fall had come suddenly, probably in the month of
December in the year 546. We do not know how the
city was taken, for Greek accounts are at variance. The
simplest and presumably the most probable is that an
entrance was first forced by a soldier who had observed
a place in the wall on the side toward Tmolus down
which an inhabitant had climbed and successfully returned. He essayed it, and was followed by others who
formed a force sufficient to rush a section of the city;

and the rest of it was then soon taken. The blockade had lasted but fourteen days,—a fortnight had ended a proud empire, and the world's richest king had gone down before men who had lived rude lives in a hard country and were like to be among earth's poorest.

The fate of Crœsus is clouded by many legends, some of which may contain reminiscences of actual facts, but most are of such quality as might be expected to cluster about a personality so manifestly appealing to those whose minds weave legends as looms do silk. What seems most probable is that the political wisdom and honorable character of Cyrus kept him alive, treated him gently and generously, and gave him such posts of honor as he might fill without danger to the now wide-extended empire, or without imperiling the prestige of a conqueror. If Crœsus had accepted, without fighting, the inclusion of his kingdom in the Persian Empire he would now have been made satrap of a province formed of his kingdom. He had, however, trusted to the arbitrament of war and the decision was overwhelmingly against him. He must now be removed far from the scenes of his former power; and Cyrus appointed him the important city of Barene as his appanage. Its location near the ancient Median capital of Media gave Cyrus opportunity to keep him under observation, if necessary, and to win him, if that might be, to loyalty by close contact with a great imperial centre. There he enjoyed a part of his original royal income, and maintained a semi-regal state, with a guard of five thousand cavalry and ten thousand footmen of various orders. Crœsus was wise and prudent, and became a loyal friend of Cyrus, engaged in his councils, participated in his campaigns, and lived on in similar relations in the reign of Cambyses.

So ended the royal house of Gyges; so closed the career of the Lydian kingdom which had made many contributions to the advance of civilization in the Mediterranean basin, and had affected the imagination of men as had no other neighboring commonwealth. The sudden collapse of Crœsus fairly stupefied the Greeks. He had power, riches, and the liberal hand. Cultivated Greeks had met welcome at his court, and reported him in the number of lovers of their country. Commercial intercourse between Greece and Lydia had been fostered by him. His fall could not be other than a public calamity in the eyes of Greeks,[1] and it would have been strange if many of the more thoughtful had not paused to consider gravely whether this new conqueror Cyrus might not be a portent, awesome and solemn, to all Hellas.

Cyrus knew little and cared less for the Greeks, and their thoughts of him or of Crœsus, but set himself to bring into orderly obedience to his rule the whole of Lydia, a problem which would have been comparatively easy but for the Ionians on the shores of Asia Minor, and their allies the Æolians. They offered to Cyrus the same allegiance which they had given to Crœsus and no more. From Miletus he accepted it, but of the others demanded unconditional surrender. They decided to fight for their independence, or at least for better terms, and sent envoys to Sparta to plead for assistance. It was refused, but the Lacedæmonians sent Lacrines to investigate, and to report to Cyrus that they would hold him responsible for any harm done to any city on Greek territory and would punish him for it. The threat was laughable in its inconsequence, and shows how little the Greeks had learned of what Cyrus had already

[1] Justin, I, 7, 9 (ed. Ruehl, p. 9 f. Teubner).

wrought upon those who had confronted him. If the army of Astyages, and the well-disciplined and splendidly organized forces of Crœsus could not withstand him, what were the Lacedæmonians to do? The answer that Lacrines received had a tragic ring, for Cyrus replied that if he kept his health, "the Lacedæmonians shall not have the misfortunes of the Ionians to talk of, but their own."[1] It was a sharp return and Cyrus acted as though it were likely to be effectual. He appointed one of his officers, whose name was Tabalos, to be governor of Sardes, and a Lydian named Pactyes, who had somehow won his confidence, to bring the gold, other treasures, and riches to Ecbatana, while he set out to face boldly difficulties in the east.

These were numerous enough, though most of them were not pressing for any immediate solution. He might well enough neglect Amasis and the Egyptians, who were not very likely to fall on his flank and still less to invade Persia; and what we have come to know of Nabonidus personally eliminates him as a source of any possible danger. But there may have been a serious threat from the Bactrians and the Sacae, as the Greeks[2] mention their names as a menace. Whatever the immediate cause, Cyrus left his new western conquests and set out on the long march eastward. He was but well away when Pactyes forgot his pledges, turned traitor to his chief, and headed a revolt. He hired mercenaries on the coast, and laid siege to Tabalos in the acropolis of Sardes. This was a serious situation, for if Sardes fell all Lydia would be lost and a campaign of reconquest would be necessary. Cyrus sent Mazares, a

---

[1]Herodotus, I, 152, 153. There is also an allusion to this embassy in Diodorus Siculus, IX, 36 (ed. Vogel, II, p. 191. Teubner), which has been supposed to have reached him through Ephorus.

[2]Herodotus, I, 53.

Mede, with troops to succor Tabalos, and went on to
the hills of Persia. On the approach of help Pactyes
fled to Cyme, and Mazares disarmed the citizens and
restored peace and Persian authority. After many vi-
cissitudes and efforts to escape, Pactyes fell into the
hands of the Persians and Mazares set about reducing
the Greek cities, but death claimed him when he had
done no more than reduce Priene and ravage the plains
of Menander and of Magnesia to feed his men. The
command then fell to Harpagos, who made better
shrift of a difficult situation, though with curious in-
terludes in his successes. The inhabitants of Phocæa
and Teos fled their little cities, preferring exile to slavery and sailing away with all their portable goods, the
former to find new homes in the Mediterranean basin
or to contribute people and goods to Tarshish on the
far Atlantic shores at the mouth of the Guadalquivir,
the latter to lay fresh foundations in Thrace. The cities
in which they had dwelt in Asia Minor fell empty into
Persian hands, and added no glory to their conqueror.
Harpagos found better fortune elsewhere, for without
difficulty he reduced every other Ionian and Æolian
city. The Samians alone successfully resisted, for they
were upon a fair and goodly island, and the sea protected them against a commander who had no ships to
command the sea. Other islands whose people had less
boldness were soon in Persian hands, as Cos and
Rhodes. For a time the Lycians, amid sequestered valleys, sheltered by mountain chains, held out, but when
Xanthos gave way they yielded, and the whole penin-
sula was part and parcel of the Empire of Cyrus.

The period of conquest had been brief, and little had
it cost the conqueror. Cyrus had been well served by
his generals, and Harpagos was richly rewarded, for he

ruled in vice-regal state in Sardes, and secured great provinces in Lycia and Caria as an appanage of his family. But the fall of Lydia was a tragedy for civilization, and the obscuration of Ionian culture by the semi-barbaric customs and laws of Persia a lamentable thing. Here, as often since in the story of European peoples, beauty had gone down before might, with promises of future greatness left sadly unfulfilled.

While his generals were busy with Ionians and Æolians or with the remaining remnants of Lydian independence, Cyrus pushed steadily eastward and north-eastward into upper Asia,[1] to conquer Iran. No story of this campaign has been preserved, but of its brilliant success there need be no doubt. When Darius I came to the throne he enumerated twenty-three lands over which he ruled. Among these were Media, Sardes, as representative of Lydia, Ionia, and Cappadocia, all of which were taken by Cyrus either in person or by his generals. To these he adds Bactria and Saca, which must now have been reduced by Cyrus, for they are not connected in any way with the wars of Cambyses. With Bactria Darius[2] associates Margiana as ruled by a Persian satrap. All these must have come to Persian rule before the reign of Cambyses; and so had been taken and set in orderly rule by Cyrus. Indeed Cyrus had now pushed his domains all the way to the Jaxartes; at one of its principal fords there rose a city named Kyropolis, in its Greek form bearing the conqueror's own name. On the way thither or upon the return he had coasted Atropatene (the modern Azerbai-

---

[1] So does Herodotus (I, 177) distinguish by a phrase the vast territories of upper Iran, without naming them severally.
[2] Darius, The Great Inscription of Behistun (Bisitun or Bisutun), par. 6. King and Thompson, *The Sculptures and Inscriptions of Darius the Great*, etc. London, 1907, where the texts are given in Babylonian, Persian, and Elamite.

jan) and so passed the land to be forever sacred to millions as the birthplace, or the early home or the scene of the early ministry, of Zoroaster, whose faith would later transform the empire. His name in its Persian form, Zarathustra, may well have reached the royal ears, but Cyrus could have had no dream of how much greater would be the influence on later generations of this obscure religious enthusiast than his own.

From 546 to 539 had Cyrus marched and countermarched, fought, conquered, received submissions, and crowded willing or unwilling folk into this new empire. He came back into his capital city and rich trains must have followed him, for the Sacæ[1] at least were famous for their wealth in the east as Lydians had been in the west. Cyrus might now well have taken his ease in Ecbatana, and there have received messengers to report the progress of his empire from the blue waters of the Ægean to the turbulent muddy stream of Jaxartes, or some humble embassy from a tribe whose borders touched his own and would now desire incorporation. He was, however, like other conquerors who have not known where to rest from conquest and carry on construction and consolidation; or like many masters in vast commercial or industrial forms of modern business, who know not how to cease combining, uniting, consolidating until the concern is too great for any mind to control successfully, or until that which seemed built for all time must again be split into component parts or go down into ruin. Cyrus could not forget that

---

[1]The location of the Sacæ has long been a debatable question. There are to be found in antiquity no less than four separate views as to their homeland. Two of them, those of Megasthenes, who places them north of the Himalayas, and Ptolemy and Eratosthenes, who set them rather indefinitely beyond the Jaxartes, may be brought into some relation, but the other two views are discordant. Modern investigators locate them generally in the Pamirs. The best summary of the whole case is given in the elaborate article by Herrman, *Sakäen*, in Paulv-Wissowa, 1920, s. v.

an empire possessing every prestige of age, every suggestion of splendor, yet possessed the rich valleys of Tigris and Euphrates and was ruled from Babylon. He knew that when the Assyrian empire had fallen before the Medes in 612 some of its fairest, most desirable provinces had come to the Babylonians. He was himself master of the coasts of Ionia and of her waters, but he had no sea-borne commerce to bear comparison with that which sailed in and out of the Phœnician harbors, nor could his commerce by road vie with that anciently cultivated by the Aramæans, nor were the newer splendors of his own Ecbatana able to match the ancient magnificence of Babylon. We need not wonder that Cyrus should resolve to capture Babylon, and with it at one stroke seize all its fruitage, all its conquests, all its commerce by sea or land.

The way was prepared for him not by his own genius or capacity, but by the amazing fatuity of the strange man who now sat in the seats of the mighty. Babylon had had her fair share of great kings since Hammurapi (1955–1913 B. C.) had first begun to lift an obscure place by the Euphrates into a city of power and prestige, of splendor fit successfully to kindle the imagination of far distant Greece. But like every other kingdom Babylon had suffered much from the incompetence of rulers whose only claim to rule had been royal birth, who gave no sign of hereditary ability, but watched idly while greater personalities ruled in Assyria and annexed portions of Babylonia. During fifteen hundred years of glory and of decay, of power and of poverty, there came not to rule so strange a man as he who was chosen king in 555 B. C., by the conspirators who had slain Labashi-Marduk after a reign of only nine months. The king thus chosen was Nabonidus

(Nabu-naidu, i. e., "Nabu (the god Nebo) is glorious"). He came to power in days filled with dangers to the stability of his throne, and to the very continuance of his kingdom as an independent state. The time cried loudly for a man who could inspire terror in his neighbors as Nebuchadrezzar had done, and at the same time possess such skill in organization as Hammurapi had demonstrated. Instead of such gifts Nabonidus displayed a zeal not for war, nor yet for civil administration, but only for religion. His care was lavished upon the cultus of the gods, and upon the great temples for the conduct of worship and the offering of sacrifices. His predecessors had indeed erected great temples, and when insecure foundations had dragged walls out of plumb and filled their brick surfaces with cracks, had reconstructed them. Their labors seldom carried them further than restoration or embellishment, for they were content to take down a wall only as far as was needful to make it safe, and Nabonidus would never have been satisfied with work so uninteresting. He took down the walls from coping lines to the foundations. These were sometimes at water-level, and the courses of bricks had to be followed down by trenches until the big bricks first laid by kings of long ago were laid open before his eyes; savants might then be summoned to read the names and titles of the kings who had set them. From these, chronological lists were compiled, and so Nabonidus became not only a patron of the gods of his day, but likewise of the scholars of our time. All this was well enough in its way, but it was full of peril for the very existence of the state.

Nabonidus seems to have lived much of his time not in Babylon but in the obscure city of Tema, from which he went out to watch excavations at temple

sites and there to look wonderingly on the inscribed
names of kings who had built hundreds of years before him, or to offer sacrifices to gods whose forgive-
ness or whose aid he implored. Though there is no
positive statement in proof there is reason enough to
believe that affairs of state were left largely in the
hands of Belshazzar (Bel-protect-the-king) his son.
When Lydia was in imminent peril Nabonidus did
nothing to give help; yet was there nowhere among
men a greater need than that all western Asia should
unite to stem the invading tides of Persians. Cyrus was
after all a mortal man; and a coalition of every people
of the west would surely have stopped his conquering
progress for the time, and perhaps have broken the
spell of fear which drove nations to yield without a
stroke. Crœsus, Amasis, and Nabonidus, with the addition of minor peoples, not to mention the hardy Ionians, Æolians, and Lacedæmonians, might well have
saved the day. The kingdom of Nabonidus was particularly well placed to have wrecked the plans of Cyrus,
for now that Assyria had ceased to be and the old fortress of Nineveh had vanished, a determined Babylonian king might have driven a wedge into the erst-
while Median but now Persian territories of such
menace as to recall Cyrus from the conquest of Lydia,
and on his attempted return could well have given him
serious difficulties by sudden flank attacks. If it had
been difficult to give direct help to Crœsus, indirect
would have been almost as valuable, and the time thus
secured would have given opportunity to the Lacedæmonians. But Nabonidus had no such purposes as
these. He would honor the gods, and leave to them the
protection of his empire, and the welfare of his subjects. In 547 when the crisis in the fortunes of Crœsus

had come and another year would bring the stroke of dumb fate, Nabonidus was in Tema and not at the head of his army. In the spring of that year his mother died and great mourning for the dead was poured out, but no heed was paid to the army. Only ten days after her death Cyrus entered Assyria, crossing the Tigris below Arbela. Here he seized territory which had been Assyrian, had not fallen fully into Babylonian hands, but was well within its natural limits of influence. To any man but Nabonidus this would have caused serious inquiry as to what should be done to ensure his borders against an attack which this presaged. There was a Babylonian army in Akkad in the year 546 and Belshazzar, the king's son, was in command. That was the year in which Crœsus fell, and a sudden drive north-eastward would have recalled Cyrus to save his Median possessions. It was not made, and it could not be long until Cyrus would seize his opportunity.

For the brilliant success soon to come to Cyrus the way was already preparing in Babylonia, as we well know. No people resists long or well when confidence in rulers is shaken, or conviction in the resistless might of those who are attacking has once been established. We have no records to show that the Babylonians thought of their king as we who survey his deeds in so vast a perspective. Yet it could hardly have escaped wide-spread notice that his thoughts had not been upon his army but upon his gods, upon worship and not upon the sacrifices of war. That terror concerning Cyrus was spreading in the land is perhaps too much to say, but there has come down to us a series of utterances of one of the greatest of Israel's prophets, spoken in Babylonia among the captives from Jerusalem, which show what the Jews were thinking; and some echoes of this must have spread beyond the confines of Israel's sojourning by the canal of Chebar, to infect the leaders of the Babylonians with confidence in the invincibility of Cyrus, and the certainty of Babylon's downfall. The words are as moving as they are eloquent, "Thus saith the Lord to his anointed, to Cyrus, whose right hand I have holden, to subdue nations before him, and I will loose the loins of kings; to open the doors before him, and the gates shall not be shut; I will go before thee, and make the rugged places plain: I will break in pieces the doors of brass, and cut in sunder the bars of iron: and I will give thee the treasures of darkness, and hidden riches of secret places, that thou mayest know that I am the Lord, which call thee by thy name, even the God of Israel. For Jacob my servant's sake, and Israel my chosen, I have called thee by thy name; I have surnamed thee though thou hast not known me."[1] This was pointed enough to rouse not only the Jews, but any Babylonians whose ears should catch even a part of it. But the prophet had more to add and yet more pointedly. "Bel boweth down, Nebo stoopeth; their idols are upon the beasts, and upon the cattle; the things that ye carried about are made a load, a burden to the weary beast. They stoop, they bow down together; they could not deliver the burden, but themselves are gone into captivity."[2] He is saying that the gods shall not deliver them, not Bel Marduk, god of Babylon, nor yet Nebo, of Borsippa, though in them Nabonidus rested his confidence. His words grow in intensity as he returns yet again to denunciation and prediction. "Come down, and sit in the dust, O virgin daughter of Babylon; sit on the ground, there is no throne, O daughter of the Chaldeans: for thou shalt

[1] Isaiah 45, 1–4. [2] Isaiah 46, 1, 2.

no more be called tender and delicate. Take the millstones, and grind meal: remove thy veil, strip off the
train, uncover the leg, pass through the rivers. Thy
nakedness shall be uncovered, yea thy shame shall be
seen. I will take vengeance, and accept no man. Our
redeemer, the Lord of hosts is his name, the Holy One
of Israel. Sit thou silent and get thee into darkness, O
daughter of the Chaldeans; for thou shalt no more be
called the lady of kingdoms."[1] So, as the prophet foresaw, the people who had ruled would soon be reduced
to slavery, taking the millstones to grind for a foreign
conqueror.

Soon Nabonidus began to realize the danger to which
his kingdom, outside Babylon's supposedly impregnable walls, was subject. The first manifestation of his
apprehensions is shown in his desire to rescue his gods
from places exposed to danger. From Ur and Erech,
from Larsa and from ancient Eridu, from Marad and
from Kish, the images of gods, renowned of old, were
brought carefully within the walls of Babylon which
Nebuchadrezzar had built, or rebuilt and strengthened.
He would save the gods, men might save themselves.
Let the ancient cities fall into the conqueror's devour-
ing maw, the gods were safe.

Meanwhile Belshazzar was probably at Upi (Opis),
for there the army under his command was stationed.
Upon this force fell the first blow. Cyrus fell on it in
the early days of Tammuz, June-July, and met with a
resistance so slight that it scarce deserves mention.
Pushing onward toward the south the broken forces of
Babylon's army of defense fled before him. Meanwhile
a second Persian army under the immediate command
of Gobryas (Ugbaru) had come out of Elam, crossing

[1] Isaiah 47, 1-5.

the Tigris at or near the junction with the Diyala and advancing toward the west in perfect consonance with the southern movement of the other army. On the fourteenth day of Tammuz, Nabonidus, who had been in Sippar, fled, and the city fell. The only hope of independence that now remained was Babylon itself. All the other defenses which Nebuchadrezzar had built were gone; the Median wall which stretched, a great line of brick laid in bitumen, from the Euphrates to the Tigris, passing near Sippar, had not even slowed up the advance of Cyrus. The ramparts and moats east of the city and south toward Nippur had failed to arrest the army of Gobryas. There remained the vast structural defenses of Babylon begun by Nabopolassar, and carried far beyond any possible intent of his by Nebuchadrezzar. A triple rampart of brick walls completely surrounded the city, the outer wall of which, with the distinguishing name of Imgur-Bel, rose from the banks of a great moat whose waters came from the Euphrates. Behind this as one looked inwards was Nimitti-Bel, more than ninety feet high with battlements and towers, almost like a mountain chain about that great level river plain; and within this was another wall as high as Imgur-Bel and providing a last stand for any defenders who, having lost the outworks of greatness, had yet the will to sell their lives dearly in the defense of the city whose people had always had a glorious pride in her being and history. But the times had sadly changed and degenerate sons of noble sires now had inherited glories of which they were not worthy. The city was surrendered without a blow to Gobryas, governor of Gutium. Cyrus gives the story with a boast and an expression of trust in the city's chief god, though he was not his god. "Marduk, the great lord, looked

joyously on the caring for his people. To his city Babylon he caused him (that is, Cyrus) to go, he made him
take the road to Babylon, going as a friend and companion at his side. His numerous troops, in number unknown, like the waters of a river, marched armed at his
side. Without battle and conflict he permitted him to
enter Babylon. He spared his city Babylon a calamity."[1] This was the god whom Nabonidus had trusted
would save the city, who is now viewed by Cyrus as
one who delivered it to him in order to spare it a "calamity." He is silent as to how the calamity might
come, but inference is easy—he would have taken the
city without regard to any consequences. It was a fortunate escape, fortunate that it came suddenly, as indeed Isaiah of Babylon had foreseen, "and destruction
shall come upon thee suddenly."[2] Nabonidus had fled
to Borsippa, worthless and contemptible creature that
he was, unfit to be a king in time of trouble and distress. His son Belshazzar perished, and, as we may
hope, died like a man, if not fighting, at least at the
post of duty as he understood it.

The city received every possible consideration from
its conquerors. The temples were carefully guarded
against any profanation, nor was any looting permitted.
A fortnight later Cyrus made a triumphal entrance into
the city, offered worship to Marduk, its chief god, and
set himself to give benefits to the common people by
restoring their dwellings, which had fallen.[3] One may
suppose that Nabonidus had been too busily engaged
in rebuilding temples to give heed to the shelter of
men. There, in the city which had been the chief glory
of the Semites, Cyrus, the Aryan, held court and re-

[1]*Cylinder of Cyrus*, lines 14–17, Rogers, *Cuneiform Parallels*, p. 381, with
complete references to text and translations.
[2]Isaiah 47, 11.   [3]"Cylinder of Cyrus," lines 25, 26, ib., p. 382.

ceived the tribute of many peoples, from those that lived in tents to the inhabitants of ancient cities like Susa and Agade.[1] The triumph of the Aryan was complete beyond parallel, for with the fall of Babylon there fell also Semitic dominance among men. Never again was there any great Semitic kingdom or empire until the rise of Islam.

With the seizure of Babylon in 538 there had come into the hands of Cyrus not only the old territories of the Babylonian kings, but likewise also the whole Phœnician and Philistine coasts with their hinterland of Syria and Palestine. So it had come to pass that Cyrus was king of the territory of Judah which had been conquered by Nebuchadrezzar, who in 597 had taken the city of Jerusalem and carried thence eight thousand of its inhabitants, appointing one of the sons of its king, by name Zedekiah, to rule the remainder. They who were thus deported were settled in Babylonia on the banks of the Chebar, as the Jews called it, or Kabaru, the great canal, as the Babylonians knew it. When Zedekiah had proved himself faithless to the king who had given him his post of honor Nebuchadrezzar had taken Jerusalem again in 586 and had deported perhaps nearly fifty thousand of its inhabitants, carrying them off to dwell with those who had preceded them. It had now come to pass that Cyrus was king of these people, both of those who had remained in Judah, and of their fellows who had been living in Babylonia. As he was concerned for the dwellings of his newly conquered people of Babylon and for the restoration of their temples and the return of gods to the various cities of Babylonia, it is not surprising that he should take thought for the Jews of Palestine and of Babylonia. In

[1] Ib., lines 30, 31.

the year 537 B. C. he issued a decree that the temple of Jehovah in Jerusalem was to be rebuilt at the expense of his kingdom and the sacred vessels restored to it which Nebuchadrezzar had removed to Babylon.[1] At the same time he gave permission for those of the Jews in Babylonia who wished to return to go back and settle again in their fatherland. How many accepted and returned cannot be determined, for the number forty-two thousand three hundred and sixty, given as the total number in Ezra and Nehemiah, cannot be reconciled with the detailed lists which precede the summary. The number is not likely to have been so great, and was certainly much smaller than the entire number of those who had been in Babylonia. They had been much differentiated from the people left by Nebuchadrezzar in Palestine, for they who remained had continued in the practice of the religious forms usual before Josiah's time, while the people of the Exile had developed under the tuition of Ezekiel and the Deutero-Isaiah a new codification, expansion, and evolution of their laws and customs, and were in much a new people. They did not easily blend with their co-religionists in the old land, and the work of rebuilding the temple did not go forward as Cyrus had purposed. Having re-erected the altar of burnt sacrifice they were with that content, and the good will of their Persian master was frustrated. The fault was not his, and the credit of willing to do this service for a people who were not of his own faith deserves recognition.

Babylon had now become a second capital in the Persian empire, sharing with Ecbatana its honors. Cyrus appears to have lived at Babylon during the winter, and was certainly there at the beginning of the

[1]Ezra 6, 3–5.

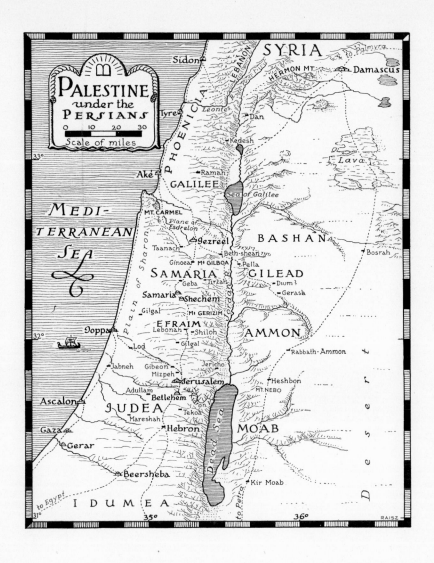

Palestine under the Persians

Scale of miles
0   10   20   30

SYRIA
Sidon
HERMON MT.
Damascus
to Palmyra
EBANON
PHOENICIA
Tyre
Leontes
Dan
Kedesh
Lava
MEDI-
TERRANEAN
SEA
Ake
Ramah
GALILEE
Sea of Galilee
MT. CARMEL
Plane of
Esdrelon
Jezreel
BASHAN
Taanach
Beth-shean
Bosrah
Ginoea
Mt GILBOA
Pella
Plain of Sharon
SAMARIA
Geba
Tirzah
GILEAD
Dium
Samaria
Shechem
Gerasa
Gilgal
Mt GERIZIM
Joppa
EFRAIM
Lebonah
Shiloh
AMMON
Jordan
Lod
Gilgal
Jabneh
Gibeon
Mizpeh
Jericho
Rabbath-Ammon
Adullam
Jerusalem
Heshbon
Betlehem
MT. NEBO
Ascalon
JUDEA
Tekoa
Dead Sea
MOAB
Mareshah
Gaza
Hebron
Gerar
Beersheba
Kir Moab
to Egypt
IDUMEA
to Petra
Desert
RAISZ
33°
32°
31°
35°
36°

New Year in the spring, for then he acknowledged in the most complete manner his wish to conform to the ancient rites and customs of the Babylonians and to respect their sensitive pride. At the New Year's festival he took the hands of Bel Marduk to signify that he had been adopted by the god as his son, and was therefore legitimate king of Babylon. In nothing did he display greater wisdom. In earlier days Sennacherib[1] by his refusal to conform to the demands of an obligation deemed sacred by priests and people had brought a great train of evil consequences upon the Oriental world. Cyrus was too wise to refuse a demand so simple, and had now made himself as confident of loyal submission as a native born king could hope to be.

Cyrus reigned ten years in Babylon, from 538 to 529, during which the ordinary business records of transactions bore his name precisely as in the case of the native kings. The last of these bears as its date, the twenty-first day of the twelfth month of his tenth year.[2] These were years richly fruitful in undertakings both small and great, and in the most skilful ordering of government and of daily life. Cyrus appointed his son Cambyses king of Babylon in the very first year of his reign, and adopted for himself the style "king of the lands," signifying thereby his wide extended rule. It is quite possible, if not probable, that this title had been suggested to him by the learned people of his new court, who would know that the early Sumerian kings had used a similar title[3] to express their possession of dominion over other lands than the homeland. If any greater title could have been found Cyrus might well

[1]Rogers, *History of Babylonia and Assyria*, II, p. 354 ff.
[2]Strassmeier, *Leide Cong.*, 17; Clay, *Babylonian Expedition of the University of Pennsylvania*, VIII, 1, p. 4.
[3]Rogers, *History of Babylonia and Assyria*, II, p. 5.

have worn it, for no king before him had ruled and administered a dominion so vast. In his hands Babylon acquired a new position of honor and power, for as the winter capital of the empire of Cyrus it was the head of a dominion vastly exceeding that of any of its former rulers from Hammurapi to Nebuchadrezzar. From it issued the orders of the greatest of kings, who ruled dominions so wide that the greatest empires of the Ramessides of Egypt or the Sargonides of Babylonia were lost in the comparison. Over this he ruled through representatives whose duties formed the beginnings of the elaborate systems of satrapies later developed by Darius. We can discern this in the rule of the Jews who returned to Jerusalem. They obeyed a representative of the great king; and he was answerable to one more highly placed than himself, who held, very likely, control over the Phœnicians and the Philistines as well. Cyrus was paying good heed to the religious susceptibilities of his new subjects, as the treatment of the Jews shows quite conclusively.

There remained yet another king with whom Cyrus might well expect to deal in turn. Amasis, king of Egypt, had shared by word if not by deed in the plans of Crœsus to defeat the plans of Cyrus. He had been a soldier in his earlier days, but was now an old man and little likely to be able to offer serious resistance to a world conqueror. Cyrus had made both safe and easy the approach to his kingdom by the great bridge of Palestine between the sea and the desert, but he did not undertake the campaign, nor has the hand of fate preserved for us any reason. We may only infer that disturbances in the eastern sections of the empire seemed more important, as they might well be more dangerous.

From Babylon or from Ecbatana Cyrus set out at the
head of his troops into the far northeast. The campaign
may well have been directed against two peoples, as the
traditions of the Greeks have reported. The first part
of the movement was directed against the Dahae of

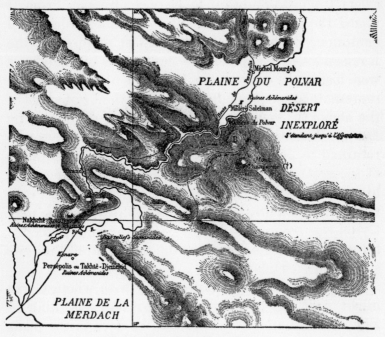

Sketch Map of the Plain of Polvar.
Copied after Dieulafoy's design, which is based upon the English surveys.

Parthia,[1] and thence, presumably, against the Massa-
getai,[2] a tribe beyond the Jaxartes. There on that great
steppe east of the Caspian Sea Cyrus fell, wounded at
first, and then dead. Faithful hands brought his body
the long journey over river, mountain, and plain, that
it might rest near the scenes of his youth and early
triumphs. A stately, dignified, and beautiful tomb rose
upon the great plain of Pasargadae. Within they laid

[1]Fragm. Hist. Gr., II, 505.   [2]Herodotus, I, 207.

his body, covered with wax as was the Persian custom,[1] or less probably embalmed, as the Egyptians would have done. Without, the tomb bore an inscription, which has long since disappeared, which may well have been in Persian, Susian, and Babylonian, and perhaps in the very form which once appeared upon the great shaft of Cyrus on the same plain.

ADAM · KURUŠ · KHŠAYA
THIYA · HAKHAMANIŠIYA

^mÚ · KURAŠ · ČUNKIK ^mAKKAMANNIŠIYA

ANA-KU ^mKU-RA-AŠ ŠARRU ^mA-HA-MAN-NIŠ-ŠI-'

This would well suit the taste of the great man whose dust was left to rest within the little stone chamber,[2] greatest of the kings of early days, yet leaving behind in his inscriptions no such boasts as those that Assyrian kings have used. It would be no honor to such as he were his tomb inscribed with words high

_____

[1] Herodotus, I, 140.

[2] The Greeks have left reports of a more elaborate inscription. Arrian (*Anabasis*, 6, 29, 8, ed. Roos, I, p. 336) gives it in the form: "O man, I am Cyrus, the son of Cambyses, who founded the Persian Empire and was king of Asia. Grudge me not therefore this monument." Strabo (*Geographica*, 15, 3, 7, ed. Meineke, III, p. 1018) repeats this in the same form, but adds that Onesicritus says the inscription was in Greek, engraved in Persian characters, and another in Persian to the same effect: "I, Cyrus, king of kings, lie here." This forms in Greek a hexameter. Plutarch (*Alexander*, 69, 2, ed. Sintenis, III, p. 355) narrates that Alexander found the tomb violated by Polymachus and ordered the inscription to be engraved in Greek and in the words: "O man, whosoever thou art, and whensoever thou comest, for come thou wilt, I know, I am Cyrus, who founded the empire of the Persians. Grudge me not therefore this little earth that covers my body." The one which seems most probably original is the form given in the text above: "I, Cyrus, King of Kings, Achæmenian," which would suit fairly well the form quoted from Onesicritus by Strabo. He would naturally supply a verb, "I, Cyrus, King of Kings (lie here)," and would very likely find the word Achæmenian unintelligible and not attempt it in Greek.

Fig. 7. Stele of Nastesen.

Fig. 8. Tomb of Cyrus the Great at Pasargadae.

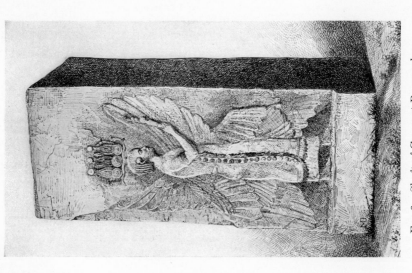

Fig. 6. Shaft of Cyrus at Pasargadae.

sounding but empty. The world was not likely soon to forget his deeds.[1] There in the stone tomb on a golden couch lay a golden coffin with the precious dust, and priests, faithful to a glorious tradition, kept watch and ward for two centuries. It is a melancholy tragedy that the tomb is now empty. When Alexander the Great was making war in India the Greek officers who were left to administer Persia were tempted by the treasures supposed to lie with the king's body and broke open the coffin, smashed the couch and table and, unable to remove them, carried off only the drinking vessels and jewels.[2] When Alexander returned, he found the work of the vandals before his eyes. The body lay thrown out of the coffin, its treasures rifled, and only the battered coffin and the golden couch remained. He ordered the body replaced, and the contents of the tomb restored as far as possible. He then closed the doorway, cemented it, and sealed it with his own signet.[3] How long this protected the lonely body we do not know, but other and more able vandals were later able to accom-

---

[1] The first description of the tomb of Cyrus which has come down to us we owe to Aristobulus, who described it, and his account has been preserved by Strabo (*Geographica*, 15, 3, 7, ed. Meineke, III, p. 1017. Teubner) and by Arrian (*Anabasis*, 6, 29, 8, ed. Roos, I, p. 336. Teubner). The latter has given a good description of it, and of the visit of Alexander to it. A version of it is given by Curzon (Persia, II, 79, 80) and a most excellent review of all the evidence by Jackson (*Persia Past and Present*, pp. 278–293). In quite recent times doubts have been expressed as to whether this was not rather the tomb of Cyrus the Younger. The best statement is that of Weissbach, *Zeitschrift der Deutschen Morgenländischen Gesellschaft*, 48, pp. 653–665. Hommel (*Grundriss*, p. 196, p. 197 n. 1) expresses the same view, and Prášek rather doubtfully appears to subscribe to it (*Geschichte*, p. 237), as does also Dhorme ("Cyrus le Grand," *Revue Biblique*, Jan., 1912, p. 47). On the other hand, Nöldeke stands by the original identification (*Aufsätze zur persischen Geschichte*, p. 24), as does also Maspero (*The Passing of the Empires*, pp. 653, 654). Stolze (*Persepolis*, plate 128) gives the tomb as of Cyrus the Great, and this view is energetically supported in Sarre and Herzfeld (*Iranische Felsreliefs*, pp. 166–180). After a thorough review of the whole case I am more than ever convinced that there is no adequate reason for doubting that the tomb is really that of Cyrus the Great. The description given by Jackson is entirely adequate and Sarre and Herzfeld do not add any material details.

[2] Arrian, *Anabasis*, 6, 29.

[3] Arrian, l. c.

plish fully the devastation, and the tomb is now quite empty.[1]

Cyrus left five children by his wife Kassandane, two sons, Cambyses and Smerdis, and three daughters, Atossa, Roxana, and Artystone, and with them the story continues.

When Cyrus was gone legends clustered quickly about his name, and fancy imputed to him every virtue which fantasy might invent. It is none too light a task to separate out the truth; yet a sure foundation exists for assigning to him a high moral character. His treatment of his conquered enemies seems always to have been humane, or even nobly generous. His people called him a father, and they had much opportunity to know how well he deserved the title. His tolerance of the religious faiths of his subjects forms a beautiful contrast to the attitude of the Assyrian kings, who counted as enemies or as rebels all who had not or would not reverence their gods. As an administrator it may be doubted whether Cyrus made much, if any, advance over the methods of the Assyrian kings after Tiglath-pileser IV, for though he did appoint his son king of Babylon, and others of his more confidential friends as governors of vast provinces there is no evidence to show that he narrowly defined their duties or made provision for their oversight. It is as a general of armies, as a strategist and commander of troops in the field that Cyrus rose to supreme distinction. The greatest of those who preceded him in these capacities are not to be named with him, neither Thotmes, nor Sargon, nor any other. It was long ere any to rival him in fame was to be seen among men.

---

[1]Trees have grown from cracks in the walls, threatening to destroy the fabric by the roots; and it is a kind gift to future generations that Brigadier-General Sykes on a recent visit has chopped them down, and procured the filling of the cracks by the services of a local mason.

CHAPTER V

CAMBYSES

WHEN Cyrus was dead the rule passed lawfully to the oldest son who was born in the purple, and this was Cambyses, as the Greeks have reproduced the name which in Persian is Kambuzia, or Kabuziya, in Susian or Elamite Kanpuzia, and in Babylonian Kambuzia. He had very probably been born about 558, about the time of his father's accession, and now in the summer of 530 he was at the very summit of early manhood, fit by age at least to take on himself the duties and assume the honors of the greatest kingship the world could then boast.

In the very beginning of his reign there were serious disturbances; and his own brother Smerdis was associated with them. How extensive or dangerous they may have been we do not know; Cambyses closed them swiftly by the murder of his brother, but concealed his death. It was quite according to common and oft-repeated Oriental custom that a younger brother should attempt to lead a rebellion against the older and legitimate brother when he became king, but the concealment of his death brought a chain of evil consequences.[1]

---

[1] There are considerable difficulties in the understanding of this whole situation, yet it does seem that the main facts as above stated should be regarded as assured. The inscription record comes from Darius, who records it thus: "He who was named Cambyses, the son of Cyrus, one of our race, was king before me. That Cambyses had a brother, Smerdis by name, of the same mother and father as Cambyses. Afterwards Cambyses slew this Smerdis. When Cambyses slew Smerdis it was not known unto the people that Smerdis was slain." (Inscription of Behistun, § 10. Compare King and Thompson, p. 164.) This suits perfectly the statement in the *Cyropædia*, VIII, 8, and it is not to be doubted because Herodotus and Ktesias have not known of it.

71

Cambyses married his two sisters Atossa and Roxana, in accord with Persian custom, desiring by one or the other to secure issue to succeed him on the throne and continue the line of Cyrus by blood on both sides. Having provided him a wife, and secured his own title to the throne by the removal of his brother, Cambyses was ready to assume the great burden of a serious campaign to which the unfulfilled plans of Cyrus called him. He must take Egypt. Egypt had long been preparing for her fate. Her kings had made sorry use of her vitality and depleted it by mad adventures or by internecine quarrels. The King, who began his reign in 589, was known to the Hebrews as Hophra, to the Greeks as Apries. A mad folly induced him to contest the supremacy of Syria and Palestine with Nebuchadrezzar, king of Babylon, though the latter's overwhelming victories over Necho II in 605 might well have given him pause. He marched up the coast to attack Tyre and Sidon and precipitated a series of misfortunes for all western Asia. Zedekiah was now nominal king of Jerusalem, appointed by Nebuchadrezzar under a pledge of loyalty which he was morally incapable of keeping. Deluded by the tradition of Egypt's greatness, which had long since passed, he threw off the Babylonian obligations and refused the annual tribute. Nebuchadrezzar marched quickly into Syria, halted at Ribla, and detached a force to besiege Jerusalem, while he overawed the whole of the northland.

Nebuchadrezzar was much more than a match for the absurd machinations of a puppet king like Zedekiah, no matter what help Hophra might plan or seek to give. His attempt to divert Nebuchadrezzar by an attack from the south was a complete failure, for it withdrew the besiegers only for a brief moment and left him in worse case than before, as Jeremiah, statesman as well as prophet, had correctly foreseen.[1] Jerusalem fell in 586 B. C., and the prestige of the Babylonians was as much increased as that of the Egyptians had suffered. This miserable fiasco had consequences at home as well as abroad, for the warrior class provided deserters against the king's authority, and though he did succeed in securing punishment for them,[2] the signs were ominous, betokening a weakening of the power to make war. This was made clear by the severe defeat of an Egyptian army sent against the Greeks, who had made a flourishing colony at Cyrene. So was produced a still more dangerous revolt of the warrior class, which the king sought to quell by the shrewd skill of Amasis, a man who held command among the troops, having risen from the ranks. The men hailed him as king, but a compromise secured an honorable station for Hophra, and a co-regency with full power to Amasis. This was a hopeful sign that there was still life in the Egyptian state and perhaps a gift for conciliation. But it was of short duration, for war began between the two and the triumph of Amasis ended in the death of Hophra, who received royal burial, while his successful rival went on with his own plans.

These lamentable quarrels were sapping the strength of the state; and there were enemies who would know how to win profit from them. It was of no great value to Egypt that Amasis should be able to conquer Cyprus; it would have been a great stroke of prosperity could he have recovered Palestine, but the great and forbidding figure of Nebuchadrezzar in the background made

[1] Jeremiah 21, 1–10; 34, 7; 37, 3–10.
[2] Breasted, *Ancient Records of Egypt*, IV, 999 f. Compare ib. *History of Egypt*, p. 589.

that hopeless. His death in 562 may have offered some
vague encouragement to Amasis, but it was short-lived.
So early as that Amasis was not likely to have known
much of what was going on beyond the Euphrates and
the Tigris, but in 558 Cyrus was king of Anshan, and
in 550 he had subdued Astyages and united Media to
his growing fortunes. There was now reason enough to
be anxious; and in 547 Amasis had entered into alliance with Crœsus and may even have meant seriously
to give him help. The great and fearsome shadow of
Cyrus was soon upon his land, for in the year that
Crœsus was defeated and his kingdom made a part of
the Persian Empire Amasis could not fail to realize his
danger. He took what precautions he could to ensure
some help. Nabonidus was apparently known to be useless. But Amasis, though his troops had fought the Cy-
renian Greeks, had found various ways of ingratiating
himself with the Greeks. When the temple of Delphi
was destroyed by fire in 548 he made handsome contributions for its rebuilding.[1] To the Greeks he thought to
turn hopefully in his testing hour. With Polycrates,
tyrant of Samos, he had a friendship, little if anything
less than an alliance. If he had any comfortable
thoughts of Greek aid he was sorely deceived. The
Ionian Greeks had experienced the terrors of Cyrus,
and the Spartans were too far from these scenes in the
eastern Mediterranean to be able to send a fleet which
might or might not be able to do anything. Polycrates,
tyrant of Samos, did worse than naught, for he foresaw
the future victories of the Persians and deliberately
placed his ships at the orders of the Persians.[2] There
was no help anywhere for Egypt.

In about four years after his accession Cambyses was

[1] Herodotus, II, 180.　　　　[2] Herodotus, III, 44.

ready to undertake the great enterprise. He had settled the rebellions in his rear, and his brother Bardiya (Smerdis), who had a dangerous capacity for making trouble, was dead. Egypt was hopelessly weakened and her aged king was helpless. The march began and Cambyses halted only at Gaza, the "outpost of Africa, the door of Asia." Before him there were serious difficulties to be surmounted before Egypt should be invaded. He must march troops over the fearful desert, which might engulf them in sinking or flying sands or stifle them with the horrible mania of thirst. Beyond the desert lay the scarcely less formidable marshes, and possible quicksands of the Delta. The distance to be covered on the desert marches was only about fifty-five miles, and they might be covered in ten days, if all went well; but ten days of thirst would be fatal. At this moment fate played into his hands and sealed the destiny of Egypt.

Phanes of Halicarnassus, who had been one of the Greek mercenaries in the employ of Amasis, quarrelled with his master for reasons unknown, and deserted his service and offered his valuable help to Cambyses. Pursued and captured, he escaped by subterfuge, and knew how to place his new master in communication with the Sheikh of the wandering tribes of the desert. He arranged to station relays of camels with water along the route of march.

Cambyses entrusted the control of the Persian government to Oropastes,[1] and left in the same hands the

[1]The name of the man thus entrusted is given by Herodotus (III, 61, 63) as Patizeithes, which is not a personal name but a title, the Persian Patikh-shayathiya, which signifies viceroy, as Maspero (*Passing of the Empires*, p. 659, foot-note 2) has shown. The name was probably Oropastes, which Pompeius Trogus (Justin, I, 9) has preserved. This would correspond to the Persian Ahura-upashta, and should be the name to be substituted for the form mistaken by Herodotus. See further Justi, *Geschichte des Alten Persiens*, p. 50.

care of the royal household. The movement across the desert began auspiciously, and the distance was easily overpassed. Meanwhile Polycrates had sent a squadron of forty galleys to join the fleet which Cambyses was causing to be assembled and equipped in Phœnician ports, that Egypt might be assailed by sea as well as by land. Had Cambyses known the Egyptian situation as we can see it over centuries of time he might have taken fewer and easier precautions. But he who had taken precautions so elaborate to ensure military success made a blunder fatal to future peace and prosperity in his empire. He set out upon the campaign not accompanied by Atossa, the elder sister, as wife, but by the younger Roxana.[1] Atossa must have felt that it was her right, as the eldest daughter of Cyrus, to bear the son who should later rule Persia, and was not likely to yield the place without a struggle or without revenge in case of failure. The plague of this unwise decision would later fall upon him and his empire.

Cambyses took the command in chief of the land forces and the campaign began in 526. It is one of the strangest circumstances in history that Cambyses was accompanied by Crœsus, now an old and broken man, but with such repute for wisdom or cleverness or both that the son of his old enemy Cyrus was glad to have him near by to give counsel if needed. Darius, son of Hystaspis, certain princes of the royal house, and Syloson of Samos completed the entourage of the king. When Pelusium was approached Cambyses learned that Amasis had not lived to meet his attack, but had died after a short illness, leaving to his son a kingdom

---

[1] Herodotus (III, 31) says specifically that it was the younger who accompanied Cambyses but does not name her. The sequel shows that it was Roxana.

in dread of disaster and filled with fear. His demise
was an irreparable loss, for his personal prestige at
home, his honor abroad among the Greeks, and his repute as a soldier were all alike irreplaceable. His son
ascended the tottering throne under the style Psammeticus III, and could do nothing to stem the flood
that then impended. His people felt themselves surrounded with ill omen. A few days after the new king's
accession rain fell at Thebes, an event declared, in their
nervous fear, to be unknown before, though it has occurred perhaps as often as thrice in a century,[1] and is
now perhaps more frequent than formerly.

Psammeticus had at least the boldness to gather such
forces as he might, including with the native troops
Libyan and Cyrenæan auxiliaries and some Greeks,
Ionians, and Carians. The battle was joined before
Pelusium and both sides fought desperately. The Egyptians knew that defeat meant the enslavement of their
country, and the Persians that for them there was no
hope if they failed, for a trackless waterless desert lay
in their rear. The Egyptians were inferior in numbers,
and at last gave way and a rout began.[2] It might still
have been possible to save his country had the Egyptian king rallied his forces and contested every foot of
ground among the tangled masses of vegetation in the
numerous channels of the lower waters of the Nile. The
Persians could not possibly know the country as did the

[1] Herodotus (III, 10) mentions it. Wilkinson declares it not so uncommon
(see Rawlinson, Herodotus, II, p. 338, n. 4), but does not make it certain that
he knew it to reach the plain so frequently. Maspero declares that he never
heard of rain at Luxor during six winters' residence there, but in one winter
(1898) I personally saw a very light shower.

[2] The fighting had been very severe (Herodotus, III, 11, 12) and eighty years
later the battle-field could be shown strewn with the bones of the dead. It
was there that Herodotus heard that Egyptian skulls were harder than Persian. Wilkinson (Manners of the Ancient Egyptians, 1878, II, 74) supports
Herodotus as respects the Egyptian skulls.

Egyptians, and their losses would speedily have become discouraging if not unendurable. But Psammeticus committed the unpardonable folly of shutting himself up in Memphis. Both ancient and modern military experience shows that this course usually leads to disaster.

Cambyses halted only long enough to reduce Pelusium, and then summoned the capital to surrender. Met with a violent refusal and the murder of his messengers, Cambyses attacked, and though a spirited resistance prolonged the siege for a time the city was compelled at last to yield; and with it at one stroke all Egypt as far as Philæ became the prize of the conqueror. The Libyans came over the mountainside of the valley, unsummoned, and brought tribute, and Cyrene and Barca followed suit. Cambyses planned to let Psammeticus live, as Cyrus had done with Crœsus, and even made comfort and ease for him and would probably have made him governor of Egypt under suitable pledges of loyalty and fidelity; but the unhappy man was discovered in an attempt to raise a rebellion and was then given over to death,[1] and a Persian named Aryandes was appointed to rule the valley.

The conquest of Egypt was a victory more spectacular than anything achieved by Persian hands since Cyrus laid the Lydian empire low. Nor could that bear any real comparison with this. Lydia was a comparatively recent creation, but Egypt had a history that swept back beyond the thoughts and dreams of any Persian, and the splendor of the scenes which met the eyes of these wild men who made up the conquering

---

[1]Herodotus (III, 15) records that he was compelled to drink bull's blood, which was supposed to coagulate and choke the victim. (Aristotle, *De animalibus Historia*, III, 19, ed. Dittmeyer, Teubner, p. 99.)

army was overpowering. The like had never been seen
by them before, and pride and wonder held sway over
their spirits. To have conquered Egypt was to have
mastered the greatest civilization that the world then
knew. The conquest had been easy; the securing of a
deep and enduring hold was quite another, and the oft-
repeated human experience that conquest was easier
than possession would soon be their fate.

Cambyses took steps at once to make himself an
Egyptian, so far as in him lay. The older civilization
had collapsed physically, but its spiritual forces were
not destroyed and would demand their own. The first
move was to ascend the throne of the Pharaohs as a
legitimate sovereign. He adopted their double cartouche, the royal costume, and laid official claim to be
the son of the sun-god Rē. How strange does his Persian name look in an Egyptian cartouche, when compared with what seems its natural form in Persian
characters of cuneiform! To complete the round of be-
coming really an Egyptian he embraced the religious
faith and usage of the land, and had himself instructed
in its mysteries and customs. The man chosen for this
honor for himself and this service to Persian autocracy
was Uzahor-resenet,[1] Admiral of the Egyptian Navy
and warden of the temple of Neith at Saïs in the western Delta, a shrine both ancient and deeply venerated,
associated with the early history of this portion of the
double kingdom and known centuries before as the
"House of the King of Lower Egypt"; it was the joy-
ous Neith there worshipped, the sky-goddess symbol
of woman and of woman's joy. Though less important

[1] Our knowledge of him comes from a statue now in the Vatican. There is a
translation of it in W. M. Flinders Petrie, *A History of Egypt*, vol. iii, 1905,
pp. 360–362. Compare also Eduard Meyer, *Die Entstehung des Judentums*,
Halle, 1896, p. 71.

than the sun-god Rē, there was dignity and honor enough in this cult. The king's teacher composed the religious or "Horus" name for Cambyses, calling him *Re-mesuti*, "she who hath given birth to Rē."[1] By the new king's orders the temple was cleared of foreigners

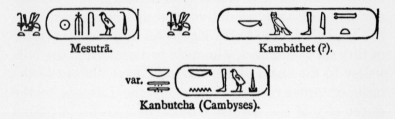

Mesutrā.   Kambâthet (?).

var. Kanbutcha (Cambyses).

who had there taken up residence, and the revenues which Amasis had removed to pay the Greek mercenaries, who had failed, were restored to the goddess and her worshippers. All these moves of Cambyses in the interest of Egyptian religion were quite of a piece with the deeds of his father Cyrus in honoring the faith of the Babylonians, and to whatever motive they be ascribed, whether as acts of policy or of religious tolerance, were profoundly wise for that day and for those conditions.

Cambyses was now impelled by the madness of world conquerors, and was ready to undertake the conquest of Africa, in so far as it was then known. As Cyrene had capitulated, and might be judged safe from evil designs, it seemed to offer a stepping-stone to Carthage, even then famous, and fully as tempting as it was renowned. To make still more complacent the people of Cyrene he sent back to them in safety and honor Ladice, who had been wife to Amasis and had

---

[1] Hall, *History of the Near East*, p. 565, calls it soundly and truly a "most uncouth and unusual appellation," for it was really a title of the goddess herself. The name appears in Egyptian thus.

come from them. The taking of Carthage, in spite of these preparations, was no small task, for it must probably be attacked from sea as well as by land. The fleets of Ionians and Tyrians were to be used, but the latter refused to join in an attack upon men of their own blood on the African coast. Abandoning hope of a success by sea Cambyses determined upon approach from the landward side. From Egypt he despatched a force of fifty thousand men, who were to march from the Nile valley to the oases of the Libyan desert, thence to the oasis of Ammon, and onward by the Libyans to the queen city of the African coast. The expedition passed successfully the oases of el-Khargeh and ed-Dakhlah and then continued the march over the fearful desert wastes. The troops were never heard of again;[1] and their utter annihilation still remains in part a mystery. It is easy enough to believe, when modern experiences in the same regions are known, that many might easily have perished, but it seems scarcely probable that none should have survived to tell the mournful tale.[2] Whatever may have befallen the remnant, there can be no doubt of the utter failure of the attempt upon Carthage.

The next effort of Cambyses was to restore Nubia to Egyptian domination and to add Ethiopia to his Empire. It was a dangerous but quite natural enterprise. The empire of Napata had severed all connections with Asia since Tanutamon had retired from Egypt, and

---

[1] Herodotus, III, 17, 25, 26. So also Diodorus Siculus, X, 14 ed., Vogel, II, p. 205 (Teubner), and Justin, I, 9, § 3.

[2] These great sandstorms are called in Egypt a *habûb*. The story of the disaster has sometimes been thought by moderns to be fabulous. There is, however, no reason to doubt aught save perhaps the numbers of men involved. Budge, who knows Egypt well, says justly (*The Mummy*, 2nd ed., p. 79): "Egyptian and Turkish military annals are full of reports of disasters of the kind and, to the writer's personal knowledge, a caravan of 700 camels with a military force was lost through a *habûb* between Korosko and Abu Hamad, and only two men escaped to tell the tale."

had been ruled by a line of princes whose names have
been preserved but their personalities lost. Attempts
on the part of Psammeticus I and II to conquer them
had failed, and Cambyses was now to essay what had
brought only disappointment or chagrin to them. The
Ethiopians had no mean reputation for skill and daring in war, and Shabaka and Tirhaka had shown no
small success in defying Assyrians; and the reports
brought to Cambyses of their stature and vigor were
alarming, if even partially true.[1] Having secured such
intelligence as he could by spies he set out up the river
on the long and hard journey. The valley appears to
have been followed only as far as Korosko, and thence
the course lay over the desert toward Napata.[2] Before
one-quarter of the distance had been covered the force
was exhausted by the nakedness of the land and the
paucity of any kind of provision. Cambyses was forced
by inexorable circumstance to give orders for the return to Egypt. He had not entered Ethiopia at all, but
he had severely shaken Nubia, and it was probably at
this time that the Nubian capital was removed to Me-
roë, though Nastasenen,[3] then king of the Nubians,
says that he "routed the man Kambasauden." The retreat, which nature rather than man compelled, would
suffice to give him excuse for a claim of victory.

[1]Herodotus, III, 20, 25.

[2]The reasons for so supposing are well summarized by Maspero (*Passing of
the Empires*), p. 667, foot-note 6. See also Rawlinson, *Herodotus*, II, p. 351,
note 4, and Justi, *Geschichte des Alten Persiens*, p. 47. Hall refuses to accept this
hypothesis and abides by the opinion that the Nile was followed all the way
(*Ancient History of the Near East*, p. 568, foot-note 1), but he does not convince me.

[3]The Stela of Nastesen was at the Gebel Barkal, but is now in Berlin.
It was published by Lepsius, *Denkmäler*, Abtheilung 5, Blatt 16. Compare
Schäfer, *Die Æthiopische Königsinschrift des Berliner Museums* (1901). The
name as it appears in the inscription of Nastasen is written K-m-b-s-w-d-n-(?)
The final sign is doubtful, and is discussed by Schäfer, op. cit., p. 45, but this
does not affect the application of the name to Cambyses, concerning which
there seems to me to be no reasonable doubt. The reference to the campaign
against Cambyses is in lines 39–41. See further Appendix.

The ghastly failure of these two great expeditions completed the wreck of the nervous system of Cambyses. He had been afflicted with epilepsy from his youth;[1] and the miseries of his present failure unhinged the mind already unstable, and he became a maniac, dangerous and forbidding. He slew the sacred Apis bull in a fury of madness, and probably committed other acts scarcely less repellant to Egyptian feelings, and quite contrary to the practice followed in his earlier attempts to win Egyptian loyalty to his person as a legitimate Pharaoh. Echoes of these and similar stories, and rumors of the failures of his great campaigns, were spread on the wings of the wind to the borders of his empire, and were heard in Media and Persia, as Darius was later to record in the words, "untruth had spread all over the country, not only in Persia and Media, but in other provinces."[2] If to these national misfortunes there were added stories of the wildest insanity, such as the Greeks have preserved, one could not wonder at any upheaval in the Empire, for they have reported that he had entered the temple and ridiculed the figure of the great god Ptah as grotesque, and had ordered the sacred statues to be burned. He had bidden them open the ancient sepulchres to expose the mummies to his vulgar gaze. He murdered his wife Roxana by a kick in the abdomen, slew the son of Prexaspes with an arrow, ordered Crœsus slain, repented and countermanded the order, but afterward

[1]Herodotus, III, 33. Various attempts have recently been made, especially by Hutecker (*Ueber den falschen Smerdis*, p. 16 f. and 30 f.) and Prašek (*Forschungen zur Geschichte des Altertums*), pp. 8–10, to deny the illness and the madness associated with it as Greek fables, but I cannot see any excuse for this scepticism. See also Hall, *History of the Near East*, p. 568.

[2]*Inscription of Behistun*, col. I, lines 32–35. See Weissbach and Bang, *Die Altpersisch. Keilns.*, pp. 14, 15, and in better form King and Thompson, *The Sculptures and Inscription of Darius the Great on the Rock of Behistûn in Persia*, 1907, p. 7.

punished the officers who had failed to execute the original command.[1] Some of these may be but tales of spite and with scanty foundation, but there appear no reasons for doubting them altogether, and to sift the certain from the uncertain is no longer possible. They all alike bear an air of verisimilitude to one who considers the varied manifestations of a brutal mind gone hopelessly mad.

Then Cambyses turned his face homeward in the spring of 522 B. C., for intelligence had reached his ears of a serious rebellion at the capital of the empire. He left Egypt in charge of Aryandes, and took with him Darius, son of Hystaspis. The journey was long and hard enough for a man in health and vigor. It was well-nigh impossible for a body weakened by the hard marching toward Ethiopia and reduced by a disordered mind to debility. The end came in Syria, perhaps at Damascus, but more probably at Hamath.[2] The final cause of death is not known, for Herodotus[3] says it resulted from a wound accidentally self-inflicted when mounting his horse, while the Persian record is at least open to the construction that he took his own life, though it may also be interpreted into agreement with the theory of accidental death held by Herodotus.[4] The wretched man had excuse enough for self-murder in his madness and the news of the appalling situation in Persia, for the whole insubstantial structure was apparently ready to collapse in a serious rebellion, the

[1]Herodotus, III, 30, 31, 32, 34, 35, 37.
[2]Josephus, *Ant. Jud.*, XI, 2, § 2, ed. Naber ii, p. 6 (Teubner), but Herodotus calls the place Agbatana in Syria (III, 64). This is probably Hamath.
[3]Herodotus, III, 64.
[4]Inscription of Behistun, col. I, line 43. The Persian text reads: *uvamàršiyuš amariyatâ*, and the Babylonian has: *mitutu ramânišu miti*. The Babylonian may be rendered, "he died his own death," which may mean he died by some act by his own hand, i. e., by some accidental act, though suicide seems on the whole the more probable meaning.

origin of which goes back to a disastrous act of Cambyses at the beginning of his reign.

Cambyses had slain, or ordered his brother Bardiya (Smerdis) slain, and then concealed his death, before he set out upon the ill-fated expedition to Egypt. The consequences of that deed were now ready to meet him. He had left the direction of the kingdom to Oropastes, called Patizeithes by Herodotus, who had a brother named Gaumâta, the very image of the dead Bardiya (Smerdis), and in earlier days frequently confused with him. As the death of Bardiya had been concealed and many believed him to be still alive there was an excellent foundation for a plot. Incited and aided by his scheming brother, Gaumâta began a revolt in the little town of Pasyauvadâ. He was accepted at once in Persia, Media, and the Iranian provinces as the legitimate king, the real Bardiya who had been in hiding since his brother Cambyses had ordered him slain. In three months he was solemnly enthroned as king over the whole Empire. Then Babylon accepted him and business tablets began to be dated in his name as reigning sovereign.[1] Having thus taken successful steps to ensure control of all the eastern portions of the empire he sent messengers into the west to proclaim him king, while others were despatched to the army of Cambyses and to the Egyptian people. They did not reach Egypt but met Cambyses with the army in Syria. It was surely weakened by the dreadful experiences of the Ethiopian campaign, and the severe marching over the desert, but was still a force to be reckoned with and quite capable of giving battle. The tradition asserts

[1]See Strassmeier, *Inscriften von Nabopolassar und Smerdis, Zeitschrift für Assyriologie*, IV, pp. 123–128.

that a herald appeared before his army and proclaimed that Cambyses, son of Cyrus, had ceased to reign, and summoned all the faithful to give allegiance to Bardiya as supreme lord and legitimate king. Cambyses believed, naturally enough, that his commands had been disobeyed and that his brother was really alive, had been in concealment, and had now declared himself; he then wept over the fruitless crime of ordering his brother's death.

Gaumâta was now rid of Cambyses, but, like every other pretender, had many and difficult problems to face. He might at any time be revealed as an impostor by the appearance of some one who had known the real Bardiya and was able to declare with a good show of positive assurance that this was not he. On the other hand, some one who had taken part in the slaying of Bardiya might arise to submit proofs that he had really been destroyed. Filled with these apprehensions, Gaumâta "slew many who had known the former Smerdis."[1] To make still more safe the subterfuge, he kept himself concealed from public gaze, and lest some word of his imposture might escape from his harem he kept his wives almost imprisoned. It seems scarcely probable that he could have hoped to keep his secret permanently, but desired that it be maintained until he had strengthened his hold on the country and might then safely defy the dangers of discovery. All went well, apparently, with the common people, who could easily be satisfied with any ruler who gave them reasonable opportunities for subsistence and lightened any of their burdens. This he did by exempting the distant provinces from the payment of taxes, and from military

---

[1] *Inscription of Behistun*, ed. King and Thompson, § I, par. XIII, pp. 10, 11.

service for three years.[1] The plans were well conceived but hopeless in execution, and in eight months discovery overtook him.

The story is told picturesquely and at much length in Herodotus[2] and need not be quite without the adornment of legend; yet are the main outlines probably soundly based. According to this Greek story Phædime, wife of Cambyses and now a member of the harem of the false Bardiya, and daugher of Otanes, secured the evidence. To rid the empire and the world of him was a resolve easily and speedily taken, and the man who executed the decision and assassinated Gaumâta, the false Smerdis, was none other than Darius, son of Hystaspis, who had been on the Egyptian expedition of Cambyses. Gaumâta was slain at Sikayauvatish, in the district of Nisaya, near Ecbatana, on the 10th of Bâgayadîsh, 521 B. C.[3] So ended in ignominious collapse one of the greatest and not least successful frauds of historic time.

But Cambyses also was dead, and could not profit from the end of this menace to the stability of the Persian Empire. He had fallen too soon, but perhaps not too soon for his own reputation. Not so great as man or soldier as was his father, he yet held together the Empire and even extended it by the conquest of Egypt. He was no mean figure, and deserves more than he has commonly received at the hands of historians.

[1]Herodotus, III, 67, and compare Justin, I, 9, who is there repeating from Pompeius Trogus, who has almost literally reproduced Herodotus.
[2]Herodotus, III, 68 ff.
[3]Behistun, I, § XIII, ed. King and Thompson, pp. 12, 13.

CHAPTER VI

DARIUS I

THE man who slew Gaumâta was made king. His own Persian inscriptions call him Darayavaush, the Babylonian text knows him as Dariyamush, the Susian as Tariyamaush, the Jews as Daryavesh, and the Greeks as Dareios. He has taken the greatest pains to declare himself a scion of the ancient house of Achæmenes, beginning his most important text with the boastful and high-sounding pedigree, "My father is Hystaspis; the father of Hystaspis was Arsames; the father of Arsames was Ariyaramnes; the father of Ariyaramnes was Teispes; the father of Teispes was Achæmenes . . . on that account are we called Achæmenians; from antiquity are we descended; from antiquity hath our race been kings. . . . Eight of my race were kings before me, I am the ninth."[1] The genealogical tree thus declared may be represented thus:

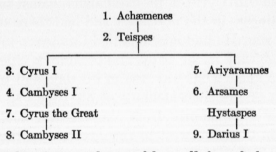

```
                    1. Achæmenes
                          |
                    2. Teispes
                          |
        ┌─────────────────────────────────────┐
   3. Cyrus I                            5. Ariyaramnes
        |                                      |
   4. Cambyses I                         6. Arsames
        |                                      |
   7. Cyrus the Great                     Hystaspes
        |                                      |
   8. Cambyses II                        9. Darius I
```

and whether it was thoroughly well founded or not it served the purpose and gave Darius a claim on the ground of blood relationship which enhanced his pres-

---

[1] The Behistun Inscription, §§ II–IV, ed. King & Thompson, pp. 1–3.

tige when confronted with the necessity of making a bold attempt to put down rebellions and establish a sure dominion over wide-spread and very diverse peoples.

Darius had to fight to establish his rule, for he had assumed the throne over a series of peoples conquered in the first instance by Cyrus or Cambyses but never brought under any thoroughly organized rule. The governors of distant provinces had a large measure of autonomy. They had troops under their command, and in one or perhaps more cases had fleets as well. The temptation to try to form separate monarchies each for himself was very great, and the troubled state of affairs after the death of the false Smerdis may well have seemed to offer a golden opportunity, certain to be seized by some if not by many. The stability of the empire was really in danger, and Darius had come to rule at a dangerous hour. A man of less experience and of hesitant nature might well have quailed before the threatening situation. But he had been well trained for the task before him. When but twenty years of age[1] he had been with Cyrus in the campaigns against the fierce mountaineers in the northeast and had there seen service in war. He had accompanied Cambyses to Egypt, held high rank in the army, and became its chief at the end. He knew what war was in his day, and probably no man of the Achæmenians of his time had seen so much of the Empire from the farthest confines of Egypt in the southwest to the Jaxartes on the northeast. He had all the personal prestige which blood could give and was careful in his inscriptions to make mention of his relationship with the reigning house which had made Persia great, and greatly feared. His own

[1]Herodotus, I, 209.

family ties were carefully chosen so as to give him
every political assistance which marriage could bring.
His first wife was a daughter of Gabryas, who led the
forces of Cyrus in the taking of Babylon. She had borne
him three sons, before he became king, Artobazanes,[1]
Ariabignes,[2] and the third of unknown name. Under
Persian law or custom none of these might inherit
the throne, only the first-born after the father's en-
thronement being eligible. As soon as Darius was king
he took steps to assure issue, and of distinguished family. He married Atossa, widow of Cambyses, daughter
of Cyrus, and Artystone,[3] a second daughter of Cyrus,
and Parmys, daughter of Bardiya, and Phaidyme,
daughter of Otanes, who had the honor of revealing the
fraud of the false Bardiya and had also been a wife of
Cambyses. The fifth wife of Darius was Phratagune,[4]
daughter of his brother Artanes. A sixth wife bore him
a son Arsamenes,[5] but the mother's name is unknown.

With family prestige and long training in war, with
some experience in administration, Darius set himself
to meet his responsibilities. There were some fortunate
advantages on his side. He had made an end of Gaumâta soon enough to forestall a very menacing issue. A
few years of his rule would have so established him
that overthrow would have been almost, if not quite,
impossible. Fortunate also was it that there was no
man left in the Gaumâta conspiracy with capacity for
leadership, or a new pretender might have arisen at
once.

The storms of revolt broke first in Elam and Babylon. In the former the leader was Atrina, or in Susian,
Ashina, son of Uparadanma, who proclaimed himself

---

[1]Herodotus, VII, 2; VIII, 126 f.   [2]Ib., VII, 97; VIII, 89.
[3]Herodotus, III, 88.   [4]Herodotus, VII, 224.   [5]Ib., VII, 69.

king in Susiana, the chief city of the province.[1] His
reign was brief, perhaps not more than six weeks, when
he was surrendered to Darius, probably by his own
people, and then slain by the king. In Babylon the
rebel leader was Nidintu-Bel, who posed as Nebuchadrezzar and in some way gained control of the city and
mustered an army which he deployed on the Tigris.
He got popular support because the Babylonians had
become convinced that their acceptance of Cyrus had
been a mistake, and their hope of transforming him
into a real Babylonian a delusion. He had fostered the
idea by the attention shown their customs, and the
worship offered their gods. But there still remained the
unspanned gulf of language and of many diverse customs, and a people who possessed so strong a conception of their own glory and a feeling for nationality
scarcely paralleled elsewhere in the ancient Orient were
not easily persuaded that a Persian could be one of
them. The forces commanding the Tigris were too
great for Darius to venture a frontal attack, and the
situation was further complicated by the boats which
Nidintu-Bel had secured to patrol the river, and so
make a crossing difficult. Darius brought the bulk of
his forces, and prepared for immediate assault. With
his army were detachments mounted on horses and
others on camels; and by making a feint he successfully
deceived his enemy and gained the opposite bank. Nidintu-Bel was too prudent to permit an attack on flank
or rear, and withdrew, to make a fresh stand at Zazanu
on the Euphrates. Defeated there, he met with heavy
losses in the river, and only escaped with his own life
and a few horsemen to shut himself up within the immense fortifications of Babylon. The city did not open

[1]Inscription of Behistun, I, 74, 82, ed. King and Thompson, pp. 15–17.

its gates to Darius as it had done to Cyrus and a regular siege had to begin, and the city was taken with great difficulty. And so one other revolt ended.[1]

There were however troubles enough elsewhere, for while Darius was engaged in reducing Babylon rebellions began in Persia, Susiana, Media, Assyria, Egypt, Parthia, Margiana, Sattagydia, and Scythia. The revolt in Susiana was not begun by a native of the city, but by a Persian named Martiya, who came from the Persian city Kuganaka, and posed in Susiana as Ummanish, their legitimate ruler.[2] The inhabitants, fearing Darius, seized the pretender and slew him. This quick end was not attained in Media, where a certain Fravartish (Phraortes) assumed the personality of Khshathrita, of the family of Cyaxares. The people accepted him and made him king of Media.[3] This was even more menacing than the Babylonian problem, for the Medes were a fighting race who had not forgotten the independence they had enjoyed before Cyrus had swept them unwilling into his net. This rebellion spread also into Armenia and Darius, unable to leave Babylon, had to send two commanders to represent him and reduce the rebels to subjection. The command of the forces against Media proper was entrusted to Vidarna (Hydarnes), who marched into the country and encountered the enemy near Marush, in a mountainous region. He claimed a victory, but it was not sufficient to enable him to move on, and he was forced to wait at Kampada for reinforcements. In the meantime Dadarshish had been sent against the Armenians. He fought at Zuzza, and then at Tigra, and again at Uyama. That the Armenians should be able to fight

---

[1]Inscription of Behistun, col. I, § XIX; col. II, § XXI.
[2]Ib., §§ XXII, XXIII.   [3]Ib., § XXIV.

thrice shows that they were determined, and must also have been well equipped. It was certainly not a Persian victory thus far, for like his fellow general in Media he also had to halt for fresh troops. Darius must have been dissatisfied with the conduct of the campaign, for he sent Vaumisa to replace Dadarshish. The rebels did not wait for him to attack but met him at Izatya in the old Assyrian territory. The new commander "utterly overthrew the rebel host."[1] This victory would seem not to have been so decisive, for the rebels gave battle again,[2] and Vaumisa was forced to await reinforcements.

It was now full time for Darius to appear in person on the scene, and released by the defeat of Nidintu-Bel he came to take command. The decisive battle was fought at Kundurush and Phraortes, driven from the field, gathered a few horsemen and fled northward, doubtless hoping to continue the struggle amid the almost trackless mountains of Elburz. He was, however, captured at Raga and carried to Ecbatana. There he was horribly mutilated, for Darius "cut off his nose, and his ears, and his tongue and put out his eyes,"[3] and then cast into fetters at the royal court, to be gazed at by the people as a warning to any who might be tempted into rebellion. In the end he was crucified and his misery ended. The most barbarous of the Assyrian kings[4] could have done no worse, and this recrudescence of the crudest savagery is a sickening blot on Darius. There had been no such record written of Cyrus.

Fed with barbarism Darius, having once committed such deeds, was soon ready for more and similar ones;

[1] Inscription of Behistun, II, § XXIX.
[2] This time at Thuravahara.
[3] Inscription of Behistun, II, § XXXII.
[4] See Rogers, *History of Babylonia and Assyria*, 6th ed., II, p. 196.

and the next opportunity that occurred was due to an uprising in Sagartia, where a pretender arose who claimed to be of the family of Cyaxares, whose name evidently continued to wield power over the people of Media. Against him Darius launched an army partly Persian and partly Median, and under Median command, saying to their commander, "Go, smite the host which is in revolt and doth not acknowledge me." The victory was quick and decisive and the unhappy pretender was delivered to Darius, who "cut off his nose, and his ears, and put out his eyes," then exposed him to the people and finally crucified him. So ended another rebellion, and Darius[1] could conclude the matter with the boastful words, "This is what was done by me in Media."

The next revolts to be dealt with were in Parthia against Hystaspis, father of Darius, and in Margiana in Bactria, both of which were quickly ended, though no individual brutal human sacrifices were demanded.[2] Much more serious than these was the rising in Eastern Persia led by Vahyazdata, who spoke unto the people, "I am Bardiya, son of Cyrus." It seems almost incredible that it would be possible again to fool the people with such a claim after all that had happened before, but it had really again come to pass, for even people in the royal palace went over to this man, and he was actually proclaimed king in Persia. Against him Darius despatched a force of Persians and Medes, by whom he claims a victory. The end was not yet, for the new false Smerdis detached forces to occupy Paishiyauvada and

---

[1]The leader of this rebellion was named Citrantakhma, and the Median general who defeated and captured him was Takhmaspâda. Inscription of Behistun, II, § XXXIII, ed. King and Thompson, pp. 37–39.

[2]Inscription of Behistun, II, § XXXV; III, § XXXVI-XXXIX, ed. King and Thompson, pp. 40–46.

Fig. 10.   Darius the Great.

Fig. 9.   View of Columns I-IV of the Persian Text
at Behistun.

was soon ready to give battle again. This time his career ended, and his life ceased by crucifixion, but not
before he had sent men into Arachosia who were subdued with difficulty.[1]

When Darius set out upon these Median and Persian campaigns he left only a weak garrison in Babylon, and this offered opportunity for a second revolt
there. Arakha, an Armenian by race, declared himself
to be "Nebuchadrezzar, the son of Nabonidus," and,
seizing Babylon, had himself proclaimed king. The issue was not long delayed, for Darius found a competent
general to end the rebellion and sent orders to crucify
the chief leader and some of his followers in Babylon.[2]

The greatest rebellions were now all subdued, and
the whole empire would soon be aware that a monarch
had arisen whom it was dangerous to defy, for the
power of life and death was in his hands, and he had
no compunctions about its use. Darius was doubtless
anxious that he should be so judged, for the inspiring
of fear in his subjects would yield rich return if they
dared not rise in rebellion against such a king. But he
took great pains also that men should read the story
of these campaigns, and posterity, as well as his immediate present. He chose a mountainside on which to
record his great deeds in imperishable stone, and no
better or more conspicuous place could have been found
in all Persia. He selected "the last peak of a long narrow range which skirts the plain of Karmanshah on
the east" (King) on the main caravan road between

[1]Inscription of Behistun, III, §§ XL–XLVIII, ed. King and Thompson, pp.
46–55.

[2]This is all told briefly in the Behistun text (III, §§ XLIX–LI, King and
Thompson, pp. 50–60), but it was a matter of no small importance, for the
prestige of Babylon was great, and successful rebellion there would have meant
imperial disaster.

the city of Baghdad and Tehran, and sixty-five miles
from Hamadan, the city which now preserves the name
and some antiquities of Ecbatana. There in front of the
mountain and at its base lies the wretched caravan
road traversed for centuries by caravans peaceful or
warlike, and by the side of the road there is a spring of
water, and there every company halts for refreshment
on the weary way. As they rest and drink, behind them
at an altitude of five hundred feet there stretches upon
the smoothed surface of the mountains a series of sculptures and inscriptions for a space of rather more than
fifty-eight feet and six inches. There beneath the symbolic figure of his god Ahuramazda stands Darius, his
foot resting on the prostrate form of the miserable
Gaumâta, the false Bardiya or Smerdis, while his up-
lifted hand seems to call attention and demand that all
and several should look and then read. Behind Gaumâta
prostrate, nine men in file march to face the king, their
arms bound upon their backs, and cords about their
necks. They are the pretenders and rebels whom he has
defeated and put to death, Atrina, Nidintu-Bel, Fravartish (Phraortes), Martiya, Citrantakhma, Vahyazdata, Arakha, Frada, Skunkha. Did ever king so array
his defeated enemies and set them up for a gazing-
stock in stone, as some of them had been displayed
maimed while yet alive? Beneath the figures in long
ranks stand the cuneiform inscriptions which record
the great king's achievements. In three languages are
they written, in Persian, the official language of the
kingdom; in Susian, the language of the great province
of Elam, a part of which bore the name of Anshan, and
gave Cyrus title, and may be said to have been the
motherland of a world-wide empire; and in the Babylonian tongue, speech of that great culture land whose

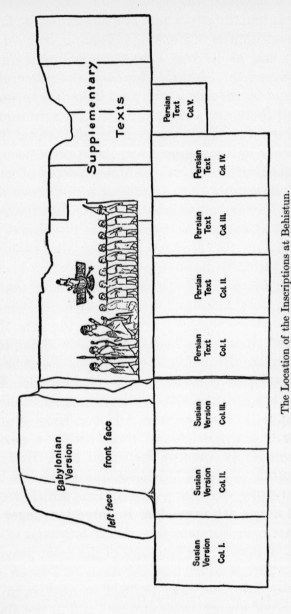

The Location of the Inscriptions at Behistun.

From King and Thompson, *The Sculptures and Inscriptions of Darius the Great on the Rock of Behistun* (London, 1907). Reproduced by permission of the Trustees of the British Museum.

greatness Hammurapi began and ages fostered. It is indeed a noble and impressive presentation of a king's claim to remembrance.[1]

The destruction of the rebels left the whole empire in peace, and Darius was now free to give heed to provinces which had not risen in rebellion, but were taking rather a free hand in their own administration and were in great need of discipline. The first of these was Egypt, left in charge of Aryandes. He had not usurped the title of king but he had more and more acted as an independent ruler, and was showing all the manners of an ancient Pharaoh. He had even caused silver coins to be minted with his portrait seated in a chariot, with his name in Greek, and hieroglyphic dates in the V, VI, and VII years.[2] The inhabitants of Cyrene had slain their king Arkesilas III because they thought he had yielded too much to the Persians, and when he was dead his mother Pheretime came to Egypt to ask aid of Aryandes. It was a good excuse for an attack on Cyrenaica, to lay it under tribute, and to it an army and fleet were despatched. Barca offered an heroic resistance and occupied the Persians nine months in a siege. The troops much desired to push on further in the hope of rich reward in plunder, but were recalled. The return march was sorely harassed by the Libyans, but they finally won through to Memphis laden with loot. The prisoners taken from Barca Aryandes, desiring to propitiate Darius, sent into Persia; they were settled in Bactriana, where they founded a new city of Barca.

[1]For an account of the inscriptions, photographs of the sculptures, and the most perfect copies of the texts in cuneiform character and in English translation, see King and Thompson, *The Sculptures and Inscriptions of Darius the Great on the Rock of Behistun in Persia.* The British Museum, London, 1907. For the processes of decipherment see Rogers, *History of Babylonia and Assyria,* 6th edition, I, pp. 83 ff.

[2]Lenormant, *Essai sur les Monnaies des Lagides,* 169. Hultsch, *Metrologie,* 380.

Fig. 11. Seal of King Darius.

Fig. 12. General View of Darius and the Rebel Leaders.

This trick availed nothing. Darius came to Egypt and executed his refractory subject.[1] He then set himself to win the province to personal loyalty to himself. The method was the old and oft used policy of honoring the gods and attending to the religious scruples of a people. Cyrus had used it with great success, and in the beginning of his reign Cambyses did the same. The problem set Darius was more difficult, for he had to undo the mistakes made during the madness of Cambyses, who, having profited much from the instructions of Uzahor-resenet, had banished him to Elam,[2] whence he was now returned by royal order, under honorable escort. The escheated revenues of the temple of Neith were restored, and the king showed every honor to the gods and gave all manner of assistance in their worship. There is no reason to doubt that immediately on his arrival in Egypt in 517 B. C., he had taken part in the mourning for the death of an Apis, and promised a reward of a hundred talents of gold to whomsoever should discover the successor of the bull.[3] It was just such an action as might be expected of Darius, and would be most effective.

The policies of Darius were useful and accomplished much, and that quickly. The Egyptians placidly accepted his rule, and in due time numbered him with the memorable legislators of their history, Menes, Sasychis, Sesoois, Bacahoris, Amasis, Darius.[4] What greater

[1]The whole story is in Herodotus, IV, 200 ff.

[2]E. de Rougé, *Inscription de la Statuette Naophore*, p. 22. Wiedemann reads Aram instead of Elam (*Geschichte Aegyptens*, p. 239), but I believe wrongly. Elam was the royal residence of Cambyses, in Susa, where the exile might be watched. There would be no point in sending him to Syria.

[3]Polyænus, *Strategemata*, VII, 11, § 7, ed. Melber, pp. 323, 324 (Teubner). This episode was skilfully used by Wiedemann (*Geschichte Aegyptens*, pp. 236, 237) to determine the date of Darius' visit to Egypt. The Apis in question must be the one which died in the fourth year of the king (S. 2274), or 517 B. C.

[4]Diodorus Siculus, I, 94, 95, ed. Vogel, I, pp. 158, 159. Teubner.

honors could they offer? And now the whole empire had added to its glories a peaceful Egypt. There remained only that Darius should take cognizance of conditions somewhat similar in Lydia to those which had been so happily ended in Egypt. In Sardes Oroetes had assumed authority which amounted almost to complete autonomy. He must be summarily reduced to order. Darius showed his usual skill in this as before. Oroetes had about him as personal guard a body of Persians. It was not known how much loyalty they might feel for him, and it were therefore prudent to move cautiously. Bagaeus was sent to the task with precise instructions, and they were carried out to the letter. Bagaeus first presented a royal rescript which relieved the guard from any further attendance on Oroetes, and when this was read, they laid down immediately their spears. Emboldened by this success, Bagaeus gave the last roll to the scribe, to read the fatal words, "King Darius charges the Persians in Sardes to kill Oroetes."[1] The command was instantly obeyed, and Oroetes lay dead beneath blows of the scimitars of the men who had been his guard. By such a sure stroke Lydia received her warning, and dared show no further evidence of any striving after autonomy.

While the processes of punishment or of pacification were in progress in Iran, in Egypt, or in Lydia a most interesting movement was in progress in one of the least of the king's territories. Cyrus had permitted such of the Jews as wished, to return to their homeland,[2] and severe had been the trials of those who accepted his of-

---

[1]Herodotus, III, 126–128. The date is quite uncertain. Maspero (*Passing of the Empires*, p. 678, note 1) dates it at "520 at the latest," but the slight indications found in Herodotus are quite insufficient. I have placed it with the punishment of Aryandes as a similar case, and perhaps about the same time.
[2]See p. 64.

fer. Many, if not most, of them had been born in Babylonia, and were ill adapted by personal experience to face the problems of a different climate, a population none too willing to receive newcomers, and a social and religious situation different from that to which they had been accustomed. The Jews in exile in Babylonia had made profound religious progress under the instruction, especially of Ezekiel and the Second Isaiah, and their law codes had been codified in part at least, and were in process of expansion and elucidation. They now found themselves amid a population to whom these gains were strange, who needed to be taught the larger view that had come to them. The struggle for maintenance was not easy, for many who returned were among the poor, and the securing of land to till, and houses to cover them was difficult. In 536 they had to be content to rebuild the altar of burnt sacrifice, and to establish such offerings as could be secured. Their political dependence was absolutely Persian, and they would need to walk warily lest they arouse suspicion. All these and other factors, great or small, operated to prevent development, and to postpone the rebuilding of the temple. As the years sped by, it became more and more certain that if the temple were not rebuilt as a rallying point not only for religion but almost, if not quite, as much for the securing of national unity, the race would lose its identity and be absorbed into the body of its neighbors. The men who roused the governor, the priests, and people to a sense of responsibility and to action were two prophets, Haggai and Zechariah, who were so fully conscious of the dangers and so sure of the way out of them, that they began to speak in public and private and to urge that the rebuilding of the temple begin at once. It was no easy

task. They used invective, scorn, persuasion, and promise, beginning their work in the second year of Darius
(520 B. C.), and finally securing persuasion and action.
The work could not go on without arousing envy in
some, and quick counter movements in others, and it
was not long until marplots had attempted to persuade
Darius that these poor Jews were meditating some sort
of breach of authority, or perhaps even rebellion. The
governor of Judah—Zerubbabel, whose name, which
means "seed of Babylon," shows that he had been born
in exile—was of Jewish race; he was persuaded by the
two prophets, and had taken an active share in the enterprise. At length, the Persian governor "beyond the
river" (he is called Tattenai in the Jewish record,[1] but
was perhaps Thithinaia in Persian[2]) learned of the af-
fair, and perhaps urged by those who desired to cause
a suspension of the work, decided to investigate for
himself, and made a visit to Jerusalem. He was ready to
defend his royal master's kingdom by instituting in-
quiries. "Who gave you a decree to build this house,
and to finish this wall?"[3] The Jews appealed to the decree of Cyrus, and made request that the archives be
searched for it. The search was successful and the permission was granted to proceed with the work, and a
subvention promised from the royal revenues.[4] It is no
small testimony to the wise statecraft of Darius that he
had so acted toward these people. He did not know the
influence which he was fostering, the restoration of the
old and the beginning of a new Judaism, which should
endure for ages and give birth to Christianity and Mu-
hammedanism. He may well have been content with

---

[1] Ezra 5, 3.
[2] Compare Eduard Meyer, *Die Entstehung des Judentums*, p. 32.
[3] Ezra 5, 3.　　　　　　　　　　　　　　　　　[4] Ezra 6, 8.

the gain to his own empire which came from the satisfaction of these Jews. He had made one little enclave in a larger province happy, and that was no small gain.

The empire was now fully restored to as much unity and stability as it had ever possessed, and the power was fixed in the hands of one man. He was justified in words of boastful enthusiasm as he thought of its extent; in an inscription written in Persian, New Elamite, and Babylonian, and inscribed upon plates of gold, silver, and perhaps also upon some baser material, he bursts out in the ringing words:

> Darius the great king, king of kings, king of the lands, son of Hystaspis, the Achæmenian. Darius the king says: This kingship that I hold, from Scythia which is beyond Sogdiana to Kush [Ethiopia], from India to Sardis, which Ahuramazda gave [me] who is the greatest of the gods. May Ahuramazda protect me and my household.[1]

But the difficulties inherited from Cambyses, the rebellions attending the succession of Darius, and the general confusion of authority in which, as in Egypt and Lydia, governors had become kings in all but style or title showed that the method of rule which worked well enough in a small kingdom was hopelessly inefficient or unsuitable for an empire of such vast extent comprising so many diverse peoples. The system had changed little or none since Tiglathpileser III had introduced it in Assyria, and had worked successfully

[1]This interesting text was discovered in some remains of the ancient city of Ecbatana, and apparently about 1922, but was not made known until 1925, when Dr. Sand made a communication concerning it to Dr. Cowley, supplying a photograph of the gold tablet. The gold tablet is somewhat broken, and a photograph of the silver tablet has been used to supply lacunæ. Sidney Smith published an account of it with transcription and translation (Assyriological Notes, *Journal of the Royal Asiatic Society*, July, 1926, pp. 433–436). It is worth adding that the Babylonian text, as he points out, has a variant in the last line which reads, "May Ahuramazda protect me with the gods and my household." Carl D. Buck has discussed the text of the Persian and annotated it. (*Language*, III, 1, March, 1927, p. 1 ff.)

even in the larger kingdom of Sargon. But analogy breaks down at last, and it had certainly no bearing on such a kingdom or empire as Darius now ruled. A new system must be discovered and introduced. Darius must find it, or the future was without assurance. He was himself a genius, or he had the wisest counsel, and was so wise as to accept its leading. It shows Darius as far more than a successful and victorious general. He was still more an administrator of the first order. His task was the reorganization of the provincial governments, their extension, and the provision of new forms of administration with checks and balances which were admirably chosen and skilfully adapted to prevent the concentration, in the hands of some provincial governor, of power which might ultimately tempt him to seek independence of the empire.

Darius found on assuming this task that Cyrus had already begun some such system, for he had provided Media, Babylon, Lydia, and perhaps Bactria and Parthia, with viceroys, whom he intended should rule in strict subservience to himself, yet have sufficient power of independent action to meet any sudden emergency. The system had failed. Darius must find a better way. When he became king the great province of Bactria was administered by Dadarshish, who bore the title *Khshatrapava*,[1] and Vivana in Arachosia was likewise so called.[2] This Persian word passed into Greek Satrapes, Satrap in English. This became the title of the king's representative in each province, both in civil and in military authority, save in certain instances where a check was specially provided. If we begin at the head we shall perhaps the better secure a view of the method

---

[1] Inscription of Behistun, III, XXXVIII, King and Thompson, p. 44.
[2] Ib., III, XIV, p. 52.

of government. The king was the head, and nominally
his authority was not only supreme but absolute. Yet
there can be no such thing as absolute authority, for
distance and the multiplicity of concerns would in
themselves make it impossible to exercise. But there
were other limitations upon the Persian king, some of
which may be called legal, while others are merely customary—and one was entirely extralegal and inhuman.
To name this last first, the Persian king needed ever to
keep well in mind the danger of assassination, which
has always been most likely to end the most despotic
rulers. This was no light danger in Persia, for three of
the nine successors of Darius thus met death. Among
the legal or customary restrictions upon the king were
some to which he would do well to give heed; others
had gradually become almost a resistless demand. Darius was made king in a great conspiracy of seven men,
and when he accepted the throne he put himself under
obligations for life to the other six. They each received
great grants of territory, and their descendants long
continued to hold almost royal power over these lands.
Above this they received the right to provide the king's
wives, and he was permitted to marry only the daughters of these men, save as he continued, as did Darius,
to marry in the royal Achæmenian line. This marriage
restriction seems to have been closely followed. Beyond this social or family requirement the king was
expected, on all important occasions, to consult the
body of Persian nobles.[1] To secure their loyalty was in
times of strain very important, and this could be the
more easily secured if they had been consulted and
their advice accepted. On matters of less importance
the seven[2] counsellors might be consulted. On points of

[1] Herodotus, VII, 8. [2] Ezra 7, 14.

law the seven judges[1] must be taken in counsel, who, as
they were appointed for life, had great and growing
power and influence. And finally the king was bound
by his own decisions, and this has passed into the pro-
verbial expression, "the law of the Medes and Persians,
which altereth not,"[2] though there must often have been
cases in which the king used his discretion and changed
what had once been ordered. It must be remembered
that the proverb is based upon a biblical book written
centuries after the time of Darius and representative
of what was then thought among the Jews to be customary; it has here been elevated into a sort of hy-
perbole.

Beneath the king in administrative influence and
labors were the satraps, whose dominion was restricted
each to his own satrapy. These varied in number, being
at one time only 20, at another 23, and again 24, and
finally 29, increasing in number as they were suces-
sively divided and reapportioned. Persia was placed at
the head of the list, but had different treatment, and is
scarcely to be reckoned a satrapy. Herodotus[3] has preserved a list of 20 satrapies, of priceless value, derived
we know not whence. Upon his list Ionia stands first,
comprising not only the Ionians properly so called, but
also the Magnesians, Æolians, Carians, Lycians. It was
almost wholly Greek, or, at the very least, Hellenized.
They were permitted to retain their constitutions derived from the Lydian kings, and in no way was there
any interference with their language, customs, or religion. The satrapy paid 300 talents of silver annually
to the royal exchequer. The second satrapy covered

[1]Herodotus, III, 31. Compare Esther 1, 14.
[2]Daniel 6, 8, 14, 15. See also Esther 1, 19, and 8, 8.
[3]Herodotus, III, 89-94.

Mysia and Lydia, and paid 500 talents as a richer province since the days of Crœsus. The third comprised Phrygia, with the Paphlagonians and Syrians, and must pay 360 talents. The fourth was Cilicia, a province with a strangely interesting history. It had its native kings whose title was Syennesis, and it somehow managed to maintain a certain amount of independence, down to the beginning of the fourth century. Such Persian control as existed was maintained by a Persian cavalry guard, and the satrapy contributed annually 360 white horses and 500 talents, of which 360 went to Persia, the remainder being used to maintain the guard. The fifth satrapy bore no name, but covered lands of the highest interest, for it comprised all of Phœnicia, Palestine, and the island of Cyprus. It paid 350 talents. The sixth was Egypt with the Libyans, and Cyrene and Barca, paying 700 talents of silver and a large supply of grain for the use of the Persian forces occupying the country and stationed at Memphis. The seventh comprised peoples in the far east, many of them still unknown to us, but called by Herodotus, the Sattagydæ, Gandarii, Dadicæ, and Aparytæ, who were plainly far below the great western provinces in resources, and were required to pay only 170 talents. The eighth brings us back into lands known and famous—to Susa; here the king was wont to spend part of the year in residence, and might therefore, one would think, have been willing to lighten its burdens and not require so heavy a contribution as 300 talents. Yet even that was small when compared with the ninth satrapy, comprising Babylon and all Assyria and paying 1,000 talents, and to them adding in human flesh 500 boys to be eunuchs. Media was divided into two satrapies, Ecbatana and some other portions near by being the tenth province, paying 450 talents, while another, or eleventh satrapy, was formed of its more northerly portions and paid 200 talents. The twelfth satrapy was Bactria with 300 talents, and the thirteenth Armenia and contiguous lands as far as the Euxine sea with a requirement of 400 talents. The fourteenth satrapy was very large, comprising many diverse peoples such as the Sagartii, Sarangeis, Utii, and others, who lived as far south and west as the Red Sea, and some of whom had been deported thither for revolting in other and particularly western lands. Upon these was laid the heavy requirement of 600 talents. The Sacae and the Caspii formed the fifteenth, and paid only 250 talents. Their territory lay in the great valley of Kabul. The sixteenth satrapy held the Parthians, the Sogdi, and the Arii, paying 300 talents, and very curiously divided by Bactria as a sort of geographical wedge between their districts. The Paricanii and the Asiatic Ethiopians made up the seventeenth satrapy and were taxed with 400 talents per annum. They are for us obscure in location and in racial character, but may have inhabited the district now known as Beluchistan. The people of the eighteenth satrapy, Matieni, Saspiri, and Alarodii, were dwellers in the region of the upper Aras, and extended downward to the upper reaches of the Tigris and Euphrates; of them the Alarodii would seem to have been Semites, whose mountainous and infertile lands could yield little for the empire, for a charge of only 200 talents was laid upon them. The nineteenth province enclosed the Moschi and Tibareni, the Tubal and Meshech of the Hebrews,[1] most of them, except the Moschi, being on the coast of the Black Sea; 300 talents were required of them. The twentieth satrapy was formed of the In-

[1]Ezekiel 27, 13; compare 32, 26.

dians, by whom Herodotus probably meant the peoples
of the northeastern part of that vast land. He knew
them vaguely enough, yet had sufficient information
concerning them to say that, "these are more in number
than any nation known to me, and they paid a greater
tribute than any other province, namely 360 talents of
gold dust,"[1] which must be multiplied by thirteen[2] to
compare it with the silver talents paid by other peoples.

The revenues derived from these twenty satrapies
would amount to about 14,560 talents, a magnificent income, to which were added large gifts from many portions of the empire now comprised in the satrapies, yet
reminded by neighboring satraps of the duty of contributing to the maintenance of the empire in its integrity. Persia alone, the very heart of the empire, was
free of all direct taxation, but was expected to give
gifts when the king made royal visitations. The collection of the revenues was no slight matter, but was fa-
cilitated by the issue of gold and silver coins called
Darics, and so known by the king's own name. Each
daric weighed normally .2788 oz. Troy, and was intended to have the value of twenty silver drachmæ or
Median shekels, and the relationship was 3,000 gold
darics to one talent. The earliest coined darics were
thick and irregular, rude in design and execution, but
extraordinarily fine, the alloy never being more than
three per cent. The coinage never came into any general use save in the countries bordering on the Mediterranean, where Lydian coinage had prepared the way
and commercial transactions were common enough to
make such a medium of exchange very useful and
highly appreciated. In the interior, on the other hand,

[1]Herodotus, III, 94.
[2]The modern proportion would be 15½: 1.

the coinage came but little into use, the older method
of weighing lumps or pieces of metal and using them
for exchange being continued. The royal treasury gave
no support by example, for there it was the custom
to pour the melted gold into clay moulds and cut off
these ingots either for use in lumps and pieces or to be
minted for exchange in the west. The revenues of the
empire would reach in actual silver talents about \$16,-
000,000 per annum, and if we consider the far higher
value of silver in antiquity would represent in modern
terms about \$130,000,000. Besides these revenues paid
in money there were large contributions in kind, of
which Herodotus makes mention at times, and must
have omitted many instances. The king's army received its rations from the provinces over and above
the payment of the taxes; for four months in the year
its food was supplied by Babylon,[1] the other eight
months by the rest of the empire. The provinces had
also to support the satraps, many of whom maintained
a style almost regal, and must besides feed the armies
which were quartered upon them. The drain must have
been very heavy, both in money and in kind. The securing of silver to pay taxes must often have been very
difficult, for it had to be bought in the market of money-
dealers who, in times of scarcity, might charge almost
whatever they willed of the satraps, who must secure
the funds and pass them onward by the regular channels to the centre of the empire.

The position and power of the satrap extended far
beyond these questions of finance, for the superinten-
dence of the whole life of his province came up before
him in the ultimate issue, however much might be done
by subordinates. He was the supreme judge in every-

[1] Herodotus, I, 192.

thing civil or criminal, and except in cases where he
was himself more or less suspect and a general was
appointed over the troops in his province, he was also
commander of the local detachments of soldiers and
was expected to deal with rebellion should signs appear.
He entered into negotiations of mutual concern with
other satraps, or with neighboring independent states,
and even undertook conquests.[1] Men with such powers
or capacities as these were occupying offices of great po-
tential danger to the central state, and means must be
devised to place checks upon them. These were found
in devices both direct and indirect. In the first instance,
members of the royal house were usually appointed to
the chief satrapies. If such were in any instance not
available, one of the king's own daughters might be
married to a satrap, and so opportunity be found for
securing allegiance to the great king by ties of the
strongest social bond. To this was added the check provided by the presence of subordinate governors who
had the right of direct access to the king, and might
convey to him information against their superior, while
the neighboring satraps were often jealous and disposed
to keep watch over satraps who held dominion in more
desirable places. Some of the subordinates had received
great land grants from the king for services rendered
in war, and there are known instances in which they
were even dispensed from the tribute.[2] Such financial
independence gave also reasons and opportunities for
mutual jealousies between a satrap and his rich sub-

[1]There is an interesting example of this in the case of Aryandes, satrap of
Egypt, who by a pretext undertook the conquest of the Libyans. (See Herodotus, IV, 167 and compare note by How and Wells, Herodotus, vol. I, p. 356.)
For this deed he was not punished, but for the issue of a silver coinage superior
to the gold coins of Darius. (Herodotus, IV, 166.)
[2]Such were Otanes in Cappadocia, Herodotus, III, 83, and Hydarnes in
Armenia.

ordinate, and retaliation on the upper by the watching
of his every move was quite likely. The king often interfered in the government of the satrapies, at times
very probably because of information received, but at
others because he preferred to give orders direct, and
so make sure of their fulfillment.[1] So complete was the
process of appointing in the first instance and of hedg-
ing about with surveillance within and without that we
hear astonishingly little of malfeasance in office among
the satraps.

To make more sure and rapid the control of the empire Darius paid great heed to the roads, which he
greatly extended and much improved. He inherited
from Assyrian rule great roads such as the old royal
road which ran from Babylon to Carchemish with a
connecting spur to Nineveh, and was prolonged westward and southward to Egypt. Another road extended
from Musasir to Parsua and Media, and still another
bound Babylon with the heart of Media.[2] The road
which connected Nineveh with Ecbatana, passing over
the Zagros, was rebuilt, as was also, in whole or part,
the road from Ecbatana to Sardes, passing through
Harran and carried by a spur down to Susa. Yet another road ran from Sardes to Smyrna.[3] For the complete utilization of roads so laboriously constructed or
renewed there was devised the splendid courier or post
system, which far surpassed everything before at-

[1]There are quite interesting instances of such interference in the case of the
returned Jews, such as the decree for rebuilding the temple (ch. 6), which posi-
tively orders Tatnai, the local governor beyond the river, not to interfere, and
in another case (Ezra 7, 26) the Jewish law of Jehovah is made the royal law
of the kingdom. That which was true of the Jews in their influence with
the king has parallels in the case of other religions. Gadatas, a local magistrate,
had interfered with the temple of Apollo at Magnesia, and Darius issues a
rescript commending him otherwise but ordering him to desist. (Hicks, *A
Manual of Greek Inscriptions*, 2nd edition, 20.)
[2]See Rawlinson, *The Five Great Monarchies*, III, 426.
[3]Herodotus, V, 52.

tempted of its kind. By this plan the whole network of roads was divided into post routes with horsemen stationed at regular intervals, so that any message from king to satrap or satrap to king would be carried from one stage to the next, and then passed to other horsemen to convey it the next stage. "These neither snow nor rain nor heat nor darkness of night prevent from accomplishing each one the task proposed to him, with the very utmost speed."[1]

The organization of the army was not equal to that of the government in other respects. Darius was not equally a soldier with Cyrus or Cambyses, and seems never to have been able to conceive or produce an army fit to cope with dominions now become so vast. He had a personal bodyguard recruited from Medes and Persians, consisting of 2,000 cavalry and 2,000 infantry men of noble birth, and beneath these 10,000 "immortals" in ten battalions.[2] This guard was intended to form the nucleus of a standing army to be increased by men of Median or Persian nobility summoned according to need. Besides these the forces of the standing army were kept at the most important fortresses, such as Sardes, Memphis, Elephantinæ, Daphnæ, Babylon, and other less important but perhaps equally dangerous places. This comprised the entire national army, and it was quite insufficient for any serious attack on the integrity of the empire. If minor rebellions occurred, the satraps, either severally or by the co-operation of one or more in the neighborhood, sought means to end them. But in any larger threat the command had to be taken by the king in person, who then mobilized his guard and made a localized or even general levy,

[1]Herodotus, VIII, 98.
[2]Heraclides of Cumæ, Frag. 1, in Müller-Didot, Frag. Hist. Græc, II, pp. 95, 96.

and the recruits poured in great numbers into the ranks. These were not armed as were the regular troops, and however brave or zealous to serve they might be, could not easily be licked into military shape or co-ordinated with ranks of the well-trained men with whom soldiering had become a business. Endurance and courage could not take the place of training, organization, and experience. With a military organization so loose and inefficient the empire could only stand if not attacked by some country better in equipment, in detail, and in direction. There was none such for a long period, and the empire survived lesser attacks and went on its career.

As a part and share in the military guard of the king there developed formulas of court etiquette not merely unknown to his predecessors, but even foreign to their whole manner of life. Darius took every possible occasion or opportunity to remind his kingdom of his relationship with the Achæmenians, but did not forget that he belonged personally to a separate branch of the family and was therefore the founder, in a sense, of a new dynasty. It was now as difficult to approach the great king, as formerly it had been easy in the days of Cyrus and Cambyses, and this would surely spare him many annoyances and petty interruptions. It had, however, great disadvantages, as kings and other rulers have often come to know, for it gave access to sycophants, to members of the family, to generals or governors, who all had some personal ends to serve, and would often be led to give wrong advice or ill counsel, and to conceal matters that should come for reckoning before the king gave decisions. The losses were greater than the gains in the growth of a system of court etiquette.

The king had now set a great empire in order, and

given it a government far superior to anything that the
ancient Orient had known before. If he could hold it
together, continue the perfecting of its organization,
protect its common people against rapacious satraps,
and find newer and better means of developing its resources, a period of great peace might ensue, and the
wonders of the later Pax Romana come upon the weary
world of eastern men. But it was not to be. The Persian
king, like his predecessors in Assyria, was haunted at
intervals by the stalking ghost of inactivity. He had
armies, and nothing could be more disastrous for them
than inactivity. They might be used to fight, and were
likely to seethe with internal rebellion if they were not
so used. Herodotus[1] puts the case picturesquely, but a
deep truth lies beneath his happy and colorful phrases.
"Sire, you are a mighty ruler; why sit you idle, winning
neither new dominions nor new power for your Persians?" So said Atossa, as Herodotus reports; but it
was really Fate that so spake, and the king heard it day
and night. It was all well enough to seek the ways of
peace and give the common folk something for their
souls and bodies, but the empire had been built by the
sword and by the sword it must be kept in being. The
only question was where a blow should fall. That question Darius faced about the year 512 B. C., and the
decision taken was to attack the Scythians, known
vaguely enough to him and still not very clearly known
to us.[2] It seems, at least, moderately certain, or perhaps only very probable, that they were a people of
Mongolian origin and general type who came southward and westward from the vast steppes of Russia and

[1]Herodotus, III, 134.
[2]There is an excellent summary of our present knowledge of this strange
people, by E. H. Minns, "The Scythians and Northern Nomads," in the
Cambridge Ancient History, III, pp. 187–205.

settled among the Cimmerians north of the Euxine
and west and south as far as the Danube. As in many
other invasions in other places, history repeated itself
in them. They brought freshness and vigor, made homes
for themselves by conquest or by a certain indefinable
pushing force, and were in turn conquered by a civilization superior to their own. This accounts for the presence among them of so many Aryan and Iranian names
of men, rivers, and places, as well as for their possession
of a religion distinctively Aryan in character. They had
now become a dangerous menace to the empire of the
Persians. Before them lay Thrace, which it were easy
for them to occupy, as they had the lands to the north;
and if it came into their possession the Hellespont was
not far away, and moving nomads would soon be
sweeping down the coasts of Asia Minor. This was no
fanciful danger, and Darius saw it closely. He would attack them and teach them a lesson not to be easily forgotten, setting a good example for any of their neighbors who might some day be tempted to make trouble
for the empire. The knowledge which Darius could secure of these Scythians was small, but alarming on the
one side and seductive on another. The whole world
seemed filled with fear of the Scythians. Tales of the
horrors committed by them were everywhere current
in Media, Persia, among the Ionians and the Egyptians. To these stories there was added also a report
spread by Greek traders that they possessed great
wealth;[1] gold mines were said to be scattered over their
regions, which were guarded by griffins and worked by
harmless ants as large as foxes! Surely the gold would
look well cast in great masses in the Persian treasury or

[1]Herodotus, IV, 13, 27; III, 116. Ctesias, *Frag.*, in Müller-Didot, *Ctesiæ
Cnidii Fragmenta*, pp. 82, 95–97. Strabo, XI, viii, § 4.

minted into darics. And to all this there was added also
a more direct testimony concerning these strange nomads. Ariaramnes, satrap of Cappadocia,[1] commanding
a flotilla of thirty ships, sailed out upon the Euxine to
explore its opposite coast. He landed some men, took
a few prisoners, had a glimpse of the coast line of Europe, learned something of its character and fertility,
and brought back the prisoners as witnesses to land
and people. Equipped with such scanty intelligence as
could be obtained in this way and from current gossip
of gold mines and great riches, the king resolved upon
a most serious expedition.

In the year 512 Darius assumed personal command
of forces estimated by tradition, but doubtless greatly
exaggerated, at 800,000 men. No sound of the happen-
ings on the long march over mountains with narrow
passes, over wild prospects and great valleys, has come
down to us. Arduous must have been the way and very
doubtful at times the issue, but he was no mean man,
and undaunted pressed on. When the swift waters that
separate the Asian shore from the European were
crossed, he was on European soil, and his expedition
the first of Asia to assail Europe. The Bosphorus was
crossed by a bridge erected by the Samian engineer
Mandrokles, at a point near the modern Stenia.[2] Darius
himself had sailed in a Greek ship over the waters near
by, had erected monuments by the bridge inscribed in
Persian cuneiform and in Greek,[3] with the names of all
the peoples who comprised his army. The tribes of eastern Thrace were easily conquered, only one offering

[1] Our only knowledge of this expedition is derived from Ctesias, Frag. 30,
§ 47, Gilmore.
[2] Herodotus, IV, 87.
[3] Herodotus, IV, 87. He says that one was in Assyrian, but the Greeks never
learned the difference between Assyrian and Persian cuneiform characters.

any resistance, and the march was then northward close to the Black Sea until the great mouth of the Danube was attained. A crossing there was obviously impossible, and the course of the stream must be followed westward. At or near the head of the Danube delta another bridge was erected by the Ionian contingents, and Darius crossed into the great unknown. The Scythians would not stand to give battle, but withdrew before the Persians, and so led them ever further from a safe base into a country almost sterile in places, and in no accessible place fitted to support an army attempting to live directly from the land. We do not know how far or how long the advance was, but it produced nothing of value either in the conquest of territory or in plunder. At length Darius was compelled to give up the vain pursuit of fleeing nomads and fall back to the Danube bridge, which fortunately had not been destroyed and was now a much needed refuge. The army must have suffered severely from great deprivations, and was glad to be on the return.

Darius detached from the main body before recrossing the Bosphorus a force estimated at 80,000 men to complete the conquest of Thrace, and this was successfully carried out. The addition of Thrace was the only result of the expedition for the empire. It brought the boundaries of the Persians into contact with northern Greece, and was in that a threat of the movements which were later to come in the attempts of Persia to conquer the Greeks. Darius had personally surely lost prestige, for his campaign against the Scythians was a complete failure, and his army would know it.

At about this same time (512 B. C.) the Persians who had been looking out from the Iranian plateau over the vast plain of the Punjab, at last determined to descend and conquer it. It was easily accomplished, and of it was formed a satrapy,[1] from which immense revenues were derived. This conquest had carried Darius as far as the Indus, and there was now a call to push on to the Ganges; but it was most wisely resisted, and Darius turned his thoughts toward the southeast. A fleet was built at Penkêla, and under command of Scylax, a Greek admiral of Caryanda, set out upon a voyage of exploration down stream to see whither its waters might lead. He fought the natives along its banks, passed safely their attacks and at length sailed out on the waters of the Indian Ocean, and turned westward. In less than thirty months he had explored the coasts of Gedrosia and Arabia, and went so far as the waters of the Red Sea, returning safely to recount his exploits.[2] It was a wonderful achievement, and surely no Persian, born far from the sea, would have dared so great an adventure. But Scylax had the Greek instinct for the sea, and it would be his pleasure to know strange waters and watch with wondering eyes new headlands. Besides he would wish to serve and please his Persian master, who had set him a great task. It was the desire of Darius to connect Egypt with the rest of his empire, and the plan was to dig a canal from the Nile to the Red Sea. The commission given Scylax was to discover what was the relation between the Red Sea, as known at its upper part, with the waters which touched

[1]See p. 109.
[2]Scylax wrote an account of his experiences which was still in existence in the time of Aristotle (*Politics*, VII, 14. 2, ed. Susemihl-Immisch, p. 257. Teubner). It has been questioned in modern times, notably by Hugo Berger (*Geschichte der Wissenschaftlichen Erdkunde der Griechen*, I, pp. 47–49), but on insufficient grounds. Scepticism concerning it is of a piece with the doubts concerning the navigation about Africa ordered by Necho. On this see Bunbury (*History of Ancient Geography*, I, 289 ff., 317), who leaves the question open, and E. J. Webb (*English Historical Review*, Jan., 1907), who opposes the authenticity. Meyer (*Geschichte des Altertums*, III, p. 99 ff.) accepts both the African journey and this of Scylax as true.

other parts of his dominion. The result of the explorations of Scylax might have been useless or at least not to be connected with this matter of the Red Sea. But the issue was really very different, for he sailed the Red Sea and came out from his journeyings just where the canal should be dug. Darius ordered the canal to be dug, and on its banks at several points set up inscriptions, of which sorely broken specimens have survived the ruin of the ages. Upon one of them Darius speaks[1] of his achievement in the bold and impressive words, "I am a Persian. From Persia I captured Egypt. I commanded this canal to be built from the Nile, which flows in Egypt, to the sea which comes from Persia. So was this canal built, as I had commanded, and ships passed from Egypt through this canal to Persia, as was my purpose."

Darius made his name known in Egypt by other means as well, for he built the temple of Hibis in the Oasis of el-Khargeh,[2] and there introduced a Persian method of irrigation by means of underground conduits fed by water from the strata of sandstone where it collected in faults. This was the beginning of a movement which has shown the way to modern methods of boring artesian wells by which a sufficient water supply is now obtained to support a population of about 8,000 in our time, with 60,000 palm trees, producing dates, and irrigated lands growing rice, barley, and wheat.[3] This work of Darius and the contributions otherwise made by his rule of Egypt will entitle him to have his name enrolled among the Pharaohs of Egypt as Setetu-Ra

[1] Inscription from Suez. See Weissbach u. Bang, *Die altpersischen Inschriften*, pp. 7, 39, and Weissbach, *Die Keilinschriften der Achämeniden*, pp. 103–105. This inscription was discovered by Lepsius while digging the Suez Canal near kilometer 150.

[2] See H. J. L. Beadnell, *An Egyptian Oasis*, London, 1909.

[3] See Beadnell's very interesting book above mentioned.

FIG. 13. Island of Elephantine.

FIG. 14. View across the Amon-Oasis, or Siwa.

("Ra hath begotten him") Ntariaush,[1] the latter part
of which seems to the eye strange as a representation
of Darius. His name appears in Egyptian thus:

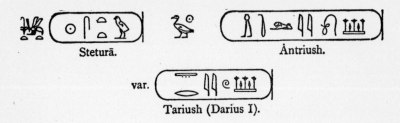

Steturā.   Ảntriush.

var.

Tariush (Darius I).

Herodotus has preserved a story flattering alike to
Egyptian vanity and to the conciliatory temper of Darius, according to which Darius wished to set up a
statue of himself before the stone statues of Sesostris
at the temple of Hephæstus; but the priest forbade
him, saying that he had achieved nothing to equal the
deeds of Sesostris, who had subdued the Scythians,
which Darius was not able to do; and Darius let the
priest have his way.[2]

In spite of every effort, whether of conciliation or
of repression, Egypt was a difficult problem for Darius.
Conciliation seems to have won little, if any, success,
and increasingly it was necessary to have recourse to
force, or the threat of it. Darius maintained a large
army in Egypt, chiefly composed of Egyptian troops
under Persian control. These were stationed at Memphis,[3] from which the country was probably ruled,
where the Persian governor lived and needed a body-

[1]The Greek delta (d) is represented in Egyptian by Nt, for which there is
a parallel in modern Greek which represents the Latin "d" by ντ. So Hall in
Ancient History of the Near East, p. 571, note 4.
[2]Herodotus, II, 110. In Herodotus the name Sesostris is really a legendary
mixture of different Egyptian kings. In this case H. is talking of kings who
ruled Ethiopia, and the confusion is of Senwosret III and Rameses II.
[3]Herodotus, III, 91.

guard, while a second body was at Daphnæ[1] of Pelusium, that is, on the northeastern part of the Delta so as to command any movements from Arabia or Palestine; a third body was at Marea on the side of the Delta toward Libya, and a fourth at the island of Elephantine as a protection against inroads from Ethiopia. The number of men in the entire force is given by Herodotus[2] as 240,000, which is surely an exaggeration, but we have no means of correcting it. Even with an army of occupation it was not possible to make Persian control both secure and permanent. The Egyptians had too keen a sense of their nationality to yield to such a dominion as that of semi-barbarous Persians without recurrent attempts to achieve their independence. While Darius yet reigned the Egyptians began a series of struggles which still remain obscure to us, but were plainly enough in being long after the days of the great king. Very dimly are we able to discern the threatening situation. A rebellion began in Egypt and at the same time there appeared a new pretender in Babylon named Belshimanni, who had himself proclaimed "king of Babylon and of the lands."[3] It would seem that Darius met that issue promptly enough and put down the new attempt at independent rule, for Herodotus[4] preserves a story that Darius threatened to remove a statue of a god, but did not do it—this being the sort of thing that kings were wont to do to conquered peoples. That there was some connection between this rebellion in Babylon and that in Egypt is highly probable, and one would likewise be justified

[1]Daphnæ is the modern Tell Defenneh on the Pelusiac arm of the Nile, now a canal. See Petrie, Egypt Exploration Fund, iv (1888).
[2]Herodotus, II, 30.
[3]In Babylonian the phrase is šar Babili u mâtâte, which successfully imitates an ancient style used in Sumerian times.
[4]Herodotus, I, 183.

in a surmise that the Greeks had a hand in the Egyptian rebellion, for they were justly alarmed for their own safety after it had been seen that Darius was able to move an army over the Bosphorus; however great was his failure against the Scythians he might be none the less a danger to Greece.

If we turn backwards and see the results that followed the Scythian campaign we shall the more readily conceive the Greek attitude of mind. When Darius returned to Asia he had left 80,000 men under Megabazos to continue the campaign southward into Thrace and Macedonia, both of which were conquered. From the hands of the successful military commander Thrace was transferred to Otanes, satrap of Lydia, as a part of the empire, and organized as a satrapy. He had already reduced Chalcedon, Byzantium, and their immediate neighbors and added the islands of Lemnos and Imbros to Persia. There was, however, an island far richer than either of these, Naxos, and ways or excuses must be found for its subjection. Whether the chief excuse was really that of faction in the island by which some of its richest citizens were exiled and then stirred up Miletus to find some way to get them home again,[1] we know not. But whatever was the exciting cause, Artaphrenes sent an expedition against Naxos which met with no real success, for the island maintained its independence. This might well seem encouraging on the surface to the Greeks who heard of it, but it was in very truth quite the opposite, for Naxos had not been conquered because it possessed unity and had prepared for the onslaught, while Greece was divided and ill prepared for such war as the Persians had made in their world-wide conquests. It was

[1]Herodotus, V, 28 f.

therefore natural enough that they should fish in troubled waters and hope to gain help against the Persians by stirring up rebellion in Egypt to disturb the great king. And well they might so desire, for by this time Darius was fully persuaded to move against Greece, a resolution greatly strengthened by the actions of Athens. From Miletus Aristagoras had gone away to Sparta and to Athens to seek help for the Ionian cities in a rebellion against Persia. The ruler of Sparta at this time was Kleomenes, who was not moved by the appeal but rather by prudence. He doubted whether it would be possible to get his foot-soldiers to the Ionian cities and after so long a march have them fit to meet the Persians who should be sent to the defence of Persian rule on the Ægean Sea. He refused. Better fortune came to the efforts at Athens. Aristagoras pleaded that the Milesians were colonists from Athens, and therefore that a blood relationship cried out for help, and that the Persians would really not be able to defend themselves because of their manner of fighting; and so won the Athenians to a decision to despatch twenty ships. In the spring of 499 the Athenian ships landed their men, and the rebels joined forces with them to attack Sardes, defended by Artaphrenes, who saw that it was necessary to retire within the citadel and leave the main part of the city to its fate. It was burned. The inhabitants, pushed together in the market-place, fought bravely and finally forced their assailants to retreat. Overtaken in pursuit by Persian troops who came too late to save Sardes they were routed near Ephesus and destroyed. The burning city of Sardes finally gave flames to the temple of Kybele and this was destroyed. This catastrophe was charged against the Greeks and long remembered as an act of vandalism. When Persians invaded Greece in the Persian wars they burned Greek temples in retaliation, so early among western civilized peoples began the stupid and futile business of reprisals.

When the Athenians had sailed homeward convinced of the folly of this enterprise the Ionian rebellion nevertheless continued longer. Some successes fell to their share, but they were not likely to have any great final result in setting them free from their overlords. Their larger hope seemed at sea rather than on land. They gathered a considerable fleet composed of contributions of ships and men from the mainland of Greece and from her islands and formed with these a rendezvous in the noble harbor of Miletus. The total number of ships was no less than 353 according to the Greek account,[1] but the number is surely exaggerated. To oppose these the Persians had gathered ships from Phœnicia, Egypt, and Cyprus, the number of which is given at the conventional 600, a sort of standard reckoning for the Persians in Herodotus.[2] For weeks the opposing fleets lay in opposition, neither venturing to attack. Delay was clearly on the side of the Persians, for the common tendency of Greeks to come to some controversial break was likely to operate. At last the united command of the allied ships fell into the capable and daring hands of Dionysius, who put heart into his men, and began a series of maneuvers to exercise the ships and men for a decisive fight. The Ionians at first submitted to his severe regimen but later objected and refused. To make the case worse the Samians yielded

[1]Herodotus, VI, 8.
[2]Herodotus, VI, 9. As to this being a conventional estimate and not the exact number one may compare the number of ships that accompanied Darius on the Scythian expedition (IV, 87–89) and that of Datis to Marathon (VI, 95). Compare How and Wells, *Herodotus*, II, p. 365.

to the temptations of the Persian emissaries and privately arranged to leave the Ionians to their fate. The Persians were then encouraged to attack. At the first onset the Samians for the greater part sailed away, leaving behind only eleven ships that remained faithful. The evil example was imitated by the Lesbians, who also sailed away. The rest of the fleet met the Persians and at their hands suffered a disastrous defeat, the Chians especially fighting bravely and being severely punished. Miletus was now left invested by sea and land, and after a siege was carried by storm. A large part of the inhabitants, and especially those who were deemed influential, were deported and settled on the Tigris, only the poor and those who were helpless to restore one of the most beautiful and prosperous of the Greek coastal cities remained, and the former glory of the city returned no more. The others who had joined in the rebellion were readily overcome, Caria was subdued, and Chios, Lesbos, and Tenedos suffered likewise. Then the Persian fleet sailed along the upper part of the Ægean Sea, burning and destroying Perinthos, Selymbria, and Byzantium. It was a campaign of savagery and the report of it must have thundered in the ears of every Greek in Athens who was capable of thinking in terms of other lands. What the Persians had done to Greeks outside Greece they might well some day seek to do to those living more remotely on the mainland. If there were any political wisdom in Athens the conditions called loudly for its exercise.

Darius now saw clearly the menace which the Greeks of the mainland offered to his empire. The Athenians had sent ships to help the Ionians. What they had once done might again be done, should similar circumstances arise. Furthermore it was plain to be seen that the

FIG. 15.   Persepolis from the Southeast.

FIG. 16.   The Great Staircase and the Doorway of Xerxes.

cities of western Asia Minor which had held out for
six years against him would be likely to remember that
men of their own race were living in independence on
the opposite shores of their sea and to draw the conclusion that it might be worth while to make on some
more propitious day another struggle for freedom. It
was obvious that the way to ensure the continued existence of Persian domination over Greeks in Asia was
to reduce to subjection the Greeks in Greece. Darius
was not a man lightly to forget the trouble which the
Athenians had made for him, and a pretty legend early
grew up to reveal the mind which was supposed to be
his. The story was that when he had heard of the burning of Sardes, he called for a bow and when it was
placed in his hands he fitted an arrow to the string and
shot it heavenward, saying, "O Zeus, that it may be
granted me to take vengeance upon the Athenians,"
and this he followed by a command to one of his at-
tendants that when dinner was set before the king he
should say three times, "Master, remember the Athenians."[1] The story is, if not true, very happily imagined,
and well represents the mind which now came to expression.

Darius determined to take up energetically the project long contemplated and to send an expedition against
Greece. The command was entrusted to Mardonios,
son of Gobryas, and but lately honored by the king's
consent for his marriage with Artozostra, daughter of
Darius. There was to be an assault both by land and
sea, and the land forces were despatched by way of the
Hellespont, while the large fleet sailed for the Greek
coast. The land forces met with much success, reducing Thrace, and meeting with serious opposition only

[1]Herodotus, V, 105.

from the Brugi between the Strymon and Mount Athos; and when these were finally beaten, Macedonia fell and its king, Alexander I, was compelled to submit to the same heavy conditions which had been laid upon his father Amyntas. Thus far the campaign had been successful, even though perhaps not brilliant. Very different was the story by sea.

The fleet, large certainly and perhaps much larger than that which had been victorious at Ladé, sailed from Thasos and Akanthos and had to round Mount Athos. There the currents are dangerous, and the sea often rough and sometimes heavy, and ill luck pursued these voyagers. A northeast gale swept the cape at the critical hour and the fleet was wrecked. Herodotus heard a report that 300 ships were lost and 20,000 men perished.[1] The ships that remained, however great the loss may have been, were insufficient for what was likely to prove an onerous campaign, and the whole expedition had to end at that point. The proposed or intended punishment of Athens and Eretria had failed for the present. Darius would have to reconsider the whole matter and find another plan. The judgment arrived at was that the plan had been far more broad than prudent and that a totally different scheme and much more modest must be drawn up. The campaign of Mardonios had failed of its larger purpose, but fairly judged on the basis of what might reasonably be expected it was far from a failure. The reconquest of Macedonia was important, and the subjection of southern Thrace was so complete that it remained under complete Persian control for thirteen years, and besides these Thaos was annexed. Mardonios had only

[1] VI, 44. The form in which Herodotus makes the statement shows that he was doubtful about the numbers.

failed to do the impossible, but like many another commander of later days was punished for not doing what none could have done. He was removed and the command of the next expedition assigned to Datis the Mede and Artaphernes the Persian, brother of Darius.

The new plan of campaign was not to attempt a cooperated movement by land and sea, but to move against Greece by stages, and always by sea. As the ships of that day would be quite incapable of transporting a sufficient number of men to make a direct attack upon Athens, it was necessary to make the apparent object of the expedition not directed against Athens but only against those states which had taken side with the Ionians. The first move was in accordance with Persian policy, often successful, to detach as many states as possible from the enemy and so minimize the difficulties. In the year 491 Persian heralds were sent to many cities of Greece asking that earth and water be sent to the great king. How many yielded we do not know, but the broad statement of Herodotus that "many of those who dwelt on the mainland gave that for which the Persians made demand and all those who dwelt in the islands did so,"[1] must be an exaggeration, though some surely did, and among them probably Thessaly, Bœotia, and perhaps Delos, and the islands must chiefly be those which had already been conquered. The most important of all the surrenders was that of Ægina. This action justly aroused alarm at Athens and representations were made at once to Sparta against these who were proving recreant to their trust and faithless to the motherland of all. This was a recognition of the position of Sparta as the chief power in Greece, and as possessing some sort of head-

[1] Herodotus, VI, 49.

ship over Athens.[1] Kleomenes acted at once, visiting
Ægina, but meeting a rebuff, due in large measure, if
not as a whole, to the action of his colleague Demaratos, who had in a letter to Ægina intimated that he was
not in agreement with his associate. The result was a
contest in Sparta which cast Demaratos out of office,
and supplanted him with Leotychides, who accompanied Demaratos on a second visit, which met with
success. The people of Ægina had to give up ten prominent men as hostages, who were then handed over to
their "greatest enemies," the Athenians.[2] This would
appear to have been sufficient to control the situation,
for in the ensuing campaign Ægina remained passive.

Darius was now ready to make the great attempt on
which so much depended. He would not attempt to conquer Greece, that were far too much to hope for. He
would only attempt to punish Athens and Eretrea for
their share in assisting the Ionian revolt. The army recruited was moved from Susa to the Cilician plain,
where the fleet was to meet it. The rendezvous was
well chosen, for no Greek fleet would reach the scene
without discovery and much time would be occupied
in any such attempt. The troops were successfully embarked, and the expedition, under Datis the Mede and
Artaphernes the Persian, son of Artaphernes, satrap
of Sardes, made a most propitious start. The number of
triremes is said by Herodotus to have been 600, a conventional number without significance.[3] There were
special transports for the cavalry horses, and the men
were somehow crowded upon the ordinary fighting-ves-
sels. There can be no satisfactory estimate for the num-

---

[1]Grundy (*The Great Persian War*, p. 154, foot-note) argues that this "assumption is possible, but not necessary," but I do not see how the conclusion can
be avoided.

[2]Herodotus, VI, 73.   [3]See p. 125.

bers of men, for Herodotus gives no estimate and modern efforts are the merest baseless speculation. There
may have been 15,000 men,[1] scarcely more when one
considers the possible capacity of the ships. The fleet
made for Samos, and there, further organized and probably provisioned, was made ready for action and sailed
out on the sea in the early summer of 490 B. C.[2] The
first point of attack was Naxos, whence the population
got away safely to the hills, and the city was laid waste.
Then Delos was approached and its inhabitants fled,
leaving the city to its fate. Datis was too shrewd or
too well advised to yield to passion. He offered sacrifice instead, and so honored religious feelings of much
moment. Politically also this was very wise, for it
would convey to Greeks in general the desired impression that this was only a punitive expedition and
that none need fear to suffer but those who had in-
sulted and outraged the Great King by giving aid and
comfort to his rebellious subjects. The next landing
was at Karystos, on the southern point of Eubœa,
which was speedily brought to terms by the ravaging
of its territory. Eretria was now justly alarmed and
appealed for aid to Athens, which was a poor hope, for
no men could be spared from Attica, and the Athenian
Kleruchs resident in Eretria promptly fled home. Hoping to escape condign punishment, the city opened its
gates to the Persians after a very short siege, but re-

[1]Later writers give high figures such as 200,000 infantry and 10,000 cavalry
(Nepos), and 600,000 (Justin). Modern writers, reduced to speculation, vary
greatly in their estimates. Grundy suggested about 40,000; Munro, 25,000
infantry and 1,000 cavalry; Eduard Meyer, 20,000. The Athenian force may
be estimated with a little more hope of success. Herodotus gives no number,
but later writers, as Pompeius Trogus in Justin, Cornelius Nepos, and Plutarch
give 10,000 or 9,000. These seem quite plausible.

[2]This has always been supposed to have been the year, and still is so commonly held. Munro (*Cambridge Ancient History*, p. 232 *et seq.*) advances the
suggestion that it should be 491, and supports it skilfully by argument. I am,
however, not convinced, and must retain the date 490.

ceived no mercy. The city was laid in ashes, and so many of its people as could be rounded up were deported to Susa. The way was now open to Attica, and Datis and Artaphernes probably hoped for a similar decisive victory there and for a like treatment of the Athenians. Hippias, son of Peisistratos, advised them to land upon the plain of Marathon, as being near Eretria and having a terrain suitable for a cavalry attack—so at least is the traditional account of the plan, though there is no reason to believe that cavalry was used at all. Whatever the reason, there was the landing made and successfully. Athens was now fully alive to her danger, and could not fail to remember what had happened to Eretria. The first move was to send a professional despatch runner to Sparta, in the person of Phidippides, who made an extraordinary quick run and laid before the Spartan authorities the plea for aid. The reply was that though anxious to give aid the Spartans could not start before the full moon, which would mean at least a week's delay. There was then nothing for it but for Athens to despatch at once whatever force could be collected. The distance was about twenty-four miles, and the upper road was exceedingly rough, and to cover it in one day was immensely difficult. It was done. The Athenians chose their encampment with great skill. It lay in front of the Heracleion and astride of the upper road to Athens by which they had come, which they now fully commanded by this position. Furthermore, they were in an admirable strategic position to attack the Persians by flank should they attempt to advance by the shore road, the main road toward Athens. They were now joined from the Bœotian town of Platæa,[1] and the situation was clear.

[1]Herodotus, VI, 108.

Fig. 17. Gateway, Palace of Darius.

The Persians must fight, for any attempt to re-embark and sail around Sunium to make a more direct or closer attack on Athens would give an instant and admirable opportunity for the Athenian attack. The only question was whether the Greeks should await developments or attack the Persians as matters then stood. An attack by the Greeks would require them to descend from a position almost impregnable to the plain where they would give the Persians a great tactical advantage in permitting the use of cavalry, and a possible flank attack. On the other hand the Persians would have great difficulty in any attempt at a direct assault on the Athenian position in the hills. The Persian plan was obviously to wait, for delay was on their side. There was a chance of treachery in Athens. But if they delayed too long they would lose, not gain, for at full moon on the 15th of the month the Spartans would start. It would not be necessary for the Spartans to reach Marathon. If they reached Athens the result would be decisive. There seemed to the Persians an absolute necessity of action and preparations were made to attack as the only recourse. It was probably on the 16th that the Persian line was formed on the plain of Marathon, and it was their duty to cover the embarkation of another portion of the Persian army who were to sail round Sunium and attack Athens while the Athenian troops were held at Marathon, and before the Spartans could reach Athens. It was strategically a good plan, and if well carried through tactically might prove successful. The battle line of the Persians was a challenge not to be denied. Any attempt to retreat along that rough road harassed by pursuing Persians would be madness. The Greeks descended the valley and deployed, facing the Persian line, forming a line of exactly the same length. Miltiades was in supreme command; Kallimachos, the polemarch, commanded the right wing, the left wing was held by the Platæans, and the two wings were made much heavier than the centre, which was intentionally thin, only a few ranks deep. The two forces were then "not less than eight stades,"[1] slightly less than one mile apart. The sacrifices being favorable the Greeks advanced to the attack, in hand-to-hand conflict. So quick had been the Greek advance that they suffered but little from the Persian arrows. The Greek centre gave way before the best Persian troops, who were according to their custom massed heaviest in the centre. The break through was not a reverse for the Greeks, but precisely according to a plan soundly based on experience, for it gave the Greek wings their chance to attack by an enveloping movement. Brave men fought on both sides and the battle was long and hotly contested. The superiority of the Greek wings won the victory, for they overwhelmed the weaker Persian wings and were able to fall upon the seemingly victorious centre, which was utterly defeated, its fugitives fleeing to regain their ships as the only means of escape. The Persians left 6,400 dead on the field, the Greeks only 192, among whom were the polemach Kallimachos, the general Stesilaos, and a number of the most prominent citizens.

The Persians were beaten but not undone, and Datis had the courage to go on; and with such forces as had not been engaged at all, or had found safe refuge on the ships, he sailed round Sunium, hoping to attack Athens before her victorious veterans could return overland from Marathon. Soon after the battle 2,000 Spartans came on the scene, in time only to hail the victorious

[1]Herodotus, VI, 112.

Athenians, but too late to join in the fighting. The
Athenians deserved all the praise that human hearts
could imagine, human lips frame. They had defeated
world conquerors, laid their repute as invincible in the
dust, and enheartened the whole of Greece with the
sublime confidence that they who fought for their
home fought on the side of justice and right, and had
a sound claim upon the help of the gods. In Athens the
name of Miltiades was on every lip. His was the strategy which had won the battle, and to him belonged
the recognition and the gratitude.

Both the Persians and the Greeks had underesti-
mated the power and the possibilities of the other, but
the Persians had made the greater miscalculation.
They would have something to learn and much to un-
learn before they might dare again to attempt to fulfil
their dream of adding Greece to the Great King's dominions. Yet this was a dream not lightly to be set
aside. He must have this territory to round out his
borders, to give a point of defense against the Scythians
or other possible marauders, and for the strengthening of his hold on the rest of his empire. If the Greeks
were permitted to defy him, would not defiance soon
appear elsewhere—in Lydia, or in Ionia, or in Egypt?
He was driven by inexorable fate to take Greece or destroy his empire in the attempt, for the empire would
in the other case go to pieces in a series of rebellions.
He must prepare for a new and far greater campaign.
He had now satisfied himself that the attack by sea
was useless without a large land force. The transports
could not carry men enough. The fleet would be a most
useful adjuvant, but was in itself insufficient, and the
land forces previously used by Mardonios were likewise too small. He must have a larger force by sea and

by land. He was more than ever determined upon success, for his own nature ran in common with fate and was not to be denied. He had also learned that while the Greeks appeared to have no natural cohesion, but were continually at odds, the one part with the other, they were on the other hand capable of being forced by external dangers into a formidable temporary unity. He must not depend on any hope of setting them so much apart as to win over them in detail. His only hope lay in the use of forces sufficient to destroy them when they had achieved the utmost unity both of forces and of command.

When the news of the failure of Datis and Artaphernes reached Darius a grim determination and not a supine relaxation came on him. He began the most extensive preparations, and began them immediately. Persia possessed the man power for the making of a great army, yet a great army she did not possess, and this, just this, it was, which had led to so much ill success for Darius as for Cambyses. He must first create an army. During the space of three years he collected men, laying the whole empire under a severe bondage for their supply. He had arms fashioned, provisions laid by, horses levied, vessels built or secured. Nothing before attempted was to be compared with these preparations. He would fall upon Greece with a weight certain to crush her. Would he personally take command? Surely he would so desire. The hands of generals had failed him, his own had never failed. But it is not probable that he hoped to lead in this his greatest enterprise. He was probably already in failing health, for the end was near; though he might not know how near, he would not be wholly ignorant that he was no longer what he had been. He must find another to command,

and he must remain behind awaiting with intense so-
licitude the first news of success or failure. In the
spring of 487 B. C. he was ready to launch the attack.
The men and fleets were prepared. The hour to strike
had come. Had he assured success? Was there any
other factor not provided for in the direct estimates?
There was.

The danger point was Egypt. The country had enjoyed an uncommon prosperity under Persian rule. It
formed the sixth satrapy associated with Cyrene, the
Libyan coast, and with some loosely attached Nubian
tribes on its southern frontier; it paid only 700 silver
talents yearly, which was a small contribution to the
imperial treasury from a province so rich. It had
therein no just cause of complaint. But it had no power
to forget its past, its independence, its glory under native kings, and could now only think that barbarians
controlled its destinies. To hold it in the empire it must
be held down by force, with an army of 120,000 men
occupying the land. Yet was there no real repression of
the land as a whole. The temples retained their rights
and their incomes, and outside the three military stations of Daphnæ, Marea, and Elephantine, the old
feudal system was unimpaired, and the great nobles
retained not only their civil rites but were so free that
insurrection was a dream with them chiefly because
there was no fear in their hearts, nor feeling of the imperial power. The land was not suffering more than under its own kings, but quite the contrary. It was reap-
ing great harvests of money by its share in an empire
that spread widely over Europe, Asia, and Africa.
Never before had so many markets been open to Egypt
as now were hers. She had become an emporium,
through which passed all the products of Nubia, Ethi-

opia, and the Sudan to their customers in the ends of
the world. Arabia found the passage through Suez
easier than the overland route through Asia to Europe.
But prosperity does not bring contentment to nations,
it does not to men. Egypt would rather be free, or
thinks it would, than be prosperous, or it vainly imagines a greater prosperity under freedom. The forces
were all laid for an insurrection. The oracle of Buto
gave the aid of a prediction, and the rebellion began
under the leadership of Khabbisha, who proclaimed
himself as king at Sais and at Memphis. His origin is
entirely unknown to us. His name sounds as though he
were an Arab, but this is highly improbable, for how
should such an outbreak happen in Egypt unless the
leader could lay some colorable claim to relationship
with the ancient rulers of Egypt? It has been supposed
that he belonged in some way to the family of Psammeticus—and this seems probable, though we have
naught but conjecture for its support.[1] How extensive
was the popular or aristocratic adhesion to him remains
unknown, but the rebellion did not seem to alarm
Darius. He went on with his preparations to make war
on Greece, and assembled a second army to reduce
Egypt, commencing war there and in Greece simul-
taneously. He would certainly have been successful in
repressing the Egyptian revolt. The result in other less
competent hands shows that. He would also very likely
have met a large even if not a complete success in
Greece, and so have altered the whole course of history.
But death claimed her own and laid him low before
either expedition could begin.

[1]Révillout (*Chronique Égyptienne*, p. 5, n. 2) supports an Arabian origin on
the basis of the name. Maspero (*The Passing of the Empires*, p. 713) conjectures
a relationship with the family of Psammeticus, but gives no reason. Stein
(Ægypt. Zeitschr., 1883, p. 25) thinks him to be a Libyan.

Fig. 18. Bas-Relief, King and Lion, Palace of Darius.

On that day died the greatest Oriental ruler from then until now. He had obviously been influenced by Cyrus and his career, and had perhaps made him his model, but in achievement as an organizer of civil or governmental life he had far surpassed him. He had not conquered so much new territory, but he had held it against severe attacks and he had made it rich and prosperous. If compared with any of his predecessors in the Orient he shines by the severest tests. Among the Egyptians only Thotmes III may be set even near him, and though he was a successful conqueror over a considerable territory in Asia he had never been able to give it any stable government. In comparison with the Assyrians his career is resplendent. Only Sargon II comes into consideration, but his range of effort was far less, both civil and military, and his savagery in the punishment of rebels is only in a relatively small measure found in Darius. Esarhaddon, a much nobler figure than Sargon, conquered Egypt, and showed a very wise as well as merciful side in the rebuilding of Babylon. Nebuchadrezzar had a spectacular career chiefly because of his sudden and overwhelming victory over the Egyptians at Carchemish; he was a builder of immense structures both palaces and temples, but none of them now survive save as shapeless masses of ruins, and he never was able to devise plans for the government of all that he had won by the sword. When brought side by side with any of these, with all of them, Darius must be allowed to be greater than they.

The character of Darius was mixed of elements good and evil. He was more often kind and gentle, forbearing and patient than savage, yet he could and did crucify Fravartish, and when roused by what he deemed insults to his person or infractions of his authority

could be furious. His determination to reduce Greece
to slavery must not be judged by what his son, Xerxes,
attempted. He had a later day and more light than
Darius to show him the way. Darius knew nothing of
the culture of Greece or of its value to the world. To
him the Greeks were little else than a pestiferous race
of seamen who persisted in giving aid to his enemies.
They and their ways would disturb the balance of empire and perhaps bring down in ruin the best scheme
of government the world had yet seen, and he would
think, and with some show of justice, that they well deserved to be reduced to order, and forcibly thrust into a
system of order and prosperity which would terminate
their squabbles among themselves and end their disturbances in the Ægean Sea and on the Asia Minor coasts.

As Darius surpassed Cyrus and Cambyses in war
and in civil government, so also did he far exceed them
as a builder of great structures. The greatest of these
was at Persepolis, about forty miles northeast of Shi-
raz. There he laid foundations upon which his successors were glad to build. Darius was able to say that the
site was new when he began, "On this platform was this
fortress built. Before this there was no fortress built.
According to the will of Ahuramazda did I build this
fortress, and Ahuramazda commanded it so with all
gods, that this fortress should be built, and I built it,
and built it entire and beautiful and precisely as I ordered."[1] This was no empty boast. He had chosen a
site splendidly suitable for noble and majestic building but so vast as to dwarf into insignificance anything
less grand than man's greatest efforts. He cut away a

[1]The text is cut on the southern wall of the terrace, and in this full form
only in Susian or Elamite. See Weissbach, *Die achämeniden Inschriften zweiter
Art*, pp. 76, 77. Weissbach, *Die Keilinschriften der Achämeniden*, pp. 82, 83.
Stolze, *Persepolis*, II, pl. 95.

FIG. 20. The Kerman Inscription of Darius.

FIG. 21. Metal Knuckle Bone with Dedication to the Didymaean Apollo at Miletus.

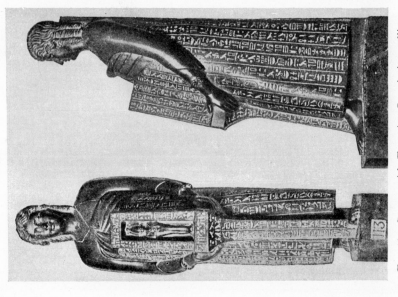

FIG. 19. Statue with Egyptian Inscription telling of Cambyses and Darius.

space at the foot of the mountain, quarried stone from
above, and then in front of the steep mountain wall
built a great platform which stretches from northwest
to southeast 1,523 feet, and has a breadth of 920 feet.
On the northeast or rear part of the platform the
mountain rock of dark gray limestone forms a barrier,
on the other sides a wall, varying from 20 to 50 feet,
according to the slope of the ground, retains and makes
level the platform. The wall is built of stones, some of
which "have been measured as much as 50 feet in
length by 6 to 10 feet in width," laid without mortar,
but originally bound together on the outer surface by
clamps of iron soldered with lead. The wall is broken
into bays and angles. The platform is approached by a
staircase wide enough and easy enough in elevation
for a troop of ten horsemen to ride up it, as it has been
quaintly and picturesquely described.[1] This was on the
western side, while a second approach by a ramp is on
the northeastern side, and a third much narrower than
these is on the southeastern corner and was probably
intended only for pedestrians. The platform had four
distinct levels, the highest in the middle, and on three
of these buildings were erected. Though dwarfed by the
mountain when viewed from a distance, as indeed are
all the works of man everywhere by the greater con-
structions of nature, when seen near at hand "we can
well believe that no more sumptuous framework was
ever wrought by man" (Curzon).

Upon this noble and spacious foundation Darius
erected two of the greatest structures which ever graced
it. The first of these was his royal palace, a building
$132\frac{1}{2}$ feet long by 96 feet broad, which was so strong
in construction and so excellent in engineering plan

[1]So Barbier de Meynard, *Dict. Geog.*, p. 48, n. 2.

that it has withstood the crash of time better than any other building of any period in this place. At the entrance Darius had deeply and finely engraved in Persian cuneiform characters the words, "Darius the great king, king of kings, king of the lands, son of Hystaspis, the Achæmenian, who built this winter palace."[1] Richly decorated were its stone doorways with combats with a lion, or a bull, and with Persian figures who stood to guard the entrance. There is good reason to believe that the structure was never completely finished, death overcoming the artificer of the building, as it did the empire maker, before his work was done.[2] Other kings used it and placed their inscriptions upon its stone surfaces.

Besides the palace for his own residence Darius built an audience room, the largest of all the buildings on the platform, the Hall of a Hundred Columns. There, according to age-long oriental custom, the king was expected to sit twice daily to grant audience, receive complaints, and right injustice. The edifice covered an area 225 feet square. The roof was supported on a hundred columns, and the main entrance on the north side had a vestibule with a roof supported by sixteen columns. The columns are nearly all gone now, the walls, which were probably of brick glazed with enamelled tiles, are gone. Some of the door-jambs and window-sills remain, and portions of the entrance. There Darius is portrayed in the act of slaying fabled beasts on the eastern and western portals, while on the north and south he appears seated on his throne, supported by subject nations bearing arms to defend their ruler. On his head is a tiara and above it the winged symbol of

[1] Weissbach, *Die Keilinschriften der Achämeniden*, pp. 80, 81.
[2] For pictures of this palace in its present state see Stolze, *Persepolis*, plates 29 ff., and Sarre and Herzfeld, *Iranische Felsreliefs*, pl. 21.

FIG. 23.   A Persian Soldier.

FIG. 22.   The Tomb of Darius.

his god Ahuramazda. All the rest has gone. But the glory of it seems even in its rack and ruin to bear witness to the greatness of the man who had it built that he might greatly dispense justice.

There was naught else that Darius must needs build but his tomb. About five or six miles north of the platform that bore his winter palace and audience chamber a rocky cliff over 500 feet long and between 100 and 200 feet high was found, and there out of the solid rock the tomb was made. The shape of the façade was that of a Greek cross about 70 feet high and 60 feet wide. The doorway was relatively small, and on either side of it cut out of the rock were four columns with the heads of bulls upon them, supporting an entablature, with ornamental architecture, frieze, and cornice. The upper limb of the cross is richly carved with bas-reliefs representing the subject nations in two rows, one above the other, supporting a platform on which stands the king, with a bow in his hand, and before him the sacred fire, above which is the winged symbol of Ahuramazda. Two splendid inscriptions are near the king and around the doorway on both sides. They begin with ascriptions of praise to Ahuramazda, "A great god is Ahuramazda, who created this earth, who created these heavens, who created man, who created blessings for men, who made Darius king, one king over many, the one ruler over many." After that came the king's own description of himself in high-sounding phrases, and then an account of the proud achievements of his reign, and at the end the solemn warning to the men who should come after him. "O man, that which Ahuramazda commands, to that show not thyself opposed. Forsake not the straight way. Sin not."[1]

[1]Weissbach, *Die Keilinschriften der Achämeniden*, p. 86 ff.

There in the tomb which he had made, and inscribed with praises of his god, a warning to his fellow men, and stately record of his own deeds, the hands of faithful men laid the great king's body. There would not be another so great as he in his line.

CHAPTER VII

XERXES I

BEFORE the hand of death was laid upon him Darius foresaw, as did others, the shadow of its approach, and was confronted by the problem of the succession. Claim was made by, or in behalf of, Artobazanes, as the eldest son of his father, but a stronger claim was offered for Xerxes on the ostensible ground that he was the son first born after his father came to the throne, and that it was in accordance with Persian custom, if not of law, that it was the son of a reigning sovereign who must succeed. The choice fell on Xerxes, and it is highly probable that his success was largely if not wholly due to the great influence of his mother, the famous Atossa, daughter of Cyrus—the blood of Cyrus still had influence and power.[1]

Xerxes became king in 485, his name in Persian being Khshayarsha, in Babylonian Khishi'arsha, in Hebrew Ahasuerus,[2] though that is probably a misreading and the name was originally in Hebrew Akhashyarsh or Akhshayarsh,[3] which corresponds more closely to the Persian form. He was thirty-five years of age, in the very flower of young manhood, admired of his own people, and, as was declared by Herodotus, "not one was for beauty and stature more worthy to possess this

[1]Herodotus (VII, 2) gives in characteristic detail the story of the appointment of a successor, and dates it before the death of Darius. On the other hand Plutarch (Mor., 488, ed. Bernardakis, III, p. 267, Teubner) and Justin (II, 10, ed. Ruehl, p. 24, Teubner) give the eldest son's name as Ariamenes, and place the decision after Darius' death.

[2]Ezra 4, 6 and Esther passim.

[3]Compare Bevan, *Daniel*, p. 149. His name in Egyptian was written thus.

power."[1] He had inherited great power indeed, but responsibilities no less great, and of dangers not a few. Egypt was in rebellion and there could be no campaign against Greece, such as his father had purposed, until

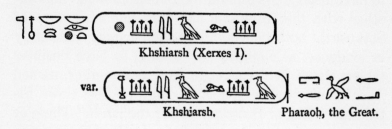

Khshiarsh (Xerxes I).

var. Khshiarsh.   Pharaoh, the Great.

Egypt was reduced to subjection. It was not an easy task, so far as one could then see, for it must have been gathering strength as time went by, having begun in the spring of 486, and rebellions have a bad habit of gaining momentum unless repressed early. There was neither time nor energy to lose, and the king took command in person and set out for Egypt. We know nothing of this campaign but its successful issue in the restoration of Persian power, and the severe punishment meted out for the revolt. The government was placed in the hands of Achæmenes, a younger brother of the king, and the hands of Xerxes were free to deal with the next problem, which was Babylon.

The last year or more of the reign of Darius was troubled by a recrudescence of rebellion in Babylon. Dark and uncertain are the hints which have reached us concerning this new folly of an effort to set up independent rule. There was no hope for its success until there arose in Persia a king weak enough to permit the empire of his fathers to fall to pieces, or until rebellions in many parts should make the suppression of some one

[1] Herodotus, VII, 187.

impossible. Neither of these contingencies had arisen while Darius lived and reigned, and it is a matter of astonishment that any man should undertake to lead an uprising. But there was such a man and his name seems to have been Bel-shimanni or Bel-shimmana,[1] and another with the enigmatic and very doubtful name of Shikushti,[2] both of whom had their names sufficiently in evidence, as claiming to be king, to have business tablets dated in their reign. And yet another, named Akshimaksu,[3] made the same claim and set down his titles as "King of Babylon, and of the lands." These or some one or two of them used the death of Darius as a stepping-stone, but with ill success. No one of them has left even one bit of clay dated beyond the year of accession, and then come the business tablets dated in the name of Xerxes and in his accession year with the title "king of Babylon, king of the lands,"[4] to show how swift had been the recognition of him as the real ruler of the country. He seems to have appointed Zopyros as satrap, and in a brief visit to the refractory capital believed he had set it in order. Zopyros, however, was speedily slain, and in his room Xerxes appointed the dead man's son, Megabyzos, as successor. It was quite likely as punishment for this mixed and obscure series of uprisings that Xerxes razed the great temple of Esagila.[5] This would be an appalling deed in the eyes of Babylonians, and when he had removed the statue of Marduk,[6] used for ages as a divine symbol whose

[1]Ungnad, *Vorderasiatische Schriftdenkmäler*, VI, No. 331.
[2]*Verhandlungen des XIII* (Leiden) *Orientalisten-Kongress*, 1902, No. 268.
[3]Ungnad, ib., Nos. 177, 178.
[4]Strassmeier, *Actes du huitième congrès international des Orientalistes*, II, Nos. 16, 17, 18.
[5]Arrian, III, 16; VII, 17 (ed. Roos, pp. 143, 368, Teubner); Ælian, *Varia Historia*, XIII, 3, ed. Hercher, p. 147 (Teubner), and Strabo, *Geographica*, XVI, 1, 538, ed. Meineke, III, p. 1029 (Teubner). This temple is called by Strabo and by others ὁ τοῦ Βήλου τάφος.
[6]Herodotus, I, 183.

carved hands every king who claimed to be a legitimate
ruler must take every year on New Year's day, he had
taken away that which symbolized in the most profound manner the very existence of a real state. Henceforth there could be no lawful king of Babylon, and
this was precisely what Xerxes was planning to accomplish. He had borne the title "King of Babylon," he is
now "King of Persia and Media"; Babylon has wholly
disappeared, absorbed into the general mass of the empire. Xerxes had pacified it with a strong hand. As a
political move the removal of the statue was quite natural from the Persian point of view. It would make
difficult if not impossible the move of some new pretender, grasping the hands of Bel Marduk, and then
laying claim to be the only lawful king of Babylon.
Some new symbolic rite must be invented, and it would
not be easy to find one quickly which should have any
such magical power as the old one. Xerxes had made
a good imperial beginning.

Xerxes had not so thoroughly seated himself on a
stable throne with Egypt and Babylon in subjection
and without any suggestion of rebellion elsewhere that
he could give himself unreservedly to the immense task
of preparing an attack upon Greece. After the reduction of Egypt Xerxes gave full three years to the work,
and upon a scale never attempted by Persia before.
The plan was a return to that of Darius in 492; it was
to use both land and sea forces in co-operation and
prodigious efforts were made to avoid the dangers
which had to be met and to keep in mind the errors
which had caused disasters before.

The wrecking of the Persian fleet off Athos caused
the resolve to avoid a repetition of such a disaster, and
the obvious way was to make it unnecessary for the

fleet to round that tempestuous cape. To avoid this it
was necessary to dig a canal for the ships to pass within
and Xerxes had the boldness to attempt it, and the
ability to carry it out. The distance to be dug out was,
as shown by modern measurements, to be about 2,500
yards,[1] and one may still see faint signs of a line of
ponds from 2 to 8 feet deep and 60 to 90 feet wide.[2]
It is therefore not improbable that the original width
was about 100 feet, which would suffice for the passage
of triremes. The digging was done by men of various
races from various parts of the empire, as well as by
men impressed near the spot and working under the
lash.

While this work went laboriously forward Xerxes
was busy gathering materials from the whole vast empire for other great works of preparation. A bridge was
built over the river Strymon and ropes and other gear
for the construction of the great bridges which were to
move the army across the Hellespont. Magazines of
provisions were assembled at Leuké Akté on the Propontis in Thrace, at Tyrodiza in the Hellespontine district, at Doriscus, at Eion, and in Macedonia.

The fleet had to be built for this purpose, as none too
much remained of those which had served and suffered
before. The fleet now prepared numbered 1,207[3] fighting vessels, and besides these there were some larger
ships driven by thirty and even by fifty oars, and about
3,000 transports—whose numbers may be exaggerated,
but there is no sound reason for doubting the number of
ships in the main fleet. The manning of this vast fleet

[1]This corresponds closely to the 12 stades given by Herodotus, VII, 23, and
there is no real justification for ancient or modern doubts that the canal was
really dug.
[2]On this canal compare the notes in Rawlinson's *Herodotus*, IV, pp. 24, 25,
and How and Wells, *Herodotus*, II, p. 135.
[3]Herodotus, VII, 184.

was given to the peoples who knew the sea by a long tradition, who had it in their blood, the best of them being the Phœnicians, though scarcely less accustomed to its vagaries were the Cypriotes, the Ionians, the Cilicians, and the Hellespontines; there were even 407 Greek ships and few were better sailors than they.

With the preparation of the fleet there went also the gathering and arming of the land forces, the calling up of men from every quarter of the empire, the determining of the places where each contingent should form, and the deciding upon the route it should follow. Never before among men had any campaign been so carefully planned, so systematically carried out. The campaigns of Esarhaddon or of Nebuchadrezzar were mere raids in comparison. Generals were chosen from Persians, as were the admirals for the fleet; there was no chance taken that might issue in some act of disloyalty or of treason. If the men to whom high command was entrusted were not so able as some that might have come from subject peoples, their loyalty at least must be unquestioned.

During the winter of 481 B. C. the preparations were completed and in the early spring of 480 B. C. the corps began to move. At Kritalla[1] in Cappadocia the forces from the east had collected and moved thence toward Sardes, where Xerxes awaited during the winter of 481–480 B. C. their arrival and union with troops from the southeast and south. The number of men in this combined force cannot now be determined, but is not likely to have exceeded 100,000 of all ranks. So great a

---

[1]The location of Kritalla is unknown, and the route is therefore uncertain. Munro (*Camb. An. Hist.*, IV, 268) suggests that the king probably came through the Cilician gates and that "Critalla lay not far from the exit from the pass, perhaps near Tyana or Cybistra." The evidence is, however, insufficient for a positive identification.

Fig. 24. General View of the Palaces at Persepolis.

Fig. 25. Bas-Relief from the Apadana of Xerxes.

force as that would seem utterly overwhelming to the
Greeks; yet were they not so content, but wildly exaggerated the number of their opponents, as have peoples
of all lands both before and since their day.[1]

From Sardes Xerxes despatched heralds to Greece to
demand earth and water from the several states, a
move which would have the great value of enabling
him to determine how much unity existed in Greece
and what opposition he was likely to meet. While they
made their troubled way westward and the army
crawled heavily along the plains of Asia Minor, the
Phœnicians and Egyptians finished the two bridges
over the Hellespont near Abydos where the strait is
narrowest, but be it remembered where the current is
dangerously swift. The bridges first erected were destroyed by a storm, and the work had to be done again.
The two bridges began on the Asiatic side close together; the western one, nearest the Ægean, spanned
the strait in a direct line, and was about three-quarters
of a mile long. The other went in an oblique direction
up the strait toward the Propontis and landed on the
European shore a considerable distance from its fellow. The western bridge was built of 314 vessels and
the eastern of 360, triremes and penteconters, slung
together with ropes of flax or papyrus and anchored

[1]Herodotus (VII, 60) gives a most amusing account of the method by which
the army was numbered. Ten thousand men were packed together as closely
as possible and a line drawn about them, and a wall built on the line. Troops
were then driven in to fill this big measuring pen in batches, until all had so
filled the pen. One hundred and seventy times was it so filled, a myriad or ten
thousand each time. This would make a total of 1,700,000. To which Herodotus
adds 80,000 cavalry and 20,000 chariot and camel corps, which brings the total
to 1,800,000 for the entire army. To this he adds the crews of the fleet, and
additions made in Europe, and the non-combatants, which latter he doubles,
and finally secures the wildly impossible number of 5,283,220 (VII, 186). This
has been subjected to an acute, penetrating and ingenious criticism by J. A.
R. Munro (*Cambridge Ancient History*, IV, p. 271 f.), who arrives at the final
conclusion that the expeditionary army numbered 180,000 combatants. Even
this seems to me far too large, but I have nothing but conjecture to offer in
its stead.

both at bow and stern, the prows turned toward the oncoming current running toward the Ægean. Trunks of trees connected the boats, and a roadway was formed by laying brushwood over them, and tamping it down with earth. The way was now really repaired, and having wintered at Sardes (481–480), in the early spring Xerxes set the forces in motion, northward over the river Caikos, into Mysia through the plain of Thebe, passing Adramytteion and so on to Abydos. There lay the two bridges over the Hellespont and Europe on the other side. Here a grand review was held and a whole month passed. In the month of May or early June the crossing was made without mishap, the troops passing by one bridge, and the baggage trains by the other. Surely no such spectacle as that had ever before been seen by men. The scene is noble, the rushing current of water swirling about the boats as they swung at their moorings, the hills of Europe and of Asia, and the obedient masses of men from Asia ready to assail a civilization superior to their own, yet of which they had no knowledge and less appreciation. What would the fates now do with this situation?

The fleet was at the Hellespont, and sailed thence to Sarpedon, when the bridges had been crossed. The Thracian Chersonese was before the men as they marched and severe must many of the problems have been. There were indeed stores of provisions assembled and located, but a greater problem was the water supply. Herodotus takes occasion more than once to remark that the waters of the rivers did not suffice to supply water for the host,[1] and this may well be the case, for in the summer many of these streams are very low and some have beds nearly or quite dry, though he

[1]Herodotus, VII, 58, is an example where he speaks thus of the river Melas.

is, of course, mentioning the matter only to emphasize the great size of the army which Greece must encounter. When the army reached Doriscos, the fleet lay off shore, and Xerxes held another review and numbered his men, using a quaint method, so described by Herodotus as to add color to the fictions of number, and to delight the Greek reader by its picturesqueness.

From Doriskos to Therma (Saloniki) the distance is about 300 miles; and the army marched in three divisions, one in sight of the coast most of the way, the other two inland. The fleet passed successfully through the canal, escaping the dangers of Mount Athos, and met the land forces at Therma, where a halt of a good many days occurred, while the heralds were received on their return from Greece, some bearing earth and water, while others had made a fruitless journey. This report, while not pleasing, could hardly have been unexpected, and at the beginning of August the move forward began again.

Up to this point there had been no serious difficulty. The country was under Persian rule, no attack upon the army could well be made, new levies of troops could be made to fill the places of those who had died by the way, and the terrain was well suited for marching near the coast. Now the case would be greatly altered. The men must march as best they could over a land far less fertile and unable to provide anything like so much for foraging; nor would it offer much opportunity for the impressment of men; and its coast was rugged, unfit for marching, and hence provided no opportunities for co-operation with the fleet; yet if the Greeks could put a force into the field there might be some sudden call to action. Conditions favorable in many ways had now changed for the worse.

The arrival of the Persian army at Therma was well calculated to rouse all Greece into a fury of apprehension, and a wild tempest of discussion arose. The reputation of the Medes and Persians as possessing invincible armies had received a shock at Marathon, but there was enough of it left to cause alarm. On the other hand, it would be fatal if confidence should be excessive, if the meaning of Marathon should be exaggerated, and men think that it were a light matter to oppose the Persians and overwhelm them, as many thought had been done with the army of Datis and Artaphernes. This was a far more difficult case. Whatever may be the exaggeration of the Persian numbers now there need be no doubt that the army to be faced was both larger and better equipped than that which broke down at Marathon. Athens was in a particularly difficult position. She had laid claim to the glory which came of planning and carrying out the victory at Marathon; it would be disastrous if the rest of Greece were to leave to her the present problem and not take seriously the menace. Yet it was sweet to claim the glory and honor and hard to admit that it had been a victory much exaggerated and needing now much to be discounted that the future might be safe. A Persian victory would not be easy to face. It was not, so far as we can see, the purpose of Xerxes to attempt the mad folly of destroying the Greeks; he would desire only to reduce them to quiet and orderliness according to Persian ideas and then to confer upon them such great blessings as had come to Egypt. But to Athens it would mean the end of an independence grown more precious with the passing years, and to Sparta the close of a hegemony for which she had struggled long and hard. Athens might even fear utter destruction for the part she had taken in supporting or aiding the rebels against Persian rule, and even if there were no such bitter feeling against Sparta her glory as the chief military state of the Peloponnesus would be gone.

Athens and Sparta formed a coalition to fight the Barbarians and set themselves to making such preparations as time might serve. Of the Greeks who had sent earth and water to Xerxes the most important were the Thessalians, who must not be too harshly judged. They had no assurance of help from the people of their own blood, were helpless adequately to defend themselves and lay directly in the king's path; they would later, however grudgingly or fearfully, take the national side. Now was an appeal made to all Greeks to take up arms in defense of a cause which ought to rally all. No Greek state dared to come out openly on the side of Persia, but Argos and Crete had the boldness, the stupidity, and the folly to declare for neutrality. Should not the gods punish them, if man should fail to accomplish a vengeance so deserved?

A plan of campaign had to be devised to meet the problem now presented. They must remember that on any computation the Greek forces would be greatly inferior to the Persian. It would therefore be important to make good use of any means of defense which the lay of the land might afford. They had three lines of defense, Mount Olympus, Mount Œta, and the isthmus of Corinth. The Thessalians had sent earth and water, but it was their leaders who had done it, and now as the Persians were drawing near the people sent an appeal to their brethren for aid, giving as a reason that if not helped they must yield to the Persians.[1] The council at the isthmus decided that the plea was justi-

[1]Herodotus, VII, 172.

fied and determined to send 10,000 heavy armed infantry (hoplites) to guard the vale of Tempe. These men came round by sea, landed at Halos, on the Pagasætic gulf, and marched thence to Tempe. The force was too small, even though the Thessalians could add some men to it, to hold back the Persians. The true strategic plan would have been to send the major part, by far the major part, of all the fighting men whom the Peloponnesus could muster to these mountain passes, and then boldly attack the Persians, not waiting to be attacked, and so have some fair chance of keeping them out of any part of Greece. But the Peloponnesians had not the stomach for such a move; they would keep their men near at home for defense, not send them out for offense, as all later experience has shown to be the only safe course. The plan failed, as it deserved. As the Persians marched onward it was soon evident that the 10,000 were useless and they withdrew, leaving all Thessaly to the Persians, with whom, naturally enough, the Thessalians must co-operate, and to whom they were useful.

Having left Thessaly to the Persians the next question to be settled was whether the middle of Greece should also be vacated or an attempt made to hold it. The council at the isthmus determined to hold Mount Œta, which was flanked on the extreme right by the Eubœan straits and the Gulf of Malis. There the only road passes through the pass of Thermopylæ, and to that point 10,000 men were sent under command of Leonidas to hold the pass, while a fleet was sent to Artemisium to meet the Persian ships. It was then quite clear to the Greeks that it was useless to hold the pass against a land army if the Persian fleet were allowed to sail by and land men beyond the pass on Greek soil.

FIG. 26. The Great King on his Throne.
(Cast in the Metropolitan Museum.)

The Greek fleet was nominally under the command of the Lacedæmonian admiral, Euribyades, but really under Themistocles.

About the end of July the Persians approached. A reconnoitre showed Xerxes that he might meet formidable opposition and induced him to delay a few days and carefully consider.

The Greeks despatched three ships to locate the Persian fleet if possible, one being supplied by Corinth, one by Ægina, and the third by Athens. All three were lost, and the Athenian crew alone were saved. It was ill fortune, but worse befell the Persians, for when their entire fleet reached the promontory of Artemisium a storm, which raged for three days, destroyed 400 ships of war and a larger number of transports, and the remaining vessels, seeking refuge, lost fifteen by capture to the Greeks. It had indeed begun to look dark for the Persians, but the fleet might now rest and recuperate while the scene was set on land.

Xerxes learned from spies that the Spartans were taking cheerfully the situation, indulging in athletic sports and combing their hair as though about to engage in some festival. He waited four days more and then ordered an assault on the Greek position by the Medes and Cissians. They were repulsed. The terrain was ill adapted for any fighting but by small numbers and hand to hand, and at this the Greeks were easily superior. Their spears were longer than those of their enemies and they knew the land. They numbered 5,200, counting all but the Locrians, whose numbers remain unknown, but it is not likely that the total force exceeded 6,000. Against them for a second attempt Xerxes sent his immortals and they were driven back. Xerxes may well have been disturbed and discouraged. Then

there came to him a Malian by name Ephialtes, who
offered to lead the Persians by a path over the mountains to the rear of the Greeks. Xerxes accepted and
gave him a division under Hydarnes. At dawn they
reached the summit of the pass, and found it held by
1,000 Phocians, who retreated without striking a blow.
The Persians were soon in possession of a post which
commanded the pass of Thermopylæ. The Greeks,
seeing the fearful state to which they were now reduced, held a consultation, and all but the Spartans,
Thespians, and Thebans retired. While the Persian
flanking party led by Ephialtes were still at a distance
fighting was resumed, and Leonidas fell. His men retired to a spot between two defiles and fought until almost the last man was cut down. The Spartans were
but mortal men and their reputation for invincibility
was lost, the Persians had beaten them. Leonidas had
died like a brave men, but only as any Spartan had
done. He deserves, nevertheless, the glory which has
been his from that day to this, but as a strategist his
rank is low. He had mistaken the situation, believing it
far stronger than it really was, and had taken insufficient precautions to guard attack from flank or rear.
The Greeks are believed to have lost about 4,000 men,
and though the Persians must have suffered far greater,
they had more lives to give and relatively had come off
better. Besides that they had won an unrestricted entrance into central Greece.

While the struggle on land was in progress the sea
had its story to tell. At first the allies were disposed to
flee when they saw how large and how formidable was
the Persian fleet. If they did the Eubœans would fall at
once into Persian hands, and they besought Eurybiades
to hold the fleet together, and meet the Persians like

men. To accomplish this the leaders were bribed, Themistocles receiving thirty talents, Eurybiades five, and Adeimantus, the Corinthian admiral, three. The Persians now drew up a plan to capture the whole Greek fleet, by sending 200 ships round Eubœa. The Greeks determined to fight the rest of the Persian fleet where it was, and displaying uncommon skill captured thirty Persian ships. On the following night a storm burst on the Persians sailing round Eubœa and destroyed the fleet. On the next day the Persians attacked but the result was indecisive. What would have been the final result we shall never know, for when the news of the terrible catastrophe of Thermopylæ reached the fleet it sailed home and left the waters of Eubœa to the Persians.

Xerxes was now completely master of the situation, for the Thessalians who had medized perhaps more from necessity than from desire led his way through the territory of the Dorians, into that of the Phocians, which was devastated. Athens was now in a sad plight. It was quite a hopeless task to attempt to defend the city. Its circle of walls was far too small to admit of sheltering all the folk of the countryside, and there was naught for it but to put all the men of fighting value on the ships and send women and children away. In the middle of August Xerxes entered the city without opposition, and burned the temples on the Acropolis in revenge for the burning of Sardes.[1] The Greek fleet was concentrated at Salamis and there Xerxes determined to bring the whole matter to a conclusion, being confident of victory. The issue was joined and there were many advantages on the side of the Greeks. They had about 380 ships, the enemy full twice as many, but

[1]Herodotus, VIII, 50–55.

the extra numbers were of little advantage, as the
waters were close and an opportunity for the skilful
maneuvering poor. The moral advantages were all on
the Greek side, for they fought for home, religion, and
the culture founded and built up by their fathers. The
battle was fought probably on the 27th or 28th of September, 480, and the Greek victory was overwhelming
and conclusive, though the details are, alas! lost forever. When morning dawned on the next day the Persians had fled. Xerxes, while the fight was still unfin-
ished, held a council of war, in which Mardonius advo-
cated the sending home of the fleet, the return of the
king in person, while he be left with a large force to
complete the conquest of Greece.

In spite of the defeat at Salamis the gains to Persia
had been very great. Athens had been fearfully punished. The victory at Thermopylæ was good cause for
boasting, and in comparison the losses of men, material, and ships were insignificant. Greece had felt the
heavy hand of Barbarian might and Xerxes might well
think that the lesson would be kept in mind. It was not
possible to find winter quarters for his army in devastated Attica, and he withdrew his land forces to the
plains of Thessaly. There Mardonius selected the men
whom he wished to retain for the continuation of the
war on the independence of Greece, and Xerxes returned in safety to Asia Minor by the same route as
that by which he had come, purposing to spend the
winter in Sardes, and so be nearer the next campaign
than if he had gone on to Susa.

The Greek army soon returned from the pursuit of
the retreating Persians, and the Greek fleet likewise returned to Salamis to divide the spoil and prepare suitable honors for the gods. Themistocles went to Sparta,

where the greatest honors were paid to him, and the Greeks began carefully to consider plans for the next inevitable campaign. It was clear that they must at all hazards keep the enemy out of central Greece, and to this defensive scheme the share of the fleet was arranged. Its ships now numbered only 110, under command of the Spartan king, Leotychidas. It sailed in the early spring to Delos to defend the Cyclades and watch the Persian fleet assembled at Samos. The army, on the other hand, was to seize the offensive as early as possible. It was however soon clear that the poverty of the land would permit no movement earlier than the gathering for the harvest.

Mardonius knew as by instinct that an assault on the fortifications of the isthmus was hopeless without the support of a fleet from Asia, and of that there was no hope for this year. It seemed to him a time for diplomacy rather than fighting and he therefore attempted by great promises to range the Athenians on his side.[1] The plan failed. Therefore as soon as ripening harvests permitted he began the southerly march to attack Athens, or if the Peloponnesians could be drawn out of the isthmus into a big battle he felt sure of a complete victory in the open field without the help of a fleet. The Athenians were far too weak to attempt to hold their city against such forces as were under the command of Mardonius, and had no recourse but to flee once more to Salamis, and so leave their city to be reoccupied by the Persians. In June, and probably near its beginning, the Persian troops were in occupation, and thence Mardonius made offers to the fugitive inhabitants to leave their city unharmed if they would now accept the overtures previously made, but again was refused.[2]

[1] Herodotus, VIII, 136, 140–144. [2] Herodotus, IX, 1–6.

In the meantime the Peloponnesians despatched an army to the isthmus under command of Pausanias, cousin and guardian of the young king, Pleistarchus, son of Leonidas. Mardonius destroyed whatever remained of Athens, desolated Attica, and retired by a circuitous march into Bœotia. The Peloponnesians, without waiting for the complete assembling of their allies, took the offensive and determined to attack Meggara. Success was swift and before Mardonius could strike their forces were safe within its city walls. Mardonius had failed to administer a lesson to the Lacedæmonians, and he had now to prepare for an attack, which he anticipated, by the Greeks.

He chose for his defensive position the ground near Platæa, and between the little city and the river Asopus. There he was exceedingly well placed. He had a stockaded camp, a well-fortified base in a fertile country, and one well adapted for the use of cavalry, in which he was especially strong. He had 50,000 Asiatic troops, and besides these 10,000, or even more, of the Greek allies such as the Bœotians, Locrians, Phocians, Thessalians, and Macedonians. He had done as much damage to Athens and Attica as would satisfy his lust for vengeance. He could now in safety and self-satisfaction await the worst that Greece could do.

In the meantime Sparta had been fully aroused to the danger, for it had gradually become plain that if the Persians were not really defeated an invasion of the Peloponnesus could not be prevented. The isthmus, no matter whether defended by a wall of stone or by the breasts of men, would not arrest the strangers, as the Spartans called the Persians. Thoroughly aroused, Sparta forsook the isthmus and marched northward with about 12,000 heavy armed men of her own troops,

Fig. 27. The Royal Throne Supported by the Subject Peoples.
(Cast in the Metropolitan Museum.)

with some contingents from Tegetæ and the isthmus. To these were added such men of Megara as might be secured, and at Eleusis the Athenians joined also, adding with Megara about 8,000 men. With the large numbers of light armed troops the total force now comprised about 50,000 men, the largest force which Greece had ever put into the field. The force indeed was probably equal in numbers to that of Mardonius, but was entirely without cavalry, in which he was strong. This might prove a deciding factor, and the Greeks would need carefully to choose their ground because of this lack. The Greeks advanced over the passes of the Cithæron range and took up a position on its northern slope where the main road from Athens to Thebes debouches from the mountains. The army of Mardonius was now in sight and the Greeks were deployed to face it; the Lacedæmonians were opposite the Persians, while the Athenians faced the Greek allies of the barbarians. The omens on both sides were unfavorable for the offensive, and both hesitated, waiting for some change. So for ten days they stood, and on the eleventh Mardonius decided to attack the Greek centre with his cavalry. During the night Alexander of Macedon passed on the word of what was going to happen to the Athenians. The Greeks made a lucky hit against the Persian cavalry, which had come forward too far and too suddenly. The Greeks were now suffering from lack of water, for the Persians had filled the springs near by, and so a change of position was attempted. The centre executed the movement very badly, coming much farther to the southwest than had been intended, while the Spartans had been far too slow because one of their commanders in charge of a division judged it disgraceful to seem to retreat before an enemy. The Athenians

desired to join the Spartans in order to make up for
the mistaken movement of the centre, but failed to find
them, and finally took position northwest of the centre,
with their left wing toward the Asopus. Mardonius
had by this time discovered that the Spartans had left
their place and advanced to attack their new position.
But the Spartans anticipated the move and charged.
The Persians were defeated and Mardonius was slain.
His men fled, some toward Thebes, and some to the
encampment, or fort. Meanwhile the Athenians had
defeated the Greek allies of Persia, but not without
difficulty. There could however be no doubt of the results. It was a Persian debacle. Artabazus fled with a
considerable remnant to Phocis, and then pushed on as
swiftly as possible toward Asia. When the Athenians
had finally beaten their opponents they united with
the other Greeks and besieged the wooden encampment where many Persians had taken refuge, and soon
overcame the feeble resistance. The fleeing Persians
left an immense number dead. Herodotus would have
it that not 3,000 remained alive, but this, like the other
numbers, is surely incorrect. Artabazus carried off far
more. Yet the Greek loss of 1,360[1] must have been very
small in comparison with the Persian loss, for the
Greek military skill was far superior and every other
possible advantage was on their side. The Persians left
immense booty on the field. They had made war, in this
respect like the Assyrians, to gather plunder, and now
that an overwhelming defeat had come upon them it
was impossible to carry off the loot of many cities. The
Greeks gave liberally to the general, Pausanias, divided

[1]Herodotus (IX, 20–85) gives the Greek loss as 91 Spartans, 16 Tegetæ, and
52 Athenians, and Plutarch (*Aristides*, 19 ed., Lindskog and Ziegler, I, p. 300,
Teubner), on the authority of Cleidemus, says that all the Athenians were of
the tribe of Æantis, and gives the total Greek dead as 1,360.

among themselves much, and devoted splendid portions
to the gods. To Delphi they sent a golden tripod
mounted on a pillar formed of three brazen serpents.
It endures to this day, having long remained in Con-
stantinople, brought thither by Constantine. It bears
still the names of the Greek communities which presented it. It is a precious memorial of great deeds and
of mighty sacrifices, though now marred and broken.[1]
At Olympia and on the isthmus other devoted objects
were set up, while on the field of battle was built an
altar to Zeus. In Platæa there was founded an annual
festival, the Eleutheria, and to the Platæans a guaran-
tee of neutrality was made.

The Greek fleet[2] under Leotychidas was stationed at
Delos, while the fate of the country was in decision at
Platæa, and the Persian fleet at Samos; and near by on
Cape Mycale was a Persian army, said to have been
60,000 strong. The Greeks long awaited an attack from
the Persian fleet, but it was not strong enough to take
so rash a venture. Some of its ships had gone to their
own harbors after Salamis, and perhaps among them
the Phœnicians,[3] who were easily the best. The Greeks
now received urgent appeals from Samos and Chios to
sail to Ionia, which was ready for an uprising. Leotychidas sailed for Samos, but before his arrival the Persians made off to the near-by coast on the northern
edge of the Latmian gulf opposite Miletus, where they

---

[1]Herodotus, IX, 81. Compare *Inscriptiones Græcæ Antiquissimæ*, ed. Röhl,
1882, 70 (with a picture). Hicks, *A Manual of Greek Inscriptions*, 19, and see
the excellent note in How and Wells, Herodotus, II, pp. 321 ff.

[2]The ships of which it was composed may now have numbered as many as
250, since Xanthippus and the Athenians had joined after Mardonius had
evacuated Attica (Diodorus, XI, 34).

[3]Herodotus (IX, 96) locates the departure of the Phœnicians for the home
ports from Samos, but it is very probable that Diodorus (XI, 19, ed. Vogel, II,
p. 251, Teubner) is right in placing their departure immediately after Salamis.
On this point compare How and Wells, Herodotus, II, p. 329, and Beloch,
Griechische Geschichte, 2nd ed., II, p. 59, note 1.

drew their ships on shore and made a fortified camp.
Here they hoped to be able to defend themselves, and
if the worst came to have a way open for flight by
land. The Greeks, seeing that a battle by sea was refused, set their men ashore and speedily carried the en-
trenchments, and the Persians, setting their ships afire,
escaped, so many as were able.[1] The result of this was
the fall of all Ionia from the Persians; and the islands
of Samos, Lesbos, and Chios were received into the
Hellenic confederation, while the Athenians made a
separate treaty with the people of the mainland. As
autumn had now come the Peloponnesians sailed home-
wards, but the Athenians, remaining a while longer,
beseiged Sestos, opposite Abydos, which had a Persian
garrison which was starved out. By this time the Hellespont was entirely in Greek hands and Artabazus,
with the rest of the Persian land forces, had to retreat
by way of Byzantium. It was now late in the autumn
and the Athenians made for home to escape the storms
of the winter.

When the spring of 478 dawned there were some
bits of Greek land and some of Greek blood still in Persian hands. Then there sallied forth from the Peloponnesus a small fleet of twenty triremes under command
of Pausanias, the victor of Platæa. Thirty Attic ships
joined, and to them were added the ships that had won
the victories in the preceding year in setting free the
Ionians and Lesbians. This fleet delivered from Persian bondage the islands on the Carian coast, and then
sailed to Cyprus, most of which was likewise liberated.
Then Byzantium[2] was beleaguered and after a long de-

---

[1] It is surely impossible that the Greeks fired the ships, while on the other
hand it would be a very natural act for the Persians, to prevent the ships falling into the hands of an enemy.
[2] Thucydides, I, 94, 128, 5.

fense taken, and with it the last of the Persian strong-
holds was once more Greek. With this taken from the
Persians there remained but few points to which any
Persian claim could be made. Perhaps the most important was the Thracian city of Eion on the Strymon,
which Cimon, the commander of the Athenian League,
took in 476.

The Greeks had delivered Greece from the Persians
in a long and serious struggle in which every nerve and
muscle had been strained to the utmost. They had won
the contest not merely by fighting, not merely by skill
in battle on sea and shore, but because in the deepest
of all fundamental things they were a superior people,
in civilization indeed, as all later centuries have securely
judged and determined, and also in a number of the
higher moral qualities. They had suffered defeat nobly
and had risen to renew the struggle boldly. They had
had poor commanders and they lived to produce better.
They won because they deserved victory. It is however not to belittle the decisiveness of the result, or to
diminish its glory, if we remind ourselves that even if
Persia had triumphed Greek civilization would not
have perished. Ionia had long lain under Persian rule
and her Greek culture had survived. Even though
Sparta and Athens had fallen, their civilization would
have endured, and they would have risen again to
claim and win their freedom.

From the bright morning, nay, even the full noon-
tide glory of Greek victory, glory, and honor, one must
turn away to follow Xerxes into the ever-deepening
shadows. He had fled to Sardes, there to remain for a
time, but never to regain even the temporary use of
any real energy. What he had attempted against Greece
was an ignominious failure. It is perhaps idle to specu-

late upon what might have been. Yet it is tempting to suppose, to imagine, to picture another figure, even that of Darius the Great, in the place of Xerxes when the great attempt was made. It were churlish not to recognize and admit that Xerxes had made immense preparations for the campaigns against Greece. Whether this were done by him, or by the greater skill of one or more of those who served and represented him, we shall never know, but done they were and the credit must be given him. But when he took personal command the task was far too great for his powers, and defeat followed on defeat, as night the day. If Darius the Great had commanded such an army and a fleet so great all signs point to the probability that he would have utterly overwhelmed the Greeks. Even Xerxes had severely punished Athens; what should a man of the military capacity of Darius have done with such weapons? Would he not have laid Sparta in ruins and sowed the whole of Greece with salt? It was well for the future of European civilization that the sceptre of Persia was in hands less able. Yet had Darius triumphed, Greece must, by the very assurance of a superior life, ultimately have come again into her own, though the losses would surely have been heavy, and some of them would have been irreparable.

Xerxes had hopelessly failed in the greater enterprise, but he retired to Sardes with much left whereof to boast. The borders of the empire which he had inherited from his father had not yet shrunken. The Athenians had, it is true, won a certain independence for the Ionians, but its importance was restricted to the port cities, and at the best was precariously held. It was a writ of freedom that ran only within sound of the sea, for the Persian power still controlled the

land behind, and whatever the coast cities might have
of freedom must be held subject to the quick exercise
of military force to repel a Persian invasion which
might come at any time. Xerxes had when the Greek
defeat came still fourteen years to live. It may and
probably was impossible for him to rouse the whole
empire to pour out its strength in another great effort
to destroy the Greek state and add its territory to Persia, for Xerxes had lost all repute as a man likely to
rival Cyrus, Cambyses, and Darius in extending the
borders of the empire. Other lands there were that
felt but a loose attachment to Persia which might have
been brought into subjection complete and final, but
the king had felt enough of the sting of defeat and
dared not take the field again. Nor could he in any
measure rival the splendid achievements of Darius in
civil or political organization. The government of the
empire was left as Darius had made it, and only the
administration of it without improvement or serious
amendment satisfied Xerxes.

As he had failed in war and in civil organization so
also did Xerxes fail to surpass his great predecessor in
buildings. Yet it is but just to say that if the eyes of
men had never seen the works of Darius some of these
which Xerxes built would seem very impressive, perhaps even majestic. On the great platform at Persepolis and facing the wide staircase that leads from the
plain, Xerxes built a porch, a propylæum of stone,
guarded back and front by colossal winged bulls. These
are based for design upon Assyrian models, but do not
stand detached as at Nineveh, but are cut in high relief. Above them on the stone face is an inscription in
three languages, four times repeated. The content is
almost the same as those of Darius, beginning with

praise of Ahuramazda, going on with his reasons for
building and concluding with the words, "May Ahuramazda protect me and my rule, may Ahuramazda
protect that which I have built, and that which my
father has built."[1] Through this great portal messengers from many lands filed in solemn procession toward the audience chamber bearing gifts to the master
of their destinies. It was a gateway for all nations. Behind it and about fifty yards to the south Xerxes built
his audience chamber, with seventy-two columns to
support its roof, and an inscription in Persian only, of
similar form to that which adorns the propylæum. It
had been in its day of glory a splendid building, its
walls probably hung with tapestries or carpets.[2] Still
further south Xerxes built his palace, richly adorned
with sculptured slabs, inscribed tablets, and columns,
and bearing but a simple phrasing of the oft-repeated
form. It is all a solemn ruin to-day, yet to the eye of
imagination almost ghostly in its suggestion of a grandeur that it once possessed. At Susa Xerxes built himself a palace, of which but small remains yet exist,
with an inscription in three languages, repeating almost identically the phrases used at Persepolis.

At Naksh-i-Rustam there are four tombs all hewn
from the native rock, all alike in design and execution.
In one of them lay the bones of Darius[3] till impious
hands removed them; the other tombs cannot be identified, but it seems highly probable that one of them
may have been built for Xerxes, and that there his
body lay, when a kind death removed him from a
world too great for his efforts, too large for his com-

---

[1]Weissbach, *Die Keilinschriften der Achämeniden*, pp. 106–109.
[2]See Blundell, *Persepolis*, Ninth International Congress of Orientalists, II,
pp. 542–547, and compare Jackson, *Persia Past and Present*, p. 314.
[3]See p. 144.

FIG. 28.   The Palace of Darius Restored.

FIG. 29.   The Apadana of a Hundred Columns Restored.

prehension. He had at least held together the empire which greater hands than his had built, but nothing but defeats had met his efforts to make it greater. The

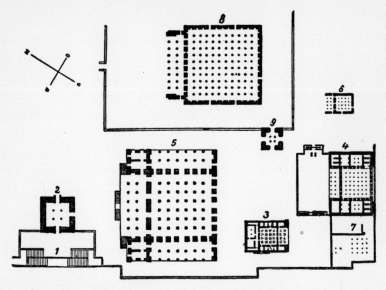

Plan of the Palace Ruins at Persepolis.

1. Stairway of Xerxes.
2. Doorway of Xerxes.
3. Palace of Darius.
4. Palace of Xerxes.
5. Hall of Xerxes.
6. Southeastern building.
7. Building of Artaxerxes III.
8. Hall of a hundred columns.
9. Central building.

last years of his life were spent in luxury and debauchery. His harem was of more interest than the moving interests of millions of subjects, and having defiled the ancient codes of honor by base intrigues to win a woman's love, he was murdered by Artabanus, who attempted to seize the throne.

We know very little of the family of Xerxes. He had as wife Amestris, daughter of Otanes, who belonged to the Achæmenian family; the names of his other wives are not known to us save for Artynte, who was judged to have been received into the royal family unlawfully, having been the wife of his son Darius and married to him by Xerxes' command in the hope of thereby inducing her mother, wife of his brother Masistes, to yield to his desires. Among the sons of Xerxes was Darius, eldest of the family and born before his father had become king and therefore not eligible to the throne. Another son, Hystaspes, also probably born while Darius I was still reigning, was governor of Bactria. The third son was Artaxerxes, born after his father became king, and therefore lawfully entitled to reign after him. We know of two daughters of Xerxes, Amytis, wife of Megabyzos, and a second by name Rhodogune.

The murderer of Xerxes, Artabanus, attempted to place himself on the throne which he had made empty, and by some chronologists is set down as king with a reign of seven months, though he had no real claim to royal title, and could only masquerade as a power behind the throne of the only lawful king, Artaxerxes. When he had heard the true story of the death of his father Xerxes and his brother Darius at the hands of this man he slew him and his sons in a palace fight and reigned supreme.

CHAPTER VIII

ARTAXERXES I (LONGIMANUS)

ARTAXERXES, as the Greeks gave his name, is represented in Persian as Artakhshatra, "he whose empire is perfected," and was called by the Hebrews Artakshasta, in Babylonian Artakshatsu, in Susian Irtakshashsha. He was surnamed Macrocheir, Longimanus, long hand, because his right hand was longer than his left.[1] He came to rule over an empire exhausted with the long struggles against Greece, wearied by internal strife in the royal family, and needing the rest and refreshment of a long peace, and the direction of a master hand, of a king who could energize the whole scheme of government. But not such a man had now come to rule.

The problems which first confronted the new king were those which had troubled more than one of his predecessors—rebellions against the central authority. The one which first claimed attention was in the far northeast in Bactria, where the king's own brother, Hystaspes, who though not lawfully entitled to rule according to Persian law and custom, thought he might hope to make himself independent in his distant province. The weakness of Xerxes had permitted the whole governmental system of satrapies so to be weakened that rebellions were now much easier. The check upon a satrap provided by the arrangement for placing at his side a military commander directly responsible to the king had gradually lapsed, and the satraps were now to all intents and purposes kings subject only to

[1]Plutarch, Artaxerxes I, ed. Sintenis, V, p. 105, Teubner.

such pressure as a strong king could bring to bear, but a weak one would not. Hystaspes, supposing that his brother was too weak to attempt his repression, had taken the chance. He reckoned without his host, for Artaxerxes rose to the occasion and ordered his destruction, which was accomplished in two bloody battles in the year 462 B. C. The king's authority in Bactria was re-established, and it might be hoped that other satraps would learn the lesson which this was intended to teach. Some may well have taken it to heart, but Egypt did not.

To the Egyptians there were many encouraging signs. Their connections with Greece were sufficiently numerous to have made known the great victory over Persia, and the internal difficulties in Persia about the time of the assassination of Xerxes led to the belief that a vigorous movement might make Egypt as free as Greece. At this time the eastern nomes of the Delta formed a compact body under the government of Inaros, son of Psammeticus[1]—called by the Greeks the kingdom of Libya, and he king. The other inhabitants of the Delta had been oppressed by Achæmenes, son of Darius and full brother of Xerxes, and were ready to turn to any such deliverer as Inaros might prove to be. Thus reinforced, Inaros defied Persia. Achæmenes left the country in haste for Persia to secure assistance in reducing the formidable rebellion. At this moment Artaxerxes was heavily burdened with the campaign against Bactria, but roused himself to save Egypt,[2] and even purposed to make the journey thither and assume personal command of his army. Dissuaded by wiser counsels, he entrusted a force to Achæmenes to return

---

[1]Thucydides, I, 104, ed. Hude, I, p. 96, Teubner, ib., Edition Minor, p. 81.
[2]Herodotus, VII, 7, and 97. See also III, 12.

and win again complete Persian control over the refractory Egyptians. The rebellion, fortunately for Persia, was confined to the Delta, the Persian garrisons in Memphis and in Upper Egypt proving sufficient to hold the rest of the land in leash. In the first test of strength Achæmenes defeated Inaros. The hour seemed dark for Inaros, when the Athenians, learning of his plight, ordered their fleet of 200 vessels then lying at Cyprus to sail to Egypt and give help. They sailed up the Nile to Memphis, attacked the Persian garrison, and carried the city save for a part called by the ancient name White Wall, where the Persians made a last stand and successfully held out. Artaxerxes, now thoroughly aroused, began to raise an army in Cilicia, and also to bring about such a diversion in Greece as would dissuade Athenians from a further pursuit of any designs upon Egypt. In 456 B. C. the new Persian force was ready and marched upon Egypt under the very capable leadership of Megabyzos. Upon the news of its approach the allies raised the siege of the White Wall, and turned to meet the new menace. The army of Megabyzos was now forced to rely on its own strength and effort, as Artaxerxes had failed to induce Sparta to attack Athens, for the memory of their united victories at Salamis and Platæa was too vivid. The forces under Megabyzos were described by the Greeks as numbering 300,000 men, with a support of 300 Phœnician ships under Artabazos—a number quite impossible to have assembled or to move. However large or small it may have been, it was sufficient for the immediate need. The decisive battle was fought in the Delta and Megabyzos defeated the enemy, Inaros himself being wounded. The Egyptians and allied Greeks retired to Prosopitis, where they barricaded themselves and withstood all assaults for eighteen months. Having failed in direct attack the Persians diverted the branch of the Nile in which lay the Athenian fleet, which was left high and dry, to be burned by its desperate crews. Hopeless of any aid, the 6,000 survivors capitulated on terms mutually honorable and were carried off to Susa to await a decision at the hands of the Great King. A fleet of 50 Greek triremes sent for reinforcement was sunk by the Phœnicians in an arm of the Nile. This brought the Egyptian revolt to an end, but it had cost Persia much to retain the province, and the struggle might well give Artaxerxes grave concern for the future well-being of his empire, while on the other hand the success of the Persians in destroying a Greek fleet and defeating Greek veterans shows plainly enough how seriously jeopardized the Greek independence might still be should a Persian king arise who could wield the forces of his empire as Darius had done. Fortunately for Greece and Ionia, Artaxerxes was not such a ruler.

The reduction of Egypt was so complete, in spite of minor evidences of local attempts at the maintenance of a certain independence, that the name of Artaxerxes appears in the Canon as a legitimate ruler of the land. He was called, as was his father, by the title "great," and twice is mentioned in national Egyptian texts as "King of the South and North," though no throne name, after the Egyptian usage, was given to him, or at any rate none has come down to us.[1] His one cartouche contains only a bald transcription of his Persian name in hieroglyphic character, and though he is called Pharaoh the Great, there is no mark in all Egypt of his having made any clear contribution to the life or glory of the ancient land of wonders. No building of

[1]See Budge, *History of Egypt*, VII, pp. 79 ff.

any kind was erected by him, nor does his name appear among those who made offerings to the temple of Ptah at Memphis or to the temple of El-Kharga which Darius I had built to Amen Re. Yet when this has been

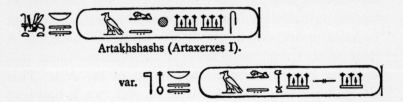

Artakhshashs (Artaxerxes I).

var.

said it must also be remembered that his rule brought the blessings of peace and quiet to the troubled land.

During his reign the greatest and most distinguished traveler of the ancient world visited Egypt. Herodotus traversed the land as far as Elephantine, and the picture which he presents displays a land well governed, and in the full acceptance of a mild and gentle though strong rule. However full of blunders Herodotus[1] may be when he attempts to set down the names and deeds of kings as he follows Hecatæus, there need be no reasonable doubt that he saw the land and the people with discerning eyes and sound judgment, and his testimony may safely be accepted as a sufficient defense of Artaxerxes as a king, foreign indeed, yet able to rule Egypt quite as well as some of the very best of its native princes of earlier days.

In Babylonia Artaxerxes had still among his subjects a not inconsiderable body of Jews. The wish of Cyrus[2] to restore them to their own land had been but partially effected. It would seem that the company

[1]On Herodotus and his visit to Egypt his second book *Euterpe* is the original witness. For judgment of it see Wiedemann, A., *Herodot's Zweites Buch,* and compare Wilhelm Spiegelberg, *The Credibility of Herodotus,* Oxford, 1927.

[2]See above, p. 64.

which accepted his permission must have been largely
composed of the religious, not to say fanatical, and the
poor who had enjoyed but small success in the land
of exile. They who voluntarily remained in Babylonia
were equally mixed, but it was on the one side a body
largely composed of the prosperous. The industry and
capacity for business everywhere displayed by this extraordinary people had found eminent expression in
Babylonia. Great business houses such as those of Igibi
and Murashu had come to distinction and even to eminence, and their business records show the prosperous
and multiform ramifications of their affairs.[1] They who
had thus wrought their lives into the fabric of Babylonian life were little likely to provide many members
to re-settle in the land of Judah. With them however
there also remained behind a numerous body of learned
and religious men who were deeply concerned for the
faith of their fathers and were busily engaged in garnering the traditions and codifying law and custom.
They were interested in everything that concerned the
development of their brethren who had made the great
adventure in 536 and returned to the sacred land. Small
had been their prosperity and difficult their situation.
The land had not been stripped of inhabitants in 597
or yet in 586 by Nebuchadrezzar, and the portions
whose people had disappeared into exile had long since
been occupied by their neighbors or by peoples living
near by and entering as immigrants. They who came
under the decree of Cyrus had to make such shrift as
they might. Some bits of land could doubtless be bought
by those who brought the means from Babylonia, while

---

[1]See for the original texts H. V. Hilprecht and A. T. Clay, *Business Documents of Murashu Sons of Nippur*, Philadelphia, 1898. Also separate and additional texts by A. T. Clay, Philadelphia, 1912.

others must seek such employ as time and circumstance might offer.

It is not surprising that the utmost that could be done for religious reconstruction was the rebuilding of the altar of burnt sacrifice. This accomplished, all hands turned toward the building of shelter, for in a land of varying winds, rains, and even snows women and children, to say nothing of men, had great need of housing. When the first essentials were met it is not surprising that poor human nature o'erstepped the bond of necessity and went on to modest beginnings of luxury. So the years dragged on their weary course until 520 B. C., and still the temple was not rebuilt. Then two prophets, Haggai and Zechariah, burst into protestations, admonitions, and incitements until the work was begun and going forward auspiciously. In 516 the happy issue came and the new structure was finished and dedicated to Jehovah's worship.

In Babylonia meanwhile under a benign Persian rule the perfecting of new codes of laws went forward, and not the Jews only, but the world of Christians and of Mohammedans have profited much by these unselfish labors. News of movements travelled back and forth and they who were living in Babylonia could not but be moved by the narratives of the struggles in far-distant Judah, where conspiracies and envyings and strifes had embittered the lives of the faithful. Yet so wanting are our sources that we do not know what efforts may have been made to give substantial help or even encouragement during these years of sore trial. These must have been, or the greater movements which now begin would be left without basis or preparation and be quite unintelligible.

Among the Jews in Babylonia were two men of eminence, Ezra and Nehemiah, portions of whose memoirs have most fortunately been preserved in the composite biblical books which bear their names. Ezra was a scribe by profession, learned in the law, and doubtless one of those who had contributed largely to its elaboration and codification. Nehemiah was one of the king's own ministers, his title as preserved for us being cup-bearer, but his functions obscure, though obviously much more important than such a style would in modern language imply. It was, however, not he but Ezra who made the first bold move. In the seventh year of Artaxerxes I, 458 B. C., he gathered a company of 1,500 Babylonian Jews, making a rendezvous at Ahava, a district of Babylonia with a river of the same name. These have not been identified, but the district was probably not far from Babylon, and the river one of the numerous large canals which covered the land. There a stay of three days made an organization possible, and the taking of proper precautions against any robbery on the long journey. He was bearing gifts for his fellows in Jerusalem and vessels for the religious services which he was expecting to establish on a larger scale in Jerusalem. He was travelling under royal decree, freed of tolls and customs charges and proud and grateful for the king's assistance. He had not asked for military escort, preferring to rely upon his God's protection, proud of his faith, and confident in his mission.

He arrived safely in Jerusalem, on the 12th day of the seventh month (Tishri) and set energetically to work his reforms, hoping also to be able at once to change into far more elaborate forms the simple religious ceremonies, which still conformed, in whole or large part, to the codes of Deuteronomy. He found difficulties between the older inhabitants and those who had returned from Babylonia, and these would not be lessened by the company which he was now adding. The point of special interest at this moment is that he was acting under Persian royal decree, and it is most interesting to observe how great was the king's interest in these people who inhabited so distant a portion of his empire. It says much for the thoroughness, and not a little for the beneficence of Persian rule.

Ezra's first move was political, and of such a character as he could not have dared but for royal support. He found many mixed marriages. Men who returned from Babylonia had often divorced their lawful wives and married women of the land. These wives Ezra drove out, and the severe application of this new rule must have wrought cruel hardship to many, and this alone would have roused local opposition to anything else that he might propose to accomplish. His larger purpose was undoubtedly the introduction of the great body of religious practice and order which we know under the style of the Priest Codex, which he had brought from Babylonia. Whatever the cause or causes, he saw that this had become impossible for the time and must be postponed.[1] His harsh determination to carry through at all costs had defeated the higher ends.

While Ezra was thus occupied in Jerusalem help of distinguished character and of the highest value was preparing in the east. In the winter of 445/444 the Persian court was in Susa, and there before the king was Nehemiah performing his state functions. From Jerusalem there returned a company of Jews, among whom was Hanani, own brother to Nehemiah. To eager questioning Hanani reported the city of their fathers

---

[1]There is a discussion of this point under similar lines in Stade, *Geschichte*, ii, p. 127 f.   Cf. Rogers on Ezra Nehemiah in Abingdon Commentary.

in a sorry state. "The remnant which is left from the captivity there in the province are in evil plight and in great reproach; the wall of Jerusalem is broken down, and its gates are burned with fire" (Neh. 1:1–3).[1] Nehemiah was overwhelmed, and "sat down and wept and mourned for days, fasting and praying before the God of Heaven" (Neh. 1:4 f.). Four months did Nehemiah wait before an opportunity occurred which seemed favorable for laying before the king the troubles of his people and the anxieties of his own heart. The king was moved and granted Nehemiah a leave of absence with permission to go to Jerusalem and undertake the rebuilding of the city. He was fortified by letters to the governors west of the Euphrates, and to Asaph, keeper of the royal forest, to supply timber for the gates of the city wall and of the temple. The letters to the governors would serve as passports, and the gifts of materials be a great encouragement to a poor people.

Nehemiah, unlike Ezra, set out with an armed escort from the king, and reached the sacred city in safety. For three days he studied the situation and made then a night inspection of the city walls, presenting a figure which has caught the imagination and touched the heart of later ages. Having confirmed by his own vision the reports of Hanani, he summoned the leaders of his people, saying to them, in burning words, "You see the distress that we are in, how Jerusalem is waste, and its gates burned with fire" (Neh. 2:17), and gave them the immense encouragement that he had royal authority behind him and a deeper assurance that God's hand

---

[1]There is some doubt as to when this destruction of the walls had taken place. But on the whole the most probable view is that it was under Nebuchadrezzar in 586. At any rate we possess no record of any other. For discussion pro and con, see Stade, *Geschichte*, ii, 161. Montefiore, *Hibbert Lectures*, p. 311. Cheyne, *Bampton Lectures*, pp. 71, 82, 231 f.

was with him. Aroused by these incitements the work
began with enthusiasm, yet had he quickly to face
great dangers and difficulties. Sanballat and Tobiah,
old enemies of the Jewish people, were ready at once to
interpose, and with them there joined a certain Geshem,
or Goshem,[1] of one of the Arabian tribes. Their plan
was to charge Nehemiah with rebellion against the
king, using doubtless the old and oft-repeated slander
that the rebuilding of the walls meant an attempt to
constitute a fortress of the city which might set up
independence of the Persian empire. Their charges
failed to move Nehemiah or to deter his helpers. All
Jerusalem was roused and set to work by the administrative skill of this master of men. Many who could
have had no previous experience of hard manual labor
were enlisted. Here were priests and levites, goldsmiths
and perfumers, rulers of districts, people from Jericho,
Tekoa, Gibeon, Mizpah, Zanoah, and Keilah. The new
spirit had swept miles away from the city and pride in
the capital and a growth of a fresh national spirit were
at hand. To all these who worked a severe trial was at
hand, and a test of endurance that must call forth their
utmost strength.

The enemies had no intention of giving over their opposition without a serious struggle. The cry of rebellion
had failed. Ridicule was next essayed. Tobiah scoffed
at the work they were doing, declaring it too weak to
be of value as a defence, "Even that which they build
if a jackal go up he shall break down their stone wall"
(Neh. 4:3). Even so "the people had a mind to work"

---

[1]The names of the fellow-conspirators are interesting: Sanballat is the Assyrian Sin-uballit, i. e., "Sin (the moon god) gives life." He is called a Hor-
onite, which means perhaps of Beth-horon, in Samaria. Tobiah is "goodness
of Jahweh," a Hebrew name, and Geshem, or Goshen (so Wellhausen, *Geschichte*, 2nd ed., p. 169), or Gashmu, of some unknown Arabic tribe.

(ib., vs. 6). Severer measures must now be attempted. When the wall was half-way up Sanballat decided to use force to prevent its completion. He raised a force of Arabians, Ammonites, and Ashdodites, and planned a sudden attack after a secret advance. The news reached Nehemiah, who unabashed prepared to fight, and laid skilful plans to arm his workpeople and train them for whatever fighting might ensue. When the enemy approached and discovered that their scheme was known and that adequate preparations had been made to receive with courage and with no mean force their assault, they shifted their plans, as cowards usually do, and determined to await some change which might give them hope of success. They now held the territory about the city and within it must be contained all workers from the outlying villages. Nehemiah was acting safely under royal order and authority, while Sanballat and his motley crew had now made themselves, by their acts, rebels against the Persian empire. It was a curious reversal.

The next move of Sanballat was a shrewd attempt to induce Nehemiah to enter a conference in the valley of Ono in the tribe of Benjamin, the modern *Kefr Anâ*, an ancient site known even to the Egyptians[1] 1500 B. C. Four times was this invitation repeated, only to meet with a courteous but firm refusal. Nehemiah had no intention of putting himself in the hands of these plotters. Then there followed a fifth appeal, in which Sanballat declared that there were rumors abroad that Nehemiah was plotting to make himself king, and that he would do well to meet the writer, who would give him help in disproving the charge. This was a dangerous de-

---

[1] Neh. 6. 2. The location is near Lydda, about 12 miles north of Jerusalem. The name appears also in Ezra 2. 33; Neh. 7. 37; 11. 35; I Chron. 8. 12.

vice. Nehemiah's experience at the court would certainly have taught him that Oriental monarchs were much given to the ready acceptance of such suspicions, and little likely to investigate them carefully, choosing rather to act sharply at once, and take no risk of a possible even if improbable uprising. Nevertheless, Nehemiah chose to take the risk with Artaxerxes and did nothing to clear himself of the charge.

These trials were enough in themselves to try a man's soul, but there were internal difficulties among the Jews themselves. There were prophets ready to act traitorously against the greatest leader of their people whom these times had produced. The name of only one has been preserved, Shemiah (Neh. 6:10), but there may have been many others. They would be indeed sorry figures if brought into comparison with mighty personalities like Isaiah and Jeremiah. Yet it must be admitted that these men had some semblance of excuse for an honorable opposition to their present governor. His plans as they developed showed clearly that the new Judaism which he was furthering bore scant resemblance to the form which their religion took in the minds of the great spiritual and ethical prophets of earlier days. Their mistake lay not in opposing Nehemiah, but in the manner of their doing it. Not by such scheming as theirs did Isaiah oppose Ahaz, or Jeremiah King Jehoiakim. Let Shemiah and his followers speak the true word of prophecy and the truth must ultimately prevail.

In spite of all schemes and devices the masterful policies of Nehemiah went steadily forward, and the walls were restored, the gates set up, and the city able once more to reckon itself a real city according to the standards of its time. The time which the whole work had required for this happy result cannot be known. The record set down in the Memoirs is obviously insufficient, "So the wall was finished in the twenty and fifth day of Elul (August-September), in fifty and two days" (Neh. 6:15). It is noteworthy that the year is not given, and the sentence may only refer to some portion of the great enterprise, or be but a fragment of a larger statement. Josephus (*Ant.*, xi, v, 8) gives two years and four months for the period of building, and even this is probably far too small for work not light in itself and carried forward under stress of intrigue, threats of war, and much internal confusion.[1] The completion was celebrated with much acclaim. Two processions moved round the circuit of the walls, in opposite directions, Ezra at the head of one and Nehemiah of the other, until they met near the ancient site of the temple of Jehovah. "And they offered great sacrifices that day, and rejoiced; for God had made them rejoice with great joy; and the women also and the children rejoiced: so that the joy of Jerusalem was heard even afar off" (Neh. 12:43). Well indeed might they acclaim that day, for Jerusalem had known none to compare with it since the days of their fathers.

Nehemiah had now fully prepared the way for Ezra, whose great and beneficent plans need wait no longer. He was ready to seize the moment of national and religious enthusiasm to proclaim the newly codified book of Laws which he had brought from Babylonia. Nehemiah had provided the stage, and the setting was easily prepared. With every possible pomp and ceremony Ezra and Nehemiah had the new book read publicly in

[1]Ewald (*History*, V, p. 157) ingeniously computes the time occupied as nearly five years, and this would suit better not only the magnitude of the task, but also accord better with the time assigned for the whole stay of Nehemiah in the province.

the ears of the people assembled in solemn concourse
in the temple courts (Neh. 8–10). This was the book
which is now commonly known as the Priest Codex,
with which the early writings were incorporated in the
later revisions resulting in the Pentateuch, a book
whose influence exceeds that of any other book that
ever was written. Three great militant religions root in
it, Judaism, Christianity, and Mohammedanism. A
great day in the history of mankind was this in which
Ezra offered and Nehemiah supported the offering. The
people accepted it as God's law for them by acclama-
tion, and in token of their acquiescence arranged at
once to celebrate the feast of the booths, and by its
token and their own declarations to free themselves
from evil deeds, and to constitute themselves a separate people. So began, with solemn ceremony, a new
era in the religious history of the Jewish people. Hence-
forward they were to be the people of a book, and not
again men attending on the spoken word of the
prophets. The prophet must decrease, and the scribe,
the lawyer, the interpreter of written law must increase.

Ezra and Nehemiah had worked well together. Their
ultimate aim was to better their people, Ezra by re-
ligious motives and works and Nehemiah by political.
Each had done well, and great must be the after effects.
In permanence Ezra's work would far outlast that of
Nehemiah, as religion would survive the state.

Nehemiah had fully proved to his people his natural right to be their governor, to which office the Persian king had appointed him; to the king it was now
his duty to make report of his stewardship. He had
been twelve years in the province, and must return to
the king. He left his charge in good order, and in far

better state than he had found it. The enemies of Jerusalem without her gates had been hopelessly scattered, and Sanballat, the worst of them, had been defeated in all his measures. But so soon as the strong hand of Nehemiah was removed by absence internal difficulties were renewed and increased. The temple precincts were profaned by the presence of Tobiah (Neh. 13:4 f.); the Levites suffered in the payment of their lawful dues, and wandered away to seek what livelihood they might in the fields (Neh. 13:10, compare Mal. 3:7–12); and the laws of Sabbath quiet and peace were set at naught (Neh. 13:15, 16); and what was perhaps worst of all from the view-points of Ezra and Nehemiah foreign marriages were common, and the children spoke partly in the language of their mothers (Neh. 13:23, 24). The whole great complicated scheme of political and religious life, instituted with such care and patience, seemed to be breaking down. The situation called loudly for the governor's personal presence, and in the year 433 B. C. he made his way once more to Jerusalem, quick to take vigorous measures to stamp out evils and enforce the sacred Book of the Law. Nehemiah had no lingering doubt of the value of his services, and could conclude his labors with the bold words, "Remember me, O my God, for good" (Neh. 13:31).

So ends an episode in Persian history crowded with interest on its own account and full also of instruction concerning the policy of the empire and the ways of its king. There is no sound reason for believing that the favor shown to Nehemiah and the Jews was in any special way significant of the attitude of Persians to this one people. Much has sometimes been made of analogies between Zoroastrianism and Judaism, and the

inference drawn that this accounts for the favor shown
the Jews. The resemblances are to be admitted, but
far too much has been made of them. It is much more
probable that the Persians treated the Jews well because they treated well all their subject peoples. We
know the history of the Jews as we do not know the life
of any other people in the empire save the Greeks. If
we knew others so well, we should find that a settled
policy of consideration for other peoples and races existed and found expression whenever circumstances
would permit. If nations rebelled, the strong arm was
ready to reduce them, and the story of the war would
find mention, but many must have been the examples
of the contrary method, when there was no question of
force, but only of the exercise of the ordinary functions
of government, and the ways of peace.

The problems which the Jews had made for Artaxerxes were of relatively small moment when brought
into comparison with the much more grave difficulties
which the relations with Greece were likely to produce
at any moment. Artaxerxes was in no fit state either
personally or nationally to undertake efforts to
strengthen his hold on the far west, and must rely on
whatever diplomacy might secure for his benefit. At
or about 448 B. C., or perhaps as late as 445 B. C.,
Athens, as the head of the Delian league, was anxious
to make regular, and to put so far as might be in treaty
form, the gains which Greece had made as against Persia. Athens decided to negotiate a treaty and sent a
deputation to Susa, headed by Callias and with full
powers. We do not know what form the negotiations
may have taken, nor in what form they were ultimately
cast, but they were apparently ill received at Athens,
and a fine of fifty talents was imposed upon Callias for

what was deemed a failure on his part.[1] The sequel,
however, shows that Persia was losing her power, not
gaining, and whether this is to be associated in any way
with the efforts of Callias, or whatever the cause, or
however much of a treaty there may have been in a
formal way, there can be no doubt of the diminution of
Persian dominion and authority. Persia still held by
a tenuous thread Egypt and the island of Cyprus, but
almost all else was gone. All Thrace was lost forever,
save for the single stronghold of Doriskos, still held by
Maskames, and soon like the rest to fall into the hands
of the Thracians.[2] The great conquests of Cyrus in
Ionia were in Greek hands, and the Athenian fleet
sailed not only along its shores of never-ending fas-
cination, but dominated the whole eastern Mediterranean Sea. There could be no better sign of the decay
of Persian power. The vast empire which men of
genius had founded, extended, and solidified was filled
with cracks, and the signs of its ruin were many. Artaxerxes was unfitted by nature and by the life he had
lived to sway the sceptre of mightier men, and his own
end was soon to come.

In the month of March-April 424 Artaxerxes I died,

[1]There is no sufficient reason for doubting this treaty or for denying its
existence. It is true that the earliest allusion to it is to be found in Isocrates,
Paneg., 118 and 120, but there is otherwise sufficient support for it. See Herodotus, VII, 151. (Compare an excellent note in How and Wells, II, pp. 189–191.)
Diodorus Sic. xii, 4; Demosthenes, *De falsa Legatione*, p. 428. Among modern
discussions reference may be made to Grote, *History of Greece*, ch. XIV, who
accepts it, while Curtius, III, ch. ii, denies a formal treaty. The objections
recently raised spring apparently for the most part out of the apparent fact
that Thucydides ignores it. This is true; yet he does imply a definite understanding in a most unmistakable way (viii, 56, 4) to which attention has
been drawn by Bury (*Hermathena*, 1898, No. xxiv, p. 153, 154). For discussion pro and con see Busolt, *Griech. Ges.*, III, 1, 346 ff. Ed. Meyer, *Gesch. d.
Altert.*, III, 615 ff. It is indeed not probable that a formal treaty which could
be set up publicly at Athens was drawn up, yet in some written form the Persian king must have given consent to a curtailment of the movements of his
fleet, and this would serve to indicate a gain for Athens and the league, even
though it were not sufficiently spectacular to bring any popular acclaim.
[2]Herodotus, VII, 105 f. Compare Busolt, III, 1, 104.

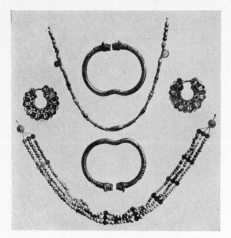

FIG. 30. Persian Jewelry.

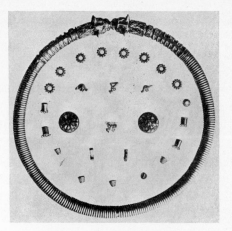

FIG. 31. Persian Jewelry.

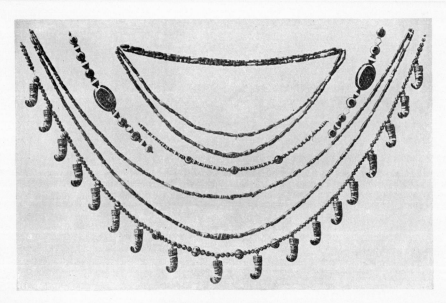

FIG. 32. Persian Jewelry.

and the story is that on that same day there also ex-
pired his wife Damaspia,[1] who alone of his wives has
left her name to posterity. The others were but lay figures, and had little or no influence upon affairs of state.
It was his mother Amestris and his sister Amytis, wife
of Megabyzos, who were most influential at court—
which, in the case of his mother, at least, but followed
a custom wide-spread in the Orient. The traditions concerning the king's person are all cast in a favorable
tone. He is called a brave[2] man, and much disposed to
take a personal part in war, but was less renowned in
the chase.[3] He was much more disposed to follow the
later Persian customs and spent his time among his
subordinate wives or concubines, of whose names there
have been preserved Alogune, Andia or Andria, and
Kosmartidine, all Babylonians.[4] He had seventeen sons,
but only five are now known by name, Xerxes or rather
Artaxerxes, Arsites, Bagapaios, Sogdianos or Sekydianos, and Ochos. One daughter only is still known,
Parysatis,[5] whose mother was Andia.

Artaxerxes had lived at Susa in the earlier part of his
reign, but transferred his residence to Babylon, when
fire made him homeless in the city of first Persian
choice. Thereafter he seems to have lived by prefer-
ence in Babylon. There he built a palace, and there
resided for the remainder of his days among his Babylonian wives. To this residence he makes proud reference in the only long inscription of his which still
remains. At Persepolis in badly mutilated form and in
the Babylonian language are these haughty words:

"The only one, [among many rulers] am I [Ar-

---

[1]Ktesias, Fragment 30, Gilmore.   [2]Cornelius Nep., I, 3.
[3]Ktesias, Fragment 30, § 71, Gilmore.   [4]Ktesias, ib.
[5]The name as given by Strabo (785) is Pharziris.

taxerxes, the great king, king] of kings, king of countries [of all tongues], king [of the great wide] earth, [son of] Xerxes, [the king, son of Darius the king], the Achæmenian. Artaxerxes [the great king, says]: Under the protection [of Ahuramazda have I] built for myself this house, [which king Xerxes] my father had built. May [Ahuramazda with the gods] protect me and my rulership [and what I have built]."[1]

Besides this fragment there remain with the name of Artaxerxes only three vases, one containing the simple legend, "Artaxerxes the great king." This is all that forty-one years of absolute rule has been able to bequeath us. It is a poor inheritance.

[1]For the text and translation compare Weissbach, *Keilinschriften der Achämeniden*, 121.

CHAPTER IX

XERXES II AND DARIUS II

IMMEDIATELY upon his father's death his lawful heir and eldest son succeeded to the throne under the style of Xerxes II. He was the only son of Damaspia, but for him there was naught but disaster in store. His rule was brief[1] and his end a tragedy. He fell a victim to the ambition of his half-brother Sekydianos or Sogdianos, who sought to make himself king. His hopes were speedily dashed, for another half-brother of Xerxes II, Vahuka, called Ochos by the Greeks, took the field against him. Artaxerxes had appointed him governor of Hyrcania, and he had taken as wife his sister Parysatis, whose name has come down to us in the form Purusshatu,[2] the only Persian Queen whose name appears in cuneiform characters. He knew how to knit his province into loyalty to his person, and had attached also to his fortunes Artoxares, his father's favorite eunuch and evidently a man of force and energy. Ochos began the formation of an army, and paid no heed to the efforts of Sogdianos, who invited him to court, and was evidently minded to take advantage and anticipate him. Ochos was far the more skilful and won over to his cause Arbasios, then in command of the royal cavalry, and Arsames, governor of Egypt. The

---

[1]The length of his reign is uncertain, for the traditions vary greatly. According to Diodorus (XII, 64, ed. Vogel, II, 432, Teubner) his reign covered one year, though, as he says, others reckoned it as only two months (ib., 71). Ktesias (Frag. 31, § 76, Gilmore) makes it 45 days. There is no certainty, but Justi (*Grundriss der iran. Philol.*, II, 461) follows Ktesias.

[2]See Meissner, *Orientalistische Lit. Zeitung*, 1904, 384 f.

combined forces were too much for Xerxes and Sogdianos, and Ochos won the purple. He ascended the
throne under the name of Darius II, and began a disturbed reign, with fewer glories than troubles. He was
controlled by his wife, Parysatis, soon to become no-
torious for bloody cruelties, and by the eunuchs Artoxares, Artibarzanes, and Athoos.

Rebellions against his authority began in different
parts of the empire, which was really too widely extended for the rule of one man unless he were a supreme genius, and too loosely organized to be controlled over so many leagues of roadless territory. The
first was apparently that of his own brother Arsites,
who won the help of Artyphios, son of Megabysos, then
governor of the district or province beyond the Euphrates. The combination made a serious threat, and
Darius would need his utmost effort to put it down.
He ordered Artasyras into the field with such a force
as could be collected. He attacked the rebels and was
defeated. The situation was now serious, and the throne
in danger. The turn of fortune came when Greek mercenaries went over to the king's side and with their
help Artasyras won a notable victory. Artyphios surrendered and under oath was assured that his life
would be spared. He was sent to the royal tent, and
there met a reception which gave him additional assurance. Darius awaited the surrender of Arsites,
which soon followed, and he also received the promise
of life under the confirmation of an oath. The king desired to give effect to the oath which had been given in
his name, but Parysatis was relentless, the weak king
yielded, and both men were hanged. So ended the rebellion, but with the king weakened personally and in
authority by the breach of an oath given in his name.

It would be followed by other and perhaps more serious uprisings.

The next movement was in Lydia, where Pissuthnes was governor, himself allied by blood to the royal house.[1] He had been twenty years in office, and had made a strong position for himself. He had a body of Greek mercenaries under command of an Athenian named Lykon. The king was well served by his general in the field, Tissaphernes, son of Hydarnes. He succeeded by bribery in detaching Lykon from his loyalty to Pissuthnes, who was then easily driven into a surrender also under the oath that his life would be safe. As in the former instance, the pledge was broken and he was hanged by royal order. In his room Tissaphernes was appointed Satrap, and Lykon received as his reward certain cities and their districts.[2] The rebellion was not yet quelled, for a natural son of Pissuthnes, by name Amorges, took up the cause of his dead father[3] and with help given by the Athenians[4] prolonged the conflict into the next year until he was captured in Iasos by Tissaphernes, and like his father was probably hanged.[5] These successful movements gave a temporary strength to the empire in the west, and may well have strengthened Persian confidence. Yet there is evidence enough that decay of serious character was proceeding elsewhere.

In 410/9 a rebellion appeared in Media which was promptly suppressed.[6] This was well enough in itself, but it was certainly ominous that so near the centre of authority it should have seemed worth while even to

---

[1]He was quite probably a son of Hystaspes of Bactria. See Justi, *Iran. Namenbuch*, 398 f., and Cauer, in Paully-Wissowa.
[2]Ktesias, Frag. 31, § 83, Gilmore.
[3]Thucydides, VIII, 5, ed. Hude, I, p. 261, Teubner.
[4]Andokides, III, 29, ed. Blass, p. 85, Teubner.   [5]Thucydides, VIII, 28.
[6]Xenophon, *Hellenica*, I, 2, 19, ed. Keller, p. 10, Teubner.

make the attempt. At the same time, whether connected or not with this futile attempt, there were intrigues in the court itself, which produced a sort of rebellion against the king. The leading figure was Terituchmes, of the house of Hydarnes. Court intrigues have always been common in the Orient and this had no more importance than many others. It gave occasion, however, for a fresh outburst of the passion of Parysatis, who saw to it that the leaders were for the greater part slain, yet curiously spared the life of Stateira, sister of Terituchmes, with her brother Tissaphernes.[1]

These very moderate successes were entirely overbalanced by the loss of Egypt. Since the days of Inaros the destinies of Egypt escape our efforts to understand them. Persian domination seems to have been more or less restored, and the imperial satraps ruled the land and gathered its taxes. Their names have generally disappeared, except for the last of them, Arsam, who was in possession in the year 408 B. C. His control could not have extended over the whole land, for the Athenians had good reason for attempting to keep a hand in the affairs of the nomes in the northwestern Delta. The Athenians had given help to Amyrtaios,[2] and now that he was dead a second of the same name had succeeded to his efforts. He is set down in Manetho's list as the only king of Dynasty XXVIII,[3] and a reign of six years is ascribed to him, with his seat in Sais. It seems natural to regard him as the head of a national movement to free Egypt from the foreign yoke and give the land once more into the hands of native rulers. A national

[1]Ktesias, Frag. 32, § 54–56, Gilmore.
[2]Yet the king's name in Egyptian has come down to us in the form Amurteos. Compare H. Gauthier, Livre des Rois IV, premier fasc., p. 158.
[3]Manetho's record reaches us through Africanus in the Syncellus, 142, 10, and from Eusebius in the same, 144, 8.

party was always in existence, or ready to spring into being, and any occasion might rouse it to action. In this instance a convenient opportunity was afforded by the presence in upper Egypt of a body of Jews settled mainly on the island of Elephantine and about Syene

Meri Åmenrā.   Åntriush (Darius II).

(Assuan). They were the descendants of mercenaries from Judah who had been employed by Psammeticus II (594–589 B. C.) in his Nubian wars. As a reward for their services those who did not desire to go home received grants of land and made for themselves homes in Egypt. They were, however, never regarded as Egyptians and since the period of Cambyses had further separated themselves from their neighbors by the earnest exercise of the Jewish religion. They had built a temple of great, or at least of considerable, size on the island of Elephantine and had furnished it richly. The protection of the Persians gave them great opportunities, but proved also a source of danger, for it excited envy and awakened hatred among the native Egyptians, who coupled them with the Persians and regarded them with equal hostility.

The Persian rule over Egypt was now represented by the person of Arsames, as Satrap. When he left the land temporarily to make report to Darius II, in the year 411 B. C., the opportunity was afforded for an outbreak against the Jews. There was a temple, or at least a shrine of the god Chnub (Khum or Khemu) on the island of Elephantine, whose priests would naturally feel aggrieved that this great god of the cataracts should be compelled to share his island with the god

Yaho (Yahweh, Jehovah) of these Jewish friends of
Persia. It was an insult to their god that these Jews
should sacrifice sheep and goats, which were animals
sacred to Chnub, and any effort to stop these sacri-
legious practices was worth the effort. The priests
headed the uprising and won Waidrang, local governor,
to their side. He gave orders to his son Nephayan, commander of the garrison in the fortress of Syene, to destroy the Jewish temple. It was done, and the Jews left
to mourn in sackcloth and ashes their most precious
possession. Three years later, 408 B. C., they addressed
a long letter to Bigvai, the Persian governor in Jerusalem, to solicit his aid in securing from Persia permission to rebuild. They were careful to state that when
Cambyses was in Egypt (525 B. C.) and the temples
of Egyptian gods were destroyed no hand was laid on
their temple. Here once again we come upon the evidence for a certain Persian friendliness for the Jews,[1]
which we are left to explain as best we may. It seems
probable that it was a part of a general Persian policy,
yet in this particular case the Egyptians seem to have
been ill treated by contrast. Even so we do not know
how much the Egyptian temples may really have suffered, nor what the provocation to Persian severity
may have been, and the after treatment of Egypt was
as friendly as well could be. However this may be, the
Aramaic papyri which have revealed to us something of
the life of these Jews in Egypt are important witness to
the kind treatment meted out to this people during the
long period of Persian rule in the Nile valley.[2]

[1]See also above, p. 188.
[2]These papyri were first discovered on the island of Elephantine in the
years 1898 to 1908. The earliest recovered was published by Euting, *Mémoires
présentés . . . à l'Academie des Inscriptions* (Paris, 1903); the next by Cowley,
Proceedings of the Society of Biblical Archæology, 1903; yet others by Sayce and
Cowley, *Aramaic Papyri Discovered at Assuan* (London, 1906), and the rest by

Almost at the very end of his reign Darius left his palace and harem to take the field against a people who had never properly bent the neck beneath the Persian yoke. These were the Karduchoi, inhabiting a wild mountain region on the upper Tigris, corresponding fairly well with the modern Bohtan. Against them he led a force said, with the usual exaggeration, to have numbered 120,000 men. There amid inaccessible clefts of rocks, where not even a passage might be secured along the river bank, he flung his men against the little villages of hardy mountaineers. Years afterward when Xenophon[1] led homeward his fragment of 10,000 men he was to hear how the Persian army had been annihilated, and Xenophon's own men suffered much in a seven days' march through this inhospitable land.

This was the last effort in the reign of Darius. His health was broken and the end drawing nigh. The time had come to consider the claims of rivals to the succession and appoint the next king. In this case the problem was difficult. Parysatis, wife of the king, had borne him two sons, the elder, by name Arsikas or Arsakas, was born before his father became king, and was therefore not eligible according to the old Persian law and custom, but was none the less likely to make an effort to secure the coveted prize. To contend with him was his younger brother, born after his father had become king and blest with the splendid name Cyrus. He was far the cleverer of the two and enjoyed the preferential love of an ambitious, intriguing, and powerful mother. She had begun, well in advance, a campaign

Sachau, *Aramäische Papyrus* . . . (Leipzig, 1911), followed by the first translation of the entire find by Cowley, *Jewish Documents of the Time of Ezra, Translated from the Aramaic* (London, 1919), and a definitive edition with translation and notes, Cowley, *Aramaic Papyri of the Fifth Century B. C.*, Oxford, 1923.

[1] Xenophon, *Anabasis*, III, 5, 16, ed. Gemoll, p. 124, Teubner.

in favor of this son, taking the method of securing for him a post in which his talent for rule might be displayed, and he be advanced in popular opinion as alone capable of swaying the royal sceptre. In 408 B. C. he was made satrap over a territory in Lydia[1] where Persian forces had been in the habit of assembling. This would seem to imply that these military forces were under his command and at his disposal. Into the confused politics of Greece he was quick to enter, giving his support to Sparta as against Athens. His aim was evidently to secure Spartan support for his projected schemes to secure the throne on his father's approaching death. The Spartan general Lysander was quite ready to enter into relations with him, hoping thereby to further with Persian help in turn his ambition to become absolute ruler in Greece. Cyrus gave his help to Lysander without stint in the Peloponnesian war, but when he was replaced by Callicratidas withheld it. He then gave his help in Sparta with such success that after the battle of Arginusæ Lysander was sent out as the real commander of the Spartan fleet, though under a nominal control,[2] in the year 405. Before Cyrus had time more perfectly to arrange his designs he was summoned to his father's death-bed in Susa, where he appeared in company with three hundred Greek mercenaries under command of Xenias. Then ensued a series of intrigues for the personal advancement of one or the other of the rivals, concerning which we are very imperfectly instructed, nor is this a matter of moment.

---

[1]Xenophon, *Anabasis*, I, 2. The mention here is of a people called the Kastolloi, which appears to be a Lydian name for Dorians. I do not know on what grounds Prašek (*Geschichte*, p. 180) extends the rule of Cyrus over Lydia, Phrygia, and Cappadocia. This is, however, repeated by Tarn (*Camb. An. Hist.*, VI, p. 4).

[2]Xenophon, *Hellenica*, II, 1–14, ed. Keller, p. 35, Teubner.

Fig. 34. Lion Weight.

Fig. 35. Model Chariot in Gold.

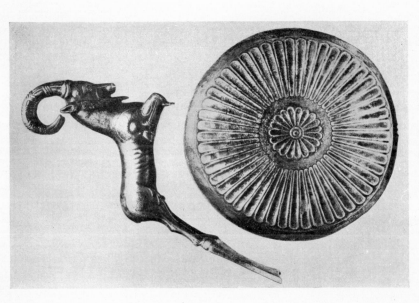

Fig. 33. Silver Handle and Bowl.

Before Darius could give a final decision he was claimed by death in the springtime of the year 404 B. C.

The personal characteristics of Darius II are but little known to us. To him was attached the mocking style Nothus, bastard, because his mother was not a Persian. His wife Parysatis is said to have borne him thirteen children, but only Arsikas and Cyrus have any historical importance. Darius made no serious contribution to the strengthening of his empire, and his death left it weaker in many essentials than it had been when he ascended a throne already tottering.

CHAPTER X

ARTAXERXES II

THE death of Darius II, Nothus, came before Parysatis had been able to carry to a successful conclusion her plans to make Cyrus king, and Arsikas succeeded, adopting the name and style of Artaxerxes II. The only hint of his personal qualities as a youth comes from the nickname Abiyatāka bestowed upon him because of his remarkable memory, which the Greeks transferred into the form Mnemon. He was probably about forty years of age when he became king, and lived only to see his empire gradually weakening and breaking to pieces amid an almost continuous series of rebellions.

Cyrus feigned obedience to the new king and was present at his crowning, accompanied by his Greek soldiers. All would have gone well for the moment but for Tissaphernes, long the intimate friend of Cyrus, but now become his bitterest enemy. He laid before the king reasons for believing that Cyrus intended to murder him at the first opportunity. Then and there, whether justly or unjustly, Cyrus would have fallen a bloody victim to his brother's suspicion, save for Parysatis, who secured for him in some way a discharge from danger, and a restoration to his satrapy. There restored to power, he rapidly increased his influence. Lysander had broken the Athenian power over the coastal cities of Asia Minor, and these for the greater part gave in their allegiance to Cyrus. Miletus alone resisted all blandishments, for Tissaphernes had there established himself in control, ready to watch

Cyrus and so be able to act as spy for Artaxerxes. Cyrus
secured the help of Pharnabazos, then satrap of the
Hellespontine province, and besieged Miletus, but with
ill success. Alcibiades was now in Asia Minor, a fugitive
from Athens, and he was keen enough to see and comprehend the plots of Cyrus. Eager to inform the Persian king he attempted to make his way toward Susa
but was detained by Pharnabazos, and afterward murdered.[1]

The queen mother, Parysatis, was able in some way
to protect the absent Cyrus from his brother, who
seemed blind to what was going on in his western dominions. The ignorance of the king was deepened by
the shrewdness with which Cyrus carried on his plans.
He paid regularly the tribute to his brother, and all the
earlier moves were so made as to convince Artaxerxes
that Cyrus was loyally governing his satrapy and eager
only to further the king's interests. Perhaps no one of
his acts was more adroitly managed than his attack on
Tissaphernes, who had shut himself up in the fortified
Miletus. Cyrus besieged him by land and sea, and contrived by the help of Parysatis to convince the king
that he was merely taking necessary steps to make the
coast lands absolutely loyal to Persia, and not at any
point in a state of turbulence such as Tissaphernes had
brought Miletus into. The siege of Tissaphernes had
given Cyrus an admirable excuse for increasing his
forces, by adding Greek mercenaries. These were readily secured, for the end of the Peloponnesian war had
left many Greeks, veterans of the war, without occupation, and they were ready for any employ in the adventure of war. Though the campaign against Miletus
failed to dislodge and destroy Tissaphernes, it had nev-

[1]Plutarch, Alcibiades, XXXVII ff., ed. Sintenis, I, p. 415 (Teubner).

ertheless great value for Cyrus in the steady increase of his army.

Elsewhere events were being skilfully handled in the same interest. Lysander had made himself dictator in Sparta, and was keenly pursuing an imperialistic policy in Greece everywhere. He took many steps to help Cyrus, and it may have been at his command, as it certainly was not without his knowledge and consent, that Clearchus in the Chersonese took the side of Cyrus and gathered troops committed to his cause. In Thessaly also Aristippus, who belonged to the distinguished family of the Aleuadæ,[1] won to the cause of Cyrus by large gifts of money,[2] plunged his country into sore straits by an internecine struggle with Hellenokrates, who fled to Macedonia,[3] and left Aristippus with a victorious army ready to serve the purposes of Cyrus. In Bœotia Proxinus was busy in the same interest, ostensibly, however, making war on the Pisidians, because they had disturbed the peace of their neighbors. In the Peloponnesus, Sophainetos of Styphale, and Socrates of Achæa,[4] were busy with warlike preparations, whose aim they represented as the helping of fugitives from Miletus prepare an attack upon Tissaphernes.

Cyrus was now ready to strike, yet even so was too adroit to move openly, but gathered an army in rendezvous at Sardes, ostensibly to march upon Pisidia and restore that province by arms to the acknowledgement of his royal brother's authority, or according to another version against other princes who had rebelled against Persia.[5] At the same time he applied to Sparta for help

[1]Herodotus (VII, 6) calls them kings, but scarcely with sufficient justification.
[2]Xenophon, *Anabasis*, I, 1, 10.
[3]Aristotle, *Politics*, V, 8, 12, ed. Immisch, p. 190 f. (Teubner).
[4]Xenophon, *Anabasis*, I, 1, 6–11.
[5]Diodorus, XIV, 19, ed. Vogel, III, p. 211 f. (Teubner).

against his brother, and the government ordered Samos, the admiral in command of twenty-five ships, to give Cyrus every assistance. He added his fleet to the squadron which Cyrus had assembled at Ephesus under the command of Tamos. Sparta sent also eighteen hundred foot soldiers under Cheirisophus to Sardes.

Coincident with the gathering of the forces of Cyrus the king played unknowingly into his hands. He determined upon a foolish attempt to regain Egypt for his empire, and sent to make the necessary preparations his general Abrokomas, who was to assemble an army in Syria for the proposed attack. He crossed the Euphrates at Thapsacus and made the long and laborious journey into Phœnicia, where he gathered an army, estimated with the usual exaggeration at three hundred thousand men.[1] The hour had now come for the open breach with his brother, and Cyrus was ready to act. He must have thought that as Artaxerxes had divested himself of his best troops for the campaign against Egypt, it would be easy to dethrone and destroy him. In Sardes he had now assembled a considerable force, comprising 7,300 heavy armed Greek hoplites, 300 men bearing the light shield or target, with 500 other light armed men. There could be no further doubt concerning the purposes of Cyrus, and Tissaphernes, with 500 horsemen, set out to warn the king of the threatening danger.[2]

In the spring of 401 B. C., Cyrus was ready for the great adventure. He had concealed with more or less success his ultimate aim long enough to have put his brother the king at a great disadvantage. From his Greek mercenaries the greater purpose was also unknown, they thinking that he was determined only to

[1] Xenophon, *Anabasis*, I, 4, 5.   [2] Xenophon, *Anabasis*, II, 2, 5.

punish some of the states of Asia Minor which had
given him concern. Their officers, necessarily better instructed, guarded the secret, and the command moved
out of Sardes. Cyrus seems as well fitted to administer
as to command, and every precaution had been taken
to leave his provinces in safe and capable hands. Over
Lydia and Phrygia he set some of his own family connections, and entrusted the rule of the Greek coast
cities to the Admiral Tamos. With the rear in good control, he began with confidence the difficult and dangerous enterprise. His goal was Babylon, a march not
only long, but over country difficult ever, as it still is,
and no man not as bold as the greater Cyrus, whose
name he bore, would have dared to undertake it. The
route to be taken offered a choice between two roads.
The easier would clearly have been to go northward
from Sardes to reach the high road which ran from
the Bosphorus, over the upper part of Asia Minor to
the Euphrates. The shorter and much more difficult
road lay through southern Phrygia and penetrated the
Taurus range at the Cilician gates. This famous pass
was under the control of the Syennesis of Cilicia, whose
opposition if it were offered would be likely to prove a
serious matter. In spite of the disadvantages, Cyrus
had the boldness to choose the shorter road. He crossed
the Meander and made a halt at Colosse, where Menon
joined him, bringing 1,000 heavy armed, and 500 light
armed men. Thence the way led onward to Celænæ,
where the Marsyas, one of the sources of the Meander,
takes its rise. Here Cyrus received a substantial addition to his growing army, for Clearchus brought him
1,000 heavy armed men, 800 light armed, and 200 Cretan bowmen, while Sosis of Syracuse added 300 heavy
armed, and Sophænetus 1,000 more. There in the royal

park a review showed that he had now under his command 11,000 heavy armed and 2,000 light armed, all Greek—a formidable force and far superior, man for man, to any Persians whom Artaxerxes could muster.

When he had reorganized his forces and placed the newly added men in due order, Cyrus marched by way of Pelta to Keramon Agora in Phrygia, which though still unidentified seems to have been situated near the borders of Mysia. Meanwhile the fleet, numbering 75 good warships, sailed along the coast of Asia Minor toward Cilicia, where it might serve a good purpose, if needed, in threatening the coast line of the Syennesis. By this time Artaxerxes had yielded reluctant faith to the reports of Tissaphernes concerning Cyrus, and renounced trust in the soft assurances of his mother Parysatis. He began now feverishly to prepare for the supreme issue, which was clearly impending. He took steps at once to raise and equip a body fit to meet Cyrus in the field. Believing that the Syennesis would be both able and willing to hold the Cilician gates, he prepared to defend the Syrian gates by summoning Abrokomas and entrusting this important mission to him. The problem now set for the Syennesis was difficult, for he wished to gain the good will of the victor in the approaching conquest, and was not certain which of the two it might be. In the end he tried to please both. He took publicly the side of Artaxerxes, yet made provision for other eventualities by sending his wife Epyaxa to meet Cyrus at Kaystrion Pedion and offer to him substantial gifts. At Tyriacon Cyrus held a great review of all his forces, Persian as well as Greek, and pushed on thence by way of Iconium to Lycaonia, which he treated as enemy country, and handed over to the Greeks to be plundered. At Tyana, a famous site

in the days of Hittite rule and civilization, Cyrus
handed over to trial Megaphernes, a distinguished Persian who was accused with another fellow countryman
of traitorous designs, and there also Cyrus determined
to force the Cilician gates. This was not necessary, for
the Syennesis fled to the mountains, leaving the pass
open to Cyrus, and Tarsus to his fleet. The city was
given over to plunder, and Cyrus was left free to march
undisturbed through what might have been an almost
impassable mountain fastness. Furthermore the Syennesis made a contribution of troops, under command
of one of his sons, to the advancing army, yet secretly
sent a deputation to Artaxerxes to say that a great
army was on the march against him to which he had
been compelled to make a personal addition which
would, however, be withdrawn at the first opportunity.[1]

The successful passing of the Cilician gates opened
now before Cyrus a country much more level, easier
to traverse, and stretching away in great rolling land
toward the majestic stream of the Euphrates, which he
reached and followed along its banks, not pursuing its
numerous windings but touching the stream on its
western side and crossing strips of land between the
curving course. At Thapsacus he found that Abrokomas
had destroyed the bridge of boats built by Xerxes.
Here the true object of the expedition was finally revealed to the Greeks, and their loyal continuance assured by promises of great rewards, and the skilful
pleading of Clearchus. The loss of the bridge did not
daunt the intrepid commander. The water was low, and
it was decided to attempt to ford it. "As they forded,
never a man was wetted above the chest: nor ever until

[1]Ktesias, Pers., 58, Gilmore; Diodorus, XIV, 20, ed. Vogel, III, 214
(Teubner).

this moment, said the men of Thapsacus, had the river been so crossed on foot, boats had always been required. . . . Thus the passage was looked upon as a thing miraculous; the river had manifestly retired before the face of Cyrus, like a courtier bowing to his future king."[1] On the other side of the great river they found villages "full of corn and wine," and remained three days to provision the army at the expense of the poor villagers. It was now midsummer, and the waves of heat that rise out of the soil and the cruel rays of the sun must have wrought havoc among the men who had spent their lives looking out upon the blue waters of the Ægean. There was and could be no halt, for time was fighting on the side of the Persian king, and haste was essential for Cyrus. Nine days of hard marching brought the expedition to the river Chabur, where wild asses and bustards were taken, and the diet varied by their flesh. Nature seemed to be fighting for the invaders, and no serious dangers were impeding their progress.

Now at last Mesopotamia proper, called by Xenophon Syria and Arabia, was left behind, and Babylonia was entered. It seemed probable that the king must soon show signs of active resistance. He had been gathering from every possible source an army sufficient to meet his brother, and now had perhaps thirty or even forty thousand men of all ranks.[2] There would seem to have been some doubt among the men of Cyrus as to the king's courage, and whether he would meet his brother in battle at all, for Clearchus had said, "Do you think your brother will give battle to you, Cyrus?" and

[1] Xenophon, *Anabasis*, I, 4, 18, ed. Gemoll, p. 23 (Teubner).
[2] Xenophon (*Anab.*, I, 7) gives the numbers of the King's army as 1,200,000, and besides his Greek forces assigns to Cyrus 100,000 barbarians. The numbers are as impossible as they are absurd.

Cyrus answered: "Not without a battle, be assured, shall the prize be won; if he be the son of Darius and Parysatis and a brother of mine."

There were still no signs of the appearance of the king to give battle, but a serious danger to the forces of Cyrus had to be met, filled with a greater menace than open war, for Orontas, of a distinguished Persian family, was detected in a plot to desert, with so many men as he could induce to follow, and deliver himself and them to the king's service. His disloyalty was punished with death, the closest of his own followers giving their assent.

After this sharp measure of safety, men who had deserted the king to join Cyrus began to arrive with reports of the proximity of the king's forces, and Cyrus ordered quickly a review, which showed that of the Greeks he had 10,400 heavy infantry and 2,500 light armed men, 20 scythe-chariots, 2,600 horses, a total of perhaps 28,000 men. Cyrus was now convinced that the king's army might come in sight at any hour, and the advance was made with greatest caution. As no signs appeared, less and less caution was used, and Cyrus began to think that his brother had abandoned all intention of a test of arms. This idea was increased when a great trench was met, no less than 30 feet wide and 18 feet deep, which seemed to have been dug to be filled with water from a canal in front of the Median wall, on the one side, and the Euphrates on the other, though it did not reach the river by about twenty feet. This must have been designed to halt Cyrus, and give the king a place favorable for battle. But the king made no stand here, and Cyrus passed it successfully and safely, and beyond it were numerous signs of a retreating army. Cyrus now advanced with still less caution, and three days later was suddenly confronted with a report of the king's army in line of battle. Temporary confusion ensued, from which Cyrus quickly organized a defense, with Clearchus in command of the right wing resting on the Euphrates, and with him a body of Paphlagonian cavalry 1,000 strong. Next these came Prosenus, and on the left was Ariæus, with Menon on the Greek left, while Cyrus himself, with a bodyguard of 600 cavalry, held the centre. The news of the approach of Artaxerxes had been received between nine and ten in the morning, and at noon there was still no sight of the enemy, but "with the approach of afternoon was seen dust like a white cloud, and after a considerable interval a black pall, as it were, spread far and high over the plain."[1] The fateful moment had come at last, and it must now be decided whether Artaxerxes or Cyrus was to rule so much of the Persian empire as might yet be held together. The decision now to be taken would be fateful for many peoples in diverse and widely separated lands. If the judgment of those who were nearest the contest is just, and there is no sound reason for doubting, it were far better for man and beast that Cyrus should come off victor. But the decision must now be left to the arbitrament of war, and human experience has often discovered its fallibility.

The scene of the battle was Cunaxa,[2] which lay quite probably at or near the modern ruin Kunisch, about fifty-one miles north of Babylon.[3] The plain was well suited for easy maneuver, and the battle was soon joined. The king's forces possessed an obvious superi-

---

[1]Xenophon, *Anabasis*, I, 8, 9.
[2]Xenophon does not name the place, which is preserved by Plutarch, Artaxerxes, VIII, ed. Sintenis, p. 111 (Teubner).
[3]See Bewsher, *Journal of the Royal Geographical Society*, XXXVII, 1867, p. 166 ff.

ority in numbers, for the Persian centre came opposite
the left wing of the body of Cyrus, who knew well that
there the king himself was likely to have his station,
and that his death or capture would swiftly end the
struggle. He therefore ordered Clearchus to attack the
centre, for "if we strike home at this point, our work is
finished." The command was based on sound tactical
grounds, but Clearchus disobeyed, for seeing that the
left wing of Cyrus was in grave danger of being turned
by the superior forces of the king, feared to expose the
right to a similar danger, and directed his attack
straight in front of his position. The Persians who opposed were unable to sustain their position, and gave
way in a rout. It seemed the moment of an overwhelming victory, and Cyrus was saluted by his followers as
king. Then he saw the king, and with a shout, "I see
the man," rushed upon him, delivering a quick blow
upon the king's chest, and in another moment would
have given him the death blow, but rather fell himself
with a javelin thrust, and eight of his trustiest followers upon him. "So died Cyrus; a man the kingliest
and most worthy to rule of all the Persians who have
lived since the elder Cyrus: according to the concurrent
testimony of all who are reputed to have known him
intimately."[1]

The death of Cyrus ended the expedition and Artaxerxes was left master and king, yet was it far from
a victory in other respects. The Greeks had proven superior to the Persians in battle; the king's losses (reckoned at 15,000, while the forces of Cyrus had lost but
3,000) are a fair measure of this.

It was the army of Artaxerxes that had suffered most,
but was the better able to bear its losses because of its

[1]Xenophon, *Anabasis*, I, 9.

numbers, and also because it had fought nearer its own territory and under climatic conditions to which it was more accustomed. The Greeks were thrown into a partial confusion and, falling back, left their baggage train and bivouac exposed to the plunder of the Persians, who looted at will and carried off all that was readily movable.

At nightfall the Greeks rested arms and believed that the victory belonged to them, and that, as Cyrus was not with them, he was in pursuit or garnering the fruits of victory; yet did they marvel that there was no message from him. At daybreak there was still no word from their idolized commander, and the generals held a meeting to decide future action. To them came a messenger with the appalling news that Cyrus was dead and that Ariæus, in command of the barbarians who had come with them out of the west, had retreated to the last halting place before the battle, and now gave them news of his intention to return to Ionia, inviting them to join him, for which he would wait one day. The defiant reply, moved by Clearchus, was that they were victors, and but for this word from him would be already in pursuit of the fleeing forces of Artaxerxes. "Would that Cyrus were still alive! But since he is dead, take back this answer to Ariæus, that we, at any rate, have conquered the king; and as you yourselves may see, there is not a man left in the field to meet us. . . . Now we can promise to Ariæus that, if he will join us here, we will place him on the king's throne. Surely to those who conquer, empire pertains."[1] Ariæus refused the crown, and on motion of Clearchus, who alone among the Greek generals had shown marked evidence of manifold gifts of leadership, the Greeks de-

[1] Xenophon, *Anabasis*, II, 4 f.

termined to join him and make such arrangements as
were possible looking to the long and sad homeward
journey. His also was the plan adopted for the journey,
which was not to return by the way which had been
traversed on the outward journey, because of the extreme difficulty experienced in the later stages to secure
provisions for man and beast, but to try for a passage
over a country more likely to afford better forage. The
route selected was to cross the valley and go northward
along the Tigris, rather than by the Euphrates as they
had come.

The king was now deeply concerned to win the
Greeks to his own rule, and so to end possible uprising
on their part when once they had returned to Ionia. To
these negotiations every possible means was given,
and the conduct of them was placed in the hands of
Tissaphernes. When Clearchus had already begun the
homeward march and was resting in villages to partake
of the good of the land in grain and date wine, a deputation arrived from the king headed by Tissaphernes,
with the king's brother-in-law and three other Persians.
These proposed a truce during which the Greeks might
pursue unmolested their homeward way. The motives
were plainer later, for this was but a ruse to entrap the
unwary if possible and open the way to a destruction
of the whole body. The truce arranged, Tissaphernes
returned from the king ready, as he declared, to lead
them back to Greece, and to see that wherever possible
in the king's dominions a market should be arranged
for them, and where this could not be, they should have
leave to take provision peaceably from the country
which they were traversing.

There was, however, no real confidence among the
Greeks either in Tissaphernes or in the Persians under

FIG. 36.   A Persian Sacrifice.

FIG. 37.   Tribute-bearing Sacae.

FIG. 38.   Women Riding.

Ariæus, who had made the fateful expedition with
them. As the march began the two bodies kept respect-
ful distance, and when camp was made at night the
Greeks were careful to place a wide strip between them
and their supposed friends and companions. In this
mood and manner the valley was crossed, the great
river Tigris came in view and was passed successfully,
and then with the river on the left flank the march
northward began and went forward without any breach
of faith on the part either of Tissaphernes or of the
Persians. So was Opis passed, and the Greater Zab
crossed where it pours its muddy flood into the Tigris.
Shortly after Clearchus, disturbed by the feeling
among his own men that Tissaphernes was not to be
trusted, and observing that on the other hand Tissaphernes or his followers seemed ever to be eyeing himself and the Greeks askance, secured an interview, and
frankly laid before him what seemed to be the folly of
the situation and desired to find means to end this dis-
trust on both sides. In the discussion which followed
Tissaphernes successfully removed all his doubts, and
Clearchus was persuaded that he might trust both himself and his followers to Tissaphernes, and that he was
especially high in the regard of the leader. Tissaphernes
was now in a position to venture upon a bold stroke,
and the method adopted was shrewdly conceived and
skilfully executed. He proposed to Clearchus that "in
some open and public way" a meeting should be arranged in which it would be possible to determine who
were causing bad blood by stirring up among the
Greeks hatred and suspicion of Tissaphernes. Clearchus accepted the suggestion, and proceeded to arrange
a meeting. Some of the Greeks protested, foreseeing a
plot and mistrusting Tissaphernes. But Clearchus won

over them, and it was arranged that five generals and
twenty captains should go to the conference, followed
by about two hundred soldiers who were to take the
opportunity for marketing.

"On arrival at the doors of Tissaphernes's quarters
the generals were summoned inside. They were Prosenus the Bœotian, Menon the Thessalian, Agias the
Arcadian, Clearchus the Laconian, and Socrates the
Achæan; while the captains remained at the doors.
Not long after, at one and the same signal, those within
were seized and those without cut down."[1] The generals were taken up to the king and there decapitated,
Menon only being spared because he was believed to
have been on the side of Tissaphernes, but his life was
extended but a year, and as a prisoner he died.

To complete the scheme which Tissaphernes had
planned, it was now necessary to secure from the
Greeks who remained a surrender of their arms and
submission to the king. There were, however, still remaining among them leaders of courage and wisdom
who advised an indignant refusal, and an attempt to
reach home by a long and hard march through hostile
territory to the Black Sea. All obstacles were successfully overcome, and with leaders chosen by themselves
in the room of the betrayed dead they came out at long
last to the glorious sight of the sea. No one of the new
leaders was so distinguished then and afterwards as
Xenophon, whose glory it was that of the original 10,-
000 about 8,600 came through to the sea.[2]

The plan of Cyrus to dethrone his brother and rule
in his place had failed miserably after untold sufferings

[1]Xenophon, *Anabasis*, II, 5, 32, 32.
[2]For the geographical and topographical details of the expedition see especially Félix Robiou, *Itinéraire des Dix-Mille*, Bibliothèque de l'École des
Hautes Études, Quatorzième fascicule. Paris, 1873.

of those who, by choice or by deceit, had followed him, yet the after effects upon the Persian empire were beyond all exaggeration. As soldiers the Greeks had conclusively proved their superiority over the Persians. They had shown also that they were capable of producing leaders out of the humbler ranks, and their resourcefulness on the march, their skill in foraging on the country, and their courageous daring under difficulties and against great odds had shown how easily a larger force could have broken the empire in pieces. Time would provide a leader able to do it, and until that day arrived the loosely attached members, geographical and ethnographical, might continue their decadent ways.

When the retreating Greeks disappeared northward Artaxerxes turned to reward those who had been faithful to him, to reorganize provinces that had been weakened, and to punish such as could be reached of those who had given aid or encouragement to Cyrus and his enterprise. To Tissaphernes as his reward came the great post in western Asia Minor, which had been in the better hands of Cyrus. To those who had helped Cyrus he meted out severe punishment, and required of them a complete surrender. Alone among them Tamos escaped and fled with all his movable possessions to Egypt. Cilicia was reduced to subjection and brought under a thoroughly Persian ruler, and never more do we hear of a king under the native title of Syennesis. The Greeks of the Ægean littoral had sent an embassy to Sparta for help, when they saw the direction of his plans. Sparta, on the other hand, sent ambassadors to Tissaphernes hoping to entice him into some arrangement which might strengthen her general position in the Hellenic world. He was too crafty himself not to

see and understand the craft of others, and declined
negotiations to attack Cyme, which would probably
have fallen but for the onset of winter.[1]

Sparta met this challenge with a declaration of war
upon Tissaphernes, not upon Artaxerxes or his empire,
and despatched Thibron with 5,000 heavy armed infantry and 300 cavalry to Ephesus. The time was aus-
picious, for there was acute rivalry between Tissaphernes and his near neighbor in rule, Pharnabazos.
To the Spartan body the Greek cities gave contributions of men, and in the spring of 399 B. C. there were
added also about 6,000 veterans of Xenophon's men,
who were ready for any adventure.[2] The little army
was now large enough to attract others to its standard,
and the men of Pergamon, Teuthrania, and Halisarna,
joined forces. Thus reinforced Thibron besieged La-
risa, whence having had but small prospect of any immediate success he withdrew and decided to launch an
attack upon Caria. At this juncture there suddenly appeared Derkylidas with orders to supersede him. The
campaign against Caria was abandoned, and after a
conference with Tissaphernes, he led his troops against
Pharnabazos in Æolis, and in but nine days' swift campaigning won eight cities of the Troad, nearly all coming over to him without a struggle, and so brought
Pharnabazos to an armistice, in spite of which the
Spartans continued the campaign against Bithynia,
which properly belonged to the same satrapy. He plundered, ravaged, and burnt ruthlessly this province. He
was now apparently invincible, and in the spring of
398 B. C., he went to Lampsakos, where he received the
Lacedæmonian embassy which came to prolong the pe-

[1]Diodorus, XIV, 35, ed. Vogel, III, p. 240 (Teubner).
[2]Xenophon, *Anabasis*, VII, 8, 26.

riod of his command, and to bring him a commission to protect the Chersonese against the incursions of the Thracians. In pursuance of these orders he crossed into Europe, after an engagement with Pharnabazos to lengthen the armistice period, and set his army the task of building a wall across the Chersonese, which was successfully completed by the last summer or in the autumn.[1] Soon thereafter he had recrossed into Asia and was ready to besiege Atarneus. In eight months he had reduced it, and turned thence to Ephesus. By this time it had become clear that the Persian court was moving toward war, and in the spring of 397 he received orders to open war upon Tissaphernes and with the help of the Admiral Pharax to attack Caria. This plan had to be altered speedily, for Pharnabazos and Tissaphernes had united their commands and were attacking Ephesus. For its help Derkylidas entered the Meander valley and came suddenly and unexpectedly in sight of the Persian army. The situation was fraught with danger, but as he kept his head and the Persians lost theirs, he came off well, if not brilliantly. Negotiations for peace followed, in which Tissaphernes demanded the withdrawal of the Spartan troops, and Derkylidas countered with an insistence upon the autonomy of the Ionian cities. The demands had to be submitted to the home governments, and meanwhile an armistice was proclaimed.[2]

Into the turmoil of the Hellenistic cities and states, and the Persian empire a new figure appeared in the year 410, when Evagoras regained the rather shaky throne of his ancestors and proclaimed himself king of

---

[1]Xenophon, *Hellenica*, III, 2, 6 ff., ed. Keller, p. 75 f. (Teubner). Diodorus, XIV, 38, 7, ed. Vogel, III, p. 244 (Teubner).
[2]Xenophon, *Hellenica*, III, 2, 12 ff.; Diodorus, XIV, 39, 4 ff.

Salamis in Cyprus, through the overthrow of Abdemon, who had been supported by the Persians. Evagoras would have less of Persian influence in his tiny kingdom, but cultivated the friendship of Athens, and for Athens sought the aid of Artaxerxes II against Sparta. After the defeat of Conon at Ægospotomi he gave him refuge. The swift rise of Evagoras to general influence, even outside his island, soon awakened the jealousy of Persia, which would probably be enhanced by the news that after the battle of Conidus, in which Evagoras had participated, his statue was set up in Athens side by side with that of Conon. To add fury to the Persian flame he refused the annual tribute to the great king, and still further aggravated the situation by causing coins to be struck[1] with his own name, and the magical word "king" with it. These acts together would have been deemed a *casus belli*, but Ktesias was now at the Persian court and eagerly pursued a policy intended to produce a reconciliation. To this same intent Conon also was working and at length successfully, at least in part, for Evagoras resumed the payment of tribute, and with it sent gifts to prominent members of the Persian court.

After this a lively exchange of letters took place between Ktesias on the one side and Evagoras and Conon on the other, with Pharbazos assisting the general case. As a result Ktesias journeyed to Cyrus and carried to Conon a commission as Persian admiral. Artaxerxes had now resolved to make war energetically upon Sparta, and to this end enter into conventions with Athens, and with all her friends. But Evagoras was no easy person to handle. He was little by little with one sure stroke after another gaining a complete control of

[1]Babelon, *Les Perses Achéménides*, p. 86 ff.; compare ib., cxx.

Cyprus, and was soon in a virtual state of war with

Persia, for he crossed into Asia Minor and persuaded the Cicilians to revolt.

It was impossible that Artaxerxes could tolerate such a situation, yet he was ill situated to resist it directly. There was a rebellion in Egypt with which he must deal, and he chose the only possible method of dealing immediately with Evagoras, entrusting to Hekatomnos, satrap of Caria, with Autophradates to make war on Cyprus. The former was not true to his Persian master, and actually gave financial assistance to Evagoras while he was pretending to make war upon him.

King Hachoris at Medinet Habu.
From Lepsius, *Denkmäler aus Ægypten*, Vol. VIII.

With Athens Evagoras made a treaty and secured promise of aid, and ten ships were actually despatched, though
they did not reach him. Nevertheless the campaign of
Artaxerxes failed, and Cyprus remained in the hands
of Evagoras, who went forward to greater achievements. He formed an alliance with Achoris, the rebel
king of Egypt, who sent men to him and ships, and thus
strengthened he could the more readily win over Cilicia
and even Phœnicia, whence the Persians were wont to
draw ships for their fleet. Tyre was taken by force,[1] and
while thus engaged Athens once more attempted to
give assistance, despatching a new fleet of ten ships
with 800 light armed infantry under Chabrias. Evagoras had now a force of no mean size and quality, reckoned at 90 triremes, 20 secured from Tyre, and no less
than 6,000 Cyprian troops,[2] with an indeterminate
number of mercenaries.

Persia was busy with peace negotiations with Athens,
and greatly improved her situation by the peace of
Antalcidas, the disgraceful King's Peace, which con-
ceded the west coast of Asia Minor to her rule, and ex-
pressly gave Cyprus to her. This definitely prevented
any further hope of Athenian aid to Evagoras, and
shows the sudden shifts in these disturbed times. The
Persians were now free to gather a large force, counted,
with characteristic exaggeration at 300,000 men, including cavalry, and more than 300 triremes.[3] The fleet
had to be recruited from the Greeks of Asia Minor. In
command of the land forces was Orontes, with Tiribazos over the fleet. The first point of attack was Ci-

---

[1]Isocrates, IX, 60–62, 65, ed. Blass, I, p. 220 f. (Teubner), with which
compare also ib., IV, 161, ed. Blass, p. 80.
[2]The numbers come from Diodorus, XIV, 110, 5. On the other hand Isocrates
credits him with but 3,000, in order, doubtless, to enhance his glory (IV, 141).
[3]Diodorus, XV, 2, 1.

licia, which had been lost to Evagoras. We have no knowledge of the course or issue of events there; but after a time the attack was directed against Cyprus, making the city of Kition the scene of operations. As Evagoras had now no fleet sufficient in size or strength to attack he contented himself with harassing the ships by which the Persians were supplied with food, and to such success that a severe deprivation began and induced disturbances among the mercenaries. He now secured the promised help from Egypt, 50 ships, and hastily built 60 more in Cyprian waters, and with these added to those already under his command mustered a force of 200 ships. With these he had the boldness to attack the Persian fleet off Kition, and after a first successful onset met with defeat in the end. His situation was now precarious, and help was sorely needed from some quarter, from any quarter. He was tightly besieged by the Persian forces, shut up in Salamis, and in this extremity decided to risk an attempt to break through the cordon, and personally seek aid from Egypt. He appointed his son Pnytagoras in command of the island, and with ten ships broke through by night and reached Egypt. Achoris gave him money only and no other help for continuing the struggle, nor was assistance to be secured elsewhere. He had now no recourse but to seek negotiations for peace, on such terms as were obtainable. The discussion was first with Tiribazos, who demanded of Evagoras to yield the claim of kingship over the whole island, remaining only in possession of Salamis as a servant of the Persian king. Evagoras refused, but was willing to yield supreme authority to Persia on condition only that he retain the style of King in the island. Evagoras was now shrewd and skilful enough to engineer difficulties between the two Persian commanders, and Tiribazos was recalled to Susa to make report, while Orontes remained in supreme command. With him the negotiations were easier, and Evagoras accepted a peace which left him with much power still. So ended a war which cost Persia much treasure, and had lasted, not indeed through ten full years,[1] yet sufficiently long to be less of advantage than disadvantage, for Evagoras was left to rule for years to come, and Persia had neither profit nor glory for all her spending of men and means. This new failure of Persian arms stands in vivid contrast to the successes of the earlier kings.

In spite of so great a failure it must be observed that Artaxerxes had made a great gain by the peace of Antalcidas, for the concession of the Greek coastal cities of Asia Minor once more to Persian rule was no small matter. If he had the genius of Darius I or Xerxes I he might make great use of a peace so valuable in many ways. This king was, however, no man of genius, and the advantage thus won would soon be frittered away.

It was Egypt that delivered the next severe stroke against the continuance of Persian rule in the world. Artaxerxes during all the confused warfare with Evagoras, with Athens, and with Sparta never wholly abandoned the hope of destroying the independence which the Nile valley had secured while Persia was so deeply enmeshed in other difficulties. He kept alive in himself, and presumably also in his entourage, a lively desire to emulate the great achievements of earlier kings, and to rule as acknowledged master in that incomparable valley. There were indeed very great dangers and many difficulties. Not the least of these was

[1] Isocrates (IX, 64) gives the length at ten years, but this is obviously a round number.

the strength of Evagoras and the strategic position of his island. It would be dangerous to attempt the assembling of a fleet off the Phœnician coast if its vessels might be harassed by swift, light ships sailing out from the stronghold of Salamis in Cyprus. Of what use or value was the peace of Antalcidas which gave the western coast of Asia Minor as a Persian possession if ships there built and manned could not safely pass Cyprus? It was during his reign that a visitor of the highest distinction, to whom all ages owe a great debt, appeared in Egypt. Herodotus could hardly have entered Egypt, as a part of the Persian Empire, earlier than 448 B. C., but the exact year of his visit is not known. He found the land peaceful and fairly prosperous as a whole, and wrote of it, its manners and customs and history, as none had ever written before. His was a master hand in narrative as in description, and his second book, called Euterpe, can never lose its glamour or its interest for thoughtful readers, who are able to find instruction and entertainment gracefully commingled.

Egypt had had a sad experience of human folly in the failure to secure once more a real national unity under a king who could rule both north and south, and organize the whole land for a united defense. There had been kinglets a plenty, rivals seeking personal profit and not national advantage. In the king lists there appears only one name as sole representative of Dynasty XXVIII, and this is Amyrtaios II, whose rule began, such as it was, about 404 B. C. For six years he maintained his position, and under him the land achieved some increase of strength and power of resistance against foes within and without. When he was gone anarchy took his place, and the list of rulers of Dynasty XXIX, with names like Nepherites, Achoris, Psamuthis, displays nothing but the hopeless state of inner confusion with no king strong enough to destroy his rivals. In this situation lay whatever hope there might be of a reassertion of Persian rule.

In the year 380 B. C. began active preparations for an assault upon Egypt, but for one cause or another there were many delays, and not until 374 was a move made. Artaxerxes placed Pharnabazos in supreme command of an army assembled near Acco, and said to number 200,000 men,[1] to whom were added 12,000 mercenaries under the Athenian Iphikrates. But the times were far from favorable for a victorious outcome. Egypt had now a king, Nectanebos I, of Dynasty XXX, who displayed considerable skill in preparing his land for the anticipated invasion. The way had been to a certain degree prepared for him, as Achoris had made an alliance with the ever energetic Evagoras, and now Nectanebos was able to follow this with a similar treaty with Sparta. Furthermore he had in his service an Athenian Chabrias, who had apparently come into Egyptian service on the invitation of Achoris.[2] He was a soldier of much repute and skilled in the arts of defense. He directed the building of fortifications at the mouth of the Nile and in the eastern desert lines of Egypt which might confidently be expected to hinder, if not entirely arrest, the Persian forces. When news of these activities reached Artaxerxes, he entered complaint at Athens and Chabrias was recalled from Egypt, but the works of his brain and hands remained behind.

Even yet the Persians hesitated to make an advance, waiting for the efforts of Artaxerxes to secure a stable

---

[1]Diodorus, XV, 42.
[2]So Diodorus, XV, 29, but Cornelius Nepos (Chabrias, 2) ascribes his entrance to Nectanebos.

peace among the Greek states which should remove all
danger of an attack by Sparta. And now for some reason
Pharnabazos was removed from the command of the
army which he was forming, and from the satrapy of
Cappadocia Datames was summoned to the command.
He was the son of a Carian named Kamisares who had
lost his life in the Cadusian war. In the withdrawal of
Pharnabazos, Iphicrates seems also to have disappeared. It seemed now as though the long delayed expedition might really begin an advance, yet was another postponement the result. In Cataonia a dynast
named Aspis had revolted, and Datames was ordered
by Artaxerxes to attack him. He had ravaged Persian
territory and allied himself with the Pisidians and was
now become a serious disturber of whatever peace there
might be in the quaking Persian empire. Datames fulfilled this mission with overwhelming energy, and so instead of glory secured only the envy of the court party
in Susa, and the suspicion that he might have become
dangerous himself. He recognized the situation and delivered the command of the Egyptian expedition to
Mandrokles, a Magnesian, and made off to Cappadocia
to secure for himself independent rule.[1]

After the withdrawal of Datames there reappeared
Pharnabazos and Iphikrates in Ake to resume command, and in the summer of 374 B. C.[2] camp was broken
and the long-deferred march on Egypt was begun. The
natural defenses of Egypt were great. The desert has
always been a difficult problem for armies small or
great, and the seven mouths of the Nile were easy to
fortify and very difficult for any army. The fortifica-

[1] Cornelius Nepos, Datames, 4 f.
[2] Diodorus (XV, 41) gives the date as under the Archon Sokratides, 374/373
B. C. (i. e., Ol., 101, 3).

tions along the Pelusian branch of the river were especially strong and they were held by a large body of troops, for Nectanebos expected there an attack by the land forces and an effort to enter the stream by the ships which sailed down the coast accompanying the Persian army. Pharnabazos had a sufficiently good intelligence service to be advised not to attempt Pelusium, and accordingly effected successfully the landing of 3,000 men at the Mendesian mouth to find that this also had been fortified and was held by an Egyptian force which fought bravely until overwhelmed by superior numbers[1] and cut down. Egypt lay now at the mercy of the Persians, and might readily be overrun. But at the moment of triumph Pharnabazos would not venture to push on into the country until the main body of the Persian army had come up, while Iphicrates desired to push the success already achieved to a conclusion and press on to Memphis while the land was disturbed by the flight of its defeated and discouraged army. He was disposed to ignore the caution of Pharnabazos and believed that he could take the capital with his Greek mercenaries operating alone. This excited the suspicion and perhaps also the rising jealousy of Pharnabazos, who thought the Athenian willed to conquer the land for his own purposes.

The hesitation and the dispute were fatal for the enterprise. The Egyptians rallied on Memphis and made quick preparations to attack the camp at the Mendesian arm of the river, and to their efforts the great river added splendid assistance. It was now the height of the summer and the Nile flood had begun, and proved as great or greater a defense than the breasts of fighting men. The Persians were compelled to retreat,

[1]Diodorus, XV, 42, Polyænus, III, 9, 38, ed. Melber, pp. 130, 131. Teubner.

FIG. 39. Gold Armlet.

FIG. 40. Persian Head in Gold.

Courtesy of the Yale Babylonian Collection.

FIG. 41. Vase of Xerxes.

FIG. 42. Silver Rhyton.

and Iphicrates slipped away in disgust to Athens. What happened to Pharnabazos we know not. He vanishes in the cheerless collapse of the whole grandiose plan so long in preparation, so empty of result. Egypt remained independent. The Persians had too many troubles elsewhere to waste time in dwelling on this catastrophe.

The most threatening of these was the steady increase in the independent spirit of satraps, particularly those in the west. This was a very serious menace to imperial unity and to the power of the throne, and Artaxerxes was at length compelled to take some notice of it. The satraps of Asia Minor had long been disposed to go their own way without consulting Susa unless a contingency arose in which the satrap preferred to leave the chances of possible disaster to the king, and so referred to him the question in advance. This course would have been impossible under the kings who had been founders of the empire but had become common since the reign of Darius II. The beginning of a great uprising of the satraps against the empire is most easily recognized in the contest begun by Ariobazanes. He was as distinguished in life as in birth, the son of a certain Mithridates, prince of Kios and Arrhina,[1] and the successor of Pharnabazos, to whom he was probably related, in the satrapy of Daskyleion[2] in the year 387 B. C. The earlier years of his rule have left us no hint of any special activity, but in 368 he was busily attempting to win some sort of recognition from both Athens and Sparta at the same time. In the next year he was ready to raise the standard of rebellion, having secured the assistance of Datames.[3] To their assistance came an Athenian fleet under Timotheos, and the dis-

[1]Diodorus, XV, 90, 3, compare XX, 111, 4.
[2]Xenophon, *Hellenica*, I, 4, 7.   [3]Diodorus, XV, 90, 3.

tinguished Spartan leader, King Agesilaos, joined in
the defense against the Persian satraps Autophradates
and Mausollos,[1] who had received command to sup-
press the rebellion, but failed in the effort. For this
valuable assistance Ariobazanes transferred to Athens
the cities of Sestos and Krithote in the Chersonese, and
rewarded Agesilaos with gold.[2] In his turn he, his sons,
and his chief counsellors received the bestowal of
Athenian citizenship. The success of Ariobazanes encouraged other satraps to revolt, and soon Thuys of
Paphlagonia made ready to rebel, but met with ill fortune, for Datames took him prisoner. Aspis of Kataonia
met a similar defeat at the same hands. The rebellion
was now in a sad state, but Datames himself had come
under suspicion at the Persian court, and now turned
his talents and arms against the king, whose valuable
servant he had been. He was now satrap of Cappadocia, and speedily conquered Paphlagonia. He was
strong enough after these successes to be regarded as
the natural head of the greater series of rebellions
which followed.[3] It was probably about the year 370
that he raised the standard of rebellion, and drew into
an offensive and defensive alliance a great cordon of
states, large and small. In this coalition were Ariobarzanes, satrap of Daskyleion, Mausollos, who hoped
from a general success to make for himself an independent kingdom in Caria, with the Greek coasts ad-
joining and Halicarnassus as his capital. Furthermore
there joined also the satraps Orontes of Mysia, Auto-

[1]Xenophon, Agesilaos, II, 29, ed. Thalbeim, p. 190. Teubner.
[2]Cornelius Nepos, Timotheos, 1, 3, and Agesilaos, 7, 2. Compare Polyænus,
VII, 26.
[3]*Primum Datamen praefectum* [*Paphlagoniae*], Justin, Epitoma . . . Pompei
Trogi, Prologus libri x, ed. Ruehl, p. 254 (Teubner). Compare Cornelius Nepos,
Datames, 5.

phradates of Lydia, and with them Ionians, Lycians,
Pisidians, Pamphilians, Cilicians, Syrians, Phœnicians,
and almost all of the inhabitants of the coast line.[1]
The king of Egypt was now Tachos (Zedhor), who
seems to have made considerable show of rule, for a
gold coin with his name upon it, and of an Athenian
type, has come down to our day.[2] He also joined in this
rebellion in yet another effort to free Egypt from all
Persian influence. This would mean that practically
the whole section of the empire west of the Euphrates
was in rebellion, and through so great a revolt perhaps
half of the expected annual tribute of the empire must
fail, for this was by far the richer portion of the king's
dominions, nor could he hope to draw from the remainder taxes sufficient to put a force into the field to cope
with adversaries so numerous or likely to be so well
equipped for war. Never before was the empire in such
imminent danger of collapse. Never before had a man
with the qualities or ability of Datames succeeded in
winning so wide an accession of confederates. His danger would be that this loose confederation had no single definite aim. These rebel satraps had each his own
ambitions. They were not making war on Artaxerxes
with the intention of founding a new kingdom with
Datames on the throne. So different was this from the
expedition of Cyrus, whose person was sacred in his followers' eyes, whom they meant to make king in his
brother's room. If Datames should win a conspicuous
success other satraps, who considered themselves as
good or better than he, would be filled with envy, and
eager to exploit for selfish ends whatever he won. This
situation was fraught with a serious threat of possible
treachery, and just here it was that the beginning of

[1]Diodorus, XV, 90.   [2]This unique coin is in the British Museum.

failure was shown. An attack on Artaxerxes made by so
large forces as this coalition could muster, if delivered
with singleness of purpose and absolute loyalty one to
another, would surely bring down the empire in a hopeless crash.

The rebellion began before complete unity and a perfected organization were achieved, and it may be that
Datames took the step too soon, perhaps because he
did not trust his own son Sysinas;[1] and the sequel shows
that he certainly had no reason to have any confidence
in him. The king stood his ground and offered such resistance as he could. The fighting took place chiefly in
Mesopotamia and Pamphylia,[2] but only an echo of it
reaches our day, and the clash of arms cannot be heard.
In this preliminary contest Datames seems to have
been in command. To his forces Mausollos added a
contingent and here also Autophradates of Lydia gave
aid.[3] We do not know the issue of these first battles.
But to Datames headship over the whole coalition was
not to come. Rather did it fall on Orontes, of the distinguished family of Hydarnes. The choice was melancholy, for he proved traitor to the cause. When he had
received money from the common chest to hire 20,000
Greek mercenaries, he turned them over to the king,
together with some Greek cities, hoping by this detest-
able trick to secure from the king appointment as Ka-
ranos, and so outreach all his fellows.

At about the same time Artabazos, who was now Persian general in command at Cappadocia, and was the
son of Pharnabazos, and his wife Apama, daughter of

---

[1]This suggestion comes from Judeich, in Paully-Wissowa sub Datames, and
is adopted by Prašek, *Geschichte*, II, p. 213. I have ventured to accept it with
a "perhaps," though it is really not much more than an inference.
[2]Polyænus, VII, 21, 3. Cornelius Nepos, Datames, 8, 9.
[3]Diodorus, XV, 90.

Artaxerxes, formed a plot which resulted in the treachery of Mithrobarzanes, father-in-law of Datames, and captain of his cavalry. Datames made great promises to his men, and fell upon the traitor, who was on the point of going over to Artabazos. Then turning on Artabazos he hunted him off the field.[1] It was a swift retribution.

Meanwhile Riomithres was commissioned by the rebels to visit Egypt in their interest, and from King Tachos secured a contribution of money and no less than fifty war-ships. This accomplished, his head was turned and he also proved a traitor to the common cause. He shut himself up in Leuka, and invited thither some of his former companions who did not understand his purposes. These he threw into chains and handed over to Artaxerxes. It would be difficult to provide a parallel in the tangled politics of the Orient to this long series of treacheries. What hope was there for a success against Artaxerxes when such men as these were among the rebels? Then to cap the long series of treacheries Artaxerxes contrived to secure the murder of Datames, the greatest leader and the noblest spirit among his enemies.[2]

The moment of his death was well chosen. The king of Egypt, who is called Tachos, was ready to send 80,000 men against Syria, stiffened by 10,000 Greek mercenaries under King Agesilaos, and a fleet of ships under Chabrias. This combined force under the Egyptian prince Nectanebos was already in Phœnicia and waited only the word to advance. But the whole allied movement was at the mercy of Persian intrigue, and Artaxerxes succeeded in stirring up a rebellion in Egypt against its king, which incited Nectanebos to try for

[1] Diodorus, XV, 91.   [2] Cornelius Nepos, Datames, 7–9.

the throne and oust his own father.[1] The plot was well carried out, for Agesilaos took the treacherous prince's side, as did also Chabrias. The king fled, and finally reached Susa, where Artaxerxes received him, succored him in his need, and appointed him to chief command in an expedition which he proposed to send against Egypt.

The death of Datames, and the change in the occupancy of the throne in Egypt under Nectanebos II, ended the rebellion in western Asia, and the king was once more free to set his provinces in order. To rule in the room of Datames his son Sysinas was appointed, who is under reasonable suspicion of having been faithless to his father. Autophradates and Mausollos, who could never have been more than half-hearted in the support of the great rebellion, declared allegiance to the Empire and were confirmed in their former posts.

One small spark of fire remained, for Orontes, son-in-law to Artaxerxes, attempted to continue the rebellion, and was joined by Artabazos, the king's grandson by his daughter Apama. These men were quite obviously planning a coup which might result in the securing of the throne by one or the other when the death of Artaxerxes should occur, and this seemed not likely to be long postponed. In Susa, however, they had a serious rival in the king's son Ochos, who had already much power in his hands and was quite likely to have been in some sort co-regent. He had sufficient energy to strike first, and marched through Arabia to head off an alliance between Orontes and the Egyptian king. Orontes, seeing the hopelessness of his situation, surrendered and was accepted in friendly fashion, while Artabazos was seized by Autophradates, and held

[1] Diodorus, XV, 92.

prisoner. So ends the last spark of fire in the great rebellion, with Artaxerxes master a while longer, left,
however, only in possession of troubles incident to the
approaching end of his long and troubled reign.

The death of his wife Stateira left him without her
counsel and in this he turned once more to place himself under the influence of Parysatis. But her position
lacked singleness of authority and influence, for he had
many concubines, numbering, so it is said,[1] no less than
360, of whom Aspasia, the younger, and once a favorite of his brother Cyrus, seems to have won his special
attention. As wife, after Stateira's death he took his
youngest daughter Atossa, but he is said also to have
married another of his daughters, Amestris. Among his
legitimate sons were Darius, Ariaspes, and Ochos, and
among the illegitimate only the name of Arsames is
preserved, and there were 115[2] others of similar status.
Here, then, in the family relationships and ties was a
fine opportunity for court intrigue and every form of
deceit. The king's later days were surrounded and embittered with the struggles for the succession. As Darius was the eldest son the first claim was rightly his,
and so apparently the king desired and appointed. He
seemingly made him a sort of co-regent,[3] where he was
certain to come into conflict with Ochos. Darius desired Aspasia to wife, and this produced a breach between father and son, which Ochos was quick to seize
and turn to his own advantage. He was shrewd enough
to win the favor of Atossa, and to promise her marriage, by which in the event of the king's death or removal and his accession she would still be queen. The

[1]Plutarch, Artaxerxes, 27, 2.
[2]Justin, X, 1, 1. Compare Curtius, X, 5, 23. Justin gives instead of Arsames
the name Ariaratus.
[3]Plutarch, *Artaxerxes*, 26, 1, 2. Justin, X, 1, 2, 3.

response which Darius made to this was to enter into
a conspiracy against the king.[1] When this was discovered Darius was hanged. In this base plot Tiribazos
had been partner because no one of the numerous royal
progeny had been given him to wife. He lost his life
also, and the field was left fairly clear for Ochos, who
was quick to seize whatever loose reins of power there
were, and so to assure his succession.

Amid all this wretched mess the king died. Whether
his death was really the natural consequence of the
painful experiences of the later days, added to the
weaknesses of age, or whether he fell a victim to the
anxieties of Ochos to seize the throne, and so his willingness to put his father secretly to death, we do not
know. There are reasons aplenty for evil suspicions,
and there the case must rest. The date of the king's
death is not quite certain, but it occurred apparently
in the year 358, after a long reign of forty-five years.[2]
It was a period filled with war, rebellion, and internal
distress, and the works of peace of which we have any
hint were few. In Susa he built a hall of columns of
which a few poor remains were discovered by Loftus,
and later described by Dieulafoy,[3] and there also was
found a seven-line inscription which declares that he
built a palace in the same place. In Hamadan, the ancient Ecbatana, he has left a seven-line inscription,
written on the mouldings of pedestals, now in the British Museum. It is a sad commentary on the pathetic
struggles of the king to call to remembrance himself

[1]Justin, X, I, 4, 5. Plutarch, *Artaxerxes*, 26–29.
[2]The length of reign is placed at forty-five years in *Corpus Inscriptionum
Graecarum*, 2691, d. (Compare Dittenberger, *Sylloge Inscriptionum Graecarum*,
I, p. 227, No. 167.) The Persian Royal Canon gives forty-six years, see Clinton, *Fast. Hell.*, II, 3, p. 378.
[3]Loftus, *Travels and Researches in Chaldea and Susiana* (1857), p. 364 ff.
Marcel Dieulafoy, *L'Acropole de Suse* (Paris, 1890), Chap. XII, with beautiful
restorations and admirable descriptions.

Fig. 47. Silver Statuette of King.

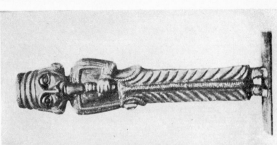

Figs. 45 and 46. Persian Kings.

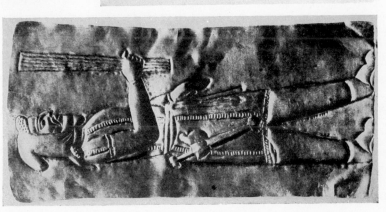

Fig. 44. Gold Plaques.

Fig. 43. Gold Plaque with Persian Figure.

and his royal house and to pray for the continuance of that which his hands had wrought. Its words are these:

"Says Artaxerxes, the great king, king of kings, king of countries, king of this earth, son of Darius the king: Darius (was) the son of Artaxerxes the king; Artaxerxes (was) the son of Xerxes the king; Xerxes (was) the son of Darius the king; Darius (was) the son of Hystaspis, the Achæmenian; this *apadana* by the will of Auramazda, Anahita and Mithra we made: let Auramazda, Anahita and Mithra protect me and my kingdom and this which we have done."[1]

This text shows a change in the Persian religion which is to be ascribed to the king, though the reason for its introduction remains obscure. Anahita is a goddess imported into the purer Zoroastrian religion and doubtless connected with the Babylonian goddess *Anat*. In Babylon she was worshipped as Ishtar, and a festival held in her honor has come down under the Greek name of Sakaia.[2] The impetus thus given by Artaxerxes to the worship of Anahita gave it an astounding spread. It appears speedily in Armenia, Syria, Asia Minor, especially in Pontos and Cappadocia. Then the oft-repeated process of identification with other native goddesses in one place or another spread it still more

[1] For the Cuneiform Text see Tolman, *Cuneiform Supplement*, 65–69, and compare his *Ancient Persian Lexicon*, p. 54.

[2] Our information concerning the introduction of this cult by Artaxerxes II comes from Berossos in a quotation preserved by Clement of Alexandria, Protr., I, 5, p. 19 Sylb. It is clear that Darius I invokes no deity by name but Auramazda, whereas Artaxerxes in his inscription concerning his erection of a great building at Persepolis prays "may Ahura-Mazda, Anahita and Mithra protect me." The rapidity of the spread of the Anahita cultus is remarkable, and in various lands it took different forms. Thus, for example, in Armenia it was associated with sacred prostitution (Strabo, xi, 532), while in Cappadocia and in holy cities there were both male and female sacred prostitutes in attendance (Strabo, xii, 559, xv, 733), while in Lydia the rites more nearly remained true to ancient Persian customs (Paus., v, 27, 5), and in Philadelphia and Hypaipa Greek sports were introduced. The Greeks sometimes identified her with Athena (Plut., Artax., 3) and at other times with Aphrodite (Herod., I, 131, with which 105 is to be compared). All this development is a sad outcome of Zoroaster's pure faith.

widely. Little indeed could the Persian king know how
wide would be the influence which he had thus set in
motion. Millions then unborn would be worshipping
this goddess for centuries to come. After the name of
the goddess Artaxerxes has put down the name of the
god Mithra, which his race, in common with the Hin-
dus, had worshipped many centuries, but whose cult
had received a severe setback when the purer Zoroastrianism had set Auramazda in a lonely superiority.
Darius the Great makes no mention of Anahita or of
Mithra, but now Artaxerxes has restored both. In the
Vedic hymns Mithra is invoked with Auramazda, and
this association was never wholly lost, though obscured,
driven into occlusion by Zoroastrianism. The faith
lived on underneath the better, and as Auramazda was
the god of the sky and hence of the light, and Ahriman
was god of darkness, between the two Mithra had
his place, created by Auramazda to give aid in the destruction of evil and the care of earthly and human
order. As a god of light he became also the god of truth
and of honor. For Artaxerxes to introduce again this
god into the pantheon is therefore less surprising than
would appear at first thought. It was however a return
from a better to a lower faith. Yet was Mithraism to
have an amazing influence in the world, sweeping in
vast conquests westward and in Rome especially entering into a contest with Christianity, which lasted
until the third century of the Christian era.[1]

When Artaxerxes was dead, men speedily became
busy in estimating his worth, his services, and in por-

[1]On Mithra in Persia see Windischmann, *Mithra* (Abhandlungen der
Deutsch. Morgenländischen Gesellschaft, 1857, p. 52 ff., and Spiegel, *Eranische
Altertumskunde*, 2, 1873, p. 77 ff., and for the general subject compare Cumont,
Textes et Monuments relatifs aux mystères de Mithra, Brussels, 1896, with which
may be compared the article by him in Roscher, Lexicon.

traying his character. It is difficult to judge him after
these years, but one can see strands in the complex
web of his life and work, and these must serve to iden-
tify him to our world. In the beginning of his reign he
was much under the influence of women of the family
or the court, as was so often the case in the Orient. The
first of these was Parysatis his mother, and after her
Stateira his wife, and her circle. In the later days
Ochos would seem to have dominated him. Here then
there is gradually appearing before us a figure weak
and given much to yielding to influences from the outside. It is impossible also to acquit him of the charge
of bloodguiltiness, for it will not serve the cause of
truth to charge all these horrors of murder which dis-
figure his reign upon his mother, wife, or son. It is clear
enough that whoever excited his suspicion or jealousy
soon paid the price with his life. The king was possessed of abounding energy when really roused, but was
dilatory, slow to action, willing to sit supine in his
harem in Babylon or in Susa, giving into other hands
the heavy duties of the march or the field. So did he
dally and wait while the expedition of Cyrus came onward directing a dangerous thrust at the heart of his
empire. Yet when the danger was imminent he showed
a tremendous energy, and personally appeared in the
decisive battle at Kunaxa, and afterward claimed that
he had with his own hand laid his brother dead at his
feet.[1] It is also to be remembered that Artaxerxes personally conducted a campaign against the Cadusians
in 384 in which he is reported to have endured the privations and burdens of the march with the best of

[1] On the whole case see Plutarch, *Artaxerxes*, 7, 1, 2. Xenophon, *Anabasis*, I,
7, 9, and contrast Diodorus, XIV, 22, 3, 4. Further compare the reports of
Deinon and Ktesias in Plutarch, *Artaxerxes*, 10, 11. Xenophon, *Anabasis*, I,
8, 26, 27. Diodorus, XIV, 23, 6, 7 and Justin V, 11, 8.

them.[1] To him there is also ascribed some skill and experience in the manly sport of the chase.[2] All these traits of character are sufficiently evidenced in undoubted ways. When we pass beyond them we are left to the judgments which antiquity garnered or invented, by which the king is presented as a just, mild, and gentle character,[3] fully earning and deserving the reverence of his day and the respect of posterity. It is a colored picture, as we should think, yet are there discernible certain lines in it which have an air of verisimilitude; and at least the witnesses who bear this testimony are nearer his figure than are we, and we must yield to them so much credence as we may.

The political purposes of Artaxerxes are plain enough. He aimed to hold in his grasp and to transfer to his heirs unimpaired the great empire which his forbears had won. To this purpose every move he made is clearly to be interpreted. For this he made all his wars, in Asia Minor, in Egypt, on every border. It must be admitted that his efforts were not wholly in vain. Egypt was indeed hopelessly lost, but whom could we imagine able to have held that splendid possession? That he kept practically the whole of the territories and provinces in Asia Minor which he had inherited is a striking testimony to his methods, horrible though some of them were. As he lay dead one might well be prepared to say that he was a great king, judged by the standards of his race and time.

[1]Plutarch, *Artaxerxes*, 24, 25, compare Diodorus, XV, 8, 4; 10, 1. Cornelius Nepos, *Datames*, 1, 2, and Justin, Prologos, X.
[2]Plutarch, *Artaxerxes*, 5, 2, 6, 3. Diodorus, XV, 10, 3.
[3]Plutarch, *Artaxerxes*, 1, 1; 2, 1; 4, 2–4, 5; 30, 5. Diodorus, XV, 93, 1. Ælian, var. hist., I, 32, 33, 34. Cornelius Nepos de reg., 1, 4.

FIG. 48.   Tomb of a Persian.

CHAPTER XI

ARTAXERXES III

WHEN his father was dead Ochos succeeded to the throne apparently without any serious contest. He may have been busily concerned with crushing the last bits of the great rebellion in Asia Minor when the end came, and at once caused himself to be proclaimed king under the name and style of Artaxerxes III. It appears that he concealed[1] for ten months the death of his father with the assistance of the court, using the time, of course, in making himself secure. The story must remain somewhat doubtful, yet there are parallels for various periods in many places, and we have no secure reasons for rejecting it.[2] He came to the throne in 390 B. C. according to the Royal Canon.[3]

Whenever or however he came to rule there need be no doubt of the quickness or the sureness with which he seized responsibility or the fierceness of his execution. Like so many other Oriental monarchs, he feared some assault upon his authority and took steps to remove all upon whom he could lay his hands who might be dangerous. The bloody record preserved for us is that he had eighty of his brothers slain in one day.[4]

[1] If he really did conceal his father's demise in this manner he would have the beginning of his reign, or rather the first year of his reign in 357. *Corpus Inscriptionum Graecarum*, 2919. The year 390 of the Canon would correspond to November 359–November, 358. So Nöldeke in Paully-Wissowa, II, p. 138.

[2] It comes to us from Polyænus, *Strategemata*, VII, 17, ed. Melber, pp. 330, 331 (Teubner). Polyænus was a Macedonian, and we do not know his sources. He claims to have taken great pains with his curious book, but the book itself, most of which has come down to us, hardly seems to have cost much. It is rather a careless compilation.

[3] Clinton, *Fast. Hell.*, II³, 378.

[4] Curtius Rufus, X, V, 23, ed. Hedicke, p. 372 (Teubner). Justin, X, 3.

He was now safe at least from their interference and turned at once to the serious tasks which confronted him.

The first business in war was to subdue the Cadusians, upon whom his father had wasted his fading energies. Whether he had much better fortune is not quite certain for accounts fail us, but apparently whatever was done went forward by the hand of a certain Darius of royal blood by descent from Darius Nothus, and later to be known in history. He had some success with the Cadusians[1] and as his reward was made satrap of Armenia, whence he was later to arise as a factor in political strife.

While these attempts were in progress the new king was confronted with the age-long problem of Egypt. It was far too valuable a royal possession to be suffered to slip away altogether from control, yet this had really been the result under the failures of the policies of his predecessors. He had the courage to attack the problem once more. Extensive military preparations were made, but the problem was supremely difficult and the king did well to make haste slowly. While thus engaged there arose in Egypt a situation well suited to his taste. Nectanebos II was king and against him there arose a rebellion led by a man whose name is lost, who proclaimed himself king and must have had a following sufficient to make him a dangerous menace. This would make troubled waters in which the Persian king might well fish successfully. For help Nectanebos turned to Agesilaos, who provided a large force and sent it to him.[2] Nectanebos had no stout heart, and be-

[1]Diodorus, XVII, 6, 1. Justin, X, 3, 2–4, compare Arrian, *Anabasis*, III, 8, 5; 11, 3, 19, 3. Curtius, IV, XII, 12, XIV, 3.

[2]Plutarch, *Agesilaos*, XXXVII, f. Diodorus, XV, 93 where Nectanebos is incorrectly confused with his father. The number of 100,000 men contributed to this campaign by Agesilaos is certainly exaggerated.

FIG. 49.　Tomb of Artaxerxes III.

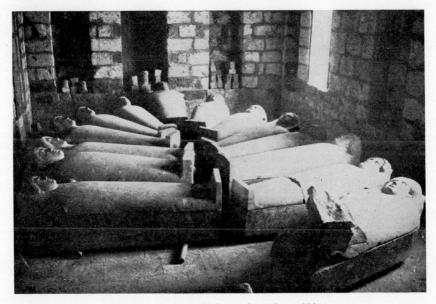

FIG. 50.　Anthropoid Sarcophagi from Sidon.

fore these allies could arrive left the open field to
whomsoever might be strong enough to seize it and retired within a strong and fortified city, where he was
besieged and reduced to dire need. Agesilaos relieved
him by a night assault and restored him to his throne.
Had Artaxerxes been ready at the right time he might
have won Egypt again.

His campaign was ready about 356 B. C.[1] and the
plan was admirably thought out. He divided his forces
in twain, took command of the chief one himself, the
one on which most depended, and left the other to his
generals. His own campaign was directed against Asia
Minor, with the purpose of bringing a stable and orderly situation, with regular tribute, to pass. Two of
the western satraps had taken to the field, and had organized a formidable force recruited with the aid lent
by Syria, Phœnicia, Judea, and Cyprus. These two satraps were Artabazos and Orontes, and they provided
no small problem for the king. Artabazos had drawn
help from Athens and Chares had come thence to his
aid. He was a helper worthy of any great occasion, for
though he had had his ill fortune in war he had also
given full proof of skill and dash, and now had against
Persian forces a quick and striking victory whose glory
brought him recognition at home in the bestowal of the
golden cross of honor, and in rich monetary reward at
the hands of Artabazos. He was now sufficiently dangerous to make it well worth while for Artaxerxes to
secure his removal if possible. The method adopted
was to threaten Athens with war, and they who were
selected to make the threat were the Thebans, to whom

[1]This date is extremely uncertain. Tarn suggests 351 but very doubtfully
(*Camb. Anc. History*, VI, p. 22). On the other hand H. R. Hall (ib., p. 153)
would date the march at 343. Amid uncertainties so great we must accept the
fact, and give over a dispute as to the date. I have been here content merely
to say that preparations were ready in 356.

he sent a gift of 300 talents of silver for this purpose. The scheme was successful and Chares was recalled from Artabazos.[1] On the other hand in the place of this very serious loss Artabazos found help from the Thebans, who sent him Pammenes and 5,000 men in the year 353 B. C.[2] They were however a poor substitute, though they had a victorious beginning. Some of the western satraps had remained faithful to the king, and these the Thebans attacked and defeated in two battles.[3] But this was the end of success for them. They were withdrawn when Artabazos himself had met defeat and fled to Philip of Macedon, whose name here appears for the first time in Persian history. It was a portent, though few if any could then have been made apprehensive by it. Artabazos was disposed of as a danger, and Orontes soon sank quietly out of sight. Artaxerxes had done well thus far and the empire was stronger than it was when his directing hand came upon it.

He had still to deal with the immensely difficult problem of Egypt. While he was busy with the tangled skein of affairs in Western lands he had placed the expedition against Egypt in the hands of his generals.[4] It was a failure and had to return without result. Artaxerxes was not discouraged but began at once preparations on an extensive scale, so soon as he was freed of the difficulty with Artabazos and Orontes. Before he was able to strike, however, the Egyptians had prepared new difficulties for him in his own dominions by assisting a rebellion in Syria and Palestine.

[1]Diodorus, XVI, 22. Schol. Dem.
[2]Diodorus, XVI, 34, 1, 2; compare Polyænus, V, 16, 2. Frontinus, *Strategemata*, II, III, 3, ed. Gundermann, p. 46. Teubner.
[3]Diodorus, XVII, 34. Compare Polyænus, VII, 33, 2.
[4]Diodorus, XVI, 40, 4; 44, 1; 48, 1, 2 with which compare Isocrates, V, 101. Justin, Prolog X.

On the Phœnician coast was the triple city, Tripolis,
with its three separate parts composed of representatives of Sidon, Tyre, and Aradus. In the Sidonian section the rebellion began, and spread thence until it involved all Phœnicia, and had entered into relation with
Nectanebos of Egypt. The Sidonians under their king,
Tennes, built or assembled a fleet, gathered food and
war supplies, and made ready for a serious attempt to
throw off the Persian dominion. The Persians first let
loose upon them three satraps, the one named Belesys
of the territory beyond the Euphrates, and the other
Mazaios of Cilicia, and the third Idrieus of Caria. Tennes received the help of 3,000 Greek mercenaries under the command of a Rhodian named Mentor, and
sent him by Nectanebos. Thus strengthened he stood
his ground and when attacked by the satraps defeated
and drove them out of Phœnicia, though not without
loss to his little country.[1] This seemed a spectacular
success and the kings of various Cyprian cities were so
greatly emboldened that they came out openly against
the Persians. Against them Artaxerxes ordered Idrieus,
satrap of Caria, who was well supplied with men and
arms. He had 40 warships and 8,000 Greek mercenaries
under the Athenian Phokion and Evagoras II,[2] who
had been driven out of Salamis, grandson of Evagoras
I, who had given the Persians so much trouble, but was
now dead.[3] With these forces, and those of the Persians
who were normally at his disposal as Satrap, he sailed
to Cyprus and besieged Salamis by land and sea. The
island was rich, for it had long enjoyed prolonged periods of peace and its people were industrious. These
riches enticed adventurers from many quarters and

[1]Diodorus, XVI, 40, 5, 6–42.
[2]Diodorus, XVI, 42, where quite erroneously Evagoras I is mentioned.
[3]Diodorus, XV, 47.

Idrieus had as many, if not more, men than he could use, and the islanders were soon driven into great need, and the cities of the island, except Salamis, laid waste. Surrender was necessary, and not merely expedient, and Evagoras, having yielded submission to Persia, caused coins to be struck with his name and the style "satrap of the Persian king,"[1] hoping by this adroit move to be left in the rule of his island. The ruse failed, for Pnytagoras had also surrendered and presumably before him, to whom the rule of the whole island was entrusted.[2] He was however later rewarded by the rule of Sidon, where he held authority for three years, and issued there coins with his own name upon them.[3] But however great may have been his gifts as a soldier he failed as administrator, fled to his native island, and there met his death.[4]

While these successes were attained in Cyprus by the empire affairs went badly on the mainland. The generals in command in Phœnicia could not withstand the local opposition, much less make headway against it, and at length Artaxerxes had to withdraw his forces, to reorganize and increase them for a greater effort. While this necessary reconstruction was in progress the king personally left Susa and spent most of his time at Babylon. When the army was ready he took the field and at its head advanced into the west, making first for the refractory city of Sidon. When the city king, Tennes, heard of the size of the advancing host he lost courage and secretly offered surrender to the Persian king, hoping by his contemptible disloyalty at least to make his own worthless self safe. He added also that he

[1]Babelon, *Les Perses*, cxxiii ff., 91 ff.   [2]Diodorus, XVI, 46, 2.
[3]Babelon, *Bull. Hell.*, XV (1891), 309 ff.; *Les Perses Achéménides*, cxxxiii ff., clxxix ff., 231 ff.
[4]Diodorus, XVI, 46, 3.

FIG. 51.   Upper row left to right: Gold Daric, Silver Siglos, Two coins of
Tissaphernes.
Lower row left to right: Two coins of Pharnabazus, Two silver
tetradrachma of the Satrap Evagoras II of Sidon.

FIG. 52.   Gold Plaque with Figure of Horse.

was eager to help the king in the expedition against Egypt, and that he knew the best point of attack and the best landing-place on the Nile. Artaxerxes accepted his help, and turned to the greater Greek states to seek help of them. Athens and Sparta both honorably refused, but Thebes, on the contrary, sent 1,000 heavy armed infantry under Lacrates, and the Argives 3,000, and these were placed under the command of Nikostratos. From the Greek cities of Asia Minor came 6,000 men. While these were still on the way Artaxerxes continued his advance, pressing on into Phœnicia and halting before Sidon to lay siege to the city whose king had failed her. Sidon had been making every possible preparation for defense while the Persians were negotiating hither and yon, and the city had strengthened its walls, dug threefold moats, and erected towers for observation or defense. Within the walls had been gathered with feverish haste and enthusiasm food and provisions and arms. Without in the sea a hundred ships, large and small, were holding the city defenses there, ready to do and die for their little fatherland. In spite of all that had been done or could be the disparity was great and the poor little city by the blue waters of the Mediterranean was cast for a sad experience; yet had she had a real king some show of defense might have been made. But the treacherous Tennes kept up his contact with the Persians through Mentor, who commanded the Egyptian mercenaries. At length, under the guise of a visit to an assembly of the Phœnician states, the king rode out of the city walls accompanied by a hundred of the chief citizens of Sidon, and when they came to a point not distant from the Persian camp he delivered the hundred into the hands of the Persians, and Artaxerxes ordered them

despatched. Tennes then returned to the city and with
help of the Egyptian mercenaries at an appointed time
opened the city gates. The city was taken and then Artaxerxes ordered Tennes hanged. If the king gave this
command because he could not think it very probable
that such a creature probably would not be of more use
to him than he had been to Sidon the judgment could
scarcely be disputed.

Before the Persians entered the city its inhabitants
determined to die where they had lived as free men,
rather than be swept off to adorn some remote corner of
the barbarous empire; they had burned all the ships lest
some should wish to escape, and then shutting themselves up in their little homes waited while fire devoured them with their possessions. The whole famous
ancient city went down in the ashes, and deprived the
world of the records which it had made during the centuries of freedom and the culture of native life. What
a sorry commentary it all is upon the savagery of man,
his cruelty, and his will to destroy.[1] Warned by the
fate of Sidon all the rest of Phœnicia capitulated, and
escaped ruthless destruction, though we know not what
otherwise they may have suffered.

Artaxerxes had now left no enemies to impede his
march along the coast of the Mediterranean, nor could
he be assaulted on either flank; not by land, for all
Syria was reduced to subjection, nor by sea, for Cyprus
had fallen. The expedition advanced with every assurance and made an assault on Egypt. But Tennes was
dead, if indeed he had really known the best point of
attack, and Artaxerxes certainly did not; the attack

[1]Diodorus, XVI, 43–45. Compare Josephus, *Antiq. Jud.*, XI, 297. Justin,
Prolog X. For a good account of this destruction of Sidon, see F. C. Eiselen,
Sidon, a Study in Oriental History, New York, 1907, pp. 65, 66.

failed,[1] for the way had been missed and a large body
of troops sank in the marshes near the great Serbonian
lake and were drowned. It was a bad beginning, and
there was nothing for it but to withdraw into Syria
and replenish his forces. He had, however, no intention
of giving up the enterprise, and the land of the Pharaohs and of an ancient culture need have no hope of
freedom from the oppressor. When once more the king
was ready to move he had found guides to guard him
against another catastrophe, and this time successfully
passed the Serbonian bogs, and entered upon the sacred
soil, and reached the neighborhood of Pelusium. Here
the Egyptians had prepared special defenses by the
Pelusiac arm of the river, and were holding them with
five thousand Greek mercenaries under command of
Philophron. Against them Artaxerxes sent his Thebans,
who attempted attack on the defenses, through a narrow and deep ditch, but met sharp resistance. This
failed, and a new plan had to be adopted for the next
day. The king divided his Greek troops under Lacrates,
Nikostratos and Mentor, and with each placed a Persian general, with Lacrates was Rosakes, a prince of
the royal house, with Nikostratos was Aristazanes, and
with Mentor Bagoas. These were to advance in three
columns, and much depended on the sort of reception
the Egyptians might give them. Nectanebos was no
mean adversary, and he had prepared as well as he
could for the test. He had 20,000 Greek mercenaries
and about the same number of Libyans, with 60,000
native troops. It was force enough to hold the Persians
to a sharp accounting, as they attempted to take the
fortifications and exposed themselves in the ditches
and trenches which lined the banks of the river. Nec-

[1]Diodorus, XVI, 46, 4, 5. Isocrates, V, 101. Frontinus, *Strat.*, II, 5, 6.

tanebos had the passion of defense in his heart, but less wisdom in his head, and in the very beginning made the mistake of not taking counsel of the experienced Greek commanders who were with his Greek mercenaries. They would know something of the method of campaign which their fellow countrymen serving under the Persians might adopt. He, however, sure in his own convictions, took personal command of a body of troops to meet the assault of the column approaching under command of Nikostratos and Aristazanes, which had the support of the Persian fleet and was entrusted with the duty of taking the entrance of the Pelusiac arm of the river, while Lacrates was to besiege Pelusium, and Bagoas attempt to turn the right flank of the Egyptians. Nikostratos in some way secured Egyptian guides and under their direction entered a Nile canal which had not been defended, and was able to put himself in a secure position. They were attacked by a detachment of Greeks under Kleinias of Cos, but without success, for they lost five thousand men, Kleinias himself among the number, and the Persians held their position. When the report of this disaster reached Nectanebos, he gave up the unequal contest without a battle and withdrew within Memphis. At Pelusium Lacrates had assaulted in vain, but here also the dreadful news of the defeat of Kleinias wrought its influence, and under pledge of permission to withdraw with the honors of war, the position was surrendered. Bagoas was instructed to accept the surrendered town, but mistreated the retiring defenders to such an extent that the men under Lacrates, consumed with pity and burning with rage, took the side of the Greek mercenaries, their fellow countrymen, and attacking the Persians drove them in flight. In due course Bagoas complained

FIG. 53. Nectanebo II.

FIG. 54. Nectanebo II.

FIG. 55. Nectanebo I.

FIG. 56. Hachoris.

to Artaxerxes, but instead of securing judgment against
the men of Lacrates, drew from the king an order to
put to death the Persians who had robbed the retiring
Greeks. It was a piece of Persian justice worthy of a
greater man and a more just than Artaxerxes.

The next move in the oncoming tragedy was made
by Mentor, who bade the Egyptians remember the example of Sidon and to surrender to Artaxerxes while
there was yet time, declaring that the king would show
mercy to those who came early to surrender, but would
deal as with Sidon with those who held out against him.
This proclamation led to a singular confusion at Bu-
bastis, whose Egyptian inhabitants desired to surrender the city to Bagoas, but the Greeks of the garrison
anticipated them and surrendered to Mentor, and when
Bagoas attempted to enter the city took him prisoner.
All the cities of the Delta surrendered, one after another, and the backbone of Egyptian resistance was
broken. Nectanebos was left without hope, and fled to
Ethiopia with such of his treasures as were portable.

For more than fifty years Egypt had, with varying
fortunes, claimed or exercised independence of Persian
authority. It was now to feel a reassertion of alien dominion in its worst form. Artaxerxes would appear to
have been filled with the fury of a demoniac. The king
of Egypt had attempted resistance of Persian authority, and his people, from the highest to the lowest, inspired with an ancient love of freedom, had supported
his efforts. For this natural loyalty to homeland the
Persian king would administer savage punishment. He
ordered the walls of defenced cities to be razed, and the
temples of Egypt's gods plundered and desecrated.
Sacred writings wrought by skilful hands upon beautiful papyri were removed, and like plundered goods

before and since, have vanished from the eyes of modern man, though some, if not many, were restored to the priests on money payments to Bagoas.[1] The tenderest and most profound religious ideas were ruthlessly trampled under foot. In Memphis he slew the Apis bull, and in its place introduced an ass.[2] It is difficult to imagine how deeply this would offend, and equally difficult to comprehend the mind of a conqueror who would be capable of ordering or permitting such an ignoble cruelty. It is, however, not surprising that Egyptians should have called him Ass, in retaliation.[3] To all these studied insults he added the worst of all punishments, for he carried off some of the population and colonized them in Persia.[4] Nectanebos had fled, yet so great was the Egyptian sense of legitimacy and so keen was the loyalty to a king, that he still from afar was regarded as king, and exercised at least a spiritual authority over his bereaved people.[5] Artaxerxes had ravaged and destroyed in Egypt as the most savage of the Assyrian kings, and was now satisfied to retire to his harem in Persia and leave to others to rule where he had ruined.

While Artaxerxes was busy in Egypt he was ably represented in certain other quarters, but in none better than in western Asia Minor, where Mentor was in command of the Persian situation. His homeland was the island of Rhodes, but he had seen much service, and to his military skill and determination the king owed many of his victories in Syria and in Egypt. He was now entrusted with the military pacification of

---

[1] Diodorus, XVI, 46, 4–51; 51, 2. Justin, Prologos X.
[2] Deinon, Fragment 30, Müller.
[3] Ælian, *Varia Historia*, IV, 8, ed. Hercher, p. 64, Teubner.
[4] Ælian, *op. cit.*, IV, 8; VI, 8.
[5] See Bergk, *Rheinisches Museum*, XXXVII, 363, and compare Prašek, *Gesch.*, II, p. 229, foot-note 2.

Asia Minor, and took up the task with characteristic
vigor and dash. Some of the satrapies were exercising
in some sort independence, and these must be reduced.
The names of their leaders have, for the greater part
perished, lost in the punishment which Mentor meted
out to them. One name only was borne by a man whose
ties of friendship have made it immortal. Hermias of
Atarneus had gained ascendance in certain towns of
Æolis and Troas, and having been a protector of Aristotle has claims on the future. He was secured by
treachery exercised by Mentor, and was executed by
order of Artaxerxes.[1] Soon after Mentor himself paid
the great demand, and was succeeded by his son. He
had rendered extraordinary services to his king, and
left all western Asia in a subjection more complete
than it had known for a long time.

The policies of Artaxerxes and their execution had
produced effects far-reaching and profound. The whole
eastern world had learned to know a conqueror worthy
of comparison with the greatest of his predecessors.
He had indeed awakened a new outburst of hatred, a
new tremor of fear. The disgust, contempt, and apprehension of Egypt were widely shared, and with justice.[2] Yet it may be doubted whether under those circumstances in a military monarchy any other method
would have achieved what he had done by this savagery. He had, at least, put fear into the heart of rebels,
and if now there were statecraft to compare with military skill the empire might take on new life.

The greatest problem which now confronted Artaxerxes was the Greek situation. To that he might well
give thought. The Greek world knew him and had

[1]Diodorus, XVI, 52. Ps. Aristot., Oeconom., II, 1351 a. Apollod. in Diog.
Laert., V, 9. Strabo, XIII, 610. Ps. Dem., X, 32.
[2]Diodorus, XVII, 5, 3. Justin, X, 3, 1.

heard of his exploits. Athens had taken cognizance of
him and paid some deference to him. Though probably
in the year 353 B. C. Athens had given aid to Orontes,
it yet was quick to regain touch with the king,[1] and in
351 B. C. the Athenian general Phokion fought for Persia in the service of Idrieus,[2] though only a little later
when Athens reformed her friendship with Sparta no
notice was taken of the great king's request for aid.[3]
On the other hand, Thebes blew hot or cold as the moment called. She had given aid to the rebellious satraps,[4] yet in 351 had asked and received aid from Persia to help her in the war with Phocis,[5] while Argos
sent troops to be used against Egypt.[6]

If these points of contact with Grecian states are
somewhat obscure and more or less given to changes,
still more difficult for us are the relations with Macedonia. When Mentor was at the height of his power he
besought the king's influence to secure the release of
his brother Memnon from the court of Philip II of
Macedon. Memnon had married into the family of
Artabazos, one of the rebellious satraps, and on their
collapse fled with Artabazos to Philip II. This was the
beginning of friendly relationships between Artaxerxes
and Philip, which finally resulted in the making of a
treaty between them.[7] Its origin, its purpose, and its
terms are alike unknown to us. Whatever they were
they proved to have no binding force on Philip, but
were well observed by Artaxerxes. Philip went straight
forward with the plans which were intended to make
him supreme master of Greece. When he besieged Pe-

[1]Corpus Inscript. Att., II, 108, bc. Dem., XIV, 31.
[2]Diodorus, XVI, 42, 7 ff.; 46, 1.   [3]Diodorus, XVI, 44.
[4]Diodorus, XVI, 34, 1, 2.   [5]Diodorus, XVI, 40, 1, 2.
[6]Diodorus, XVI, 44, 1; 46, 4. Compare Isocrates, XII, 159; V, 126.
[7]Arrian, Anab., II, 14, 2.

rinthos, Athens appealed to Artaxerxes against him,
but was sharply repulsed with a reminder that she had
given help to the Egyptians against him, and might
now shift for herself.[1] Yet when the siege by Philip had
taken on serious proportions, and it was clearly evident
that his designs were dangerous for the peace and unity
of the Persian empire, Artaxerxes called out the satraps of Asia Minor and delivered the hard pressed
city.[2] In other ways also he took a hand in Thrace, seeking to secure means to prevent the plans of Philip; yet
nowhere else after this was he to move in Greece. He
had probably troubles enough nearer home, even in his
own court, and little opportunity to work elsewhere.

Palace intrigue which probably began much earlier
was now in full course, led as so often has been the case
by one who had enjoyed the fullest confidence of the
king. The arch plotter now was the eunuch Bagoas. He
and Memnon had for some time been in practical direction of the whole kingdom while the king was sinking deeper into the associations of his harem. The
position which thus came to Bagoas should have been
sufficient to satisfy his ambitions, but he now aspired
to the throne. To clear the path he moved a physician
to poison the king and his older sons with him.[3] So
ended in the year 337 B. C.[4] the career of a king, judged
great on the basis of his achievements and compared
with others of his line, a very great king. He had inherited an empire in a veritable chaos, full of cracks in

[1]Dem., IX, 71; XII, 6. Isocrates, II, 162. Compare Æsch., III, 238. Dem.,
XIX, 137.
[2]Diodorus, XVI, 75, 1, 2. Paus., I, 29, 10. Dem., XI, 5 f. Arr., *Anabasis*, II,
14, 5.
[3]Diodorus, XVII, 5, 3; compare Ælian, var. hist., IV, 8.
[4]The date is fairly well fixed. The Canon (Clinton, *Fast. Hell.*, II³, 378)
gives as the accession year of the next king 44 Nabon. = November 338–
November 337. See however Diodor., XV, 93, 1. Synkellus, p. 146, 486. See
also Judeich, *Kleinasiatische Studien*, 148 f., 181.

its walls like some great building about to fall. He had stayed its collapse, patched up its breaches, and given it a continuance. He had indeed displayed a ruthless severity, a savagery quite inhuman, but in this he was the same as his forbears. He had done nothing to weld the divers populations, men of many tongues under his rule into a national unity, yet in this was he in no wise different from the greatest of his predecessors. Darius the Great had not attempted it, and the Empire had never been other than a congeries of peoples reduced to subjection by the sword and by the sword held in a precarious union, ready for clever leaders of rebellion within, or in danger of attack without.

In the works of peace Artaxerxes was far behind Darius and Xerxes. He erected a palace at Persepolis, which lies now a sorry ruin, though enough remains to show that its sculptured ornament represents a great decay when contrasted with the work of Xerxes;[1] yet is his tomb at Naksh-i-Rustam in architectural design and construction fairly worthy of comparison with the best of his predecessors.

The family of Artaxerxes must have been large, but the names of most of his children disappeared with their lives when the murders of Bagoas were clearing the way for his own selfish plans. He spared the life of the youngest son, Arses, intending to use him as a lay figure while he exercised rule and power himself. The mother was Atossa, and another son called Bistanes or Bisthanes in some way escaped the murderers and later appeared before Alexander the Great.[2] Atossa and three daughters also escaped, and later were taken prisoners at the battle of Issus; one of these daughters

[1] See the pictures in Sarre und Herzfeld, *Iranische Felsreliefs*, Berlin, 1910.
[2] Arrian, III, 19, 4.

bore the historic name Parysatis, and Alexander took her to wife.[1] And a granddaughter wife of Hystaspes fell into the power of Alexander after Arbela.[2] So ended the family of one of the proudest and strangest monarchs of the ancient Oriental world.

[1]Arrian, *Anabasis*, VII, 4, 4, ed. Roos, p. 343, Teubner.
[2]Curtius, VI, 2, 7.

ALEXANDER THE GREAT

"If I were asked to make a selection from among all the men who have come to my knowledge, it seems to me I could pick out three who excel all the rest. The first is Homer. . . . The second is Alexander the Great. For, if we consider the early age at which he began his enterprises; the small means with which he carried out his glorious designs; the authority which he acquired in those youthful days among the greatest and most experienced captains in the world by whom he was followed; the extraordinary favor with which Fortune embraced and seconded so many of his hazardous, and I may almost say foolhardy, exploits;

> He bore down all that his high aims withstood
> And delighted in making a path across the ruins (LUCAN);

his greatness in having at thirty-three victoriously traversed the whole of the habitable earth, and in having, in half a lifetime, attained the whole power of human nature. . . . If we consider at the same time so many military virtues, his diligence, foresight, patience, discipline, subtlety, magnanimity, resolution, and his good fortune, wherein, even if the authority of Hannibal had not so taught us, he was the first of men; the uncommon beauty and symmetry of his person, which amounted to the miraculous; his carriage and imposing mien in a face so young, ruddy, and radiant:

> As when Lucifer, washed in Ocean's wave,
> Dearer to Venus than all stellar fires,
> Uplifts in heaven his sacred head and melts
> The darkness (VIRGIL);

the superiority of his knowledge and abilities; his great and enduring fame, pure, clean, stainless, free from blemish and envy."

—MONTAIGNE.

"I find nothing more contemptible and mortal in the life of Alexander than his fancies about his immortalization. Philotas taunted him wittily in his rejoinder. He had congratulated him by letter on his elevation to the Gods by an oracle of Jupiter Ammon. 'For your sake I am glad, but there is ground for pitying men who have to live with and obey a man, who surpasses and is not content with the proportions of a man.'

> You rule the world because that you
> Confess the gods supremacy (HORACE)."

—MONTAIGNE.

CHAPTER XII

DARIUS III

WHEN Artaxerxes III was dead, Bagoas by his machinations placed on the throne Arses, intending to be the real king himself in the background pulling the strings of a puppet. But Arses showed in a little while that no such idea was in his mind, but that he intended to be king and rule in his own proper person. Then Bagoas had him put out of the way,[1] fearing lest the king should not merely have the power but also the will to lay condign punishment upon him for his murders.

Bagoas now needed some man to place upon the throne who belonged to the great Achæmenian family, and at the same time might be expected to be sufficiently tractable to rule under his control. The man chosen was a son of Arsanes, or Arsames,[2] and of his sister and wife Sisygambis, and grandson of Ostanes, one of the sons of Darius Nothos.[3] He was born about 380 B. C., and was now in the prime of life. He had distinguished himself in the war against the Cadusians and thus attracted the attention of Artaxerxes III, and as a reward for his services was made satrap of Armenia.[4] He was a warm friend of Bagoas, who thought he might use him as a tool, and summoned him to the throne.[5] Bagoas had again chosen unwisely, for the new

[1]Diodorus, XVII, 5.
[2]The name is given as Arsames in the Ptolemaic Canon, by George the Synkellus, 392, and John Antioch fragment 38, 39, and Eusebius in Hiero. ad ann., 1652, but Diodor. gives it as Arsanes.
[3]Diodorus, XVII, 5, 5. Plutarch, *Artaxerxes*, 1, 5, 22. Ælian (var. hist., XII, 43) is certainly wrong in reporting that he had been a slave, as is also Strabo (XV, 736), who denies him royal blood.
[4]Diodorus, XVIII, 6, 1.
[5]Diodorus, XVII, 5, 5; Arrian, *Anabasis*, II, 14, 5. Curtius, VI, 3, 12. Strabo, XV, 736.

king adopted the name Darius[1] and set himself to grasp
firmly the reins of power. It was not long until he saw
clearly what Bagoas had done to others, and would be
ready to do to him, and he took quick resolve to anticipate the schemes. Bagoas was poisoned as he had poisoned others.[2]

Darius III became king in the year 336 B. C., and by
a strange coincidence this was the very year in which
Alexander the Great, then but twenty years of age, ascended the throne in far away Macedonia, with a commission from his father to make war upon Persia ringing in his ears. It was a fateful thought and commission, and sore and sad days did it predict for the new
king of Persia.

Darius in Persia and Alexander in Macedonia had
succeeded in troublous times, neither inherited a kingdom either peaceable or content, neither could sit down
calmly and expect a people to cry out allegiance and to
will to do naught that might disturb high and far-
reaching plans. Yet were these two men already facing
each the other, and upon them both lay a great demand
to prepare for eventualities. The man who first seized
the moment was Alexander. He was ready at once to
make sure his hold upon the throne, and to secure such
a complete control of the kingdom which his father
Philip had left him that he might make any use he
chose of it against enemies present or prospective anywhere. There were great dangers of rebellion, and if he
were not swift to act he might soon find himself with
but broken fragments in his hand. Before men dared
expect he was in the field with his army in Thessaly,

---

[1]He receives the name Darius Codomannus only in Justin (X, 3), and as it
would appear incorrectly, yet this has passed into most histories and hand-
books.

[2]Diodorus, XVII, 5, 3–6, 2; Justin, X, 3, 3–5.

FIG. 57. Alexander.

where he compelled recognition of himself as head of
the confederation, as was his father. Thence he marched
to Thermopylæ, summoned the Amphictyonic council,
and had himself proclaimed guardian of the Delphic
shrine and leader of all Greece. Thence he marched to
Bœotia, and his very appearance with resistless might
brought to a sudden end a threatening rebellion in
Thebes. To him then Athens sent an embassy to greet
and salute him, and with this he was content without
asking any pledges from the city that once had known
the glory and honor both of independence and of dominance. While these events were in motion, there met in
Corinth ambassadors of all the Greek states, except
Sparta, and in solemn and unanimous decision named
Alexander, in his father's room, as leader of all Greeks
against Persia.[1] It was now his duty to make sure that
all his borders were secure before he set out upon the
immense task of subduing Persia, which must on any
consideration occupy him during long years of absence.

He began by returning to Macedonia, and there followed a series of murders and butcheries in the Oriental manner, by which Alexander made his position
secure.[2] They darken the record sadly, but belong in an
age accustomed to such horrors, and need receive no
special note either of condemnation or condonation.
For the present purpose they are important only as
showing what manner of man this was who was shortly
to make war upon Persia. He had now pacified Macedonia and removed by force all danger of any uprising
there against his authority, no matter how great the
distance or how long his absence might be. His next
task was to ensure the borders of Macedonia against

[1] Diodorus, XVII, 4, 9. Arrian, I, 1, 1–3. Justin, XI, 2, 5.
[2] Justin, XI, 5, 1–2; XII, 6, 14. Diodorus, XVII, 2, 4 ff., 5, 1 f. Curt., VI,
9, 17; VII, 1, 3.

invasion by the half barbarous tribes amid the northern hills. In the spring of the year 335 B. C. he marched away from Amphipolis, and in ten days was in the Balkans, at the foot of Mount Hæmos, the chief pass of which was strongly held by the Thracians, who were still free of subjection to Macedonia. By a very skilful maneuver[1] he outflanked them and came victoriously through to the lowlands beyond, free to make war upon the Triballi, who four years earlier had experienced the horrors of war at the hand of Philip but had not been completely brought into subjection. Alexander proved himself a greater master than his father, and completely reduced them.[2] He was now able to move forward to the banks of the Danube, which he probably reached in the neighborhood of Silistria. With a part only of his forces he crossed the river and completely astonished[3] the Getæ, a people inhabiting the northern bank. This movement was intended to assure the Danube as a safe boundary against any invasion from the north, and this it accomplished. On his return journey he received the surrender of the Triballi and of other less important tribes in the Danube region, and met also an embassy of Celts,[4] and then without further incident he came through the eastern passes of the Hæmos into Pæonia. Here he received the disturbing intelligence that an insurrection had begun in Illyria, whose prince, Kleitos, son of Bardylis, had fought against Philip. With the Illyrians had united also Taulantians on the shores of the Adriatic. These had seized the important city of Pelion, near the Devol river, which commanded this river valley, and if held by hos-

[1]Arrian, I, 1, 8 ff. Polyænus, IV, 3, 11.   [2]Arrian, I, 2, 4 ff.
[3]Arrian, I, 3, 5 ff. Strabo, VIII, 301.
[4]Arrian, I, 4, 6 ff. Strabo, VII, 301.

tile hands would prove dangerous to the western borders of Macedonia. Without delay, Alexander marched
along the banks of the Erigon against Pelion, where
after several sharp encounters, he finally subdued the
Illyrians, whose king fled to the Taulantians.[1] The overwhelming defeat of these sturdy peoples roused fear
among neighboring tribes, among whom the Celts of
the upper Danube sent an embassy to swear allegiance
in the immortal words—"We will keep faith unless the
sky fall and crush us or the earth open and swallow us
or the sea rise and overwhelm us."[2]

It was now fully time for Alexander to return to
Macedonia and pursue no further for the time these
contests outside, for during this absence all sorts of
wild rumors were spreading in Greece concerning his
army and himself. It was said, and on many sides believed, that his army had been destroyed in Illyria and
that he had fallen on the field of battle.[3] Such news as
this was received with acclaim in many quarters, and
Thebes made ready at once to make an attempt to cast
off the Macedonian authority. The chiefs of the Macedonian party, Timolaos and Anemœtas, were slain, and
the Macedonian garrison in the Kadmeia besieged. As
the Thebans seemed to be leaders in the revolt the
Arcadians sent to them a contingent for the fighting
that must soon come. And now, at long last, the word
had penetrated far distant Persia that a new force had
arisen among men to threaten Persian dominion and
power. It was not news of the death of Alexander, but

---

[1] Arrian, I, 5–6.
[2] This oath was most ingeniously reconstructed by H. d'Arbois de Jubain-
ville, *Les premiers habitants de l'Europe*, II, p. 316. Yet was he mistaken in his
inference that it was an imprecation, rather than an oath of fealty, as Tarn
(*Cambridge Ancient History*, Vol. VI, p. 355, foot-note 1) has shown, to whom
I owe this reference.
[3] Arrian, I, 7, 2, 6.

rather of his prowess that came over land and sea to
Susa. The story of his exploits would not lose, but gain
in intensity as it went sweeping over the hills. His
overwhelming success in fighting far away on the banks
of the Danube, his conquests of one Greek state after
another, all this gave Persia at last a vivid impression
of impending danger. Cyrus had successfully led
Greeks into the very heart of the empire; if a greater
than Cyrus were now in command there might be serious occasion for dread of a greater attack. Artaxerxes
III was dead and Darius III must face the problem.
He discovered no new method, advanced no new policy. He knew the ancient Persian way of dealing with
the Greeks, and to it he turned. He despatched mes-
sages to various Greek states to rouse them in rebellion
against Macedonia, with promises of heavy subventions in money. In Sparta only had he any success, any
promises of co-operation. In Athens men feared Alexander too much, and refused the Persian bribes. At last
the Persian ambassadors were compelled to return
home, leaving only in the hands of Demosthenes a large
sum, said to have been 300 talents, with the request
that he use them as judgment should decide against
the Macedonians, and in the interest of the Persians.[1]
From Athens he sent weapons to the Thebans pur-
chased with Persian gold. In Elis and in Ætolia men
were ready to send help. It looked much like a serious
uprising.

Meanwhile Alexander suddenly appeared with his
army in Bœotia, having made a forced march from
Illyria; in seven days he had traversed the distance
from Pelion into Thessaly, and in seven more he stood
in front of the chief city of Bœotia. It would have been

[1]Arrian, II, 14, 6.

well worth his while to grant a quick pardon to the
Thebans, in the interest of a general peace in Greece;
but their foolish leaders could think only of how they
had once been victorious over Sparta, and were now
ready to adventure all against this youthful conqueror,
nor did they know or think what manner of man he
might be.[1] The case was indeed hopeless from the beginning, though they knew it not, but made every possible effort against fate. The Macedonian garrison was
in the Cadmeia, a stronghold on the southern side of
the city. They hastily constructed a wall outside to prevent, if possible, communication with the forces of
Alexander, but in vain. The Cadmeia was reached and
entered, the city's defenders were driven back against
the city wall and thence to the Market Place, where a
last stand was made, and then a hasty flight. In the beginning of October, 335 B. C., the city was in Alexander's hands.[2] The punishment of the city was frightful.
Alexander's men were joined by Phocians and people
of neighboring cities in Bœotia who had accounts to
settle with the Thebans. Six thousand of the inhabitants were slain at once, and 30,000 were sent away in
exile to Macedonia or sold into slavery elsewhere. The
city was laid waste, its territory divided among its
neighbors, and a Macedonian garrison re-established in
the Cadmeia.[3]

Greece was filled with terror. It was clear to the dull-
est mind that a new and resistless might had been gath-

[1]Arrian, I, 7, 4–11. Diodorus, XVII, 9, 10. Plutarch, *Alexander*, 11.
[2]Arrian, I, 8; Diodorus, XVII, 11, 12; Plutarch, *Alex.*, 11. For the time of
the taking of the city compare Arrian, I, 10, 2; Plut., *Alex.*, 13.
[3]Arrian, I, 9; Diodorus, XVII, 13, 14; XVIII, 11; Plutarch, *Alex.*, 11, 12;
Justin, XI, 3, 4. The number 30,000 is surely an exaggeration, and Tarn is
probably right in calling it "a stereotyped figure, which recurs at Tyre." But
his suggestion that the number was "perhaps 8,000, if the recorded price be
true," though quite possible, lacks any confirmation. (See *Camb. Ancient Hist.*,
vi, p. 356 and note 1.)

ering, and that the control of it lay in the hands of a man of extraordinary military capacity and of indomitable will. What could any state dare or do against him? Athens had indeed been planning to join Thebes against him, but Thebes was gone and active preparations for the field had not begun. He could safely pardon the city, but made demands that Thebans who had fled thither should be driven out, and that the men who were responsible for the conduct of the city should be handed over to him, among whom were Demosthenes, Lycurgus, and Hypereides.[1] The city assented at once to the expulsion of the Thebans, but refused to deliver into his hands her most distinguished citizens; she did consent to the exile of Charidemos, who fled to Asia and entered the service of Darius.[2]

Alexander was now absolute master in Greece and might leave its lands in the assurance that no attempt would be made to diminish his authority. He could take up the task which his father had left him and begin the destruction of the Persian empire. The need for immediate action was great. Philip had taken the first step himself, for in the year 336 B. C. he had despatched to Asia Minor an army of ten thousand men under command of Parmenion and Attalus. The war which they were making with the purpose of setting free the Greek cities of the littoral had come to a sorry pass. Memnon was now the Persian general in the coast provinces, for his brother Mentor was dead. The Persian forces were, in the beginning, too small to attack, and he had to be content to give hindrance and hold the enemy near Magnesia. When his forces were increased he took the offensive. Meanwhile Alexander recalled

---

[1]For the list see Suidas Ἀντίπατρος. Arrian (I, 10, 4) gives the same list with one exception. A somewhat different list in Plutarch, *Demos.*, 23.
[2]Arrian, I, 10, 6; Diodorus, XVII, 15.

Attalus, and later Parmenion, leaving Kalas in supreme command. He went down to defeat before Memnon and was forced to retire to the Hellespont, and make ready a hasty defense in Rhœteion and Abydos. These events had completely restored Persian supremacy in western Asia Minor, and Alexander must meet an enemy encouraged by notable victories and better prepared than for a long time before.

In the spring of the year 334 B. C. Alexander began the march toward the Hellespont. At his side, as a sort of chief of the general staff, went Parmenion, renowned as the best commander of which the Macedonian forces could boast, and destined to fill a position of the highest importance and quality in the immense undertaking.[1] The army was formidable, less indeed because of its numbers than for its quality and experience. There were 32,000 infantry and over 5,000 cavalry. Of the infantry, there were 12,000 Macedonian veterans of the wars of Philip, with 7,000 men of the Greek allies and 5,000 mercenaries, a total of 24,000 regular infantry, besides 7,000 light armed Thracians, and 1,000 bowmen and spearmen. The cavalry consisted of 18,000 heavy armed Macedonians, called the Companions, a highly honored royal guard; 1,200 Thessalian, and 600 other Greek allies, with some light armed Macedonians, Palonians, and Thracians.[2] It was a splendid force, particularly strong in cavalry, which would be especially useful in an Asiatic campaign.

The army was accompanied by a distinguished company of civilians. There was a group of philosophers and men of letters, among whom were Callisthenes of Olynthus, a philosopher and historian, nephew of Aristotle, who had personally retired to Athens. There were

[1] Curtius, VII, 1, 3; 2, 33.   [2] Arrian, I, 11, 3; Diodorus, XVII, 17.

Anaxarchus, a Democritean, and his pupil Pyrrhon, founders of the Sceptic school, and Aristobulus and Onesicritus, historians. There were geographers, scientific men, such as botanists, and most important of all was Ptolemy, son of Lagos, a man of letters who kept a *Journal*, which has been excerpted by latter writers to our great advantage.

But more valuable than any of these was a siege train, with sappers and miners, under command of Diades, who were skilled in the construction of siege-towers and rams on wheels, which were said to have been invented or improved by their leader. They secured information also about routes and camping grounds, and recorded the distances traversed.

A company of royal pages in training to be officers were with the army, and these stood guard over Alexander's sleeping quarters. It was indeed a completely organized force, fit for anything, and its like had never before been seen in Asia, or anywhere else on earth. Alexander had prepared well. The Persians could at this time not put an army into the field equal either in numbers, in equipment, or in generalship. The fleet at the service of Alexander comprised 160 war-ships,[1] most of them contributed by the Hellenic allies, and commanded by Nikanor. It was not large enough to ensure success if the Persians should show any energy or quickness of action. It would be easy for them to gather a fleet sufficiently large and mobile to harass, or perhaps altogether prevent a landing of Alexander's army on the Asiatic side of the Hellespont. If this failed, a large Persian fleet could operate along the coast of Asia Minor and raise the populations in the rear of Alexander's army. If Athens were to throw her whole sea-

[1] Arrian, I, 11, 6; 18, 4. Diodorus, XVII, 17. 2 (60 is an error for 160).

power into the expedition of Alexander the Persians
could not hope to match such a force as that would be.
But Demosthenes and his friends prevented that, and
though they had not the courage to ally the state definitely with Persia, saw to it that Athens contributed
only twenty ships, and otherwise remained neutral;[1]
and even the sending of this small contingent was opposed by Demosthenes and Hypereides.

The Persian king had issued orders long before to
have the Persian fleet made ready and assembled, but,
as so often before, delays were fatal, and no attempt
was made to prevent the crossing of the Hellespont.
While Parmenion directed this operation with great
skill and speed Alexander visited the sacred spots in
the Troad, and especially the grave of his ancestor
Achilles. Then the great eastward march began, ready
for whatever opposition the Persians might offer.
The army which Memnon commanded was soon increased by contingents raised and sent forward by the
Persian satraps west of the Taurus, especially from
Lydia, Phrygia, and Cappadocia. The body thus assembled would be strong in cavalry, perhaps equal
or even superior to this arm in Alexander's force, but
in infantry inferior alike in numbers and in quality.
Memnon was an able commander, and also prudent. He
saw that it would be folly to come to battle, and that
he must rather give way slowly, devastating the country as he went, so as to leave nothing on which the
Macedonians might live. As soon as the Persian fleet
could be made ready it should carry the war against
Greece and so compel Alexander to return. This plan,
however, was not acceptable to some of the satraps,
who did not wish to see their territories desolated in

[1] Diodorus, XVII, 22, 5.

the effort to hinder Alexander. They had confidence in their cavalry and believed that an attempt ought to be made to fight.[1] The place chosen was the river Granicus, which flows from the northern slopes of Mount Ida into the Hellespont. It was well chosen, for the river banks are rough and steep, and covered well the Persian front. On the opposite bank Alexander halted and bivouacked. Very early the next morning he crossed the river unopposed, and deployed in line of battle before the Persian cavalry could strike. A sharp fight resulted; Alexander's left wing, comprising the Thessalian squadrons, was especially distinguished. Alexander commanded the right wing in person and met the Persian attack victoriously, two of the satraps bravely fighting to the last and falling on the field. The Persian infantry was soon in hopeless flight, only the Greek mercenaries offering serious but ineffectual resistance. They were quickly surrounded and compelled to surrender. Two thousand were sent in chains to Macedonia, as punishment for having helped barbarians against Greeks. The losses of Alexander's army were extremely small, being set down as only 200 men. The booty was large, and 300 complete equipments were sent to Athens to be hung up in the Parthenon as silent witnesses to the prowess of Greek arms against mighty Persia.[2] It was indeed a most significant victory, for in it there was for the first time a demonstration of the superiority of the Greek cavalry to the Persian. It was in cavalry that the Persians had always taken their chief pride, and with this arm their victories had hitherto been

---

[1] Arrian, I, 12, 8–10; Diodorus, XVII, 18.

[2] The account of the battle in Arrian (I, 13–15) and in Plutarch (*Alex.*, 16) is little else than a dithyramb of praise of Alexander, whose figure stands out as a god or hero. In Diodorus (XVII, 19, 21, 4–5) there is a more sober account, yet in other paragraphs (20–21, 4) the same pæans of glory appear. Compare on this Konrad Lehmann (*Klio*, XI, 1911, p. 340 ff.).

Fig. 58. The Sarcophagus of Alexander from Sidon.

chiefly won. Never again could they rely with the old time confidence on their horsemen. This battle had shown the way to an overwhelming Hellenic victory, and Alexander would unhesitatingly march in it.

The victory on the Granicus bore immediate and startling results. The Persian empire began to break in pieces. Daskyleion, the chief city of the satrapy on the Hellespont, surrendered to Parmenion, and Alexander marching in person to Sardes was received as a deliverer, for the Persian commander had given up the city without a blow. Ephesus was entered, and the conqueror received with acclaim. The chief cities of Ionia and Æolis joined the procession of surrender, and only Miletus, where there was a garrison of Greek mercenaries, refused, hoping for aid from the Persian fleet, which was reported to have sailed from Phœnicia and Cyprus. Alexander anticipated them and blocked by his ships the entrance to the harbor of Miletus. When the Persian fleet arrived it could not entice the Macedonians to come out and give battle, and was compelled to stand idly by while Alexander reduced the city.[1]

While these events were in progress Memnon was not idle. He had been placed by Darius in supreme command by land and sea, and his fleet was larger than Alexander's. He chose Halicarnassus as the base for future operations, and Mauxollos turned it into a formidable fortress. Here Memnon assembled all the troops he could muster, and in the offing a large fleet which he intended to use in the spring for a descent upon Greece. These plans were likely to prove a very serious difficulty for Alexander. It was now late autumn, and the winter was in sight. It was not a propitious season for warfare by sea, and a siege by land

[1]Arrian, I, 18, 19; Diodorus, XVII, 22; Strabo, XIV, 635.

was extremely difficult, for the Persian fleet could provision the city by water. Yet Alexander must face the problem in some way. He could not move onward overland and leave Halicarnassus behind unless he could detach a considerable body of troops to hold it in a state of siege. These he could, however, ill spare. The other alternative was to besiege and then take it at last by storm. But this was likely to prove extremely difficult and might be impossible. He determined to make the attempt and encamped before the city walls.[1] In front of the walls was a broad moat, which he first filled and then over it moved the engines, which soon made the first breeches in the walls. This first assault was repulsed, but another immediately organized. It was now clear to the defenders that the end was certain unless they could destroy the engines. With this objective they determined upon a sally, but were repulsed with severe losses, one of the most serious being the death of Ephialtes,[2] the Athenian commander of the Persian troops, who had fought bravely and had even set some of the engines afire. It was upon his advice that the sally was made,[3] and he had paid the full penalty for its failure. Memnon was now convinced that it was impossible longer to hold the city. Under cover of the night he moved his troops to the island of Cos, and then set on fire the storehouses and other defenses of the city. Alexander made an unopposed entry, put out the fires, and took every possible step to relieve the suffering inhabitants. The citadel alone remained in Persian hands, and this he did not attempt to take, but left a guard of 3,000 men under command of Ptolemæos to hold it in leash.

[1] Arrian, I, 20, 1-2; Diodorus, XVII, 22, 5.
[2] Ephialtes had filled an important rôle in Athens, and was one of those whose surrender Alexander had demanded.
[3] Diodorus, XVII, 26, 1 ff.

Fig. 59. Greeks and Persians in Battle. (Sarcophagus of Alexander.)

The effect of this victory was seen at once. Practically the whole of Caria except for a very few coastwise towns surrendered. The invading army was now divided in two, of which one under Parmenion took up winter quarters in Lydia, while Alexander, at the head of the Macedonians, marched on into Lycia and Pamphylia, which surrendered without a blow. In the spring of 333 B. C. he marched through the Pisidian highlands and at Gordion, chief city of Phrygia, met Parmenion, and reunited the entire army.

The army was now considerably reinforced, for Alexander had finely prepared for this by a stroke as wise as it was kind. Many men in his forces had been newly married shortly before leaving Macedonia, and these he had furloughed at the beginning of winter and sent home under charge of Ptolemy, son of Seleucus, Cœnus, son-in-law to Parmenion, and Meleager, all married men. These now returned in fine spirits and very grateful for their king's consideration, bringing with them many recruits, as did also Cleander, who had been sent to seek men in the Peloponnesus for the great endeavor. These now found the great commander at Gordion fresh from complete winter victories in Lycia and Pamphylia, with a record of more than thirty towns reduced to subjection.

In all these conquered towns Alexander had made careful provision for the conduct of control or even of government. In most cases he left a few Macedonians, commonly men who were invalided or disabled and so entitled to the consideration of some easier task than campaigning, but were quite able to act as a nucleus and rally about them a small loyal company and by their united efforts make the place safe against Persian uprising. Whenever it seemed necessary a larger garrison was left; and there are few evidences of the king's prudence and statesmanship greater than these elementary provisions for the governing and control of all that was won piece-meal from Persia.

In Phaselis Alexander had given the end of the winter for the rest and refreshment of weary men. The choice was happy. Before it lay the blue waters of the Mediterranean and on the other sides it was protected by mountains from the cold winds of west, north, and northeast. There he gave himself with the same zest to feasts and games as he had to hard work, and it is even told that he once headed a procession through the streets and decorated the statue of the poet Theodectes,[1] recognizing thereby probably a common connection with their great friend Aristotle.

A far less happy association with these winter quarters was the discovery of the treachery of the Lyncestrian prince Alexander, who was discovered in an intrigue with the Persian king to murder the Macedonian king. He had years before been implicated in a plot to kill King Philip, but had convinced Alexander of his loyalty and had been entrusted with high command. He was now apprehended, but though the evidence was strong against him Alexander refused to yield to the advice of his officers and put him to death. He was still alive four years later in Afghanistan, still a prisoner, and there the officers, having once more interrogated him and satisfied themselves of his guilt, ran him through with their spears.[2]

The whole winter plan of war, of rest, and of furloughs had given new demonstration of the genius of this extraordinary man, commander and statesman. He

[1]Plutarch, *Alexander*, 17.
[2]Arrian, I, 25. Justin, XI, 2, 1 f.; XII, 14, 1. Curtius, VII, 1, 8 f. Diodorus, XVII, 80, 2.

FIG. 60. Battle with the Persians. (Sarcophagus of Alexander.)

knew how to exact of his men the enduring of hardships almost incredible, but equally well did he know
the gentler arts of consideration, as we have seen, and
quite as well how to turn to use the gifts of men who
might not fight because of physical disability, but were
well able to take up the burden of establishing his rule
over newly conquered cities. The success thus far
achieved was splendid enough to have filled Greece
with pride and hope. But discordant opinions were not
wanting. The ability of Memnon was well enough
known in Greece to give Alexander's opponents excuse
for saying that the successes achieved by Alexander
had been allowed by Memnon as part of a greater
strategy by which he was to be enticed farther afield
in the unknown wildernesses of Asia to his ultimate
destruction. There was no other man in all Persia so
likely to give Alexander serious trouble, or perhaps
even to blast all his hopes, and much now depended
upon his next move. As an offset to these oppositions
in Athens Alexander had shown wisdom in his treatment of the Greek cities which he had reconquered in
Asia Minor. To them all he restored at once their freedom and their old laws, and so knit them to him in a
great loyalty. They recognized the gain made by the
exchange of the Persian king for him and would make
known in Athens and in all the motherland their sense
of obligation and the expression of hope for the future
of the Greek king.[1]

The pretty story of Alexander's solution of the Gordion knot[2] finds its scene and time in these spring days
of preparation for a greater campaign. Whatever it

---

[1] Arrian, I, 18, 2; see also II, 1, 4; 2, 2. Diodorus, XVII, 24, 1.
[2] Arrian, II, 3, 1 ff. Plutarch, *Alexander*, 18. Curtius, III, 1, 14 ff. Justin, XI, 7, 15 f.

was that Alexander did he seems to have persuaded the populace that he had met the demand of King Midas, and so was inheritor of the promise that whoever should loosen the cord which wound round the yoke-pin and bound the yoke to the pole was to be the ruler of all Asia. This conviction of theirs, perhaps enforced by the belief that he was more than human, went in advance of him, weakening his enemies, heartening his friends, and contributing in no small degree to his success.

While he halted at Gordion, very probably still with some hesitation as to his next move, the Persians were not idle. They were possessed of a commander in the field of energy and of strategic skill in the person of Memnon. It was his plan to stay the advance of Alexander, not by direct opposition in the field, but by indirect means, which if successful would be still more efficacious. He willed to attack in the rear by carrying the campaign into Macedonia, and so force Alexander to return home. To this end the Persian king had placed him in sole and unlimited command in the Ægean, with a fleet formidable in itself, and far surpassing aught that Alexander had ever had at his disposal. Moving northward from his base at Halicarnassus, Memnon appeared at Chios and gained possession of the island by the treachery of Apollonides, and there re-established the oligarchy. He had made a good beginning. From Chios he sailed to Lesbos, all of whose cities but Mitylene surrendered at once. This he was compelled to besiege, which he began with intense vigor. He built a double stockade on the land side from sea to sea, and invested with five military stations. On the sea side the fleet cut off all outside help, and the end was certain. The news of it spread over all Greece with swiftness

worthy of its importance. Euboea was in alarm lest it
be attacked next. Embassies came from some of the
Cyclades proposing alliance with the new conqueror.
There were rumors that Sparta would be willing to welcome the Persians, and Persian money was again entering Greece and might well produce overturns in
some of its cities. In Greece this was by no means impossible, for in general it was the oligarchic parties that
were pro-Macedonian, while in Asia Minor the demo-
cratic were Alexander's partisans, a condition directly
the reverse. Just when it might have seemed probable
that Memnon would win a success sufficiently serious
to injure Alexander he fell ill of a fever before Mitylene
and died, leaving the temporary command to his
nephew Pharnabazus, who had as his assistant Autophradatex, probably in immediate command of the
fleet. The city finally surrendered under certain definite
conditions, that it should restore the banished to citizenship, destroy the slabs on which its treaty with
Alexander was inscribed, and be confirmed in the status
it formally enjoyed under the peace of Antalcidas
(387 B. C.).[1] This latter condition, immensely important for the city, was violated at once by the Persians,
who placed a garrison within it, named Diogenes as
tyrant, and exacted a tribute from its citizens. Pharnabazus had begun well in tactics, but badly in statesmanship. He seemed determined to pursue with vigor
the plans which Memnon had formed. He sent Datames
with ten ships to reconnoitre among the Cyclades, and
himself with Autophradatex sailed for Tenedos, which
fell quickly into his hands. He was now only about
twelve miles from the Hellespont, toward which he was
evidently moving with the purpose of cutting Alexan-

[1] Diodorus, XVII, 29 f., 31, 3. Curtius, III, 2, 1.

der's communications. A move such as this, and with a sufficient fleet, if made a year earlier might have kept Alexander out of Asia.

Darius now held a council of war to determine what steps should be taken to meet the menace of Alexander. The only man who had any wise plan was dead in the person of Memnon, and whatever advice the Greeks could have given to the Persian king was naturally enough rejected in favor of the judgment of his own people. The decision taken was to assume personal command in the field after making a levy *en masse* of the kingdom. To this end he confirmed Pharnabazus in command of the west, but hopelessly weakened his position by ordering his Greek mercenaries sent to the army now formed to meet Alexander in the field.

Alexander was well convinced before he learned of Memnon's death that his impulsive act in disbanding his fleet had been very unwise. He now took quick and decisive steps to provide a new sea force. His first move was to send Hegelochus and Amphoterus to the Hellespont to prepare a provisional fleet, even by pressing trading vessels into service and by hastily transforming them into war vessels. It was a dangerous move politically, for it was a breach of the treaty which guaranteed the free passage of the Hellespont, and Athens soon protested and was almost ready to break with the king. To Antipater, regent in Macedonia, Alexander sent funds to recruit a navy, and he responded with the appointment of Proteas to collect ships in Eubœa and the Peloponnesus to protect the Greek coast against the threatened Persian attack.[1]

His army completely reorganized, Alexander now took the field, when spring was sufficiently advanced,

---

[1]Arrian, II, 1 f.; compare III, 2, 3 ff. Curtius, III, 1, 19 ff.

and moved against Ancyra (Angora), fully eighty miles
away and over a rough country. On this march, or at its
end, he learned of the death of Memnon, and took quick
resolve to make immediate use of the opportunity.
He must have had some reason for believing that Persia had no other commander whom he needed to fear.
What he had seen or experienced of others would surely
confirm such a conviction. He had in one brief year
conquered a tract of territory 250 miles square, about
double the extent of the Greek mainland. He was free
from Memnon. He would hesitate no longer. He would
turn his back upon Europe and plunge on into the Asiatic empire which he saw crumbling before him. At
Ancyra he received the submission of the Paphlagonians, who were then placed under command of the satraps of the Hellespontine Phrygia. From Ancyra his
march led directly into Cappadocia and on toward Cilicia.[1] He was now master of the whole of Asia Minor
west of the Taurus, and that without serious Persian
opposition. He might now elect to await on the defensive whatever move the enemy might make, or force
the pass and take the offensive. It was only in the expression of a perfectly natural temper of his own that
he determined to go forward, yet was this resolve not
to be fulfilled without danger. He must now pass the
Taurus, whose chief pass was known as the Cilician
Gates, the modern Gulek Boghaz, a narrow defile 3,600
feet above the sea, and practically inexpugnable if held
by even a small force of determined men. Xenophon
indeed had expressed the opinion that the defile was
beyond human ability to take. When Cyrus the
Younger confronted it he expected to be unable to

[1]Arrian, II, 4, 2 ff., ed. A. G. Roos, p. 70 (Teubner). See also Appian, Mith-
ridateios, 8, ed. Mendelssohn, p. 447 (Teubner).

force it, and made preparations to turn it by transporting a force of troops by sea to the rear of the pass. For
such a move Alexander was unprepared either with
ships or with a sufficient force of men. The Persians
were able, did they but know it, to hold the pass and
keep Alexander west of it until the great army of defense was ready to confront him. But Arsames, satrap
of Cilicia, Darius' chief officer at the place, made no
preparations for defense, and had only a small force to
make a nominal police protection. Why was this madness possible? Had Darius not taken thought to give
special orders?—or was it not even known that Alexander had already advanced far enough to menace the
safety of this important means of defense?

Alexander left Parmenion in camp with the heavy
troops, and taking a small force of light and mobile
character attacked in the night and drove the defenders
in a rout before him. The next day the entire army filed
into Cilicia.[1] It was a fateful day in the history of Persia, and its consequences would show quickly. The
great plain of Cilicia lay like an open page before the
Greeks, and in the distance the city of Tarsus, and the
sea—a sight well fitted to charm their eager eyes. As
Alexander descended the mountain ridges he had news
that Arsames, knowing he must give up the city, had
planned to plunder it of anything of value and destroy
it, to deprive the conquering enemy of its value and
comfort. Alexander by a forced march with cavalry
and light armed infantry anticipated the design, took
the city, and put Arsames to flight.

At Tarsus the tremendous exertions, the anxieties
and cares, the doubts and difficulties of this swift campaign, bore fruit in a collapse of Alexander in a dan-

[1]Arrian, II, 4, 5. The account in Curtius, III, 4, 3 ff., is quite wrong.

gerous illness. Aristobulus ascribes it to overwork,
others to bathing, when overheated, in the chill waters
of the river Cydnus. Whatever the immediate cause,
the preparations for it are evident enough in the stren-
uous labors that preceded. There was a severe chill, and
then high fever. The physicians were alarmed, all
thought his life was about to end save one, Philip, the
doctor who had known and treated him from his boy-
hood. It was a difficult position for a medical practi-
tioner to treat a king in those days. His own life was
also in jeopardy. Later when Hephæstion died, Alexander is said to have accused his physician of mal-
practice and caused his death. The illness of Alexander
was of greatest moment not only to his army, but to
the Persian empire, whose very existence hung also on
this one life. Philip won and Alexander recovered.[1]

From Tarsus Alexander despatched Parmenion
southward with a force of Greek auxiliaries and Thracians to capture the Syrian Gates, the important pass
through the Amanus mountains, while he personally
turned westward to clear the Cilician highlands of any
possible disturbance in the rear as he should advance.
The satrapy of Cilicia was now his for any disposal he
might wish, and was given to Balakros to pacify completely and then to rule.[2]

Ever since Alexander had made Gordion his rendezvous there had been anxious consultations in Persia,
for it was even there clearly enough seen that Alexander was a dangerous enemy. Darius needed advice and
listened to much. His best adviser was a soldier of fortune, Charidemus by name, born in Oreus in Eubœa,
who had had more experience of varied wars than any

[1]Arrian, III, 4, 7 ff. Plutarch, *Alexander*, 19. Curtius, III, 5 f. Justin, XI, 8.
Diodorus, XVII, 31, 4 ff. Valerius Max., III, 8, est. 6.
[2]Arrian, II, 12, 2. Diodorus, XVIII, 22, 1.

other there present might boast. He had fought Athens,
and fought for her; he had served Thracians and Persian satraps; and now, a fugitive from his own people,
was offering professional advice based on thirty years'
or more experience. It was his advice that the emperor
should not take the field in person, and stake on one
cast his empire. An army of 100,000 was enough to
harass and hinder the advance of Alexander, retreating
before him, and leading him ever further from his national base, and wearing him down with continuous
losses. It was sound advice on principles similar to, if
not wholly the same as, those of the much lamented
Memnon. The king was at first disposed to accept it,
but his blind courtiers opposed, suspecting that Charidemus was laying plans to make himself commander
of such a force, which may indeed have been in his
mind. They accused him of treachery, and were particularly incensed at his insinuations that the Persians
were no match for the Macedonians. Charidemus lost
his temper and launched into a fury against Persian
cowardice, which sealed his doom. Led forth to death
he shouted: "The king will rue this. My revenge is at
hand. It is the overthrow of the empire."[1]

In vain Darius sought to replace Memnon with a
commander fit to take the lead, and he must soon have
lamented the madness of putting Charidemus to death,
for he might have been very useful. There was now
nothing for it but to organize his forces, and assume
command in person at Babylon. It was a body far
larger[2] than Alexander had brought so far, but it had

[1]Diodorus, XVII, 30. Curtius, III, 2, 10.

[2]It is hopeless to determine how large was this force, for the authorities do
not agree, and when they approximate unity of testimony are still surely reporting exaggerations. Arrian makes the forces at Issus 600,000 (Exp. Alex.,
II, 8), Diodorus, 500,000 (XVII, 31, 2). Curtius says the foot was 250,000
and the horse 61,200, making a tota of 311,200 (Hist. Alexand., III, 24), but
adds that the troops were counted in the same rough manner as was the
custom of Xerxes. This is enough to end confidence in his figures.

no such discipline or organization, nor was it composed
of veterans knit in bonds of common suffering and experience. When the force was ready Darius marched up
the valley of the Euphrates, and took up a strong position at Sochi, in a large open plain near the modern
lake of Antioch. There he paused, expecting an attack.
But this was at the very time that Alexander lay ill at
Tarsus, or was busily engaged in reducing Cilicia. Darius became impatient and listened very unwisely to
courtiers who were now quite confident that Alexander
would never leave Cilicia, and must there be sought out
and trampled under foot by this resistless host. Confidence waxed mightily. That which was felt there was
felt also in Greece, and Demosthenes was predicting at
Athens that the downfall of Alexander was at hand.[1]
There was, however, one sane adviser in the company
of Darius, Amyntas, a Macedonian noble, who had fled
from his people for some reason to us unknown. He
knew his own people and assured the king that Alexander was certain to face the issue, and that the Persians should remain where they now had a plain fit for
cavalry maneuvers, and better suited therefore for the
battle that must come. Unwise counsels prevailed. Darius moved northward to pass the Amanus. Alexander
was now also on the move southward, having chosen
to pass by the Syrian Gates, so called, the little mountain pass from Cilicia into northern Syria. Either he
did not know that there was another pass farther northward which led from Cilicia into the valley of the Euphrates, or he was guilty of a serious military lapse not
to have guarded it. By this pass Darius crossed the
range, while Alexander passed by the other, and as he
descended to the plain of Issus must have been aston-

---

[1] Æschines (*Against Ctesiphon*, § 164) knew how later to taunt him for this.

ished to find that he was in the rear of Alexander, for
he came upon the Macedonian hospitals. Darius and
Alexander had missed each other by less than a day,
for when Darius came to Issus, Alexander was at Myri-
andrus, scarcely twenty-five miles away.

When Alexander heard what had taken place he
summoned his chief officers and reviewed the situation
before him. He kept back nothing of the size of the enemy forces, but pointed out how ill-placed they were
in that narrow position to utilize this advantage, while
it was particularly suited to Macedonian tactics. He
reminded them that these were Persians whom they
had met and defeated at Granicus. He recalled the exploit of Xenophon and his ten thousand, who had put
Persians to rout near the walls of Babylon itself. It was
a splendid speech, and enthusiasm captured them all,
eager to be led at once against such a foe.

The night came on, and Alexander having sent a
small force in advance to hold the Syrian Gates, coun-
ter-marched the eight miles in the darkness, and rested
the remainder of the night in his rocky fastnesses, after
throwing out his outposts. In the early dawn he
marched in column through the defile toward the plain,
which stretched before him about twenty miles to Issus.
On the west it was bounded by the sea coast, on the
east by more or less rugged foothills. Small mountain
streams crossed it at intervals, and a few miles south
of Issus a considerable river, the Pinarus, swept in a
southwesterly direction. At no place is the plain wider
than a mile and a half, nor could a worse position have
been chanced upon by Darius than this. Fortune, fickle
dame, was on the Macedonian side.

From the defile Alexander marched his men, as was
his custom, in column formation upon the battle-field.

It gave men confidence to move solidly, compactly forward, as upon parade. As the plain became wider he began to deploy so as to form a battle line completely across the plain from mountain to sea, so to prevent any danger of being flanked by the superior numbers of the Persians. The infantry came forward, the phalanx sixteen deep at the centre, while the cavalry rode out to the wings. Next to them on the side toward the mountain came Nicanor with the *agéma,* or picked squad, and other hytaspists, then the brigades of Cœnus and Perdiccas, while on the left were the allies, the Cretan bowmen and the Thracian troops of Sitalcas. Here Parmenion had orders to keep his left close to the sea, that he might not be outflanked.

Darius lay south of Issus and just north of the river Pinarus, where having heard that Alexander had passed southward through the Syrian Gates, had made ready to advance and seize the pass in his rear. He was too late, for Alexander had anticipated him and returned, and was even now advancing to give or accept battle. He now threw out a body of horse and light infantry across the river as a curtain behind which he could form a line of battle. They were to return on call and retire left and right behind the flanks. He was well intrenched for defensive fighting, for the river was a ditch in front, and its high northern bank his wall. In his centre, opposite the now visible Greek phalanx, he placed his best troops, his Greek mercenaries; on their wings were his best native troops, the Cardaces. His left wing stretched along the hills to menace Alexander's right and threaten to flank it. On his own right next the sea, where alone there was any opportunity for maneuver, he placed the main body of cavalry. His worst difficulty was in the very greatness of his numbers, which could not possibly find place for any real use. His men had been assured that they were pursuing a fleeing enemy, yet here before their eyes was this very enemy advancing boldly to attack. This would not increase their courage or their confidence. Darius having made his dispositions, took his own station in the centre and behind the Greek mercenaries to await the onset.

Alexander had now the chance to survey the situation, and seeing the Persian cavalry in force opposite Parmenion on his left wing, judged that there was not sufficient force there to meet its attack. He therefore sent his Thessalian cavalry quickly behind the phalanx and placed it in support of the left. Before the battle began he despatched a body of light troops to dislodge a force which lay along the foothills on his right and was in so far a menace to his right wing. This was immediately successful, and the enemy scattered up the hillside.

In quiet the two armies faced each other, each waiting the first move. When all was ready Alexander rode down the line, giving his last exhortations to each body in words appropriate to its memories of history or experience. It was finely done, well fitted to stir pulses already tense to a new and greater effort. He gave the word and the line advanced with cheers. The river had to be crossed, but it was everywhere fordable. The phalanx advanced to music, as though upon parade, until at a preconcerted signal they dashed into the double-quick and made for the river. Alexander himself in immediate command of the companion cavalry, 1,200 strong, drove as a compact force into the Persian left which yielded ground at once. The Persian centre was still holding the assault of the Greek phalanx, but the

situation now swiftly changed, for as the Persian left
wing gave way Alexander was soon upon the flank of
the Greek mercenaries on whom Darius had chiefly
relied. The fighting was now fierce and still indecisive.
The onrush of Alexander had been so swift that the
men behind were not able to keep their alignment, and
the phalanx was in some danger from the sheer weight
opposed to it. The fighting of its way up the river bank
had been difficult, and it was Greeks, albeit mercenaries, against whom it had to throw its force. They
stood fast, and their superior numbers gave them great
advantage. At this anxious moment Alexander was
ready. He had driven the left of Darius back from the
river, and now found himself on the flank of the Greek
mercenaries, still holding his own phalanx. He struck
a sudden and tremendous blow, and the flank broke in
confusion, the phalanx regained its alignment and attacked the front with renewed intensity, and thenceforward held its own. The danger was averted. The turning point had come.

While these events were in progress the Persian cavalry had crossed the river and fallen upon the Thessalians under Parmenion. So far superior in numbers
were they that they threatened to sweep the Macedonians from the field by sheer avalanche-like impetuosity.
Parmenion was getting decidedly the worst of it,
through no fault of his own or of his men, and his position was only saved by the attack which Alexander had
made on the Persian left and on the strategic flank of
the mercenaries. This put the Persian cavalry in a serious position, and it had to give ground quickly and re-
cross the stream, leaving Parmenion victor almost by
a hair.

Alexander was then ready to follow up his advantage

to the utmost, as was his custom. He aimed straight for Darius in person. It was the manner of the Persian kings to sit in splendid prominence in the rear of the centre, and there was Darius in a splendid chariot drawn by four horses abreast, and surrounded by his whole military family under the immediate command of his brother Oxathres. For this royal group Alexander rode at the head of his Companions. Darius was quickly surrounded by the wounded and the dead that fell before the Macedonians, and with great difficulty was extricated by his brother, placed upon a lighter chariot with fresh horses, and left to flee to the rear. He was none too soon in flight, for he would certainly have been dead or captured. Descending from this temporary refuge he took to horse, and left to their fate not only the already defeated army, but even his mother, wife, daughters, and little son. With these Alexander collected also from the king's chariot his Median mantle, bow and shield, all the luxurious furnishings of his courtly splendor, robes, fabrics, utensils, armor, and a treasure estimated at 3,000 talents. He made sure of the field and all that it contained before commencing a pursuit, and by that time the November evening was turning into night, and a distant pursuit was impossible.

The losses on the two sides were disproportionate. The Persian loss was heavy, but is surely exaggerated when estimated at 100,000, including 10,000 of the cavalry. The Macedonian loss may be more readily learned. Curtius gives it as 182 killed, and Justin makes it 280. The estimates of the number of wounded vary greatly. If the average of ten to one killed be assumed, and the figure of Justin accepted for the number of the dead, the total loss would come out at less than 4,000. The loss

was serious enough for the king, who was so far from
his Macedonian homeland, but it was nevertheless a
small outlay for a victory so decisive. It had shut off
Persia into the interior of Asia beyond the mountains,
given a new glory to the Greek name, filled all Persia
with doubt or even with dread, confounded the de-
tractors in Athens and elsewhere in Greece, and produced a new world situation to astonish the minds and
blind the eyes of men. Few battles in history have produced an effect so great, perhaps none ever a greater.

Alexander on the next day rewarded handsomely by
word and deed all who had made distinguished contribution to the brilliant success, spoke words of comfort or cheer to the dying or the wounded, and conducted a great military funeral to pay the last honors
to the dead. The family of Darius were received with
great respect and treated with every dignity possible
under the circumstances. Whether this was the young
victor's natural mood, or a wise decision taken contrary to natural temper we can scarcely know, but
whatever the motive it was clearly sound policy.

The flight of Darius on relays of fresh horses continued until he had gone on through the Amanic Gates,
and across the field of Sochi, where he ought to have
awaited battle in the first instance, and thence on until
he had crossed the Euphrates at or near Thapsacus.
His army was hopelessly broken and scattered, for only
a small force of Greek mercenaries joined him by the
Euphrates. Some of his army had made off for inner
Persia, and others for the Cilician mountains. Yet
others wandered in small groups aimlessly seeking
refuge, only to be cut down by Macedonian viceroys in
various parts of Asia Minor. Eight thousand Greek
mercenaries, under command of Amyntas, alone pre-

served order and discipline, making for Tripolis, the port at which they landed when they entered the country. There they found still in the harbor the ships on which they had arrived, and taking so many as were necessary, burned the rest and sailed away as soldiers of fortune to Cyprus, and later to Egypt, where they ultimately perished at the hands of Egyptian troops.

The first signs of approaching winter saved Darius from serious or continued pursuit, and he was left, no longer a hero but a broken and defeated man, to go home and gather whatever he might of influence or of power that the sad times had left to him. The battle of Issus, as it has been commonly called, had begun the destruction of his empire, and he needed to take thought for the morrow.[1] To that Darius purposed to devote his energy. He could not count his empire lost on the issue of this one battle, great and cruelly disturbing though it was. He had been defeated, there could be no dispute about that. But he had fought under circumstances highly unfavorable. He had been able to use effectively only a small part of his army in that restricted valley. His preponderance in numbers, however great it may have been, was not an advantage under the circumstances, but a severe and dangerous handicap. He must redeem the past under other conditions.[2] There would be an opportunity, or he must make it. Alexander had achieved much, but it was after all only on the outermost fringe of the empire. There were still the vast flat plains of the Tigris and

---

[1] The chief source for the battle of Issus is Arrian, II, 8–11, with which is to be compared the report of Callisthenes in Polybius, XII, 17 ff. Besides these there are points of value in Plutarch, *Alexander*, 20, and especially in Diodorus, XVII, 33 ff. The most interesting and lively account is in Curtius, III, 9 ff. (on which compare Kaerst. *Forsch. zur Geschichte Alex.*, 44 ff.). By far the best modern discussion in Dodge, *Alexander*, xxiii, pp. 295–320. A lesser sketch in Wheeler, *Alexander*, p. 280 ff.

[2] Diodorus, XVII, 39, 3, 4.

Euphrates to be crossed by the Macedonian. On one of
these there would be space for the exercise of those
arms in which the Persian king might easily be the
stronger. There cavalry might sweep round the dimin-
ished forces of the Greeks, while chariots flung themselves upon the front line. If that should fail there were
mountain passes to be traversed familiar to Persians,
strange to Greeks, where they might be harassed at
every turn and slaughtered in gloomy defiles. Darius
had not yet shot his bolt. Yet if he considered the facts
as they really were he might well have felt that Asia
Minor was lost, and that was a splendid province in the
empire which his fathers had won and successfully defended. On the other hand, Alexander had not completed its conquest. He controlled the great central up-
land west of Cappadocia, and the coast-lands of the
south and west with the old roads into Cilicia. There
still remained much land to be possessed, for the north
had been scarcely touched at all. Southern Cappadocia
still remained more or less Persian, and Pisidia was
independent. Uprisings here or there were not merely
possible but even probable, as the future would show.

These conditions might give concern to Alexander,
for he had not troops enough to leave considerable
bodies of men to hold in complete subjection all that
the sword had conquered, and continue further the conquest of the intractable. Nor could he at once give anything like a complete civil administration to that which
had been won. He had to content himself with a proclamation of democracy, which might be hoped to bring
over to his side every city which for one cause or another, for heavy taxes or severe tyrannical suffering,
was weary of Persian rule. This worked well in a number of instances. At Zelea the citizens expelled their

Persian tyrant; Erythræ destroyed the citadel fort and sent away its mercenary garrison by a bribe. Other cities opened their gates gladly to the Macedonians and secured at once the abolition of the former tribute payments.

That so much of conquest and administration was secured in a country with few roads over rough mountain ridges is one of the marvels of history and a tribute extraordinary to the genius of Alexander, and to the enthusiasm which his personality evoked. He was the real Master of Asia Minor, even though his rule was incomplete.

The victory of Alexander at Issus did not point directly and immediately to an invasion of Mesopotamia, and there for the present Darius was personally safe, and able to survey the situation in a certain degree of calmness and decide on what his next move should be. Alexander's plan of campaign developed at once. He determined before venturing further inland to make sure of the coastline about the Mediterranean Sea. He knew and fully appreciated the danger of the Persian navy, which still had a fleet in being in the Ægean Sea. It might well harass the Greek cities of the Asian littoral, or descend upon the Greek coasts, and so expose him to the contemptuous fling that he was a king who could not protect his homeland, while he wasted its substance in schemes of distant conquest. His only security for the future lay in cutting Persian gold and intrigue and power completely off from Greece, so that Persia's only contact with the Greeks should be through territory absolutely controlled by him, and under his immediate personal rule.

This decision meant the conquest of Phœnicia, Syria, Palestine, Idumea, and Egypt, and the sweeping of

Persian ships entirely from the sea. An undertaking so
great that it would in itself have staggered the imagination of any man of even slightly less capacity. Alexander began it at once and evidently without a qualm
of hesitation.

The first move ordered was the despatching of Parmenion, with the Thessalian cavalry and other troops,
to occupy Damascus, 250 miles away to the south
around and behind the range of the Anti-Lebanon.
Thither Darius had sent heavy treasures and much
camp material before marching from Sochi on the ill-
fated move toward Issus. Damascus fell at once, and
all its great possessions became the booty of the new
conqueror. Over the new province of Cœle-Syria
Menon was appointed satrap, and Parmenion was free
to rejoin his already moving chief.[1]

While the splendid city on the edge of the desert was
occupying Parmenion, Alexander advanced southward
near the coast to Marathus in Phœnicia, and without
opposition. Darius was now at Babylon, had had time
to draw a sober breath and quietly to consider the situation. He determined now to try diplomacy before war
should actively begin directly in his front. His first
care quite naturally was for the members of his family,
still in the hands of the victor at Issus. He sent to Alexander an embassy and a letter entreating the restoration of his mother, wife, and children, and proposing
friendship and alliance. He recalled the ancient amity
between Persia and Macedonia, and himself a king
asked this boon of a king. It was a dignified request
made in fitting and stately manner. Alexander instead
of a mere curt verbal reply sent in answer an embassy
of equal rank bearing a letter so haughty that even to

[1]Arrian, II, 13, 7. Curtius, IV, 8, 11.

our day its bitter, uncompromising tone remains. There is no sound reason to doubt that it has been preserved for us substantially as it reached the hands of the Persian king.[1] Here it is as it was despatched and received.

"Your forefathers came into Macedonia and into the rest of Greece and did us harm, without any previous injury from us. Now I, having been appointed leader of the Greeks and wishing to punish the Persians, have crossed into Asia, after you had made a beginning. For you sent aid to the Perinthians, who were dealing unjustly with my father, and Ochus sent an army into Thrace, which was under our rule. My father was killed by conspirators whom you instigated, as you have boasted to everybody in your letters; and after you had slain Arses with the help of Bagoas, and wickedly and in defiance of all Persian law seized the throne and wronged your subjects, you send letters about me to the Greeks, urging them to make war upon me, and send money to the Lacedæmonians and to other of the Greeks, though none of them accepted it except the Lacedæmonians. Then as you had corrupted my friends and were seeking to destroy the peace which I had secured for the Greeks, I marched against you, you who had begun hostilities. Now that I have conquered in battle, first your generals and satraps, and now you and your power, and am in possession of your country, by gift of the gods, I am giving protection to those of your men who escaped from battle and have taken refuge with me, and they of their own accord stay with me and have joined my army. As therefore I am lord of all Asia, come to me; but if you are afraid you may be harshly treated if you come, send some of your friends to receive pledges. Come to me, then, and ask for your

[1] Arrian, II, 14, 4 f.

mother and your wife and your children, and whatever
else you will, and you shall receive. Whatsoever is just
shall be yours. And for the future, whenever you send,
send to me as King of Asia, and do not address me on
an equality, but speak to me as lord of all your possessions, if you have need of aught. If not I shall conduct
myself toward you as an evil doer. But if you dispute
my right to the kingdom, stay and fight on for it; but
do not flee, for I shall march against you, wherever you
may be."

While he yet halted at Marathus Alexander received
the welcome news of the brilliant success of Parmenion
at Damascus, whether before or after the stinging letter was sent to Darius we know not, but it was news
not likely to make Alexander more easy to approach on
any terms. These matters despatched, the victorious
army moved southward along the Phœnician coast. The
fame of Alexander had preceded his army and the important cities of Aradus, Byblus, and Sidon surrendered on his approach. So fell into his hands cities of
ancient repute long famous as centres of the ancient
Phœnician civilization. They had much cause to have
hated many foreign conquerors from the days of the
Egyptian Thotmes III (1500 B. C.) to these of Darius,
and may well have welcomed a Greek. And now before
him lay the noblest city of all these that the ancient
Phœnicians had made famous, for there was Tyre, on
its tiny island and stretching about its harbor on the
mainland, the most glorious harbor the world had yet
known when the range of its influence is considered.
At first thought the city expressed a willingness to surrender,[1] but when Alexander demanded permission to
enter within the walls, and at the temple of the city
god Melkart offer worship he was refused. He had iden-

[1]Arrian, II, 15, 6. Curtius, IV, 2, 2.

tified Melkart with Herakles (Hercules), and this god he claimed as his ancestor. On their side the citizens declined his plea on the ground that it was determined to admit neither Macedonian nor Persian but maintain neutrality.[1] It was a critical resolve, but in every way worthy of the ancient tradition of the city now to trust to its defenses and fight for its freedom. The city had every just claim to a splendid pride in its past. It had defied the Assyrians in their day, and against them sustained long and successful sieges (701–697 B. C. Sennacherib and 671–662 Esarhaddon) and even Nebuchadrezzar after thirteen years (585–573 B. C.) had not been able to reduce it to subjection. With such a history Tyre had just right to trust to the arbitrament of war and defy this new conqueror. Alexander, like the kings who had preceded, began a siege, but with far different result from that which vexed his predecessors. What they could not do after years of effort he brought to a successful conclusion in seven months, in August, 332 B. C.[2] Yet had it been no easy task, and the time occupied must have seemed long and arduous to a man who had experienced so many quick successes. He was, however, no less able to move slowly and surely. The seven months were largely consumed in reaching the city, for its inhabitants had forsaken their old town on the mainland and withdrawn to the new city on an island separated from the mainland by half a mile partly swamp, but with water eighteen feet deep near the new walls. There in a space only a little over two miles in circuit, without either water or vegetation, a hardy and determined people had shut themselves in

[1]Arrian, II, 16, 7.
[2]Arrian, II, 18 ff. Diodorus, XVII, 40 ff. Plutarch, *Alexander*, 25. Curtius, IV, 2 ff. Compare Glück *de Tyro ab Alexandro magno oppugnata*, 1886. Kaerst, *Forsch. z. Gesch. Alex.*, 49. Excellent account in Dodge, *Alexander*, 328 f.

behind strong walls. Alexander had no available ships, and determined to build a mole from the mainland to the city walls. The Lebanon forests supplied timber to be driven as piles, the old city offered its houses as a stone quarry to fill in between the piles, and the rushes from the swamps provided binding material. The work, which was easy in the shallow swamps, became more and more difficult as the depth of water increased and the wall and its defenders were brought nearer. They used every resource to hinder the work and to daunt the enterprise, but only to increase the determination of a masterful man. The work went on stubbornly in spite of every resourceful move of the defense. As new troubles appeared frequently Alexander saw more and more the need of ships, and leaving the work on the mole to his engineers and men went to Sidon to collect triremes. In this his success was immediate. The kings of Aradus and Byblus deserted the Persian navy and placed all their ships at his service. To these were added the ship of state and nine others from Rhodes, three from Soli and Mallus, towns in Cilicia, ten from Lycia, and no less than 120 from Cyprus, with nearly 80 from Sidon. He now had a magnificent fleet of 220 war-ships, exceeding in number all that Tyre could muster, and was able to blockade the sea ports while he attacked on the land side over the mole. While the fleet was assembling and refitting at Sidon Alexander in person with a small mobile force made a ten days' campaign against the mountain tribes of the Anti-Lebanon who had been disturbing the peace of the Orontes valley.[1] Swift and certain was their fate, and Alexander was free to return to the main task. On his reappearance he found a reinforcement of 4,000 Greek mercenaries

[1]Plutarch, *Alexander*, 24.

under Cleander, and the fleet nearly ready. When Alexander sailed from Sidon for Tyre an entirely new era in warfare began for him. He was now relatively as strong at sea as on land, and must prove his ability to direct movements on land and water in a unified movement. The day of fierce reckoning with Tyre had come. The little city had two harbors, that on the north called Sidonian, on the south Egyptian. The fleet was divided between the two and common action was impossible. When the wall had been breached from the mole, and a portion of the Tyrian fleet which had made a sally was sunk the end had come. Many of the inhabitants had fled to seek refuge in Carthage. The savagery which followed is the measure of Alexander's weariness and rage at the cost and the length of the siege. To the slave dealer passed sad thousands. Arrian says 13,000, and Diodorus 30,000. Over 8,000 of the defenders gave their lives, and 2,000 more were hanged or gibbeted after the city fell.

If Issus had given pause to the world, the fate of Tyre was certain to add to it. Here was indeed a new force in the person of this man, and kings, princes, common folk as well, would listen and give solemn heed. Others would be likely to imitate Aradus and Byblos, and surrender at discretion rather than fight a losing fight as Tyre had done.

While the siege was in progress Darius again approached Alexander with an embassy offering friendship and alliance. He asked only for the return of the members of his family save one; the one exception was his daughter whose hand in marriage he offered Alexander. He would pay the sum of 10,000 talents and cede all the territory west of the Euphrates.[1] Alexander

[1] Arrian, II, 25, 1 ff. These offers of peace have been doubted by Neumann, *Jahrb. f. Philol.*, CXXVII, 546, but on grounds quite insufficient. See Kaerst, *Forsch. z. Gesch. Alex.*, 7 ff.

laid these proposals before the council of Companions, and the pretty story is told that Parmenion said: "If I were Alexander I should be glad to secure peace on these terms and end the continued risk." To which Alexander replied: "So should I, if I were Parmenion; but as I am Alexander, my answer is what it is." However this may be, Darius received an answer no better than its predecessor, and seeing that no terms could be secured set himself to prepare for war.

The wrecked city of Tyre was now left behind and Alexander advanced on toward the south, receiving the submission of every city or village until Gaza was reached. It lay about 150 miles south of Tyre and was the chief among the five cities of the Philistines. It had once possessed a harbor and a considerable sea-borne commerce, but this had been long silted up before the days of Alexander, and the city was now two miles inland on a foundation more than sixty feet above the terrain, with massive walls of defense. Alexander's engineers informed him that siege engines could not be moved up against the walls and therefore it could not be taken by assault. He determined to make the attempt, and the method adopted was to select a place on the south side where the wall appeared to be weakest, and there begin the construction of a mound, probably in the form of an inclined plane, on which the siege engines could be moved up against the wall, and so be brought to bear and batter down the wall. A method the same or closely similar had been used by the Chaldeans centuries before for attacking fortified cities,[1] though there is no reason for denying to Alexander independent thought in its use here. This mound was carried to the height of 200 feet and was 1,200 feet

[1]Habakkuk 1 : 10.

wide at the base.[1] The city was in command of a faithful eunuch named Batis, who had provisioned it for a
long siege and was determined to give a good account
of himself for his master Darius. He little knew how
serious was his task.

The siege engines were brought by sea from Tyre and
landed at the small harbor of Majorma to be dragged
thence overland and pushed up the surface of the
mound. The garrison made a gallant sortie with no result of importance other than the wounding of Alexander in the shoulder by a shaft from a catapult. Once
the engines were in place a part of the walls was readily
breached and the Macedonians delivered an assault,
which was repulsed. Two more were made with like result. The fourth went forward with increased forces
and added determination. Through the breaches and
over the walls by scaling ladders poured the resistless
Macedonians, and a vicious slaughter of the defenders
began in the city streets. Ten thousand of them, so the
story runs, perished sword in hand, and the women and
children were sold into slavery. It is also narrated that
Alexander took barbarous vengeance on Batis by drag-
ging him round the walls tied to the back of his chariot,
as Achilles had done to Hector. Two months had the
siege cost, but the capture of immense stores from the
rich commercial city, long a depot at the sea end of
desert routes, was a great reward, and one more nail
had been driven into the coffin of Persian supremacy
on the Mediterranean.[2]

The month of December had now come just one year
after the battle of Issus, and Alexander had mastered

---

[1]Dodge, op. cit., p. 344, supposes that there were several of these mounds,
but there is no necessity for this, nor do the sources support it.
[2]The story of the siege of Gaza is in Arrian, II, 26 f., and Diodorus, XVII,
48, 7, with a more rhetorical account in Curtius, IV, 6, 7 ff.

the whole sea coast of Syria, Phœnicia, and Philistia.
He was free to order an advance over the desert wastes
against the storied and glorious land of Egypt. In
seven[1] days of hard marching he reached Pelusium in
the Delta, a place ill favored for health, and the breed-
ing-place of many a plague. There he had ordered his
fleet under command of Hephæstion to meet him, as
though a serious business were to be taken in hand,
though quite the opposite proved to be the case.

But a short time had elapsed since Egypt had been
reconquered by Persia, yet was it in no sense committed to its masters. The Persian satrap Mazaces had not
shown any loyalty to Darius. When the Greek mercenaries, fugitives from the army of Darius at Issus under the command of the renegade Amyntas, approached
Egypt he had met and slaughtered or dispersed them.
He had no means adequate for the repulse of Alexander, even if he had eagerly wished it, nor did the peaceful folk who lived industrious lives in the long narrow
valley of the incomparable Nile care who ruled their
country if they were but left to till their black soil in
peace. There lay the richest land of that age open to
occupation as and when Alexander wished. He ordered
his fleet up the broad river to Memphis, and leaving a
garrison in Pelusium marched along the east bank to
Heliopolis, received the submission of every settlement
on the way. Before him now lay the ancient historic
capital, Memphis, which he could enter unopposed.

The wealth and splendor of the city may well have
moved this young man to amazement. He was seeing
it in one of the best months of all the year. Its vast
temple to the chief city god Ptah, gleamed daily be-

[1]Thotmes III, in his day, required twelve days, or twenty-one. Breasted,
Hist. of Egypt, pp. 285, 286.

neath an unclouded sun. Here by immemorial rites was
the god worshipped under the living symbol of a sacred
Apis bull. For centuries as one living animal took the
place of its predecessor, the dead creature, embalmed
with manifold religious ceremonials and every skilful
process, was laid away in tombs where serried hundreds reposed in state. The city above ground has long
since perished, the tombs of the Apis bulls remain to
challenge the wonder of every cultivated beholder. The
Persians had not had the wisdom or tolerance to pay
even nominal honor to these religious customs, for
Cambyses had expressed his contempt by wounding a
sacred bull, and Darius Ochus had caused one to be
slaughtered. Alexander knew a more excellent way.
Upon entering the city he was quick to pay every honor
to the Apis worship and to hold feasts and gymnastic
contests after the Greek religious manner quite as he
would have done before any Greek temple. The effect
was richly rewarding: "The Egyptians, as the Persians
had violated their sacred rites and had dominated
rudely over them, welcomed the Macedonians gladly."[1]
It would be less than just to ascribe this act of Alexander merely to policy. In this same way he always
acted toward all religious rites and customs of all people. He was in heart a religiously minded man, and re-
spected the worship of God wherever and however he
found it. If his spirit was religiously tolerant, it had
also a discernible trace of mysticism, an indefinable
feeling for powers greater than mortal reverenced by
man under various names, and approached by varied
forms of supplication.

He might now consider himself lord of all Egypt, for
there was no power farther up the river to dispute any

[1] Diodorus, XVII, 49.

claim that he might choose to make. He sent part of
his army down the Nile to the coast, and with a small
force marched down the western river bank to the
Canopic mouth. Thence he made a circuit of Lake
Moeris, a body of water fed by numerous canals which
connected it with the Nile and no less than fifteen miles
wide, navigable for the largest vessels of that day and
forming a most important means of intercommunica-
tion. By the side of this body of water and between it
and the sea was a narrow strip of land, varying from
a mile to a mile and a half wide, and between thirteen
and fourteen miles west of Canopus (Mt. Aboukir).
There Alexander performed a feat almost miraculous
in its outcome. He determined to build a new city,
which was to bear the name Alexandria, and, however
wise and far-seeing were his hopes or aspiration, even
his mind could not have conceived the wonder that was
to come. To him at least we cannot deny that the choice
of location was amazingly wise. Landward Lake Moeris
offered at the same time an easy means of defense, and
an admirable opportunity for commercial intercourse,
for by its canal communication with the Nile and
thence by the greater canal of Necho II (609–595 B. C.)
to the Red Sea, the commerce of Egypt, Arabia, and
India might come to form connections with the western world, sea borne upon the Mediterranean. On the
sea side there were two small natural harbors, the one
opening westward, the other giving toward the east,
both protected from heavy weather by the small island
Pharos, four-fifths of a mile offshore. It would be comparatively easy to form a safe harbor, or harbors,
for the sea commerce, and the city would be without a serious rival. The nearest port on the African
coast would be the insignificant Parætonium, and on

the Asiatic Joppa, where there was no harbor at all, only an open roadstead, and Tyre, once mistress of the Mediterranean, had been destroyed. There was no rival in being and none was ever found in the eastern portion of the great sea. In less than a century after the death of its founder it was exceeded in size and population only by Antioch and by Carthage. In 60 B. C. it had a population of 300,000 freemen, or a total of half a million, and was considered the greatest city of the world.[1] Persia was confronted by a master mind whose conceptions turned into realities, not a military conqueror only, but a statesman of commanding stature.

While Alexander tarried over these great city plans he was visited by Hegelochus, commander of his new fleet, who brought news both welcome and of far-reaching importance. The island cities lost during the spring of 333 B. C. were now in the midwinter of 332–331 B. C. all recovered. The people of Tenedos, forced against their will under Persian rule, had revolted and come back to him. Chios had done the same. Cos had yielded submission to the summons of a fleet of sixty vessels sent upon its own request. Mitylene had been retaken by the fleet, and the other cities of Lesbos had voluntarily surrendered. The whole Ægean Sea was cleared of Persians.[2] But for Sparta, Alexander might have felt securely possessed of the whole Mediterranean. There was a serious possible danger of considerable moment though not to become pressing until a little later.[3]

---

[1] For the founding of the city the chief sources are Arrian, III, 1, and Plutarch, *Alexander*, 26, though usable details are to be found in Diodorus, XVII, 52, and Curtius, IV, 8, 1 ff., and Justin, XI, 11, 13, though these three erroneously set the founding of the city after the visit to the temple of Jupiter Ammon.

[2] Arrian, III, 2, 3 ff. Curtius, IV, 5, 14 ff.

[3] Arrian, III, 6, 3 and III, 2, 4. Curtius, IV, 8, 15.

While the architect Dinocrates[1] was busy with the sketching of plans for the new city Alexander set out upon a curious expedition perhaps long in contemplation. With a small body of horse and foot Alexander marched 200 miles westward along the coast of Parætonium, and thence nearly due south about the same distance over the desert wastes to visit the temple of Jupiter Ammon in its lonely oasis upon the Libyan desert (modern Siwah). Here was a famous oracle which had been consulted by Perseus and Hercules, whom Alexander counted his ancestors. He desired to learn from the oracle his own origin and future, because, as Curtius reports: "he either believed Jupiter to be his father or had a mind the world should think so, not being satisfied with his mortal grandeur." It may be safely doubted whether Alexander really held this religious fiction in any genuine way. It seems much more natural to suppose that he would be willing to spread it abroad as a part of his plan to overawe the superstitious and further his plans of conquest. It would be fitting enough to make such a claim in Egypt, where for centuries the kings had been called, one after another, son of Re. He was now a Pharaoh by conquest, why should he not be as divine as the native princes had been?[2]

From this visit Alexander returned to serious business and reappeared in Memphis. There he received deputations from Greece, and from various Greek islands. Chios and Rhodes asked that the garrisons be

[1]Vitruvius, II, pr. 1, p. 31, 7; ib., 4, p. 32. Pliny, NH, V, 62; VII, 125, though the manuscripts of Pliny read the name erroneously Dinochares.
[2]For this visit to the oracle there are diverse accounts, yet a general rough agreement in the main. Arrian, III, 3 f. Plutarch, *Alexander*, 26 f. Diodorus, XVI, 49 ff. Curtius, IV, 7. Justin, XI, 11. Among modern discussions Wheeler, *Alexander*, pp. 347 ff. may well be consulted. Grote also, and an interesting paper by Kaerst, *Historische Zeitschrift*, lxxiv (1895), pp. 1 ff., 193 ff., whose conclusions are similar to those of Grote.

withdrawn from their cities. Mitylene asked reimbursement for expenditures in war against Persians, Cyprians, and Athenians, while others had each his own particular favor to ask or congratulations to offer. To them all Alexander knew how to make some answer satisfying at least for the present, and displaying anew his diplomatic adroitness, in its way no less remarkable than his military skill.[1] At Memphis also he received small reinforcements sent by Antipater, and others were to join him in Pelusium.

There remained now but one month more of his stay in Egypt, and it was most fruitfully employed in a reorganization of the government of the whole land. The country was used to a central government based upon hundreds of much loved local customs, and with characteristic wisdom Alexander provided for the retention in every possible place and at all times of every use to which the people were accustomed. As Pharaoh he was willingly, even gladly accepted, as Persian rule had not been beloved, though probably much of the population never knew that any great change had occurred at all. As governor of the country, in his own absence he placed a native Egyptian, Doloaspis, but was careful to put the entire military control in the hands of Macedonians. This distinction between civil and military control was carried from top to bottom, and each had its province and power carefully differentiated. To the civil power was granted the levying and collection of taxes and the ordinary administration of the simple forms of justice, the religious worship, and the usual laws and customs. The military was to maintain peace, protect his rule, and enforce loyalty wherever and whenever needed, but was prevented

[1]Arrian, III, 5, 1. Compare Diodorus, XVII, 48, 6.

from the handling of monies, and from the temptations
which might thus appear. Native levies were to be
raised, trained in the Macedonian fashion and stiffened
by small bodies of trusted troops from Greece. In Memphis and in Pelusium were garrisons under complete
Macedonian control. Libya and Arabia were detached
under separate governments. It would be difficult to
conceive a government better adapted to the people,
or better suited to ensure the complete extinction of
Persian influence and the perfect establishment of
Macedonian.[1]

[1]Arrian, III, 5, 2 ff., and much less valuable Curtius, IX, 8, 4 f. For this
entire Egyptian episode Wiedemann, *Gesch. Aegyptens*, pp. 298 ff., may be
profitably consulted, though very brief. See further H. R. Hall (*Camb. Anc.
Hist.*, VI, p. 154 f.), an excellent discussion, and Tarn (ib., p. 378 f.).

THE END

We are now, reader, arrived at the last stage of our long journey. As we have, therefore, travelled together through so many pages, let us behave to one another like fellow-travellers in a stage-coach, who have passed several days in the company of each other; and who, notwithstanding any bickerings or little animosities which may have occurred on the road, generally make up all at last, and mount, for the last time, into their vehicle with cheerfulness and good-humour; since, after this one stage, it may possibly happen to us, as it commonly happens to them, never to meet more.—FIELDING.

CHAPTER XIII

ON THE WAY TO BABYLON

EARLY in the spring of 331 B. C. Alexander moved his victorious veterans out of Egypt, recrossed the desert, and marching up the coast of Philistia and Palestine halted at Tyre, where his fleet swung at anchor ready to give him welcome. Hither came the sacred state trireme bearing an embassy from Athens to pledge the city's loyalty and to beg once more the release of fellow countrymen taken prison in Persian service at Granicus, and in view of reports of a better political situation there Alexander was now ready to grant the request.[1] From the harbor a fleet was despatched to meet threatened dangers at Sparta. Sparta had all along been a cause of anxiety, and even the victory at Issus had not quieted her aspirations for independence. King Agis had kept Spartan ambassadors at the court of Darius, and while Alexander needed every man at Tyre, had seized Crete and was making of it a stronghold in the vain hope of contesting control of the Mediterranean. The full storm had not been completely made known to Alexander until he was far away in the Phœnician city, but he was now sufficiently interested to send this fleet as a sort of warning and a possible preventive of greater trouble.[2] He had accepted the news with composure, saying: "While we are here conquering Darius it seems they are having

[1] Arrian, III, 5, 1; compare Diodorus, XVII, 48, 6.
[2] Arrian, III, 6, 3, and III, 2, 4. Curtius, IV, 8, 15.

313

a war of mice in Arcadia." Swift came the news to confirm his confidence. Antipater had appeared, found the Spartans besieging the walls of Megalopolis, and a decisive battle was fought. Antipater left 5,300 Spartans dead upon the field, and King Agis among them. The submission of Sparta followed, nor did she ever fully recover from the effects of this blow.[1]

Alexander had now stripped from the once proud and puissant Persian Empire all its western possessions. Where Cyrus had builded and Cambyses extended and Darius the Great made glorious and magnificent all had fallen into hopeless fragments before this strange youth of destiny. A similar fate had befallen the Greek commonwealths, once so proud of independence and rivals in the pursuit of the finer arts of life. These all were now helpless parts of a Macedonian empire which had understood how to reduce them to dead levels of imbecility. Assured of safety behind, for none was able in all Greece or Asia Minor or Phœnicia or Egypt to rise in opposition, Alexander was now prepared to make the staggering adventure of an expedition into the vast regions of Asia to seek out Darius, destroy him and his, and add to that already won the almost fabled territories of Persia in Asia.

After two attempts to win Alexander to some peaceful solution of the differences between them Darius had recognized that the issue must be squarely met and that only one way was open. He must prepare for a renewal of active war. It was evident enough that Alexander was ruthless and determined to seek him out wherever he was and decide on the field of battle who should rule henceforth over all these diverse peoples.

[1]Plutarch, *Agis*, 3. Diodorus, XVII, 63. Curtius, VI, 1. Justin, XII, 1. This campaign begun in the spring of 331 was not finished until autumn, and its conclusion therefore followed Gaugamela.

Darius took a high and worthy resolve to meet the issue as a man and a king. Whatever final judgment must be passed upon his ability and character, it will not justly be said that he failed now to perceive destiny and duty and to prepare as well as he was able for the last trial. He knew that his family were all honorably treated by their captor,[1] and that however great were their mental sufferings for separation from home and friends there was no need to make any surrender of the state for their lives or fortunes. He must have begun to feel, after Issus, that the only hope for the future of his empire was to be sought in beginning preparations on a huge scale and in fighting to the end.

To Babylon he had retired and thence issued orders for the assembling of an army fully representative of the best that all remaining Persia might gather. It was a congeries of races rather than a unified national army, but that so many peoples of diverse tongues and still more diverse customs could be brought together shows that there was still some cohesion in the empire and that a brave fight for its continuance as an Asiatic power was possible. Here were Persians, Medes, Babylonians, and Elamites to represent the very center of the empire. With them were Armenians, from the mountains of the north, Syrians who had slipped away beneath Alexander's hand on the Orontes, Cappadocians and Albanians from the shores of the Euxine, Bactrians from the valley of the Oxus, Sogdians from the Jaxartes, Arians from Herat, Indians from the Punjab, and Sacæ from the neighborhoods of Kashgar and Yarkand, and many others to a great sum of twenty-five nations.[2] The number of the host is even reck-

[1]Arrian, II, 12; Plutarch, *Alexander*, 2; Curtius, III, 12; Diodorus, XVII, 38.
[2]Arrian, III, 8, 11. Plutarch, *Alexander*, IV, 11.

oned so high as a million or more,[1] but like so many
other estimates of orientals must be greatly reduced,
though by this we are left without any means of making an estimate of the numbers that his forces might
muster. It is more to the point, however, to learn that
he had made great efforts for renewal and improvement
of their equipment. There were issued swords and
spears longer than the Persians, to match the length
of the Macedonian weapons which had given them an
advantage at Issus.[2] Two hundred scythed chariots
were ordered[3] for fighting on a plain, and spiked balls
to cast upon the field over which the Macedonian cavalry must be fought. Darius had done what he could to
prepare for the inevitable contest. He needed only to
select a field best suited for his defense, take any possible steps the better to fit it, and then await attack.
When all was ready Darius marched out of the precincts of Babylon toward the northeast, strange as it
may appear, and crossing the Tigris made on northward
into the territories of the ancient Assyrian empire, to
Arbela, where he established his harem, magazines of
supplies, reserves, and the treasury. Thence marching
the fighting forces nearly due west he crossed the Lycus (modern Lower Zab), and chose a site for fighting
near Gaugamela on the Bumodus, seventy miles west
of Arbela, eighteen miles northeast of Mosul. The position was admirably chosen, for it was a large plain
suited well for the free evolution of chariots and of
cavalry. Darius had time to perfect it by the removal
of possible obstacles, the cutting down of brush, and

---

[1] Arrian (III, 8) makes it 1,000,000 infantry and 40,000 cavalry. Plutarch
(*Alexander*, 31) is content with the round number 1,000,000; Diodorus (XVII,
39) gives 800,000 infantry and 200,000 cavalry; Justin (XII, 5) makes the
totals 400,000 infantry and 100,000 cavalry; and Curtius (IV, 12) 600,000
infantry and 45,000 cavalry.

[2] Diodorus, XVII, 53.   [3] Curtius, IV, 9.

even the levelling of the ground in places deemed especially likely to be needed for the movement of the
chariots with their heavy scythes fastened to the axles
and great spearheads on the poles. Here also fifteen
elephants brought by the Indian contingents might be
sent against a line of men who had never before seen
these massive creatures and might be terrorized at the
sight. Perhaps never before had any commander taken
so much thought to fit any site for open field fighting.[1]
Praise must justly be given Darius for the wisdom he
was at long last displaying in the defense of an im-
perilled cause. It was all needed, for the Macedonians
were on the march, and the day of destiny could not
long be deferred.

Having completed the governmental arrangements
at Tyre in June or July, 331 B. C., Alexander was ready
for the supreme and decisive venture. With a skilfully
reorganized army, quite probably reinforced by the
addition of fit men from some of the minor garrisons
now to be left in the rear, he gave the order to advance.
The route chosen seems to have been by the great valley between the Lebanon and the Anti Lebanon, and
then by the Orontes valley to Antioch, and thence easterly over the great plain. In eleven days he had covered the 350 miles to the Euphrates and Thapsacus, a
speed almost unthinkable of thirty miles a day over a
treeless arid plain reeking in summer heat, and often
chill at night. The engineers sent in advance had un-
dertaken to build two bridges of boats, which had however not been completed, for on the opposite bank
Darius had stationed an outpost of 5,000 cavalry and
2,000 Greek mercenaries, a force only intended to reconnoitre and report the appearance of Alexander.

[1] Arrian, III, 8.

Upon the arrival of the main body these withdrew, the bridges were completed, and the crossing was accomplished without opposition. The position would seem to have been excellent for a battle to delay Alexander if not to destroy him, but Darius had not elected to seize it, the strategy followed being still that of Memnon to draw Alexander farther into the heart of the country, weakened by hard marches and compelled to fight in a strange land.

Before the actual crossing of the river Alexander founded a new city to be called Nicephonium (modern Rakka) in further pursuit of a well-defined policy to form a chain of military posts on the line of communications and introduce into barbarous lands some semblance of Greek life and culture as a preparation for the new era that was to be. The weeks spent in this enterprise were well invested, though the return is not to be compared with that received from Alexandria.

The Euphrates crossed, Alexander did not make direct for the Tigris across a territory already devastated by the Persians to impede his march, and dangerously hot, but moved northward along the Euphrates until near the Armenian mountains and thence eastward to the Tigris, which was crossed unopposed probably at or near Jezireh.[1] After this great achievement of crossing the river there occurred on September 20, 331 B. C., a lunar eclipse, which might well have been taken as an unfavorable portent by the Greeks, but Aristander, the prophet, deftly explained away its meaning, for it was

---

[1]So Ritter, *Erdkunde*, XI, 146 ff. Dodge (*Alexander*, p. 357) suggests Bezabde as the place and his opinion deserves respect; his observations concerning the feat of crossing are very interesting. He makes the point that the current was swift, perhaps six miles an hour, and the water came up to the armpits of the men, and adds: "It may be worth while to state that the limit of depth for cavalry is generally assumed to be less than four feet, and for infantry less than three."

the sun, reverenced by the Greeks, which had eclipsed
the moon, object of Persian adoration. With renewed
confidence the Macedonians entered upon the march
of eighty miles down the Tigris, with the Cadusians
mountains (modern Gordæan) on the left. After four
days the outposts of Darius, 1,000 cavalry, appeared
in front. Prisoners taken from this body reported Darius to be near, but there was no need for haste, and
Alexander made a fortified camp and rested his men
four days. On the 29th day of the month, the baggage
and non-combatants were left in the camp, and at mid-
night the fateful advance began, expecting to attack
at daybreak. At dawn the Macedonians, advancing over
a low hill, descried scarce four miles away the Persian
host filling the plain, and beginning at once to form in
battle line, expecting an immediate attack. In an hour
contact was possible. The men were keen to be sent forward, but were rather ordered to halt while a council
was held. Would it be wise to attack at once or to reconnoitre? The prudent and skilful soldier Parmenion
won over the ardent and unwise and the decision was
taken to study the disposition of the enemy's forces
and the condition of the terrain. Alexander with a small
force went forward for a reconnaissance and on his return called another council to hear his report, and to
receive final instructions. The night came on and the
Persians still maintained their line of battle, nervously
worn by the constant expectation of assault at any moment, while the Macedonians rested refreshed and in
confidence.

Darius had a vast superiority in numbers, and he
had chosen a field to suit his own tactics. His dispositions were sound, and were, as a Persian document captured among the archives after the battle showed, ap-

proximately these. In the left wing were the Bactrian cavalry under Bessus, with the Doans and Arachotians, the Persians, horse and foot; the Susians and Cardusians. In the right wing from the right under command of Mazæus were the Cœle-Syrians, the Mesopotamians, the Medes, Parthians and Socians, the Tarpurians, Hyrcanians, the Albanians, and Sacessinians. These were disposed in three main lines and in large squares or in deep masses. In the rear centre was King Darius, in front of him fifteen elephants, fifty scythed chariots, and a bodyguard of 15,000 picked men; the Persian guards with spears, the Indians, Carians, and Mardian archers. In front of the right were stationed the Armenian and Cappadocian cavalry, and fifty more scythed chariots. The Greek mercenaries, who alone were fit to meet the Macedonian phalanx, but were more or less suspect by Darius, were drawn up in two divisions, one on each side of the king and his bodyguards. Bessus held the main command on the left; Mazæus on the right wing.[1]

Darius showed himself in person to his men, using every art to encourage them and pointing out that the conditions were now far different from those at Granicus and Issus, better suited for them, ill fitted for the Macedonians. He bade them fight for home and for their families: "It has become a contest for existence, and what is dearer still, the liberty of your wives and children, who must fall like mine into the hands of the enemy, unless your bodies become a rampart to save them from captivity." It is the last audible cry of a doomed man, and though reported by Greeks after the Greek manner may well correspond to verity in its main features.

[1] Arrian, III, 8.

Darius stood ready to fight upon a field of his own choosing and prepared by his own engineers. It was on a wide plain near Gaugamela (modern Kermelis), near where the Ghazir empties into the Lower Zab. For Persian hopes and purposes no better place could be chosen. It proved to be the field of destiny. Here was to come to final judgment the long-drawn contest between East and West, between Persia with all her inheritance from venerable empires Babylonia, Assyria, and Elamite, and Greece, under the heavy hand of Macedon, rich in treasured memories of glorious achievements in art and letters.

The morning of October 1, 331 B. C., came up out of the desert hills and above the plain of Gaugamela; over the low hills in the north Alexander's force filed out, formed in line of battle, and began the measured descent toward the army of Darius. The Macedonians are said to have numbered about 40,000 infantry and 7,000 cavalry.[1] The right was held by the cavalry Companions, the royal squadron in the lead under Clitus, with Alexander in person. To the left were the squadrons of Glaucias, Sopolis, Heraclides, Demetrius, Meleager, and Hegelochus, all under the supreme command of Philotas, son of Parmenion. Then came the Macedonian phalanx in two lines, the hoplites and peltasts, first the agema of hypaspists, then the rest of them under Nicanor, son of Parmenion. After them the phalan-

---

[1] Upon this a judgment is precarious. It is, however, difficult to understand whence a force so large could have been assembled at that time. Tarn (*Camb. Anc. Hist.*, VI, p. 380) accepts the cavalry number, but doubts the infantry. I am disposed to think both too high. Tarn, however, justly observes that Alexander's "system of reinforcements is obscure; probably he received an annual draft of recruits from Macedonia, and before his death he and his satraps had enlisted the whole available supply of Greeks; these perhaps about sufficed to meet losses and supply his armies of occupation, leaving his field force roughly a constant quantity." But see the discussion by Beloch, *Griech. Geschichte*, III², 2, p. 322–352. This is an admirable discussion of the whole case, and in the present state of knowledge leaves nothing to be said.

gites under Cœnus, Perdiccas, Meleager, Polysperchon, Simmias, and Craterus, who commanded the left wing of the infantry. Next were the allied Greek cavalry under Erigyius, and the Thessalian cavalry under Philip. The left wing was formed by the Pharsalian cavalry under Parmenion himself.

The superior Persian force, though we do not know its numbers, formed a line far overlapping the Macedonian flanks. Alexander recognized the danger and to meet it formed a second or reserve line in the rear of each flank, to be used as a sort of flying column wheeling to right or left, fighting on either flank, if Darius should attempt an enveloping movement, or even be ready to meet an attack from the rear. Never before had Alexander made such a disposition and this must be counted as another evidence of his resourcefulness in meeting any new situation as it arose. In the right flying column were half the Agrianians under Attalus, and the Macedonian archers under Briso, and the veteran Macedonians under Cleander. In front of these were the light cavalry, and the Pæonians under Aretas and Aristo, and again in front of these were the newly arrived Greek mercenary cavalry under Menidas. Covering the agema and Companion cavalry were half the Agrianians and archers and Balacrus' javelin men. Upon Menidas was laid command to ride round and take the Persians in flank if they should try to surround this Macedonian wing.

On the left there was a similar flying column composed of the Thracians under Sitalces, the Greek auxiliary cavalry under Cœranus, and the Odryssian cavalry under Agatho. In front of all these stood the cavalry of the Greek mercenaries under Andromachus.[1]

[1]These dispositions are derived in the main from Arrian, with a very few hints from Curtius. (See detailed references below.) I acknowledge much very

Alexander anticipated correctly that Darius would open battle by a charge of chariots, and had instructed the phalangites to open spaces for the chariots to pass through, attacked by the javelin throwers to wound the horses, and destroy their drivers. His own first move was to open by a charge of his best cavalry opposite the left of the Persian centre. This advance was made by an obliquing movement, intended primarily to avoid spiked balls which a Persian deserter declared had been thrown in front, and secondarily probably in the hope that a gap might open between the Persian right and left. At any rate this is precisely what did happen, for Darius, fearing that Alexander might succeed in gaining higher ground where chariots could not fight, impatiently ordered their advance, following them with his centre, and at the same time sent forward 1,000 Bactrian and some Syrian cavalry to envelop the Macedonian right. To meet this move Menidas was ordered, but the superior numbers of the attacking force were too great and he was repulsed. To their aid others were sent up, the balance retrieved and after a sharp cavalry engagement, in which Alexander met heavy losses, this part of the plans of Darius was brought to failure. Meanwhile the scythe-bearing chariots came on against the centre phalanx, which opened to receive those that survived the rush of javelins, and the crash of swords. They had achieved nothing of importance save a temporary unsteadying of the Macedonian line which was quickly repaired.

This ill-fated Persian move had opened a gap in their front and Alexander saw his opportunity. From a part of the Macedonian phalanx on his right he formed a deep wedgelike column, and heading this by

valuable help in their comprehension from Dodge, *Alexander*, pp. 369–373, who has brought to the criticism of the details a soldier's expert training.

his cavalry Companions made straight for the gap at the double-quick and directly at the spot where Darius himself was posted. The onset was irresistible, though for a time the Persians fought bravely and did good execution hand to hand. The charioteer of the emperor fell dead, transfixed by a javelin. Darius lost all power to think in large terms, could not perceive how a disaster was to be averted, considered only his own safety, turned, and fled.

The flight of the great king put an end to every hope of resistance, the lines broke in a wild confusion, and a few charges of the Macedonian right began a complete clearance of the field in the centre. There was, however, still a point of serious danger. The Persian, Parthian, and Indian cavalry had burst through the cleft in the Macedonian line made by Alexander's swift advance, and cutting off the left wing, threatened it with destruction. Parmenion was hopelessly outmatched and hastily sent to Alexander for aid. The reserve column behind the left came first to aid and began a furious attack upon Mazæus and his cavalry of the Persian right. Alexander now reluctantly abandoned pursuit of the Persians fleeing before him, turned with his Companion cavalry to the help of his embarrassed lieutenant, and came upon the Persian cavalry already in retreat. These knew well that their only hope lay in hacking a way through, and the heaviest fighting of the day resulted. Few made their escape, the bulk lying dead or wounded on the field, and the Companions suffered severely enough in the struggle, for sixty fell dead, and many were severely wounded. This unexpected diversion of Alexander had, however, important consequences, for it gave Darius a long start, not to be overtaken in pursuit, making his lonely and broken way over a narrow pass through the mountains of Armenia toward Media, with the kinsmen, the remnants of the Bactrian cavalry, and some Greek mercenaries, numbering all told about 6,000 infantry and 3,000 cavalry. His one thought seems to have been to save himself. It was evident enough that Babylon was hopelessly lost, for the road to it lay open for Alexander. Susa was equally at his choice and disposal. But all was not yet lost, if the great king were but able to see and to act. There still remained a great stretch of imperial territory covered by the mountain ranges which afforded splendid opportunities for defense, if not for aggression. Ecbatana remained, and Persepolis lay behind mountain ranges which a foreign army might well hesitate to attempt against a hardy population easy to rouse in defense of its own wretched homes.

The losses in the battle had fallen heaviest upon the vanquished as is wont to be the case. The Persian slain is reported by Curtius to have been 40,000, and by Diodorus as 90,000, while the usually cautious Arrian makes the wild guess of 300,000. The Macedonian loss was 500 killed and 1,000 horses of wounds or fatigue. It was loss enough for a commander far from his natural base, but it was relatively small. But whatever the relative losses may have been there can be no doubt of the total destruction of the Persian army as a fighting force, and of the overwhelming and renewed proof of the superiority of the Macedonians, man for man, and of their discipline, training, and morale. Their commander was doubtless the greatest military genius the weary sons of men had yet known, but he was well supported by lieutenants selected mostly by himself with that almost unerring instinct seldom equalled and perhaps never exceeded by any future leader.[1]

[1] The chief sources for the battle as a whole are Arrian, III, 8–15; Plutarch, *Alexander*, 31 ff.; Diodorus, XVII, 55–61; Curtius, IV, 12 ff.; Justin, XI, 13 f.; Polyænus, IV, 3, 6, 17 f., 26. A word of praise is due Dodge (*Alexander*) for

As an immediate reward to Mazæus the satrapy was given for what could scarcely be regarded as less than treachery to his royal Persian master. But Alexander took good care that he should have small chance of any opportunity for a reversal, for he entrusted the military command and the collection of taxes to Macedonians, leaving but the dignity of satrap and its almost empty honors to the traitor.[1]

Before the battle Alexander had made as careful preparations for a possible reverse as he did for an assured victory. At a distance of about seven miles from the Persian position he had made his last great halt. There he laid out a great camp, defended by a ditch and a stockade. Here were left all the heavy baggage, the hospitals, non-combatants and prisoners, and a base for retreat most carefully provided. Among these who there remained none were so deserving of pity as the sad and weary and homesick remnants of the family of Darius. Here they were held as hostages who might be very valuable should a Macedonian defeat ensue. There is no reason to doubt that they had every possible attention, and every distinction of royalty was granted. They were safe in their persons, far safer than if left behind or turned loose to wander they knew not whither, when Darius himself had long been little else than a fugitive, and was shortly to become nothing else. But if their bodies had such comfort as the field might provide, the marches were long and full of weariness, and their minds suffered the incessant tortures of doubt and apprehension, ignorance of what the morrow might bring forth. At this sorry spot, or perhaps before, for we do not know the hour or day, Sta-

---

his description of the battle and the military criticism of its various features. The equal of his analysis is not elsewhere to be found.

[1] Arrian, III, 16, 3 f.; Diodorus, XVII, 64, 5; Curtius, V, 1, 43 ff.

teira, the wife of Darius died, able to endure no longer. It was a sad ending of all the pomp and glory that had been.

When Alexander had satisfied himself of the futility of any further pursuit he advanced across the Lycus, in whose waters many Persians had lost their lives during the swift flight and hurried pursuit, and on the farther bank encamped to give rest to an army almost drunk with victory, but overcome with fatigue. To Parmenion was left the sacking of the Persian camp at Gaugamela. As at Issus, there fell to Alexander the empty symbols of the king, his chariot, spear, and bow. There was no great treasure secured, or we should have a boastful enumeration of it. Whatever was most valuable had somehow been spirited away, and though Alexander soon advanced to Arbela, it was not secured. The king was already beyond the mountains and had left behind as a prize that vast fertile valley of the Tigris and Euphrates where once had been empires filled with story and with treasure.

Alexander turned at once to secure it for Greece and for himself. The first objective was clearly Babylon. Alexander crossed the Tigris at Upi (Opis), and having learned that the doughty Mazæus, who had already given him trouble enough, had taken possession of the city to hold it for the Persian king, anticipated a fight for its securing. Nearing the historic walls he approached cautiously and in battle array, but met the pleasant surprise of open gates and a deputation of priests and Persian officials with wreaths and presents to bid him welcome, and Mazæus himself to offer a complete surrender. Babylon had fallen again quietly and peacefully as long ago to Cyrus, and Alexander might enter to do as he willed. With a wisdom now become usual with him, if not indeed a personal characteristic from the beginning, he chose to show to every patriotic or religious impulse the highest respect.

CHAPTER XIV

ON TO THE HEART OF THE EMPIRE

In Babylon Alexander remained only long enough to give a much needed rest to an army almost worn out with colossal achievement, leaving his men to the full enjoyment of the city's luxuries, refinements, and entertainments. Here were captured great treasures which were very carefully disposed to increase loyalty, reward service, and prepare for future trials. Liberal gratuities were distributed upon a scale carefully graded. Each Macedonian cavalryman received 6 minas or 600 drachmas, a sum equal in mere face value to about $120; each Greek and light horseman 5 minas or $100; each Macedonian infantryman $40, and the allied infantry and peltasts two months' extra pay. When it is remembered that the purchasing power of these sums was several or even many times that possessed to-day, they seem like fortunes distributed among common soldiers and must have made many feel that this was indeed a commander to follow anywhere with the certainty of rewards ever greater.

But if Alexander had taken pains to buy a greater loyalty from his own he was no less careful to conciliate the populace by the recognition of every religious concern. Into the great temple of E-sagila, home and shrine of Marduk (Merodach), chief god of the city, he entered to pay homage according to the age-long and deeply reverenced ritual. Outside its solemn precincts he provided for the inhabitants a spectacle certainly long to be remembered and hugely enjoyed, by staging

races and games in the Macedonian manner. Proud
must have been his inmost soul when the priests of that
ancient shrine named to him the kings who had there
laid brick upon brick in the mighty pile, while he
thought himself to be the heir of the ages. But it was
not like him to lose time or tide, or to waste energy in
idle contemplation of his own greatness. There was
much yet to be conquered. The army was refreshed
after a month's rest, and might well be ordered forward.

The next objective was Susa, winter capital of the
proud empire. The march began out of the hot valley
up the mountain slopes, and in twenty days the city
was before him, probably in the month of November.
It had already surrendered to his lieutenant Philox-
enus, who had been sent in advance. Its immense
treasure, estimated at 50,000 talents (perhaps about
$70,000,000), had dropped like a ripe plum into his
hands. This was all in ingots and in coined darics, but
added to it was a bewildering mass of manufactured
metals, jewels, and every form of woven stuffs. Precious beyond these all there were found in the treasure
house the statues of Harmodius and Aristogiton, carried off from Athens by Xerxes, and now restored in
triumph to their old home. Here also as at Babylon
Alexander offered sacrifices in the temple of In-Shushi-
nak and celebrated races and games as he had done
in Babylon. Here he saw still standing in all its bizarre
magnificence the palace which Darius I had begun and
Artaxerxes III finished. Strange to Greek eyes must
have been the high colors of the enamelled brick walls,
whose mural decorations recovered by Dieulafoy now
repose in the Louvre.[1] These, which earlier and greater

[1]Marcel Dieulafoy, *L'Art Antique de La Perse*. Parts I to V. Paris, 1885.
Magnificently illustrated and published by the French Government.

kings than his present enemy Darius III had reared and adorned, were now his, another pledge of his greatness and power. There remained that the recovered treasure should be utilized, and of it there were despatched 3,000 talents to Antipater to carry on the war against Sparta. The reorganization of the city order was accomplished after what had now become the usual method. The Persian Arbulites, commander of the city, who had surrendered it without an attempt at defense, was made satrap, but all else was left in trusty Macedonian hands.[1] Here he domiciled the sorry remnant of the family of Darius, providing royal state and use for them, and was thus relieved of a burden of anxiety and care. There is good reason to believe that they had received every possible comfort and attention at his hands, nor have we any call to judge motives or nicely balance diverse traits of character in the case. It is sufficient that Alexander's hands were not stained by their blood, or sullied by their ill treatment.

At Susa there were welcomed considerable reinforcements brought by Amyntas, son of Andromenes, from Macedonia, and estimated to have numbered no less than 15,000 men.[2] In the process of incorporating these with the older forces he made a considerable reorganization, promoted officers who had shown capacity for command or achieved a record for bravery, boldness, or success in battle. The chief appointments were made not by Alexander in person, but by a board of judges which he had appointed to canvass the record, and were required in every case to state the reasons for a promotion that the rank and file might be convinced there was no favoritism, and only the best man chosen. It

[1] Arrian, III, 16, 7 ff.; Curtius, V, 2, 8 ff.; Diodorus, XVII, 65 f.; Plutarch, *Alexander*, 36.
[2] Arrian, III, 16, 10 f.; Diodorus, XVII, 65, 1; Curtius, V, 1, 40 f.

may well be asked what chance had Persia with her
outworn Asiatic imperialism in the army against a
body thus organized, disciplined, and individually rewarded? Her cause was hopeless, and her downfall
awaited only the stroke of the hour.

It was now time to begin the march on Persepolis,
the very centre of the homeland of this Achæmenian
Persian dynasty. Fabulous tales of the magnificence
of the place must have reached Macedonian ears, but
to Alexander far more tempting would be the thought
that its seizure would be a spectacular demonstration
of the end of the Persian dynasty and the beginning
of his own. To take Persepolis must be his next objective. But however easy might come its fall, even though
as easy as Babylon or Susa, to reach it were no such
easy problem. From Susa to Persepolis the way led
from a great plain to an austere tableland 5,000 feet
higher, and between the two lay a cruel tract of Alpine
mountain ranges, passed by but one fairly travers-
able pass, and many narrow clefts riven between cliffs
with dashing brooks or torrents, and hopeless as a scene
for a moving army. Never since Hannibal crossed the
Alps has any later commander been confronted by such
a problem. The difficulty was greatly enhanced by the
season, for winter with its snows and ice had settled
down upon the one single pass. In successive terraces
the mountain range attains a height of 14,000 feet, and
as though this were not difficulty enough there were
rivers great and small to be crossed. Yet facing all the
difficulties Alexander determined upon action. He
would hardly be suspected of such a foolhardy enterprise by Darius, and there was, therefore, some hope of
a surprise. In any case he was unwilling to give the
great king time to reorganize for a fresh defense.

It was the month of December when orders were issued to begin the advance. The route taken is in several places rather doubtful, for the Greeks have dismissed the whole enterprise with few words, but its main course is unmistakable. Immediately upon the beginning of the advance an awkward problem had to be met. The tribes which inhabited the great plains had acknowledged Persian lordship, and upon the fall of Susa had yielded unhesitating submission to the new conqueror. But there were mountain tribes who lived their own separate existence, paid no tribute to the Persian exchequer, and rather exacted toll of the Persian king when he passed through their defiles. To Alexander the Uxians sent ambassadors with the demand that he do as Darius had done. What happened is certain, but the course of events is doubtful, as the Greek authorities differ;[1] the Uxians were defeated with the destruction of their villages and their annexation to the Susian satrapy with the payment of an annual tribute. The march might now be resumed with the assurance that the news of the Uxian defeat would spread through the mountains and deter other tribes from any similar madness.

From the Uxian villages Alexander advanced in two columns. Parmenion was ordered off with the baggage and siege train to traverse the road by the foothills, in command of the Thessalian cavalry, the Greek allies and mercenaries, and a part of the phalanx, while Alexander himself, with the remaining and lighter part of the phalanx, the lancers, bowmen and archers, and as usual the Companion cavalry, moved up the shorter and more difficult mountain pass. After a march reck-

---

[1]Arrian (III, 17) gives a picturesque account of the outflanking of the Uxian stronghold, and Curtius (V, 3, ed. Hedecke, p. 117 (Teubner) a much simpler.

oned at 113 miles, he reached on the fifth day the
Persian or Susian Gates, held by Ariobarzanes with
a strong force, occupying a position additionally
strengthened by a wall built hurriedly across the defile.
Here were 700 cavalry and 40,000 infantry, all Persians
and of the best and most reliable which the empire possessed. This pass is the key to the plateau of Iran, difficult of approach and easy to defend by even a small
body of determined men. It is now called Kal eh-Safid,
"white fortress," a mass of mountainous rock, inaccessible on the sides, and battlemented like a castle. Alexander might have reached Persepolis by the winter
road over Râm Hormuz and Babehan by which he had
sent Parmenion, but it would have been unsafe to
leave Ariobarzanes in the rear, with a force about equal
to his own. Had he ventured upon this the Persians
might, after he had gone on toward Persepolis, move
upon Susa and undo all that he had there set in order.
The problem must be faced boldly.

Alexander went into camp, reconnoitred the position,
and the next day attempted to take the position by
direct assault. Through the narrow defile where but
three men might march abreast the column advanced.
At the narrowest point it was suddenly attacked from
above with arrows, sling-stones, and heavy boulders
rolled from the heights above. The Macedonians stood
the attack, and even attempted to scale the almost per-
pendicular walls, but failed, and at length Alexander
was forced to sound the retreat and withdraw four
miles to his camp. Other means must be sought. From
a prisoner he learned that by difficult footpaths it was
possible to reach the farther end of the defile in the
rear of Ariobarzanes. With the promise of a great reward if he led successfully and a threat of death if he

practised deceit, this prisoner, who was a shepherd and knew the rugged country, became guide. Alexander personally with a small mobile force set out amid December snows to scale these forbidding mountains. By two night marches he achieved the impossible and brought his men to the rear of the Persians, who lay in fancied security watching in the opposite direction the movements of the main body of Alexander's men left under command of Craterus to make demonstrations by day and keep numerous watch fires alight at night. So sudden was the appearance of Alexander and so quick his attack that the outposts were not driven in but scattered, and at dawn his cavalry assaulted in the rear while Craterus, at the sound of the bugles, attacked in front. Ariobarzanes was completely taken by surprise, his discipline shattered, and his force cut to pieces. With but a small body he cut his way to the rear, only to find himself cut off from Persepolis by Philotas, sent forward by Alexander to cross the Araxes by a bridge erected by the Macedonian engineers.[1]

The success was brilliant, and the way to Persepolis lay open. Alexander moved on immediately with the Companions to the bridge, crossed the Araxes and made for Persepolis, eager to reach it before the Persians should take flight with all the coveted treasure. The Persian governor Tiridates, mindful of his own selfish interests, and hoping to profit from whatever help he might afford Alexander, prevented Ariobarzanes from pillage, and died in the struggle. Tiridates had judged wisely, for he received as the reward of his perfidy the satrapy of Susa.

Persepolis and Pasargadæ were taken. Alexander se-

[1]Arrian, III, 18; Curtius, V, 3 f.; Diodorus, XVII, 67 f.; Polyænus, IV, 3, 2.

cured a treasure estimated in value at over $150,000,-
000, and every conceivable form of object of utility or
of beauty which Persian art had made or Persian conquest gathered elsewhere. It was conveyed to Susa
temporarily and thence later to Ecbatana, whither it
was carried, so the story goes, in 10,000 two-mule carts,
and upon the backs of 5,000 camels.

Alexander stood now at the most sacred spot in all
the Persian empire. Here in this very valley Cyrus had
overthrown the Median empire, and here won its territory. Here his body rested in a simple and dignified
tomb. Here his successors had built palaces and temples with whose size and splendor no other place in
Persia could compare. To the heart of an empire which
once had humiliated Hellas had come now at long last
her vindicator. A Persian king had burned and desecrated Athens. Alexander burned the palace of the Persian kings.[1] It was quite likely a deliberate act, ordered
by Alexander as symbolic of the end of the Persian
empire, and with that quite likely as a deed of revenge
in memory of the acts of a Persian king at Athens.[2] It
was contrary to the usual practice of Alexander so to
destroy what it had cost much to secure, but the hour
was glorious and much must be allowed of folly to a
man in the position Alexander had now attained. In
four years (March, 334 to March, 330) he had penetrated to the very heart of the Persian empire, conquering all its territory between Hellas and Persepolis.
The ancient world up to his day could show no parallel,

[1]Arrian III, 18, 10 ff.; Plutarch, *Alexander*, 38; Diodorus, XVII, 70 ff.;
Curtius, V, 6 f.
[2]Diodorus, Curtius, and Plutarch agree that it was the result of a drunken
orgy, but the more sober story of Arrian seems the better worthy of credence.
It is not thereby intended to be said that Alexander was not already beginning to give way to the seductions of drink, but merely that in this story the
lines seem overdrawn in view of what follows. See further Nöldeke, *Aufsätze
zur persischen Geschichte*, 84.

and if he who had accomplished it were drunk with pride instead of wine it were not a marvel.

Before Alexander had reached Persepolis Darius had fled. Five hundred miles away at Ecbatana (modern Hamadan) in Media he halted, there to await the next move of this amazing man of destiny. He might fight if Alexander came on, or he might flee as he had done before. Personal safety was still a dominant motive, perhaps the dominant. At Ecbatana he was safe for some time to come. Picturesquely and comfortably situate at the base of Mount Elvend it had long been the summer capital of the Persian kings. Originally the capital city of Ishtuvegu (Astyages), and taken by Cyrus in 649 B. C., there had been none to dispute its possession. Here for months dwelt Darius III, a hunted fugitive, little worthy of a seat upon the throne which Astyages had erected and Cyrus possessed. He took no steps to assemble another army, though this were quite possible. The eastern quarter of his empire was still his. He was here joined by Ariobarzanes, who could give direct information concerning Alexander, his methods of warfare, and whatever prospects there might be for the meeting of the issue. Not ill served in counsellors was the king, for besides this veteran he had Artabazus, "the first nobleman of Persia," commander of the Greek mercenaries, and his sons, and Nabarzanes of the horse guards, Bessus, satrap of Bactria, and yet others. With these to advise or command, and raw material a plenty, a force fit to give Alexander serious concern might have been prepared. His thoughts seem only to have reached as far as conservation of what remained, not of any adequate defense. His baggage train, his women folk, and whatever treasures still were his, had been sent on to the Caspian

Gates, a pass through the Caspian mountains just by the sea, narrow, easily fortified, well adopted for a stand. The king sat still and waited. One move only did he make upon the checker board of destiny. To Hellas he despatched 300 talents to induce the Lacedæmonians and Athenians to undertake an attack upon Macedonia. There seemed naught else for him but to retire before Alexander and lay waste the lands to hinder pursuit.[1]

When the winter of 330 B. C. ended Alexander was prepared to take the road. Out from the valley of Persepolis and Pasargadæ went a swift marching column and faced northward, leaving the baggage train to follow. The march lay along the eastern footlands of the mountain range. We do not know the month in which he was now on the move, but the wet season lies there from November until February, and spring would be early on this eastern front. In twelve days he was in Media, and there had word that Antipater had been victorious in the far-off homeland. The Lacedæmonians were defeated, King Agis slain at Megalopolis, and warned by events, the Cadusians and Scythians had refused aid to Darius. The signs were favorable, but there were just reasons for the exercise of caution. Darius still lived, and while he lived Persians of any patriotic mould had a rallying point in his person. About him were able men; there were almost endless places of easy defense. A small army fighting at the last ditch for families and homes might be far more formidable than the unmanageable masses of men at Issus.

On the way north a small mountain campaign reduced the Parætacæ, a tribe somewhat similar to the Uxians, and then, again unopposed as at Babylon, Susa and Persepolis, Alexander entered a royal capital and

[1]Arrian, III, 19, 1.

Ecbatana was his. Three days before the city was reached he was met by Bisthenes, son of King Ochus, who had left Darius and his sinking ship of fortune to find place with the Macedonians. He brought news that Darius was retiring eastward with but 3,000 cavalry and 6,000 infantry. There were desertions from his ranks, and men were increasingly recognizing his failure.

The march from Persepolis to Ecbatana (Hamadan) had required fifteen days, but the prize was great. The city was ancient, so old that even in antiquity men were busy inventing origins for it, in default of definite knowledge. It lay about one and a half miles east of the Elvend mountains, above a great plain, and at an elevation of about 525 feet. On the eastern end of the modern city of Hamadan rises a high hill called Musalla, on which there are still discernible remains of a citadel. The plain about the city is well watered by the Kara-su river, and its surroundings would give the city a good food supply. The Persian kings had carried treasure into it, and all that it had garnered had fallen readily into Alexander's hands. From it he could survey with keen eyes three great roads radiating to Babylon, to Susa, and to Nineveh, with minor roads to sites of lesser importance. Twenty-five miles away to the north stretched a plain to the range of mountains which bar the way to Mehreban and Sarderud. The Macedonian king was master of yet another Persian capital, and might dispose of it as he would.

At Ecbatana Alexander discharged from service the Thessalian and Greek allied cavalry, whose term of enlistment was up, paying them in full and adding a handsome bounty. He set Menes in command of arrangements for their sea transport to Hellas, yet many

elected to enlist again and go on. Here also he received
reinforcements of 6,000 Greek mercenaries under Plato
of Athens.[1] Hither were brought the captured treasures
to be stored in vaults under Harpalus, and a garrison
of 6,000 cavalry and some light troops established in
the city. The rule of Media was entrusted to native
Persians,[2] and he was ready quickly for the pursuit of
Darius.

The field was taken by Alexander at the head of the
Companion cavalry, the light armed and Greek mercenary cavalry and part of the phalanx. He marched
about twenty miles a day, and in eleven days had
reached Rhagæ, near the modern Teheran, and headed
straight for the Caspian Gates,[3] a march of thirty miles
made in one day. Darius had already passed through,
and another place well suited for defense was left open.
Beyond lay an arid desert land, and Alexander rested
his men five days and made arrangements for foraging
this land as against the difficulty of the next stage.

Darius had now perceived that flight did not shake
off this pursuer. He was losing daily by desertions. He
called a council and invited suggestions, believing himself that another attempt at resistance should be made.
But it was too late. His companions had no more faith
in him, nor courage for his empire, and treason against
his royal person was on foot. As Alexander halted at
the Caspian Gates there came renegades from the camp
of Darius with the startling intelligence that a conspiracy headed by Bessus had seized the king, bound

[1]Arrian, III, 19, 5 f.; Curtius, VI, 2, 17; Plutarch, *Alexander*, 42.
[2]Arrian, III, 20, 3.
[3]The Caspian Gates are the defiles of Sialek, and Sardar, the former the
northerly, the latter to the southward. "The entrances at both ends [of the
Sardar] are about 20 to 25 yards wide, with steep walls on both sides and an
exceedingly salt stream running through. . . . The length of the defile is
about 10 kms."—A. F. v. Stahl, *The Geographical Journal*, LXIV, No. 4,
October, 1924, p. 319.

him, and left him behind, while some scattered homeward, and others turned to Alexander. The Greek mercenaries would have saved him, but too late; as usual, he had delayed, and his hour had come.

Spurred to another outburst of speed by this news Alexander selected a *corps d'élite* of the Companions, the horse-archers and lancers, and a few men of the phalanx, mounted all on the best available horses, and set out in pursuit of the fleeing conspirators on their way toward Bactria. They were on the main road, and were marching at night. Alexander learned from the populace, well enough frightened as they must have been, that there was a short cut across the desert waste by which, if taken, he might come up with the fugitives. To make the attempt was quickly determined, and 500 picked men mounted on 500 of the best horses set out amid the terrific heat to secure the quarry. The rest had orders to follow with whatever speed they could by the same road as Bessus had taken. In the afternoon the 500 made their start, and by daybreak had covered 47 miles (400 stades), and at dawn came up with the renegades. Alexander had forged ahead with only 60 companions, and fell upon them. Thrown into hopeless confusion by the unexpected attack, they were slaughtered without mercy.

Darius, their hopeless and helpless prisoner, was in their hands, and two of them, Nabarzanes and Barsaëntes, transfixed him with their spears and made off safely lightened of their burden. The place was in a valley between Semnân and Sharud,[1] in the month of Hecatombaion (July) 330 B. C. There, as Alexander approached the prison carriage, lay dead the last of a

[1]Arrian, III, 19 ff.; Curtius, V, 8 ff.; Diodorus, XVII, 73; Justin, XI, 15; Plutarch, *Alexander*, 42 f.

distinguished line of kings, and the conqueror threw over the lifeless body his own red robe in token of royal respect. It was well for Alexander that the king was dead.[1] Alive he could hardly fail, weak though he was, to be a centre for the rallying of Persian strength and the will to war. Yet would Alexander have gladly kept him alive, in his train, as he had so long kept the sorry members of his family. As a moving spectacle in a conqueror's camp he would have been a rich display. So had Cyrus kept Crœsus. But Darius, spared this humiliation, was dignified in death, beyond his position in life. Alexander sent his body to Persepolis and gave it royal burial, and to his family showed all commiseration, and every possible honor. This was the family of a king, and was he not a king himself?

Darius was about fifty years of age when death brought silence. He was an able man on the civil side, an administrator of no mean capacity, and though slow of action gave often displays of remarkable energy and decision.[2] Against any other living man of that age he might have made a good show of resistance, and have kept much, if not all, of his empire. But it was his misfortune to be compelled to match his moderate talents against the supreme military genius of that day, and his gift of statecraft against the greatest statesman.

Alexander appointed Amminaspes, a Parthian, satrap in Parthia and Hyrcania, and with him stationed

[1] It is no longer possible to locate with any certainty the site of the tragedy. A. F. v. Stahl (*Geog. Journal*, LXIV, No. 4, October, 1924,) offers this suggestion: "From Curtius we learn that Darius was murdered not far from the military road—doubtless to the southwest of Damghan. The valley to which the car with Darius was dragged must have been on the southeast side of the present Sefid-Kuh mountains from which water is drawn to irrigate the fields of the villages of Qumish, and somewhere to the north of the present villages of Taziabad and Ahzabad."

[2] Tarn (*Camb. Anc. Hist.*, VI, p. 386) says sharply: "Darius 'great and good' is a fiction of legend. He may have possessed the domestic virtues; otherwise he was a poor type of despot, cowardly and inefficient." This seems to me unjust, and I hold to the judgment expressed above.

as general in command of the forces Tlepolemus, a
Companion. It seemed like the last stroke in Persia's
doom, but there were still dangers to be met and final
solutions found. The first problem was his own men.
They were satisfied with the death of Darius, and regarded the campaign as ended. They could see no reason for not making a return homeward, or in any case
a retirement upon Babylon. Fearful had been their ex-
posure, their pitiless privations, their outpour of
strength in almost incredible marches.[1] They would
have been more than human did they not now long for
home and family. Alexander set himself to comfort,
console, and stimulate. His record of lavish rewarding
in the past now stood him in good stead. They would
believe any promise he might make. He promised, they
believed.[2] At Hecatompylus he halted, awaited the
slower moving columns which had been left behind, and
rested. The place was forlorn enough, and the forward
look over the beyond might well have given them all
pause. It lay on the outer boundary of the cultivable
district of Semina (modern Semnân), beneath the
mountain ridges which separate Media and Parthia,
the Elburz range of our day. From it the modern post
route climbs the difficult pass of Akhori Ahuan, while
the commercial caravan route sweeps round at lower
levels. Alexander elected to take the caravan route and
pursue Bessus. He now regarded himself as the legitimate successor of the Persian kings. He had possessed
himself of their authority, and their honor was in his
care and keeping. His was the duty of punishing the
murderers of his predecessor. He now not merely accepted, but demanded the same sort of honors as were

[1] In about six days they had passed eleven ordinary daily stages.
[2] Diodorus, XVII, 74, 3; Plutarch, *Alexander*, 38; Curtius, VI, 2, 15 ff.;
Justin, XII, 3, 2.

of old given the men who sat upon the throne now become his.[1] This had its value and importance among Persians, but the case was far otherwise with Macedonians and Greeks. They could not enjoy prostrations to earth in the Oriental manner, and conflicts were soon begun over this new move.

The conspirators who had murdered Darius separated each to his own district under agreement to raise armies and form a union with Bessus in Bactria, there to elect a new Great King, and with combined forces to protect him in person and dominion. They had, however, no real coherence, nor any confidence and loyalty one to another, and were little likely to accomplish any deed of moment under such circumstances. The situation was playing safely into the hands of Alexander. We are witnessing the gasps of the dissevered portions of the Persian empire.

Alexander determined to reduce Hyrcania, and crossed the mountain ridge in three columns with orders to make a rendezvous at Zadracarta, the provincial capital. He took in person the most difficult, the westerly route, Erigyius took the central and easier public thoroughfare, with the Greek mercenaries and Craterus the eastern. Much circumspection was necessary, for barbarous peoples might easily attack from numerous defiles. Craterus subdued the Tarpurians on the way, Erigyius found little opposition, and the union at Zadracarta[2] was accomplished. There he placed in control the former satraps and received the submission of men long opposed, now reconciled by inexorable fate, to accept his rule. They were accepted in full faith, and

---

[1] Diodorus, XVII, 77, 4 ff.; Justin, XII, 3, 8; Curtius, VI, 6, 1 ff.; Plutarch, *Alexander*, 45.

[2] This place is called Zadracarta by Arrian (III, 25), but Karta by Strabo c. 508 (ed. Meineke, p. 714, Teubner), Sirynx by Polybius, X, 31, 6.

received commissions or appointments which proved
how willing he was and how trustful. The Greek mercenaries who had fought for Darius at Issus and at Arbela, convinced that the Persian cause was now lost,
came asking for terms, but were only accepted on unconditional surrender. Then censured, they were freely
pardoned and drafted into the victorious army. What
a homecoming that must have been when Greek saw
Greek and knew that Persia could have no more of
such service as that had been!

Alexander had fully recognized the possible future
value of the Caspian Sea and now took further steps to
ensure safe control of its waters. He had despatched the
able and faithful Parmenion through Carducia, and
now personally marched off westward to meet him and
grind between these two forces a human grist of Mar-
dians, a poor folk near the sea, who might become
troublesome if and when a Macedonian fleet should
sail this great inland sea. They were reduced, and we
hear no more of them,[1] but have not learned the details
of the fighting nor whether Parmenion and Alexander
had actually met in the field during this campaign.

Alexander had now deliberately to face the plans
and purposes of Bessus, who had decamped, after the
death of Darius, into his own original satrapy of Bactria.[2] His purpose soon became evident. He meant to
make himself the Great King, and under the style of
Artaxerxes, shortly raised this claim. He must not be
left even attempting such a scheme, and Alexander set
out in hot pursuit, following the valley of the Atrek
upwards into Suria,[3] purposing to pass straight over

[1]Arrian, III, 24, 1 ff.; Diodorus, XVII, 76, 3 ff.; Curtius, VI, 5, 11 ff.
[2]Arrian, III, 21 ff.; Diodorus, XVII, 73 f.; Curtius, V, 8 ff.; Plutarch, *Alexander*, 42.
[3]Arrian, III, 25, 1.

Areia and into Bactria. A diversion southward became
shortly necessary on receipt of intelligence that the satrap of Areia, Satibazarnes, had proved faithless. To
bring him to his senses Alexander made a southerly
sweep through his satrapy, scattered his forces, put him
to flight, and pushing on still further southward
through Drangiana, accomplished its subjection and
brought to an end the purposes of its satrap Barsaëntes
to join Bessus. He fled for safety, but was returned to
Alexander and put to death.

The way was now clear for the march northward
through the Caucasus in pursuit of Bessus. Alexander
took his time. On the way he was careful to ensure
safety in the rear, and at the same time plant a new
centre of Greek influence. With the greatest foresight
a spot was chosen, and the foundations laid for another
Alexandria, where cross the great army roads from
Hyrcania and Bactria, Arachotia and India.[1] It was
worth the expenditure of time and energy, but the city
would never vie with its more glorious namesake in
Egypt. It must rather be reckoned as only one more in
the long list of cities which he built in Bactriana and
in Sogdiana, which are said to have numbered eight[2] or
even twelve.[3] This one was called Alexandria Areion,
that is, Alexandria of the Arians, and its modern representative is Herat, lying at an altitude of 2,500 feet
above the sea, and with but 10,000 inhabitants, composed of a mixture of diverse races. The ancient fortifications suggest an early period, and Alexander was
probably only using an ancient site.

Meanwhile Bessus had been busily preparing for the
attack upon him which he knew to be as inevitable as

[1]Arrian, III, 28, 4 f.; IV, 22, 5; Diodorus, XVII, 87; Curtius, VII, 3, 23;
Strabo, XII, 514.
[2]Strabo, XII, 517.   [3]Justin, XII, 5.

fate. He was ravaging, destroying, laying waste great tracts of country to render difficult the approach of Alexander. The spring of 329 B. C. came over the Parapamisus (the Hindu Kush), and Alexander crossed unopposed after making a passage over the mountains that has no parallel in military history save that of Hannibal over the Alps. The sufferings of these men who followed this superhuman creature over the Hindu Kush will never be written. They lost heavily from hunger, disease, snow blindness, and came through to the first city of Bactria, by name Drapsaca, where a much needed rest was secured. Then a swift march and the Oxus lay before them, by far the largest river Alexander had dared to attempt. There were no boats to be had, for Bessus had destroyed them all. Timber was scarce, and the building of a bridge impossible. Alexander took his tent-skins, filled them with straw or other light materials, made them as nearly water tight as possible, and in five days literally floated his army across unopposed.

This immense achievement so completely overawed all the supporters of Bessus that they deserted his standard and took steps to conciliate rather than oppose Alexander. Led by Spitamenes, they sent word to Alexander that they had Bessus in custody and would deliver him up if Alexander would send a force to receive him. For this purpose Ptolemy, son of Lagus, was sent forward with a mobile force which received the person of Bessus.[1] The poor wretch was scourged, and sent back to Ecbatana, where in a council of Medes and Persians he was convicted of high treason, and later executed.[2] Bessus had never been great enough for the

[1] Arrian, III, 29, 6 f., 30, 1 ff. This account derives from Ptolemy personally, and is to be preferred to the others, as Curtius, VII, 5, 19 ff., 36 ff., and Diodorus XVII, 83, 7 ff.

[2] Arrian, III, 30, 5; IV, 7, 3; Curtius, VII, 10, 10.

plans which his fertile mind had made. He is not a grand but a pathetic figure, yet had he just enough strength to have given Alexander no small trouble to subjugate him. His entire province was now in complete subjection, and was for the moment at least highly profitable to its conqueror. It resupplied the army with horses, in which the losses had been very heavy while crossing the Hindu Kush. Furthermore, when the capital Maracanda (modern Samarcand) was reached the Macedonians found themselves in a noble and very fertile valley of Sogdiana, known to the Middle Ages as Al Sughd, the Mohammedan paradise, even to-day, in its shabby, careworn, and careless misery, a scene of wonder, whose inhabitants practise more gardening than any other labor. There Alexander could refresh tired bodies and consider what the next move was to be. Besides the capital Maracanda, he took a number of well fortified posts[1] and made himself master of the entire province in a sense attained by no Persian king. He was still not quite satisfied, for Cyrus the Great had gone farther eastward. Alexander could not think of himself as doing less. More than 100 miles farther eastward, and over another mountain range were his men ordered until they came to the banks of another great river which Alexander erroneously called the Tanais. It was, however, really the Jaxartes (modern *Syr-daria*), and there he paused, as Cyrus had done before him. But he surpassed his mighty predecessor in making a serious attempt to found a centre of civilization in this wild land. There he built another Alexandria,[2] called indeed Alexandria the Last, the most remote. There it still remains in the form of a poor

[1] Arrian, IV, 1 ff.; Curtius, VII, 6; Strabo, XI, 517.
[2] Arrian, IV, 4, 1, 3; Curtius, VII, 6, 13, 25 ff.; 7, 1 ff.; Pliny, VI, 49. It is called 'Α ἐσχάτη and even 'Αλεξανδρέσχατα. (Appian. Syr., 57.)

modern representative, Khodjend. Alexander was now
in a country which provided for him a series of difficulties far exceeding in many ways any which he had
yet met. A land which the Asiatic born and bred Persians had never completely pacified, and had assuredly
not civilized, offered many and very great problems of
conquest, and still more of administration.

While he tarried, city building, on the Jaxartes there
burst out in his rear a very serious rebellion whose
leader was Spitamenes, a native of this province of
Sogdiana, the man who was immediately responsible
for the death of Darius, had been pardoned by Alexander, and even entrusted with military command in
the province. He now was besieging the small garrison
of Maracanda. Alexander was confronted by a very serious situation, for in front from the opposite bank of
the Jaxartes he was taunted and threatened by the
warlike Scythians. The Jaxartes would have to be
crossed to attack them, before he should dare to turn
upon the treacherous Spitamenes. The river in dry sea-
sons is fordable, though with difficulty, but now must
be crossed as the Oxus had been on inflated skins or
camp equipage. The horse swam the stream. A bold
attack was made, and so swift was the advance that the
characteristic Scythian method of attack by swift riding round upon the flanks failed, and Alexander dispersed them, leaving hundreds dead upon the field. His
own losses had been considerable, for he had 160 dead
and 1,000 wounded. Worse than this, in the pursuit he
and his men drank stagnant and foul water and on the
return across the river many fell ill of fever, among
them Alexander himself very seriously. The compensa-
tion found was that envoys arrived from the king of
the Scythians tendering all sorts of friendly agreement.

Alexander received it all graciously, accepted it at full value, and restored the prisoners he had taken.

This act cemented a friendship which long endured. Alexander had no desire to extend his borders of actual administration beyond the point reached by Cyrus. He was king of Persia as Cyrus had been, and his border was the border of Cyrus. It was enough. Let the new Alexandria look across the river, and Greek culture hold that outpost. Whether any real move of Greek culture was made thither we know not, but it seems but little probable. It is a mere name that has come down the long roll of the centuries, the name of the most remote of all the many Alexandrias. But something far more strange has happened and that is the preservation of a direct tradition of the greatness of Alexander among the remote and almost inaccessible peoples in the mountains upon that country well and suitably known as the roof of the world. In Ferghana (or Fergana), a province of Russian Turkestan, formed of diverse portions in our own time and populated chiefly by Mohammedans, even their chiefs claim descent from Alexander, and "everything great and grand they still couple with the name of Alexander."[1]

The river Jaxartes was evidently considered by Alexander as the proper boundary of his empire, and the Cyrus tradition, well known to him, would confirm this. The site he had chosen for his last city was admirable, for it stood just where the mighty river takes its northern bend, and at the very point where from time immemorial the road from the far east came to cross the river westward. This great road then and now came from the mountain passes whose more easterly

[1]Franz von Scnwarz, *Alexander's Feldzüge in Turkestan*, p. 97. Quoted by Wheeler, *Alexander the Great*, p. 402.

gateway is Kashgar, the door to China. Man is after all a very conservative animal and once he has made a road holds very tenaciously to it. The eyes of Alexander would never penetrate so far, yet had he vision sufficient to provide an entrance for that far distant commercial movement into his Persian empire. Here was its eastern limit. He believed its natural southern limit was the Hindu Kush range, which he had crossed when he made this invasion of Bactria. To his geographical knowledge this was the Caucasus, and the Caucasus was but an extension of the Taurus range running east and west through the centre of Asia. South of this mountain range lay Assyria and Babylonia and the Elamite lands conquered and occupied by Persia as added territories and now become his by conquest, yet lying somewhat apart and severed by this long mountain range from Persia of old. South also lay India, the Punjab, and toward that rather than toward China did his eyes turn in longing. But to no far distant dream could he now yield attention, for there was a fire blazing in his rear which demanded immediate and very important attention.

While Alexander was busy with the war and the diplomatic negotiations with the Scythians at or beyond the Jaxartes, Spitamenes had been even more industriously at work to break all that Alexander had accomplished in Sogdiana. He had opportunity to rouse the entire province into a formidable rebellion against the rule and administration of Alexander. At the capital of the province, the city of Maracanda (modern Samarcand), Alexander had left a garrison of Macedonians, who could have seemed little else than an island in a surging sea of rebellion. When Spitamenes counted himself ready to clear the province and attacked Ma-

racanda the Macedonians not only successfully held
him at bay but made a sortie and gave him a rough
handling. This was well done, and had the garrison
been content with this achievement all would have been
well. But unfortunately boldness rather than wisdom
and prudence prevailed in the garrison, and possessing no leader of genius it made a disastrous blunder.
When word reached Spitamenes that Alexander had
despatched a relief force toward Maracanda he pru-
dently withdrew toward the west and abandoned hope
of taking the city. The Macedonians, swollen with
pride of achievement and eager for the praise of distinguishing themselves much further, sallied out in
hot pursuit. Coming upon a band of nomad Scythians,
whom they counted as allies of the hated Spitamenes,
they attacked. Infuriated by this, the Scythians of
the westerly district now turned to the support of the
rebellious Sogdianians, and, reinforced by their help,
especially in cavalry, Spitamenes was able to cease his
flight and come to a reckoning with his foolish pur-
suers.

He chose with great skill a level plain on which his
horsemen could fight with the native tactics in open
order, and then attacked the Macedonian phalanx, riding round and round in swift movements and attacking with darts and arrows, and making feints, but never
allowing the phalanx to come to grips with his swaying horsemen. The fewer horsemen which had come
from Alexander under command of Andromachus were
worn by their march and were quite unfit to match the
six hundred far better horse which the Scythians had
contributed to the Sogdianians. The Macedonians were
hopelessly beaten, and could only organize as best they
might a square and cut their way through to the river

Polytimetus (modern Sarawshan), hoping by its banks
to find some refuge. Caranus, who commanded part of
the cavalry, tried to cross the river, but failed to send
word to Andromachus of his purpose. The infantry at-
'tempted to follow. There was neither command, nor direction. Far away was the master mind of Alexander,
and none of those who were here in command could do
what he would have done. The poor men were cut to
pieces, and of the force that had sallied boldly out of
Maracanda only 60 horse and 300 foot got away. Two
thousand men were lost to Alexander—more indeed
perished in this one sorry escapade than were sacri-
ficed hitherto in the whole campaign for the conquest
of Persia.

Spitamenes was so overjoyed by the complete success of this move that he moved back to attack once
more the garrison in Maracanda with a renewed hope
of success. When news of this reached Alexander he
decided that the hour had struck to retrieve the fearful disaster already sustained by an effort to end once
for all the career of Spitamenes. With his usual decision and dash he picked a mobile body of men consisting of half the Companion cavalry, the shield-bear-
ing guards, archers, Agrianians and light-armed men
of the phalanx, and set out for the bloody scene on the
Polytimetus. To the capable hands of Craterus was
entrusted the main body of the army with instructions
to follow. In three days Alexander marched 170 miles
and on the fourth came up to Maracanda. Spitamenes
fled upon his approach, and was not overtaken, though
Alexander followed him into the desert. On the way
Alexander passed over the sad field on which his ill led
men from Maracanda had suffered slaughter and there
provided for such bodies as could be found a decent

burial with the wonted ceremonies of honor. This done
he turned upon the unhappy Sogdianians and visited
his unrestrained fury upon their lands and persons.[1]
It could hardly be said that these people were responsible for Spitamenes and the disaster to the Macedonians which he had brought about. They were more
or less helpless tools in his hands. Yet for whatever
share they had taken in the rebellion Alexander laid
their whole district waste, burning and desolating every
hamlet or village and slaying mercilessly all who could
not make escape to the fastnesses of the mountains.
It would be difficult, if not impossible, to parallel these
deeds of savagery in all the earlier career of Alexander. Oriental method and manner of the type once common among Assyrian conquerors had come into the
blood of a civilized man from the west. A newer and
more evil spirit is preparing for that nemesis which ancient Greek faith and fear might well have warned the
king to beware.

When, as he falsely believed, Sogdiana was completely pacified the winter again had fallen upon the
"roof of the world," and Alexander was compelled to
creep into winter quarters, chosen to be at Zariaspa
(modern Charjui), where in these later days the Trans-
caspian railway crosses the Oxus. Alexander was now
once more in Bactria, during the winter of 329/8, and
here received sorely needed reinforcements which had
successfully made the long march from Greece. They
numbered 17,000 infantry and 2,600 cavalry. Here
again do we meet new proof of the success with which
Alexander had planted garrisons and established order
over that vast distance. Even more striking than his
conquest of Persian military prowess is his administra-

[1]The whole narrative of this Sogdianian episode may be read in Arrian, IV,
5, 6.

tion of Persian territory. Always, when most needed, troops seem to arrive to supply the gaps made by battle or disease. It is indeed an astonishing display of organization.

The winter of 328/7 was spent at Nautaka, where preparations for a projected campaign in India went forward, as though all was peaceful in a fully conquered Sogdiana. But this was still far from the truth. He held the plains only in a grasp sufficient to prevent any serious uprising. But the hills were full of dangers to his rule. Four mountain chiefs held undisturbed possession of them, one of whom at least, Oxyartes, aspired to some sort of independence, perhaps even to the making of a kingdom of his own in this wild province. There was indeed grave need of a strong effort; and in the month of January 327, while deep snow still covered the mountain fastnesses, Alexander took the risk of a sudden assault up his fortress, called the 'Sogdian Rock.' The rock was steep, the snow heavy, and the garrison, having refused to surrender, taunted Alexander with the mocking declaration that he could never take the stronghold unless he could find men able to fly. Alexander called for volunteers, and 300 responded to attempt to scale the defenses with ropes and iron pegs, only thirty were killed, while the rest made the top, and hoisted the signal. Alexander bade the garrison look at his flying men, and a glance made them surrender at discretion. Oxyartes was absent, but his daughter Roxane was captured and married, doubtless as a stroke of policy, to Alexander. When this intelligence reached Oxyartes he came, accepted the situation, and joined with Alexander to reduce his compatriots.[1]

[1] For this episode we must rely upon Arrian, IV, 18, 4 ff., 19; Curtius, VII, 11; and Polyænus, IV, 3, 29.

There still remained the stronghold of Chorienes, protected by a swift river flowing through a deep cañon, which the garrison was confident could not be crossed. Alexander, not to be foiled, set his men to making ladders and pegs by which they climbed down the ravine, flung hurdles covered with earth over the stream, and were ready for an assault. Oxyartes now entered the lists and induced Chorienes to surrender, largely apparently by showing him how generously Alexander had dealt with himself under similar conditions.[1]

Alexander returned to Bactra, leaving to Craterus the reduction of any remaining chiefs in the hill country, which was safely accomplished, while the master was busy with arrangements for the projected campaign into India.

These later campaigns were interspersed with difficulties in his army and with outbursts of temper on the part of Alexander sadly suggestive of changes in his nature. It might well happen, indeed, that a man who had now been living in a wilderness, fighting desperate and rude men, should take up some of their weaknesses, adopt some of their savage or barbarous customs. It is to be remembered that Alexander was still a young man, still in the character-forming stage, and it is too much to expect of him the soberness and restraint of matured manhood.

The first serious outburst occurred when Bessus was captured by Ptolemy and brought to Bactra in the winter 329/8 for judgment. He was condemned, his ears and nose were cut off and the mutilated man sent off to Ecbatana and there executed. His condemnation apparently was not based upon his slaying of Darius,

[1]Arrian, IV, 21, 3 ff.; Curtius, VIII, 2, 19 ff.; Strabo, XI, 517.

but upon his attempt at the assumption of royalty.[1]
But whatever the charge the mutilation was unworthy
of Alexander. There was however a case far worse than
this, and with consequences more deplorable. The
preparations for it came slowly but surely, and the explosion was nevertheless startlingly sudden.

Alexander knew himself to be master of Persia, and
felt himself ready to assume not merely the actual disposition of all its affairs, but also to assume the dig-
nities and accept the honors which had been customary
in the land. He was certain to be surrounded by sycophants ready to support every new expression of royal
assumptions. Persians who surrendered or were captured were quick to pay to this man every honor that
had been given their own former king, now humbled
by this new king. The sight of these men prostrate
upon the ground before Alexander was most unpleasant
to Greek eyes. Symbols often have very differing inter-
pretations among diverse peoples. To the Greeks it was
not custom to bow prostrate to earth before any but a
god. They could bow before a king who however ex-
alted was still a man, but it were a humiliation not to
be borne to fall to earth in his presence. Alexander
was confronted with an awkward dilemma. Could he
hold Greek loyalty if he attempted, even on Persian
soil, to ask of them what Persians gave willingly, and
if he did not would Persians accept this situation as
impartiality? It was a problem difficult to solve, a decision hard to give. An attempt to compromise the matter by lifting a bit the Macedonian methods and de-
pressing somewhat the Persian was not appealing.
Alexander drifted for a time without a conclusion.
Anything might cause a sudden turn, and the outcome

[1]Arrian, III, 29, 6 ff., 30, 5, IV, 7, 3, and Curtius, VII, 10, 10.

be perilous. Who could say when the overturn might come?

At Maracanda there occurred an incident which brought affairs to a crisis. There were few among all the generals of Alexander superior to Cleitus, the Macedonian hipparch. Well had he served his master, and deservedly great were his honors. But fate made him now the cause of a fearful catastrophe. They were in dry Turkestan, the heat was great, the cold bitter. Water was almost unpotable, and the district supplied in abundance a fiery wine. The Macedonians drank it, and when in camp it were natural enough for weary men as they drank and made merry after fearful fatigues, to overstep the limits of safety. There is no sure reason for accepting the gossip that makes Alexander a frequent or confirmed drunkard, yet human as he had often enough shown himself to be there is also no reason to doubt that he was at times drunk. This was certainly true of others in his company. At last the inevitable came.

As they sat and drank after dinner flatterers extolled Alexander and compared him with the demigods. What else was said does not clearly appear. But they were guilty of making the fame of Alexander completely detached from Philip his father, and apparently reflected upon other Macedonians, among them probably Parmenion. Cleitus had been in the service of Philip and was proud of it. He could not endure any minishing of his fame, and believed to the full that the genius of Alexander owed much, if not all, to an inheritance from blood so distinguished. He was drunk and his loosened tongue was indiscreet. Alexander was also drunk, and a small spark might cause an explosion. He was a spoiled man, as would have been any other by victories so amazing. Cleitus was so mad as to speak out to defend Philip's men generally, and by innuendo to include Alexander among those who had owed everything to them. He seems to have been implying that Alexander had given countenance to slurs upon his human ancestry, and was rapidly making himself a demigod, and Philip's generals puppets. He was ready to glorify them, and to compare Alexander invidiously with his father. He went on boldly to declare that Alexander owed his victories to his generals. The words stung. Alexander made efforts at self-control, and said to two Greeks beside him, "Don't you feel like demigods among beasts?" But Cleitus was now in a drunken fury and beyond restraint. He thrust out his hand toward Alexander, saying "This saved your life at the Granicus"—which was quite true. Alexander could bear the taunts no longer, but springing to his feet snatched a spear from a guard, but was forcibly held while Ptolemy drove Cleitus from the hall. There was now time for appeasement, could the men be kept apart. But as Alexander continued to shout "Cleitus," the foolish man broke loose from his well-meaning captors, re-entered the hall, with the defiant words, "Here is Cleitus, Alexander." Alexander ran him through on the instant.

When Alexander was sober his remorse was more bitter than his anger had been. He would take no food for three days, and kept calling out the names of Cleitus and of his sister Lanice, who had been his own nurse, whom he had loved as a mother. Mournful now were his cries to her, "Fair return have I made in manhood's years for thy nurture and care—thou who hast seen thy sons die fighting in my behalf; and now have I slain thy brother with mine own hand." The army was now justly alarmed for their chief. He might grow mad

or die, and these men be left at the ends of the earth
without a leader. They must persuade him to eat, nurse
him back to manhood. The philosopher Anaxarchus
told him that kings could do no wrong. Arrian closes
the case with at least a word of good and the verdict
that many kings had done wrong, but he had heard of
no other who had repented.[1]

The death of Cleitus had not bettered but worsened
the whole case as related to Alexander's proper attitude
to the assumption of royal honors. Nemesis was steadily preparing for vengeance, and troubles and dissen-
sions menaced. The time had now come for a fresh
reckoning. Since the death of Darius Alexander had
adopted on occasion the Persian dress, and assumed
parts of the ceremonial which historically accompanied
it. He was introducing the Persian custom of prostration (*proskynēsis*) before the king, which, as we have
already seen, was repugnant to Macedonian ideas. The
evil genius of the piece at this juncture was Callisthenes, who had been with Alexander from the beginning of the great adventure as historian. He had sent to
Athens a life of Alexander which continued the narrative of victories up to this time. He took himself far
too seriously, and seemed to think that his portrayal
and not Alexander's deeds had made the king great.
He was anxious to keep in the king's favor, hoping to
secure from him the rebuilding of his native city of
Olynthus. His method was flattery, but ill managed. In
his history of Alexander he declared that in the march
along the Pamphylian coast, at Mount Climax the sea
itself had prostrated itself before Alexander, son of
Zeus. But Alexander merely wrote home that he "had
made a path along the Pamphylian ladders and

[1]For the whole Cleitus episode the authorities are Arrian, IV, 8 ff.; Plutarch, *Alexander*, 50 f.; Curtius, VIII, 1, 20 ff.

marched over it." Callisthenes was not to be gainsaid and took opportunities to circulate amazing stories, such as that the oracle of Ammon had told Alexander that he was not the son of Philip but in truth the very son of Zeus Ammon himself, and that the oracle of Apollo at Didyma had declared him to be the son of Zeus.

It is therefore not surprising that this man should have brought forward at Bactra the fiction of Alexander's divine descent, and could offer something in support of it. Callisthenes was a nephew of Aristotle and he, great philosopher as he was, had told Alexander that he had no peer, and with Alexander in mind had written that the supreme ruler when he came would be as a god among men. The issue now hung upon the question as to whether this man, be he god or demigod mattered little, was to force Persian royal customs upon Macedonians and compel all his subjects to adopt prostration before him. It is not known how or when the idea first took root in the mind of Alexander, whether perhaps very early or only far on in the series of incomparable victories. There were those who thought it primarily a suggestion of Callisthenes and Alexander seemed confident that he would have the support of this man. It was his purpose now to assume the fiction of divine origin as a matter of policy, though there is no reason to think that he really believed it in his heart. There were Macedonians to support him in every new move, but when prostration was actually introduced opposition arose, and in the opposition and active in it was none other than Callisthenes. Alexander was enraged. We shall never know why Callisthenes had changed his mind, and had chosen this fatal course. The sad fact stands and that is all.

In this situation there came suddenly an event which gave Alexander cause or excuse for a dreadful act of vengeance. It arose, as do tragedies so often, out of an incident trifling in itself. There had been a boar hunt and Hermolaus anticipated the king, which was quite contrary to Macedonian custom. He was deprived of his horse and whipped. Hermolaus and Sostratus, son of Amyntas, decided to assassinate Alexander the next time they were appointed to watch at his bedside, and four others joined in the conspiracy. But on the fated night Alexander, advised by some soothsayer, sat long at supper, the plot was detected, and they were put to death. Callisthenes was directly or indirectly implicated, perhaps only because of some loose talk to these unfortunate men about tyrants. Callisthenes was imprisoned, and died whether by natural causes, as Aristobulus would have it, or hanged, as Ptolemy reports.[1]

These sorry events cast lurid light upon Alexander's inner life. They are quite easy to understand, for circumstances had made changes in his moral character and he was long in danger of his life not only in war with Persians but from envy and treachery among his own. As we attempt to form some picture of the form, content, and consequences of the conquest of Persia we must think not only of the character of Persian kings and of their civilization, but also of the man who had conquered, and of the example he was to set to the men whom he appointed to govern satrapies in his name. What good or evil he was to bring the common people of the now defunct Persian Empire would in no small degree depend upon the sort of man he had now become. That which then was, would bring forth what was to be, and this man was the custodian of the situation.

[1] Arrian, IV, 10 ff.; Curtius, VIII, 5 ff.; Plutarch, *Alexander*, 52 ff.

Alexander was now to invade India. It had indeed never been a part of the Persian Empire in any true and unequivocal manner, and for the goal which he had set it was none of his care to undertake these hardships and make this great effort. But Darius the Great had invaded India and Alexander could not leave such glory as that to the king that was dead. He would grasp it for himself and show men that he could do more with it. He seems to have divined the seriousness of the problem, for the preparations were extensive and revolutionary. He introduced now in the fullest manner the use of Persians in his army. It was no longer a Macedonian but in very truth a Persian army. He was no longer merely a Macedonian king; he was king of the vast Persian Empire, and it was now the Empire making war, the Empire extending its borders, solidifying conquests made by Darius, and adding territories of wide extent to its borders, and myriads of men of diverse races to its supporters.

Yet in a fundamental sense the invasion of India was folly. The task of Persian administration was already too great for the human brain; and the sequel showed only too clearly that Alexander's real work was now done. He would do nothing with the Punjab, nor could he. He were much better employed in the consolidation of that which had already been won. There was enough of labor and care to take on any shoulders. There is no need here to follow Alexander into India. This story concerns Persia only, and India was never in any real sense a part of the Persian Empire, however much Darius may have overawed one small part of its mighty distances, its great congeries of peoples. For this present purpose it will suffice to remind us only of the simplest possible outlines of this campaign and then to meet Alexander on his return to Persia.

He crossed the Indus in the early spring of 326 B. C. If he could conquer a small territory south of the great river and pursue its course to the mouth he might fairly boast that he had done as much as Darius and Xerxes, and that no people who had ever acknowledged even the semblance of Persian authority were outside his rule. Yet was this invasion only a mere incident, a sort of by-play. Its results were small in value, if there were any, and its consequences serious, for here began the wearing down of Alexander's strength, the sapping of his vitality. The steady and uniform control of his men had ceased. The fighting was none too easy. The climate was strange and Macedonians came into no easy relation with it, or adaptation to its moods. Seventy days of rain produced a discomfort far worse than the wounds of weapons. A mutiny arose and men who had borne all and said little now pointedly refused to follow their leader further afield. They had become accustomed to the idea of conquering and ruling Persia, but this was not Persia and they knew it. Alexander was compelled to yield and declare his intention to return. The effect upon the army must have startled Alexander. "Then they shouted as a mixed multitude would shout when rejoicing; and many of them were in tears; some even approached the royal tent and implored blessings many and great upon Alexander, because, forsooth, by them alone he had let himself be conquered."[1]

On the Jhelum Alexander had a fleet in preparation, which was now completed. There were eighty triakonters, and with all the subsidiaries for the transport of horses, and of food, the total is said to have consisted of 800 vessels. Nearchus was admiral and Onesicritus

[1] Arrian, V, 29.

pilot of Alexander's ship. With much ceremony the fleet moved slowly down the stream early in November, 326 B. C., while Alexander poured libations from a golden cup to his ancestors Heracles, to Ammon, and to the rivers and the sea. When the confluence of the Jhelum and the Chenab had been passed there was a sharp campaign against the Malli (Mahlava), a people living on the Ravi who had been reported as under arms. The mass of the army were advancing on land in three divisions commanded by Craterus, Hephæstion, and Philip. Alexander landed and took the lead against a virile people who were prepared to defend themselves. Their resistance was without much effect until their well-fortified capital was attacked. There the king received a dangerous wound, was even reported as dead, to the consternation of the army. He recovered and this proved to be his last great campaign and this his last battle wound.

From the mouth of the Ravi the flotilla made its way, a hundred and fifty miles or more, to the Indus. The course of the river then was not as it is now, nor is the exact line of the ancient stream now to be identified, nor have the sites touched been discovered. We must be content with the general statement that the mouth of the great river was reached, after Alexander had founded two Alexandrias upon its banks, and that he secured at least a nominal submission of the peoples who lived by the stream.

Craterus was sent off homeward through the Mulla Pass, taking the sick and wounded, the siege train, heavy baggage and the elephants, while Alexander continued with the fleet to Patala, where he built a harbor with docks, intended to act as a port for commerce with the Persian Gulf and so make connections between this new portion of the empire. He had attempted to constitute three satrapies and to make some sort of an orderly provision for their rule. It was however a fatuous proceeding, displaying indeed his attempt everywhere of order and unity, of an empire and not of a mere congeries of peoples. But time would soon blot out all his efforts in India. It was not to be hellenized. He had overstepped the limits of possibility.

In September 325 he started with perhaps 15,000 men for the horrible march through Gedrosia, while Nearchus waited for the northeast monsoon to give him a favorable wind and smooth sea. The men on the ships were to suffer hardships, but these were naught in comparison with the frightful experience of the army toiling over desert wastes of burning sands, often without water for long stretches. Reduced to uncontrollable wretchedness, men plundered provisions which were intended to be left in caches along the shore for the use of the fleet, slew pack animals and ate them. Men died in numbers and after sixty days of indescribable torture in a land not even so much as visited by white men in modern times a miserable remnant reached the oasis of Pura. Thence stretched Carmania, a land of plenty in which food and clothing could be supplied again. But Alexander felt grave anxiety for his fleet, of which no tidings were received. Anxiety was scarcely justified so early, for the ill-assorted fleet had 750 miles to sail, and it had been late in making sail at the beginning. After delays during unfavorable winds at the mouth of the Indus they made good progress and in thirty days more lifted Ras Musandam from the sea, and skirting cautiously the coast in five days more were safely anchored in the river Anamis, near the present harbor of Bender-Abbas. It had been upon the whole a very favored voyage. Only four ships were lost, and frequent deprivations of food and even of water were soon forgotten in the joy of arrival. The army of Alexander was sixty or seventy miles inland in camp. The men disembarked in a land that looked pleasant after those that had been before their eyes, and the search for Alexander was soon rewarded with success. His joy and gratitude were unbounded, and Nearchus was laden with honors.

The fleet was despatched in January, 324 B. C., to explore the coast to the head of the Persian Gulf, and Hephæstion led the main army parallel with the fleet, while Alexander with the light troops marched by way of Pasargadæ and Persepolis. In the spring of that year all were reunited in Susa.

Alexander's return was sorely needed. There were disorders, confusions, or incipient rebellions in many parts of the empire. The tomb of Cyrus had been violated, and the sacred dust removed; many temples had been plundered. There was open rebellion in Bactria. The military commanders in Media had outraged the populace by violence and plain disregard of even elementary justice. Western satraps had collected armies, and were acting as petty kings in almost complete independence. Harpalus, who had long administered the royal treasure, had fled into Cilicia, and then into Greece, carrying with him great sums which he used for corruption, with which he left a sad mark upon various politicians, chief of all even upon Demosthenes.[1] Cleomenes had practised serious abuses in Egypt. There were pretenders in Carmania and in Media; the former was captured by Craterus, and the latter by

[1] For this episode see an excellent exposition by Tarn, *Cambridge Anc. Hist.*, VI, pp. 450 ff.

Atropates. The whole fabric of empire built by the sword and marvellously ordered while the strong hand and discerning mind were present seemed to be flying into hopeless pieces.

Alexander acted with fearful severity, and with dramatic suddenness. Aristobulus was ordered to restore the tomb of Cyrus, but it could never again be what it was. The satraps of several of the largest provinces were summarily put to death, and Macedonians took their places, for trust in the Persians for such posts was believed to be premature. The most interesting appointment was in the person of Peucestas,[1] who was made a personal royal bodyguard, and then satrap of Persis and Susiana. He adopted Persian customs, assumed native dress, learned the language, and acquired genuine popularity with his people.

At Susa there was a great feast to celebrate the conquest, and the establishment of a new monarchy. There were held numbers of marriages between Macedonian officers and Persian women as a symbol of the union of Hellas and Persia. Alexander married Barsine, daughter of Darius, and her sister Drypetis became wife to Hephæstion.[2] But it was an artificial and unreal device and there was no good in it. Plutarch[3] glorifies rhetorically the effort and contrasts it with Xerxes and his bridge of boats, in the joining of Europe and Asia, "not with rafts and timbers and senseless bonds, but by the lawful love of wedlock and by community of offspring."

When Spring came Alexander sent Hephæstion with the army by road up the Tigris to Opis, but himself embarked on ships with the hypaspists, the *agéma*, and

---

[1] On him and his fortunes see Arrian, VI, 28, 35, 30, 2 s.; VII, 6, 3, 23, 1 ss.
[2] Arrian, VII, 4, 5, 6.   [3] *De Alex. Magni Fortuna aut virtute*, I, 7.

Fig. 61. Persians at the Hunt. (Sarcophagus of Alexander.)

a few cavalry Companions down to the coast, where
he founded another Alexandria. He was seeking ac-
quaintance with these outlying portions of his empire.
Thence he sailed up the Tigris, breaking down dams
built by the natives to hinder the advance of any hostile invasion. He had none to fear but wished to render
easy the movement of commerce. He joined his army
at Opis, and there saw a new and astonishing sight. He
had held a great assembly before which he declared
that he would now send to their homes veterans who
were ill or failing, giving each one such honors or
emoluments as would make him an object of envy in
Greece. The declaration was completely misunderstood.
The Macedonians believed that he would now surround
himself with Persians and Medes, to which suspicion
color was given by his great new force of trained and
armed Orientals whom he was adding to his army in separate detachments. The discontent broke into a fury of
mutiny and Alexander addressed his men in stinging
words, and told them all to go home if so they willed
to do. Then he retired into the palace to which none of
them were admitted. Two days of confusion and doubts
intervened. They, poor deluded fellows, were without
leadership. They could not leave him, nor could they
remain. After two days he called to him the Persian
leaders and began definitely the organization of a Persian army. The Greeks could endure the strain no
longer and on the third day appeared in numbers before the palace, casting their arms upon the ground
and bidding him do as he would with them. The crisis
was over, and naught had done it but the shining personality of an incomparable man. The veterans, 10,000
men, were sent home under the command of Craterus,
and Alexander turned to go on with the work of con-

solidation, with the investigation of his dominions, with the reconstitution of a stable government.

From Opis Alexander went to Ecbatana, and there met an irreparable loss, for Hephæstion fell ill of a fever and died. He had long been closer to the king than any other, trusted beyond all others, as he deserved to be, and as able as he was faithful. The king buried him as did Achilles Patroclus, and turned from his tomb to subdue refractory mountain tribes of Cossæans and Uxians.

In the spring of 323 B. C. Alexander returned to Babylon in defiance of the warnings of Chaldean priests, who predicted mischief for him. He acted as he had always done, and without fear. He was busy with preparations for an expedition to Arabia. There were deputations from Greece, and prolonged discussion of grave political questions. His body, worn and weary with campaigns such as the world had never seen before, and his mind, exhausted with the surging of wind and wave of dispute over questions little or big, were ready for any assault of evil. He was struck down with a fever, and vitality wasted quickly. Into the palace of Nebuchadrezzar was he carried, and men who had suffered with him in the past ten years were determined to see him even on his bed. They filed by in silence to moan outside, having seen that the commanding eyes could speak recognition, but the tongue was hushed. Then at sunset on June 13, 323 B. C., he died, being not yet thirty-three years old, and having reigned twelve years and eight months.

In the last weary days of life Alexander had been full of plans for the future. He seems to have had no grandiose schemes for any extended conquests. The dream of world empire ascribed to him by later ages is without sufficient foundation. There was indeed a larger world sweeping on over limitless spaces to the Pacific Ocean, but he had no knowledge of it. One must know that one may covet. He had mastered the Persian Empire and he knew it. There remained only that he find a way to join Persia and Greece, to unite them in some fashion so that one man might rule them and transmit a unified empire to those that should come after him. He thought only of two projects. He would conquer Arabia, not because it had ever been an integral part of the empire but because he was anxious to open the seaways which surrounded it, and feared lest its untamed peoples might block the southward sea traffic of the empire. This idea is therefore to be credited to statesmanship and not to war. In precisely the same thought are we to seek explanation of the second project. He wished to conquer Scythia, of which his conceptions were vague geographically. He would find a northern connection between east and west, as he had found and traversed a southerly one. He would join the Danube and the Jaxartes. There was no certain knowledge of the Caspian Sea, but very persistent conjecture that it had outlets of some sort into the oceans that were known. This he meant to explore and settle the matter definitely. These two projects, Arabia and Scythia, offer an engaging entrance to such a brief survey of his imperial ideals, his statesmanship and administrative skill as may fitly engage the thought of one who has followed the history of ancient Persia to this point. A fuller study of Alexander himself belongs not here but to those whose care it has been to write his life.

Every conquest, every destruction by the sword of any empire, kingdom, or state always brings losses to humanity. Something that time and man's hand and brain have conceived and brought to fruition goes down in the crash. Yet has it often happened that a new creation has seemed to be worth all that it cost. Humanity has lost indeed, but mankind has gained on the whole and civilization has gone forward. However this may be in some cases there can be no serious doubt that the gain wrought by Alexander has immeasurably outweighed all losses, no matter how great they might seem to have been. Before his astounding enterprise there were but two great centres of civilization in the world. The one was located in the river valleys of the Nile and the Euphrates, the other in the free cities of Greece. It were a sorry mistake of judgment not to recognize the greatness of the first. With every passing year of excavation, translation, and interpretation the wonder at the achievements of these peoples in the arts, sciences, and letters grows and intensifies. The extraordinarily clever fingers of Egyptian artists and artizans wrought objects of exquisite beauty, and had a message concerning them well deserving the attention of Greece when the time came. In the valley of the Euphrates men had evolved a civilization represented not only in gold and silver work worthy of comparison with the best that Egypt had done, but had also devised scripts and enshrined in them records of human life and thought which were destined to abide when all the original Sumerians, Babylonians, and Assyrians had long been in the dust. These two, Egypt and Babylonia, had a very different message from that which Greece had to give. There in the struggles of cities there arose out of the strife political ideals so superior to all that the Orient had learned as to be beyond serious comparison. When to this consideration there is added the wealth

Fig. 62. The Panther Hunt. (Sarcophagus of Alexander.)

of Greek genius in founding the sciences which still endure; in working in stone as never man before or since;
in the writing of books whose recovery from their hiding places gave civilization a new start in the Renais-
sance, then the world of the East, great as it was in its
own way, needed Greece more than Greece the Orient.
It was Alexander who brought these two great centres
together when he conquered Persia. No conqueror before, nor any since, has so moved dissevered parts of
humanity together as this man. He did it also at the
right moment. Greece, when he began his work, was
still the old Greece, and it was rapidly losing driving
force. Inertia had begun. Still more was this true in
Egypt and in Babylonia. The men who had made them
great were dead, and there were no worthy successors.
Persia had conquered them, but lacked the power to
assimilate in any but a small way their civilization, and
then to advance.

Alexander founded upwards of seventy cities and began to lay in all of them so much of Greek culture as
the instruments and agents whom he could find were
able to set up. One only of the seventy attained a position of supreme importance to men. At Alexandria in
Egypt the intellectual interests of the old Greece flow-
ered anew, and it was thence and not from Athens directly that a later world learned to know the earlier
seed plantings of Hellas herself. Some of the other
Alexandrias became centres of influence, of which their
greater sister in Egypt might not justly be ashamed.
They had too great a distance from Greece easily to be
overpassed by waves of influence. We do not know
much directly about them, and are left to inference and
conjecture. They were governed in large measures by
army officers. And the modern pacifist who knows no

good in war or men of war can scarcely think how much
these men have done for civilization in many lands
during the last 2,000 years. They have so often been
silent men, content to do their work and say nothing
about it. They pass but their influence lives on. Such
men lived on after Alexander was dead, and worked in
the great silence which followed his glorious days. How
great was their share in the spread of Hellenism is only
to be inferred from a hint now and again during the
lives of the Arsacids and the Sassanids, and no man has
paused to glean the scattered evidence, here a word and
there a deed, which shows how the results of Alexander's conquest and administration had opened new
roads for civilization westward, let it not be forgotten,
as well as eastward. Persians came westward bearing
so much as they could of the spoils of culture which
had come to them from Sumerians, Babylonians, and
Assyrians. These treasures are clearly enough to be
seen in the art and letters of Greece. In the great Alexandria there was a rich inflow from all that Egypt had
gleaned and garnered. Greece gave indeed as Alexander
or his helpers and advisers intended, but she received
largess in return. Man is an acquisitive animal not
merely in money, as the moralists are wont to remind
us, but ideas as well, and Greece became a great debtor
to the Orient.

The political genius of Alexander as displayed in
Persia is too hard to measure. What he did do is fairly
easy to understand and estimate. He adopted from the
Persian kings the system of satrapies scarcely changed.
He died too soon to show whether this was his final decision as to the future. He surely did not intend that
each of the seventy Alexandrias should be the seat of
a satrap, for there were far too many of them. His con-

FIG. 63. Persians and Greeks Hunting the Deer. (Sarcophagus of Alexander.)

quest of a strip of India was administered not by a
satrap, but in a way now difficult clearly to envisage.
In Egypt the plan though also vague seems more liberal than that which was afterward administered by
the Ptolemies. Alexander was a statesman, but whether
his clearly manifested gifts would have ultimately
placed him in the front rank must ever remain doubtful. His return from India offered a loud call for renewed attention to this very type of effort, but he did
not make any great display of it. He had too much else
to do, and he was content savagely to punish the men
who had failed him, appoint new men in their places,
and let it go at that. His body was worn, doubtless often
full of pain, and the quick and agile brain was weary.
It was enough.

But whatever doubts there may justly be of his ability as a statesman there must be none as to his generalship. "He showed the world, first of all men, and
best, how to make war." (Dodge.) It is an art, a terrible art, but an art not yet outlived. And age after
age, again, and yet again, have men cried out for a
man of thought and of action to lead them against enemies. Men have in more recent days thought of each
war as the last, only to wake and fight again. Their
leaders have always turned their eyes backward to
learn from their forerunners how war must be fought
in some new day. But they never go more remotely
into times past but only to Alexander for their lessons.
He it was who taught the elements of the art to Hannibal, to Cæsar also. From these came the great tradition from captain to captain, even to Napoleon. Nor
does the line of influence cease there, for in our own age
it is once more a son of France, Ferdinand Foch, who
grasps a standard, and does the work again, while in

the shadows of the past it is still the great figure of Alexander that men see, it is he that they consciously or unconsciously emulate. Is not this one of the greatest marvels of history?

As this story comes to its intended end one might yet steal another word to say that as we look back to the earliest chapter, and survey the long line of empire builders from Cyrus and Darius, and then see that which they had erected with toil lying in ruins by Alexander's sword, there need be no cause for discouragement. The things of the spirit survived the deeds of the flesh. Religion as civilization's touchstone outlived the words and deeds of kings. Zoroaster himself, his spirit, his words, his works of kindly intent, his love of animals, survived works of brutality and savagery. Alexander's sword cut a way eastwards for Christianity and her message to come back out of the west into the east. There have been failures enough to live the life which these two, Zoroaster and Jesus, had shown, but they have not lived or died in vain. Alexander had contributed to the spread of their ideas. Neither Persia nor Macedonia had lived in vain. It is enough.

APPENDICES

APPENDIX A

We possess two different versions of the Greek legends concerning the origin of Cyrus, of which one only, that of Herodotus, has come down to us in a complete form. The other, that of Ctesias, exists only in fragments from extracts made by Nicolas of Damascus.

THE STORY FROM HERODOTUS[1]

Astyages, king of the Medes, had a daughter named Mandane. Warned in a dream thought to be portentous not to marry her to a noble of his own race he gave her to wife to Cambyses, whom Herodotus calls a Persian. In the first year of her marriage another dream warned her father that her offspring should rule in his place. He had her brought home, and when her boy child was born, gave him to a man of his household called Harpagus with instructions to kill him. Harpagus was loath to fulfil the cruel command personally, yet feared not to do his master's will in some way. To escape direct connection he sent for a cowherd named Mitradates, into whose hand he delivered the child to be exposed among wild beasts in the mountains. While Mitradates was absent from his home his wife gave birth to a still born child, and she persuaded her husband to lay it out on the mountains, and keep and rear as their own the child that was to have been slain. When the youth was ten years old he revealed in play with his comrades a temper and quality that led to his discovery and brought him before his grandfather Astyages.

Harpagus when summoned told the true story and Astyages seemed glad that Cyrus had not been slain as he had commanded, and declared his intention of giving a feast in honor of the youth's deliverance. To this feast he invited Harpagus, and served to him without his knowledge, the flesh of his son, then about thirteen years of age, who had been summoned to the palace. So was Harpagus punished.

[1]Herodotus, I, chapters 107–130. For translations compare Macaulay, G. C., *The History of Herodotus*, I, pp. 54–67. Godley, A. D., *Herodotus*, I, pp. 139–171, with Greek Text. (Loeb Library.)

Astyages now called the Magians and asked their advice concerning the further fulfillment of the dreams which had almost caused the destruction of his grandson. Reassured by them he sent the boy to his parents Cambyses and Mandane, with whom he grew to man's estate, and was most courageous and well beloved among his peers.

Harpagus determined to seek an occasion to take vengeance upon Astyages and chose Cyrus as the agent. By secret means, rather more picturesque than probable, he communicated with him, then living among the Persians who were subject to the Medes. Cyrus accepted his advice and roused the Persians to rebel. Astyages gathered his forces to reduce them, and having forgotten what he had done to make Harpagus an enemy, gave him command over his troops, who made a sufficient number of them treasonable, and brought victory to Cyrus over them. Astyages was made prisoner and Harpagus taunted him, reminding him of the ghastly banquet upon his son's flesh.

"Thus Astyages was deposed from his sovereignty after a reign of 35 years: and the Medes stooped under the yoke of the Persians because of his cruelty, after they had ruled Asia beyond the Halys for 128 years, from which must be taken the time when the Scythians held sway. . . . As for Astyages, Cyrus did him no further harm, but kept him with himself until he died."

"Thus born and bred Cyrus became king; and afterwards, as I have already said, he subdued Crœsus, who was the first to begin the quarrel, and after this victory he became ruler of all Asia."

APPENDIX B

The stele of Nastesen, as the only known record of the king's reign, is so interesting in itself, and so important as an Egyptian record of Persian campaigns in Egypt that it may well seem worth while to give here a translation of the portion relating to Cambyses, lines 39, 40.

The history of its discovery at Dongola in 1853, and of its further travels until it found place in Berlin, is given by Budge (*The Egyptian Sudan*, 1907, II, p. 84 ff.). The text first published by Lepsius (*Denkmäler*, Abth. V, Bl. 16) has been republished by Schäfer (*Regierungsbericht des Königs Nastesen*, Leipzig, 1901), who also gives a translation (*Die Æthiopische Königsinschrift des Berliner Museum*, Leipzig, 1901). It has been translated by Maspero (*Transactions Soc. Bibl. Arch.*, IV, p. 2, 1876); by Erman (*Ausführliches Verzeichnis* of the Royal Museum in Berlin, p. 402); by Budge (*The Egyptian Sudan*, II, p. 97 ff.). The translation as given by Budge is as follows; compared with that by Schäfer.

"The chief Kambasuten came, and I made my bowmen to advance against him from the city of Tchart. There was a great slaughter. I captured all his . . . I made myself master of all the boats of his captains, I routed and overthrew him. I seized all his lands, and all his oxen, bulls, cows, calves, and animals of every kind, and everything on which men live, from the city of Kartept unto the city of Taruti-pcht. . . ."

"On the upper part of the stele are sculptured two scenes: in that to the right Nastesen is standing before the ram-headed Amen of Napata, to whom he offers a necklace of beads, and a necklace with a pectoral attached, and in that to the left he makes the same offering to the man-headed Amen-Re. In the former scene he is accompanied by the Queen Sekhmakh, and in the latter by the Queen mother Pelkha. Above these scenes is the winged disk, with pendent uræi, between which is the king's name enclosed within a cartouche."

—Budge.

APPENDIX C

Æschylus fought at Marathon in the first invasion,[1] and in the second invasion at Artemisium, Salamis, and Platæa.[2] This personal participation in the defense of Greece makes Æschylus highly important as a witness to the course and meaning of the events.

His interpretation of the significance of the events is admirably summarized by Sheppard (*Æschylus & Sophocles, Their Work and Influence*. New York and London, 1927, pp. 9, 10) as follows:

"Æschylus fought at Marathon and Salamis. He saw the burning of the Athenian shrines by Xerxes, and his *Persæ* (472 B.C.) interprets the Greek victory as the work of Nemesis. The extent and luxury of the Persian Empire and the veneration which its monarchs claimed, seemed to Greek eyes a provocation of the gods. That view he shares. In this play there are even traces of the notion which he later repudiated, that the gods are jealous of all greatness and tempt men wantonly to ruin. It is easy to accept such doctrines about enemies. But the thought that arrogance sows crime and reaps death as the harvest is applied impartially to Greeks and Persians. In sober earnestness he reads the great deliverance as a proof of justice in an ordered universe.

"He lays his scene in Persia, and imagines the reception of the news by the court. The lyrical introduction, which describes the dazzling and apparently irresistible splendour of the Persian host, has an undercurrent of foreboding. It creates an atmosphere for the arrival of the Queen-Mother Atossa. That is a new and promising use of lyric. Atossa is the embodiment of pride in Xerxes and of haunting fear for him."

[1] For which the evidence is in Eustratius on Arist. Eth. Nicom., 3, 2 (Commentaria in Aristotelum Græca edita consilio et auctoritate Acad. Litt. Regiæ Borussicæ, Vol. XX, p. 145, lines 26 ff. Compare Bergk, P. L.⁴, II, 241, 4). Müller Frag. Hist. Gr., vol. II, p. 197, quotes this passage or something like it from Aspasius on the Ethics, and Bergk l. c. gives the epig. in a 4-line version from Athenæus, XIV, 627c. It may be conveniently read in Sidgwick's Æschylus (Oxford Class. Texts) at the end, or in the Teubner Æschylus (ed. Weil, p. 310 ff.).

[2] For these the evidence is found in the Vita Æschyl., which appears in the Medicean Manuscript of Æschylus (Teubner ed. of Æschylus, ed. Weil, p. 310) and in Pausanias, 1, 14, 5, and also in the Scholia in Æschyli Persæ, ed. Dähnhardt (Teubner), p. 141, where the reference is to Ion. This should appear in Müller's Fragmenta Historiorum Græcorum, II, p. 44 sqq., but apparently does not, and Ion is not yet included in Jacoby Fragmenta der Griech. Historicker.

It seems therefore worth while to print here Æschylus' account of the battle of Salamis which he puts into the mouth of a messenger telling the story to Atossa, mother of Xerxes.

THE BATTLE OF SALAMIS, AS DESCRIBED BY ÆSCHYLUS

(Quoted by kind permission of Macmillan & Co., from *The Suppliant Maidens, The Persians, The Seven Against Thebes, The Prometheus Bound of Æschylus,* translated by E. D. A. Morshead, M.A., London, 1928.)

ATOSSA

Say, how began the struggle of the ships?
Who first joined issue? did the Greeks attack,
Or Xerxes, in his numbers confident?

MESSENGER

O queen, our whole disaster thus befell,
Through intervention of some fiend or fate—
I know not what—that had ill will to us.
From the Athenian host some Greek came o'er,
To thy son Xerxes whispering this tale—
Once let the gloom of night have gathered in,
The Greeks will tarry not, but swiftly spring
Each to his galley-bench, in furtive flight
Softly contriving safety for their life.
Thy son believed the word and missed the craft
Of that Greek foeman, and the spite of Heaven,
And straight to all his captains gave this charge—
As soon as sunlight warms the ground no more,
And gloom enwraps the sanctuary of sky,
Range we our fleet in triple serried lines
To bar the passage from the seeking strait,
This way and that: let other ships surround
The isle of Ajax, with this warning word—
Smiting the swirling brine, and in a trice
They flashed upon the vision of the foe!
The right wing first in orderly advance
Came on a steady column; following then,
The rest of their array moved out and on,
And to our ears there came a burst of sound,
A clamour manifold.—*On, sons of Greece!*
On, for your country's freedom! strike to save
Wives, children, temples of ancestral gods,

Graves of your fathers! Now is all at stake.
Then from our side swelled up the mingled din
Of Persian tongues, and time brooked no delay—
Ship into ship drave hard its brazen beak
With speed of thought, a shattering blow! and first
One Grecian bark plunged straight, and sheared away
Bowsprit and stem of a Phœnician ship.
And then each galley on some other's prow
Came crushing in. Awhile our stream of ships
Held onward, till within the narrowing creek
Our jostling vessels were together driven,
And none could aid another; each on each
Drave hard their brazen beaks, or brake away
The oar-banks of each other, stem to stern,
While the Greek galleys, with no lack of skill,
Hemmed them and battered in their sides, and soon
The hulls rolled over, and the sea was hid,
Crowded with wrecks and butchery of men.
No beach nor reef but was with corpses strewn,
And every keel of our barbarian host
Hurried to flee, in utter disarray.
That if the Greeks their jeopardy should escape
By wary craft, and win their ships a road
Each Persian captain shall his failure pay
By forfeit of his head. So spake the king,
Inspired at heart with over-confidence
Unwitting of the god's predestined will.
Thereon our crews, with no disordered haste,
Did service to his bidding and purveyed
The meal of afternoon: each rower then
Over the fitted rowlock looped his oar.
Then, when the splendour of the sun had set,
And night drew on, each master of the oar
And each armed warrior straightway went aboard.
Forward the long ships moved, rank cheering rank,
Each forward set upon its ordered course.
And all night long the captains of the fleet
Kept their crews moving up and down the strait.
So the night waned, and not one Grecian ship
Made effort to elude and slip away.
But as dawn came and with her coursers white
Shone in fair radiance over all the earth,
First from the Grecian fleet rang out a cry,
A song of onset! and the island crags
Re-echoed to the shrill exulting chant,
Then on us Eastern men amazement fell
And fear in place of hope; for what we heard
Was not a call to flight! the Greeks rang out

Their holy, resolute, exulting chant,
Like men come forth to dare and do and die!
Their trumpets pealed, and fire was in that sound,
And with the dash of simultaneous oars
Replying to the war chant, on they came,
Smiting the swirling brine, and in a trice
They flashed upon the vision of the foe!
The right wing first in orderly advance
Came on, a steady column; following then,
The rest of their array moved out and on,
And to our ears there came a burst of sound,
A clamour manifold.—*On, sons of Greece!*
On, for your country's freedom! strike to save
Wives, children, temples of ancestral gods,
Graves of your fathers! now is all at stake.
Then from our side swelled up the mingled din
Of Persian tongues, and time brooked no delay—
Ship into ship drave hard its brazen beak
With speed of thought, a shattering blow! and first
One Grecian bark plunged straight, and sheared away
Bowsprit and stem of a Phœnician ship.
And then each galley on some other's prow
Came crashing in. Awhile our stream of ships
Held onward, till within the narrowing creek
Our jostling vessels were together driven
And none could aid another: each on each
Drave hard their brazen beaks, or brake away
The oar-banks of each other, stem to stern,
While the Greek galleys, with no lack of skill,
Hemmed them and battered in their sides, and soon
The hulls rolled over, and the sea was hid
Crowded with wrecks and butchery of men.
No beach nor reef but was with corpses strewn
And every keel of our barbarian host
Hurried to flee, in utter disarray.
Thereon the foe closed in upon the wrecks
And hacked and hewed, with oars and splintered planks,
As fishermen hack tunnies or a cast
Of netted dolphins, and the briny sea
Rang with the screams and shrieks of dying men,
Until the night's dark aspect hid the scene.
Had I a ten days' time to sum that count
Of carnage, 'twere too little! know this well—
One day ne'er saw such myriad forms of death!

ATOSSA

Woe on us, woe! disaster's mighty sea
Hath burst on us and all the Persian realm!

MESSENGER

Be well assured, the tale is but begun—
The further agony that on us fell
Doth twice outweigh the sufferings I have told!

ATOSSA

Nay, what disaster could be worse than this?
Say on! what woe upon the army came,
Swaying the scale to a yet further fall?

MESSENGER

The very flower and crown of Persia's race,
Gallant of soul and glorious in descent,
And highest held in trust before the king,
Lies shamefully and miserably slain.

ATOSSA

Alas for me and for this ruin, friends!
Dead, sayest thou? By what fate overthrown?

MESSENGER

An islet is there, fronting Salamis—
Strait, and with an evil anchorage: thereon
Pan treads the measure of the dance he loves
Along the sea-beach. Thither the king sent
His noblest, that, where'er the Grecian foe
Should 'scape, with shattered ships, unto the isle,
We might make easy prey of fugitives
And slay them there, and from the washing tides
Rescue our friends. It fell out otherwise
Than he divined, for when, by aid of Heaven,
The Hellenes held the victory on the sea,
Their sailors then and there begirt themselves
With brazen mail and bounded from their ships
And then enringed the islet, point by point,
So that our Persians in bewilderment
Knew not which way to turn. On every side,
Battered with stones, they fell, while arrows flew
From many a string, and smote them to the death.
Then, at the last, with simultaneous rush
The foe came bursting on us, hacked and hewed
To fragments all that miserable band,
Till not a soul of them was left alive.
Then Xerxes saw disaster's depth, and shrieked,
From where he sat on high, surveying all—
A lofty eminence, beside the brine,
Whence all his armament lay clear in view.

His robe he rent, with loud and bitter wail,
And to his land-force swiftly gave command
And fled, with shame beside him! Now lament
That second woe, upon the first imposed!

ÆSCHYLUS

The battle-field, where Persia's victim horde
First bowed beneath the brunt of Hellas' sword,
As on the morn to distant Glory dear,
When Marathon became a magic word;
Which uttered, to the hearer's eye appear
The camp, the host, the fight, the Conqueror's career,

The flying Mede, his shaftless broken bow—
The fiery Greek, his red pursuing spear;
Mountains above—Earth's, Ocean's plain below—
Death in the front, Destruction in the rear!
Such was the scene. . . .
—BYRON, *Childe Harold*, ii, Stanzas 89, 90.

INDEX

Achæmenes, 146, 174–175
Achæmenian Dynasty, 14, 114, 261, 332
Æschylus, 382–387
Africa, 80, 137
Ahasuerus, see Xerxes I
Ahura Mazda, 21–27, 96, 140, 143–144, 170, 192, 237, 238
Alcibiades, 203
Alexander of Macedon, 163
Alexander the Great, 28, 69; ascends throne, 262–263; attack on Illyria, 265–266; expedition into Bœotia, 267–268; advance on Greece, 269–278; struggle with Darius, 278–342; in Egypt, 303–309; final conquest of Persia, 329–355; march into India, 355–356, 363–367; as head of Persian empire, 356–362; last days, 367–370; estimate of, 370–376
Alexander I, 128
Alexandria, 305, 318, 373
Alexandria Areion, 346
Alexandria the last, 348–349
Alyattes, 42
Amasis, 43, 51, 57, 66, 73–77, 99
Amphictyonic Council, 263
Anshan, 36–37, 38, 74
Antioch, 305, 317
Arabia, 122, 138, 305, 309, 370, 371
Aristotle, 253, 269, 276, 361
Armenia, 92, 108, 325
Arrian, 264 n., 265 n., 266 n., 267 n., 268 n., 269 n., 270 n., 272 n., 273 n., 274 n., 276 n., 277 n., 280 n., 281 n., 282 n., 283 n., 284 n., 292 n., 295 n., 296 n., 297 n., 298 n., 300 n., 302 n., 306 n., 307 n., 309 n., 313 n., 315 n., 316 n., 320 n., 322 n., 325 n., 326 n., 331 n., 333 n., 335 n., 336 n., 338 n., 340 n., 341 n., 345 n., 347 n., 348 n., 354 n., 355 n., 356 n., 357 n., 360 n., 362 n., 364 n., 368 n.
Arsikas, 199. See also Artaxerxes II
Artabanus, 171, 172
Artabazos, 234, 243–244, 254
Artabazus, 164, 166
Artaxerxes I, 172, 193; suppresses revolt in Bactria, 173–176; Jewish policy of, 180–189; death of, 190; family of, 190–191

Artaxerxes II, ascent of throne, 202–203; struggle with Cyrus, 203–219; struggle with Evagoras, 219–224; attacks Egypt, 226–229; general revolt against, 229–235; last days of, 235–236; contribution to religion, 237–238; estimate of, 239–240
Artaxerxes III, 261, 266, 330; secures power, 241–242; threatens Athens, 243–244; subdues Egypt, 244–252; and Grecian states, 253–255; estimate of, 256; family of, 256–257
Artobazanes, 145
Aryandes, 98
Aryans, 9–10, 13, 14
Ashurbanipal, 40
Asia, 53, 117, 127, 137, 138, 268, 280, 296, 314, 368, 380
Asia Minor, 5, 11, 40, 42, 52, 116, 127, 160, 202, 203, 206, 207, 221, 222, 224, 225, 240, 241, 243, 252, 253, 268–270, 277, 279, 281, 291, 293, 294, 314
Assyria, 39, 55, 58, 103, 115, 321, 351
Astyages, 37, 39, 51, 74, 337, 379–380
Asura-deva, 17
Athens, 124, 126, 128, 129, 130, 132, 133, 135, 154, 155, 157, 159, 160, 161, 162, 163, 167, 168, 175, 189, 200, 202, 220, 221, 229, 243, 247, 254–255, 263, 266, 268, 270, 271, 272, 277, 280, 284, 285, 291, 313, 330, 336, 373
Atossa, 70–71, 76, 90, 115, 145, 382–383
Attiads, dynasty of, 41
Avesta, 18, 27, 31

Babylon, 38, 55, 64, 67, 104, 110, 112, 180, 191, 206, 239, 246, 284, 286, 295, 315, 316, 325, 332, 338, 339, 343, 370; fall of, 55–63; under Cyrus, 64–66, 72; revolts against Darius, 90, 95, 122; conquered by Xerxes, 147–148; conquered by Alexander, 327–330
Babylonia, 5, 44, 48, 63, 177–181, 186, 209, 321, 351, 372
Babylonian, language, 14; script, 14
Babylonians, 12, 14, 37, 55, 63, 80, 91, 315
Bactria, 18, 19, 53, 104, 108, 341, 344, 346, 347, 351, 354, 367